Writing & Grammar 7
Third Edition

TEACHER'S EDITION

for Christian Schools™

BJU PRESS™
GREENVILLE, SOUTH CAROLINA

NOTE:

The fact that materials produced by other publishers may be referred to in this volume does not constitute an endorsement of the content or theological position of materials produced by such publishers. Any references and ancillary materials are listed as an aid to the student or the teacher and in an attempt to maintain the accepted academic standards of the publishing industry.

**WRITING AND GRAMMAR 7 for Christian Schools® Teacher's Edition
Third Edition**

Coordinating Writers

June W. Cates

Elizabeth Rose, M.Ed., M.A.

Kimberly Y. Stegall, M.Ed.

Dawn L. Watkins, M.Ed., M.A.

Contributing Writers

Alicia M. Bernson

Eileen M. Berry

Kara D. Bixler

Jill M. Blackstock, M.Ed.

Denise Zutter Cevela, M.Ed.

Constance C. Collins, M.Ed.

Dana Gibby Gage

Wendy M. Harris

Ellen M. Howell, M.S.

Judith W. Lanier, M.A.

Erika J. Merkle, M.A.

Lois Oldenburg

Ronda Radford Preacher, M.S.

Karen Rowe, M.Ed.

Christina Hatfield Schiederer

Lesa M. Seibert, M.Ed.

Sarah Shanks

Maggie Smeltzer Sloan, M.A.

E. Anne Smith

Sandra R. Utt, M.S.

Consultants

Grace Collins Hargis, Ph.D., *Chairman of the Departments of Linguistics and English Education, Bob Jones University*

Daniel P. Olinger, Ph.D., *Professor of Theology, School of Religion, Bob Jones University*

Steven N. Skaggs, M. Ed., *Director of Product Development, BJU Press*

Editor

Kelly D. Clepper

Designer

Duane A. Nichols

Photo Acquisition

Rachel Carper

Terry Latini

Brenda Hansen

Joyce Landis

Cover Designer

Timothy French

Compositors

Nancy C. Lohr

Bonnijean Marley

Project Manager

Nathan Huffstutler

Bible Integration

Bryan Smith, Ph.D.

Will Gray, M.A

Artists

Timothy D. Banks

Vincent Barnhart

John Bjerk

Johanna Ehnis

Justin Gerard

Preston Gravely Jr.

Deborah King

Stefanie Kubina

Asher Parris

Scotty Pruitt

Dick Sheets

Lynda Slattery

Melissa Smith

Produced in cooperation with the Bob Jones University Division of English Language and Literature of the College of Arts and Science, the School of Education, and Bob Jones Academy.

for Christian Schools is a registered trademark of BJU Press.
Acknowledgements and Photograph credits appear on page x.

© 2005 BJU Press
Greenville, South Carolina 29614
First Edition © 1982 BJU Press
Second Edition © 1999 BJU Press

Printed in the United States of America

ISBN 1-59166-367-9

15 14 13 12 11 10 9 8 7 6 5 4 3 2

Congratulations

Your search for the very best educational materials available has been completely successful! You have a textbook that is the culmination of decades of research, experience, prayer, and creative energy.

The facts

Nothing overlooked. Revised and updated. Facts are used as a springboard to stimulate thoughtful questions and guide students to broader applications.

The foundation

Nothing to conflict with Truth, and everything to support it. Truth is the pathway as well as the destination.

The fun

Nothing boring about this textbook! Student (and teacher) might even forget it's a textbook! Brimming with interesting extras and sparkling with color!

TABLE OF CONTENTS

To the Teacher

WRITING AND GRAMMAR 7 for Christian Schools, Third Edition, provides students with a basis for a clear understanding of basic English grammar and for increasing proficiency in the use of English. Further, the text seeks to present material in an engaging, manageable style. Plentiful examples and exercises cover topics of interest to seventh-grade students. Special features and a wide variety of writing opportunities enrich the learning experience.

Teachers or students coming to this textbook series for the first time will find that the grammatical terms and concepts are largely familiar. The text seeks to emphasize the orderliness of language. This emphasis helps students understand that language, a gift of God, reflects the orderliness of His nature. In addition, the grammar is constructive, not just pulling sentences apart to see how they work, but also helping students build clear sentences.

Writing instruction and assignments take students through the writing process as it applies to informative writing, personal narrative, descriptive writing, creative writing, persuasive writing, and report writing.

Features of the Student Text

The student text contains three units: **Grammar, Usage,** and **Reference.**

Each chapter in the Grammar unit (Chapters 1-8) begins with a **literature excerpt,** a model of good writing featuring the part of speech taught in that chapter. Each chapter in the Usage unit (Chapters 9-16) begins with a short introduction linking communication skills to other

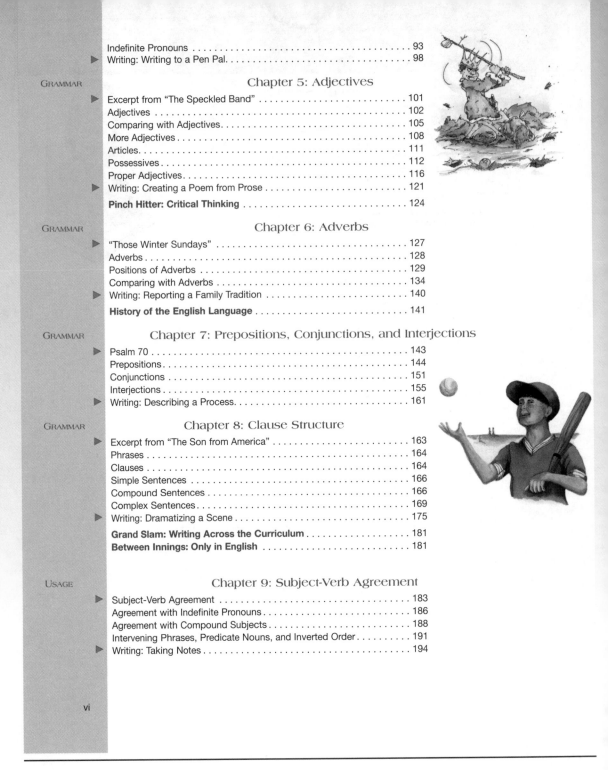

Chapter 5: Adjectives

Chapter 6: Adverbs

Chapter 7: Prepositions, Conjunctions, and Interjections

Chapter 8: Clause Structure

Chapter 9: Subject-Verb Agreement

---

areas of knowledge. In both units, discussion questions draw students into the chapter.

Every section of new material closes with an **In Summary** review of the concepts, followed by **Practice the Skill, Review the Skill, Use the Skill,** and/or **Cumulative Review** exercises.

Chapters 1-8 end the grammar instruction with **Sliding Home,** discussion questions referring to the opening literature selection. These questions allow students to see how grammar aids effective written communication. Scripture verses and accompanying discussion questions follow the literature questions and demonstrate the effective use of grammar in God's Word.

Both the Grammar unit (Chapters 1-8) and the Usage unit (Chapters 9-16) include **Writing** instruction and assignments that take students through the writing process.

The third unit, Reference (Chapters 17-20), includes information that will benefit students throughout the school year.

Throughout the textbook, **Combine the Skills** icons identify related information that is elsewhere in the textbook. The teacher can use these icons to combine instruction of skills from one chapter with related skills from another chapter. A student can use the icons to find information to aid his understanding of the concept he is studying. **Etymologies** reveal the origin of common English words. **ESL** notes provide in-depth information for the student whose native language is not English. (*ESL* is a widely used abbreviation for *English as a Second Language.*)

Periodically throughout the text, special sections supplement the basic instruction. **History of the English Language** pro-

Chapter 10: Pronoun-Antecedent Agreement

Chapter 11: Pronoun Usage

Chapter 12: Using Adjectives and Adverbs Cor

Chapter 13: Using Troublesome Words Correctly

Chapter 14: Capitalization

Chapter 15: Punctuation

---

vides a brief historical background. **Pinch Hitter: Critical Thinking** challenges students to solve a short mystery from clues in the story. **Grand Slam: Writing Across the Curriculum** enriches interdisciplinary teaching efforts by offering writing opportunities in various academic subjects. **Between Innings** features fun facts about language to help students improve their writing style.

The **Glossary** lists the definitions of many terms for ready reference.

Features of the Teacher's Edition

The Teacher's Edition contains reduced student text pages and lesson support. Also included is a Support Materials CD with bulletin board ideas and reproducible blackline masters that supplement the lessons in the Teacher's Edition. See page 460 for more information about the Support Materials CD.

Lesson Plans for each chapter offer inductive teaching strategies, opportunities for instruction in oral communication through speech activities, methods of evaluation, and sources of further information.

- Within each lesson plan, a list of *Chapter Goals* states the goals of the lesson—concepts you want your students to understand fully.

- A list of *Objectives* states the outcome of instruction in terms of student behavior.

- *Lesson Support* sections list the pages from the student text, the Teacher's Edition, and Support Materials CD for that lesson.

- *Teaching Strategy* sections suggest procedures for instruction.
- *ESL Strategy* paragraphs offer suggestions for individualized instruction of the student whose native language is not English.
- *Link* strategies suggest ways to connect the grammar and usage instruction to other disciplines, such as literature, writing, and speech.
- *Scriptural Application* ideas point to biblical principles drawn from the lesson content.

- *Reinforcement* suggestions offer methods for reinforcing the concepts in the lesson, including homework suggestions.
- *Evaluation* ideas present ways to assess students' grasp of the material presented.
- *Enrichment Activities* supplement the basic lesson plans. Many of the Enrichment Activities include an alternative *One on One* activity for those teachers who have only one student.

- Lists of *Additional Resources* recommend other sources of information for students and teachers.

The **Suggested Teaching Schedules** on pages 442-44 show how the material in *WRITING AND GRAMMAR 7 for Christian Schools,* Third Edition, can be taught in one semester or in two semesters. The schedules are flexible, allowing for adaptation to individual needs.

Sentence **Diagrams** on pages 445-50 correspond to those sentences in the student text marked with the diagram symbol. This symbol indicates that students should

Chapter Reviews

be able to diagram correctly the sentence elements that they have studied up to that lesson. Practices not marked with the diagram symbol may contain elements that students will not learn to diagram this year (such as dependent clauses).

Making Writing Assignments

Getting a good writing assignment from a student starts long before the student picks up a pen or sits at a computer. It starts with the teacher's making a thorough plan for the year, and then carrying it through,

adapting and revising as the needs and opportunities arise.

A good curriculum, of course, is a solid place to start; but every student, every class, is unique, and only the teacher can really determine what is best. Beyond a general plan, a teacher needs also to make good, specific assignments.

An assignment that gets a good response needs to be focused, inviting, and clear. "Write about your summer vacation" is not going to prompt the kind of writing that pleases. It is too general, too broad, and too overwhelming, even for the eager

writer. "Write a paragraph describing the most interesting place where you ate on your vacation" is better. It narrows the assignment; it engages the interest of the student; it looks possible, even to the least eager writer.

In clarifying the topic, it is possible, however, to put too many parameters on the assignment. "Write a five-sentence paragraph, using five adjectives, to describe the way the restaurant looked" is too limiting. Nor is it advisable to use writing to teach some grammar principle. For example, "Write two paragraphs on your

Acknowledgments

A careful effort has been made to trace the ownership of selections included in this textbook in order to secure permission to reprint copyrighted material and to make full acknowledgment of their use. If any error or omission has occurred, it is unintentional and will be corrected in subsequent editions, provided written notification is made to the publisher.

CHAPTER 1
Excerpt from "The Drummer Boy of Shiloh" by Ray Bradbury. Reprinted by permission of Don Congdon Associates, Inc. Copyright © 1960 by Curtis Publishing Company, renewed 1988 by Ray Bradbury.

CHAPTER 2
From *The Cay* by Theodore Taylor, copyright © 1969 by Theodore Taylor. Used by permission of Doubleday, a division of Random House, Inc.

CHAPTER 6
"Those Winter Sundays." Copyright © 1966 by Robert Hayden, from *Collected Poems of Robert Hayden* by Robert Hayden, edited by Frederick Glaysher. Used by permission of Liveright Publishing Corporation.

CHAPTER 8
Excerpt from "The Son from America" from *A Crown of Feathers* by Isaac Bashevis Singer. Copyright © 1973 by Isaac Bashevis Singer. Reprinted by permission of Farrar, Straus and Giroux, LLC.

CHAPTER 11
Excerpt from *The Count of Monte Cristo* by Alexandre Dumas. Used by permission of Bantam Books, a division of Random House, Inc.

CHAPTER 17
Page 1567 from *The American Heritage Dictionary*. Copyright © 1997 by Houghton Mifflin Company. Adapted and reproduced by permission from *The American Heritage College Dictionary, Third Edition.*

Photograph Credits

The following agencies and individuals have furnished materials to meet the photographic needs of this textbook. We wish to express our gratitude to them for their important contribution.

The Biltmore Company, Asheville, North Carolina
The Bob Jones University Collection
The British Library
B.W. Carper
George R. Collins
Corel Corporation
Denver Metro Convention and Visitors Bureau
The Dr Pepper Museum, Waco, TX
Dwight D. Eisenhower Library
George Bush Presidential Library and Museum
Hemera Technologies, Inc.

Brian D. Johnson
Library of Congress
NASA
National Archives
National Basketball Hall of Fame, Springfield, MA
OMF International
PhotoDisc/Getty Images
Unusual Films
Dawn L. Watkins
The White House
www.arttoday.com

Chapter 1
George R. Collins 4; Used with permission from the Biltmore Company, Asheville, North Carolina 6

Chapter 2
© 2004 Hemera Technologies, Inc. All rights reserved. 40

Chapter 3
PhotoDisc/Getty Images 52; © 2004 Hemera Technologies, Inc. All rights reserved. 53; National Basketball Hall of Fame, Springfield, MA 57; By permission of the British Library (Cott Vit A XV; folio 132) 59; OMF International 67; George Bush Presidential Library and Museum 74

Chapter 4
Corel Corporation 97

Chapter 5
www.arttoday.com 109; Denver Metro Convention & Visitors Bureau 118

Chapter 6
PhotoDisc/Getty Images 136, 138

Chapter 7
Official White House Photograph 145; Library of Congress 148; NASA 151 (both); Courtesy of the Dr Pepper Museum, Waco, TX 154

Chapter 8
PhotoDisc/Getty Images 174

Chapter 9
Brian D. Johnson 182; NASA 187; Library of Congress 189

Chapter 10
B. W. Carper 196; Corel Corporation 198; © 2004 Hemera Technologies, Inc. All rights reserved. 203

Chapter 11
Dawn L. Watkins 208

Chapter 12
Brian D. Johnson 232

Chapter 13
PhotoDisc/Getty Images 246; Unusual Films 258

Chapter 14
Dawn L. Watkins 266; Library of Congress 278; © 2004 Hemera Technologies, Inc. All rights reserved. 279

Chapter 15
Brian D. Johnson 286; George R. Collins 288; Dwight D. Eisenhower Library 296; National Archives 303, 308; Library of Congress 313; Unusual Films 314

Chapter 16
Brian D. Johnson 318

Chapter 17
PhotoDisc/Getty Images 336

Chapter 18
PhotoDisc/Getty Images 344

Chapter 19
PhotoDisc/Getty Images 358

Chapter 20
PhotoDisc/Getty Images 374; *Esther before Ahasuerus* by Claude Vignon, From the Bob Jones University Collection 380

favorite sport, using four complex sentences" not only does not teach the grammar well but also engenders bad style.

Writing assignments should prompt good writing and should communicate messages that are important to the writer. An assignment with definition and clarity spurs a writing assignment of purpose and energy. Then the evaluation of the work is far more enjoyable and useful to both the student and the teacher.

Grading Writing Assignments

The only thing harder than getting a student to write is grading that writing. The task seems overwhelming. Sometimes, perhaps, it just seems easier to cut back on writing altogether—less hassle all around.

To aid your grading, this curriculum offers reproducible **Rubrics** for each major writing assignment. The purpose of the Rubrics is twofold: to inform the students of the teacher's expectations and to give the teacher a method for evaluating fairly, yet quickly.

Additional Resources

Teachers who want a fuller understanding of the aims of Christian education should consult the following publications of BJU Press: *The Christian Philosophy of Education, Christian Teaching and Learning, Christian Educational Methods,* and *The Christian Teaching of English.*

To the STUDENT

Why do we study language? Some would argue that we need this study because people who know their language can make a lot of money. Others may say that good language training helps a person appear educated.

The Christian knows that he should take his language study seriously because of God. Our God is a God of language and communication. He brought the world into existence through language (Gen. 1:3), He made mankind in His image and called him to have dominion over the earth partly through his use of language (Gen. 1:28; 2:19-20), and He is redeeming this world to Himself through language (John 1:1-18). Christians are the instruments of God's redemption, and God has called us who love Him to use language for redemptive purposes. By taking language study seriously, a Christian may demonstrate obedience to the two most important commands in the Bible (Mark 12:29-31). The Christian who studies language shows that he loves God, who displays part of His glory in His use of language and in His gift of language to us. The Christian student also shows that he loves those around him, who will understand God's work of redemption only as they hear about it through human language.

But why do we study English? We learn how to understand and how to speak English while we are very young. Why, then, do we spend so much of our lives studying something we already know?

English is a living language. It changes—constantly. New words appear; obsolete words fade away as they are no longer needed. Usage patterns change; even rules occasionally change. Without a thorough understanding of English, we cannot communicate effectively with others.

English is also a flexible language. We use different levels of formality for different audiences. For example, we speak and write to our friends differently than we speak and write to our pastor or teacher.

WRITING AND GRAMMAR 7 for Christian Schools, Third Edition, will help you learn to communicate in English more effectively. The first step toward the goal of better speaking and writing is to acquaint yourself with the text. Take a few minutes to become familiar with these features:

> • *Combine the Skills Boxes point you to other pages with information about the topic:*
>
> *A grammar box refers to a grammar concept in Chapters 1-8.*
>
> *A usage box sends you to material in Chapters 9-16 about correct usage.*
>
> *A reference box refers to helpful tips in Chapters 17-20.*
>
> *A writing box tells you about an important writing concept.*
>
> • *Etymology boxes tell you the histories and definitions of certain English words.*
> • *ESL notes explain concepts that can be difficult for students from another language background (ESL is an abbreviation for English as a Second Language). Every student can learn more about English from these helpful explanations.*
> • *Grand Slam: Writing Across the Curriculum brings your writing skills into contact with other areas of study, such as geography, history, and science.*
> • *Between Innings offers tips for improving your writing style.*
> • *Pinch Hitter: Critical Thinking develops your critical thinking skills as you try to solve the mysteries that confront Inspector Jameson and Officer Bell.*
> • *History of the English Language explains how our language has developed.*
> • *The Glossary is a collection of definitions of the terms used throughout the book.*
> • *Learning Christianly notes encourage you to step back from what you are learning and to look at it from a Christian worldview.*

The personal satisfaction of becoming an effective communicator is a good feeling to have—just like hitting a home run in a baseball game. So go for it; make an A+ home run this year.

Learning Christianly

The title "Learning Christianly" is adapted from the phrase "Thinking Christianly," which was coined by Harry Blamires in his book *The Christian Mind*. In the following lines Blamires explains what he means by the phrase: "One prevalent confusion of thought must be swept aside in advance . . . and that is the confusion which would equate thinking christianly with thinking about Christian matters. To think secularly is to think within a frame of reference bounded by the limits of our life on earth: it is to keep one's calculations rooted in this-worldly criteria. To think christianly is to accept all things with the mind as related, directly or indirectly, to man's eternal destiny as the redeemed and chosen child of God. You can think christianly or you can think secularly about the most sacred things—the sacrament of the altar, for example. Likewise, you can think christianly or you can think secularly about the most mundane things—say, about a petrol pump" (44).

Chapter Goals

Students will

1. understand that a sentence expresses a complete thought.
2. learn the four sentence types.
3. identify simple and compound subjects and predicates.

SENTENCES

THE DRUMMER BOY OF SHILOH
BY RAY BRADBURY

Objectives

Students will

1. identify a complete sentence.
2. define and identify the four types of sentences and use correct end marks with each type.
3. recognize the two main parts of a sentence: the subject and the predicate.
4. identify the complete and simple subject.
5. identify the complete and simple predicate.
6. recognize compound subjects and predicates.
7. identify the natural order and inverted order of sentences.
8. recognize and correct fragments.
9. identify comma splices and fused sentences.
10. correctly change comma splices and fused sentences into correct sentences.

Lesson Support

Student Text
Chapter Review 1—pp. 391-93

Support Materials CD
Warm-Ups—pp. 1-2
ESL Helps—p. 43
Concept Reinforcements—pp. 51-54
Bulletin Boards—p. 205

The boy turned on his side. A moth brushed his face, but it was peach blossom. A peach blossom flicked him, but it was a moth. Nothing stayed put. Nothing had a name. Nothing was as it once was.

If he stayed very still when the dawn came up and the soldiers put on their bravery with their caps, perhaps they might go away, the war with them, and not notice him lying small here, no more than a toy himself.

"Well, by thunder now," said a voice. The boy shut his eyes to hide inside himself, but it was too late. Someone, walking by in the night, stood over him. "Well," said the voice quietly, "here's a soldier crying *before* the fight. Good. Get it over. Won't be time once it all starts."

And the voice was about to move on when the boy, startled, touched the drum at his elbow. The man above, hearing this, stopped. The boy could feel his eyes, sense him slowly bending near. A hand must have come down out of the night, for there was a little *rat-tat* as the fingernails brushed and the man's breath fanned the boy's face.

"Why, it's the drummer boy, isn't it?"

The boy nodded, not knowing if his nod was seen. "Sir, is that you?" he said.

"I assume it is." The man's knees cracked as he bent still closer. He smelled as all fathers should smell, of salt-sweat, horse and boot leather, and the earth he walked upon. He had many eyes. No, not eyes, brass buttons that watched the boy.

He could only be, and was, the general. "What's your name, boy?" he asked.

"Joby, sir," whispered the boy, starting to sit up.

"All right, Joby, don't stir." A hand pressed his chest gently, and the boy relaxed. "How long you been with us, Joby?"

"Three weeks, sir."

"Run off from home or join legitimate, boy?"

Silence.

"Fool question," said the general. "Do you shave yet, boy? Even more of a fool. There's your cheek, fell right off the tree from overhead. And the others here, not much older. Raw, raw, the lot of you. You ready for tomorrow or the next day, Joby?"

"I think so, sir."

"You want to cry some more, go on ahead. I did the same last night."

Preparation

Before beginning lesson preparation, read through Chapter 1 completely to acquaint yourself with the scope of the chapter. Assign Chapter 1 Warm-Up as a diagnostic tool to help you determine the students' skill level before they study the chapter. Use this information to plan the emphasis of your lessons.

Literature Link

Use the literature selections at the beginning of the grammar chapters as springboards for speech and writing activities. After reading the selection aloud, discuss the questions with your students.

- Answers will vary. *(The short sentences and general style are similar to the conversation of real people.)*

- Both Joby and the general ask questions. The general gives the commands.

- Answers will vary.

- Answers will vary. *(The general sounds tough, but he speaks kindly and honestly with Joby about the hardship of battle. Joby is afraid of what the next day will bring.)*

Learning Christianly

Pursuing excellence in grammar is not a waste of time. Improving grammar skills allows a student to communicate well in many settings. But the Christian has a unique opportunity to profit through studying subjects such as grammar. Learning grammar is part of pursuing wisdom. In order to learn grammar, a student has to admit that it is something worth learning and something he is not yet skilled in. God can use challenging subjects to develop the quality of humility in students. When a student realizes his imperfection in grammar or another subject, and ultimately his imperfection before God, he is in a wonderful place for God to lift him up and give him grace. God can use this subject of grammar to continue developing the admirable qualities of wisdom and humility in your students.

Learning Christianly

At the beginning of a course like this, you might wonder how important this subject really is. You may think, "Why do I have to study grammar? I can understand what I speak and write, and all my friends can too!" Is it really fair to expect students to learn standard grammar when they already understand each other? Read Proverbs 4:7 and James 4:6. In what distinctive ways can Christians profit from the study of grammar?

- *This conversation takes place in a peach orchard on the night before a bloody battle. Does the dialogue between the two characters seem realistic to you? Why or why not?*

- *Which characters in this story ask questions? Which character gives commands or requests?*

- *If you had to choose a favorite sentence from this passage, which one would it be? Why?*

- *What do you think of the general at the end of this conversation? What do you think of Joby?*

The types of sentences used in the dialogue show the relationship between the characters. Joby, who is fourteen, does not speak in commands; he is not in a position to give orders to his general. Instead he asks a polite question ("Sir, is that you?") and answers the general's questions ("Three weeks, sir"). Notice how many commands the general gives. ("Get it over. . . . All right, Joby, don't stir. . . . You want to cry some more, go on ahead.") Even though the commands are gentle, they express the general's position of authority over Joby. They paint a picture of the general as a strong, tough leader with a compassionate heart.

Sentences that are commands have a special name: *imperative.* Questions have another name: *interrogative.* In this chapter, you will learn about imperatives, interrogatives, and two other types of sentences. This excerpt from "The Drummer Boy of Shiloh" uses different kinds of sentences to make the characters real to us. At the end of this chapter, you will be able to identify the types of sentences Bradbury uses.

Sentences

There are several ways of explaining what a sentence is. One way would be to say that everything on this page that ends with a period or a question mark is a sentence. That is true, but it is not much of a definition. After all, people do make mistakes in placement of punctuation.

Another way is to say that a sentence expresses a complete thought, or a whole thought. That is not very exact, but it may help. Smaller groups of words, called phrases (such as "in the house" and "as fast as possible"), seem to express pieces of thoughts rather than whole thoughts. Of course, it sometimes takes several sentences before we really understand what a person is talking about. Still, each sentence is a complete thought-link in the chain of ideas.

Four Types of Sentences

Sentences can be of four different types, each of which serves a different purpose in our language. We vary word order and change punctuation to express statements, questions, commands, and strong emotion.

A **declarative sentence** makes a statement, usually a fact, and ends with a period.

> Andrew will go fishing.
> Jamal ran with the ball.

An **interrogative sentence** asks a question and ends with a question mark.

> Will Andrew go fishing?
> Will anyone catch Jamal?

Interrogative is a combination of the Latin words *inter*, "between," and *rogare*, "ask." The word *interrogate* means "to question formally."

An **imperative sentence** gives a command or a request and usually ends with a period.

> Go fishing, Andrew.
> Run faster, Jamal.

Imperative comes from two Latin words that mean "to prepare against." The phrase later came to mean a command or an order to prepare.

An **exclamatory sentence** expresses strong emotion or feeling and ends with an exclamation point.

> Andrew caught a huge fish!
> That was a great play, Jamal!

page 287

Endmarks

ESL: Be aware that some ESL students may have difficulty with punctuation. Some languages use different punctuation marks from what we use in English, while others use very little punctuation at all.

An emphatic imperative sentence can end with an exclamation point.

Teaching Strategies: Introduction

Remind the students that they use all four sentence types regularly. Ask students to offer examples of each sentence type. Make four categories on the board or overhead transparency and write the students' examples under the appropriate headings. Refer to the examples as you teach the lesson.

Scriptural Application

Remind the students that God's Word contains all four sentence types. Refer to the Bible verses on page 21 as examples of the sentence types.

In English, one of the major differences in the types of sentences is the rising and falling of pitch, called the *intonation*. Intonation of a sentence can be a hint about what type the sentence is.

1. Declarative sentences have falling intonation at the end.
2. Many interrogative sentences have rising intonation at the end.
3. Imperative sentences have falling intonation at the end.
4. Exclamatory sentences are stated at a higher pitch than other sentences or with a greater difference between the high and the low pitches.

ETYMOLOGY *Intonation* comes from two Latin words: *in*, meaning "in," and *tonus*, meaning "a musical sound." To intone, then, is to give words a musical sound.

 1-1 PRACTICE THE SKILL

Identify each sentence as declarative, interrogative, imperative, or exclamatory. Place the appropriate punctuation mark at the end of each sentence.

declarative	1. Deserts do not receive much rainfall.
exclamatory	2. Whew, it is hot!
interrogative	3. Have you ever lived in the desert?
declarative	4. Most people must adjust to the dry climate.
interrogative	5. Where is the Mojave Desert located?
interrogative	6. How many national parks have you visited?
declarative	7. The beautiful scenery attracts thousands of visitors to the parks every year.
imperative	8. Watch for interesting wildlife in the Great Smoky Mountains National Park.
exclamatory	9. Wow! The sequoia trees in Redwood National Park are huge!
interrogative	10. Can you trace Daniel Boone's exploration through the Cumberland Gap near the borders of Kentucky and Tennessee?

Identify each sentence as declarative, interrogative, imperative, or exclamatory. Place the appropriate punctuation mark at the end of each sentence.

_____imperative_____ 1. Listen to Rich's story of the game.

_____exclamatory_____ 2. That was an exciting game!

_____interrogative_____ 3. Why was the game so exciting?

_____declarative_____ 4. At the beginning of the fourth quarter, our team was behind by eighteen points.

_____declarative_____ 5. Well, with our best two players fouled out, there seemed to be no hope of winning.

_____declarative_____ 6. Coach Rhodes put in Doug Riselle, a new student in our school.

_____exclamatory_____ 7. Doug made fifteen points in just one quarter!

_____interrogative_____ 8. Did you see Doug's face when he sank the winning twenty-foot jump shot?

_____imperative_____ 9. Come to the game next Tuesday.

exclamatory/declarative 10. Maybe we will win again! or.

Finding Subjects and Predicates

All sentences have two main parts: a subject and a predicate. The following example is a complete sentence because it has the two parts necessary to any sentence.

The young man on the platform spoke to the audience.

The **subject** of a sentence is the person, place, thing, or idea that the sentence is about. The subject usually comes at or near the beginning of the sentence, and it may be one word or many words. In the example above, _The young man on the platform_ is the **complete subject.** _Man_ is the **simple subject** because it is the main word in the complete subject. In every sentence, the simple subject will be a noun or a pronoun.

The **predicate,** which follows the subject in most sentences, makes a statement about the subject. Every predicate has a verb. In the example, _spoke to the audience_ is the **complete predicate.** The **simple predicate** is the verb _spoke._ The complete predicate either describes the subject in some way or tells about an action of the subject.

Some imperative sentences seem to have only a predicate. The subject may not actually appear in the sentence, but we understand the sentence as if it were there. Rather than saying, "You go to the store," we usually say, "Go to the store." The _you_ is understood to be the subject even when we do not say it. Only imperative sentences can have understood subjects.

page 51

Verbs

Sentences   **5**

Teaching Strategy:
Induction

Tell the students to pay careful attention to what you say for the next thirty seconds. (Get out a piece of paper. Put your pen on your desk. Be ready to write.) Then instruct them to write from memory your exact words. Ask a volunteer to find the subjects of those sentences. If he does not answer "understood _you,_" refer to the student text discussion of understood _you_ and again ask the students to identify the subjects of the sentences.

However, not all imperative sentences have understood subjects because the *you* may actually appear in the sentence.

> You mail this letter right away.
> (you) Mail this letter right away.

Both examples are complete sentences because both include a simple subject (either *you* or understood *you*) and both include a simple predicate *(mail).*

page 164

Clauses

Predicate comes from two Latin words meaning "to say in public" or "to proclaim." A predicate in a sentence makes some "proclamation" about the subject.

ETYMOLOGY

Word Order: In English, unlike some other languages, the subject almost always comes before the verb.

1. Tim ordered pizza for dinner.
2. Tim was hungry for the pizza.
3. His mother said, "(you) Eat a sandwich now, Tim."

I N   S U M M A R Y

The **subject** of a sentence is what the sentence is about. The **simple subject** is the main noun or pronoun in a sentence.

The **predicate** of a sentence makes a statement about the subject. The **simple predicate** is the main verb in a sentence.

1-3 PRACTICE THE SKILL

A. Draw a vertical line between the complete subject and the complete predicate. One of the sentences has an understood subject. When you find it, draw a vertical line before the verb.

1. George W. Vanderbilt | built a huge mansion near Asheville, North Carolina.

2. He | named his mansion Biltmore House.

3. Beautiful European furniture | fills Biltmore House.

4. Vanderbilt's heirs | opened the house and gardens for public tours.

5. | Visit Biltmore House on your next vacation.

B. List the simple subjects and the simple predicates of the sentences above. If the subject is understood *you*, put it in parentheses.

	Subject	Predicate
1.	George W. Vanderbilt	built
2.	He	named
3.	furniture	fills
4.	heirs	opened
5.	(you)	Visit

1-4 REVIEW THE SKILL

A. Draw a vertical line between the complete subject and the complete predicate in each sentence.

B. Underline each simple subject once and each simple predicate twice.

C. If the subject is understood *you*, draw a vertical line before the sentence and write *you* in parentheses.

(you) 1. | Read about education in colonial times.

2. Few people | attended school.

3. Some children | went to school for only a short time.

4. Benjamin Franklin | left school at age ten.

5. His father | stopped his education after only two years.

6. He | studied for the rest of his life, however.

7. Franklin | taught himself mathematics and science.

8. Grammar | was another of his subjects.

9. He | learned five foreign languages.

10. His example | amazes us today.

Some sentences may have more than one subject or predicate. Look at the following examples.

> Pedro went to the parade.
> Pedro and his sister went to the parade.

If students ask why *and* is not part of the compound subject or compound predicate, explain that *and* is a conjunction, not a noun or verb, and cannot be a subject or predicate.

page 151

Conjunctions

page 188

Subject-Verb agreement

In the first sentence, *Pedro* is the subject. In the second sentence, *Pedro* is joined by *sister*. The compound simple subject of the sentence is *Pedro* and *sister*. A **compound subject** is two or more subjects joined by a conjunction.

A sentence can also have a compound predicate. A **compound predicate** is two or more simple predicates joined by a conjunction.

> Manuel buys apples at the market.
> Manuel buys apples at the market and eats them on the way home.

In the first sentence *buys* is the simple predicate. In the second sentence the subject, *Manuel,* not only *buys* apples but also *eats* them. The compound simple predicate is *buys* and *eats*.

Sentences can have both a compound subject and a compound predicate.

> George and Maria built and decorated a new house.

Be sure to look carefully at each sentence to find all the subjects and all the predicates.

IN SUMMARY

A **compound subject** is two or more subjects joined by a conjunction.
A **compound predicate** is two or more predicates joined by a conjunction.

1-5 PRACTICE THE SKILL

Underline each simple subject once. Underline each simple predicate twice.

1. Hudson Taylor preached God's Word and administered medical treatment to the wounded.

2. The China Inland Mission began under Hudson Taylor's leadership and employed John and Betty Stam.

3. John Stam and Betty Scott attended Moody Bible Institute.

4. John Stam studied the Chinese language and wrote letters to Betty Scott.

5. John and Betty Stam traveled to Suancheng and visited with the Birches there.

6. Helen Priscilla Stam and the Los' son traveled far to the Wuhu Methodist Hospital.

7. The Red forces invaded and pillaged the city of Tsingteh.

8. <u>John</u> <u>wrote</u> to the China Inland Mission about his capture and <u>requested</u> twenty thousand dollars in ransom money.

9. John's <u>faith</u> and Betty's <u>faith</u> <u>influenced</u> many Chinese.

10. <u>Evangelist Lo</u> <u>rescued</u> Helen Priscilla and <u>took</u> her to her grandparents.

 1-6 REVIEW THE SKILL

Combine the following pairs of sentences. Some sentences may need a compound subject; others may need a compound predicate.

1. Ice cream was sold commercially in 1851.
   Ice cream did not become popular until the 1900s.

   Ice cream was sold commercially in 1851 but did not become popular

   until the 1900s.

2. Whole milk can be used in ice cream.
   Two percent milk can be used in ice cream.

   Whole milk or two percent milk can be used in ice cream.

3. Flavorings are added to ice cream.
   Nuts are added to ice cream.

   Flavorings and nuts are added to ice cream.

4. Jenna baked some cookies.
   Jenna ate some cookies.

   Jenna baked and ate some cookies.

5. Sasha likes gingerbread.
   Sasha dislikes gingersnaps.

   Sasha likes gingerbread but dislikes gingersnaps.

6. Jenna made a gingerbread house.
   Jenna gave it as a gift.

   Jenna made a gingerbread house and gave it as a gift.

 Learning Christianly

Learning how sentences work may not seem very important at first. How significant can a sentence be, anyway? Pretty significant—if you take the Bible seriously. Consider the power of one of God's sentences in Genesis 1:3. What does this verse suggest about language in general?

 Learning Christianly

Genesis 1:3 reveals that language can be very powerful. God made light simply by saying the sentence "Let there be light." Of course, humans cannot use language in exactly the same way that God can. However, since we are made in God's image, we can use language in a way similar to God's way. We cannot bring things into existence with our words, but we can indirectly shape the existence of many things through our words. Because humans speak and write, bridges are built, industries are founded, churches are planted, and wars are fought. Consider mentioning James 3:1-10. This passage talks about the remarkable power humans have because of language. This power of communication can be used for good or evil, and Christians should learn how to use it well.

7. Sasha baked for the party.
   Jenna baked for the party.

   Sasha and Jenna baked for the party.
   _____

8. Jenna made a cake.
   Jenna brought some ice cream.

   Jenna made a cake and brought some ice cream.
   _____

9. Jorge came to the party.
   Sasha came to the party.

   Jorge and Sasha came to the party.
   _____

10. Jorge ate only a few cookies.
    Jorge became quite ill.

    Jorge ate only a few cookies yet became quite ill.
    _____

page 192

Inverted Order

Finding Subjects and Predicates in Inverted Order

In the natural order of most declarative sentences, the subject comes first and the predicate follows.

        S   P
The young man spoke to the audience.

      S   P
He is speaking about his trip to Australia.

Some declarative sentences reverse the **natural order:** the predicate comes first and the subject follows. These sentences are in **inverted order.**

           P   S
Behind the podium stood the young man.

       P   S
There were the notes for his speech.

Look again at the second sentence. The word *there* is almost never the subject of a sentence. If you see a sentence that begins with *there* followed by a verb, look for the subject after the predicate.

Usually, you can rearrange the words in an inverted sentence to follow natural order. Doing so may help you to find the subject and the predicate more easily.

Teaching Strategy:
Introduction

Offer examples of God's orderly creation. *(The earth rotates on its axis on a set schedule.)* Explain that exceptions to these "rules" sometimes exist. *(God stopped the earth's rotation to prolong the day while the Israelites fought the Amorites [Joshua 10:12-14].)* There are exceptions in the natural order of sentences too.

         S   **P**
The young man stood behind the podium.

       S   **P**
The notes for his speech were there.

Interrogative sentences also can be in both natural order and inverted order. Many interrogative sentences are in the same order as most declarative sentences.

     S **P**
Who spoke to the audience?

Other interrogative sentences are in inverted order.

      P   **S**
When is the program?

In many interrogative sentences with inverted order, the subject comes between the two verbs that make up the simple predicate.

   P   **S**   **P**
Did the young man speak to the audience?

   P S   **P**
Is he speaking about his trip to Australia?

You can turn inverted interrogative sentences around to make sure that you have found the subject and the verb.

      S   **P**
The program is when?

        S   **P**
The young man did speak to the audience.

   S **P**
He is speaking about his trip to Australia.

Be sure to include both parts of the simple predicate for any interrogative sentences that follow this order.

IN SUMMARY

Most sentences follow the **natural** subject/predicate order.

Some sentences, especially interrogative sentences, may use **inverted order,** with the predicate first and the subject second.

ESL Strategy

Use ESL Helps page 43 (Support Materials CD) to explain the inverted order of questions more fully.

Underline each simple subject once and each simple predicate twice.

1. Where do you live?

2. There stands your mother.

3. Into the house walks your dog.

4. Where is his leash?

5. Did you see it in the house?

6. There is the leash.

7. Where was your dog going?

8. On the porch sits your dog.

9. Who called her name?

10. Your mother called from the house.

1-8 **REVIEW THE SKILL**

Underline each simple subject once and each simple predicate twice.

1. Did you see the marines?

2. Where did they go?

3. There went the corps of marines.

4. Will they travel on a boat?

5. Yes, into the ocean went their boat.

6. Upon land walked another group of soldiers.

7. By whom were their orders issued?

8. Into the tent marched their commanding officer.

9. By his hand came the orders.

10. Where is he?

Recognizing Fragments

In formal usage a sentence needs to be complete, not a **fragment**. As you have learned, a sentence contains both a subject and a predicate. A **complete sentence** also expresses a complete thought. It is properly capitalized and punctuated.

Charles Lindbergh flew across the ocean.

The group of words above is a complete sentence because it meets all the criteria for a complete sentence.

A fragment is a group of words that is not a complete sentence but is wrongly capitalized and punctuated as if it were complete. In other words, a fragment leaves out important information. It may lack a subject or a predicate or both. Sometimes a fragment has a subject and a predicate but also includes a word or phrase that makes it too weak to stand alone. The words *after, although, as, because, if, unless,* or *while* often introduce a group of words that, unless combined with a complete sentence, will result in a sentence fragment.

Was named the *Spirit of St. Louis. (What was named?)*
The people of Paris. *(What did the people of Paris do?)*
Because he was the first pilot to cross the Atlantic Ocean alone without stopping. *(What happened because he was the first?)*

You can correct a fragment that lacks a subject or a predicate by supplying the missing element. You can correct a fragment that cannot stand alone by joining it to a sentence or adding information that completes the thought.

Lindbergh's plane was named the *Spirit of St. Louis.*
The people of Paris **welcomed him enthusiastically.**
We remember Lindbergh today because he was the first pilot to cross the Atlantic Ocean alone without stopping.

page 164

Clauses

IN SUMMARY

A **complete sentence** must express a complete thought and contain both a subject and a predicate.

Fragments are incomplete sentences. Correct a fragment by supplying the missing information or by joining it to a complete sentence.

 1-9 PRACTICE THE SKILL

A. Label each group of words *S* (sentence) or *F* (fragment). Be prepared to explain your answers.

___S___ 1. We do not know the origin of cheese making.

___F___ 2. European cheese making, a family tradition since the seventeenth century.

___F___ 3. Today the United States.

Teaching Strategy: Discussion

Recognizing fragments can be difficult for some students because they simply rely on what "sounds good" to them. Discuss the examples on page 13 of the student text. Ask students to point out the errors and to suggest ways to fix the errors to make complete sentences.

Scriptural Application

A fragment is an unfinished sentence. God does not want us to leave things undone in our lives. We are to be complete in Him. *(Colossians 2:10—"And ye are complete in him, which is the head of all principality and power.")*

Literature Link

Discuss the differences between formal and informal speech or writing. Point out fragments in "The Drummer Boy of Shiloh." Explain that authors use an informal style for many reasons. Bradbury uses dialect and casual speech as a powerful tool to add a unique flavor to "The Drummer Boy of Shiloh."

Use part B if students need additional practice.

_F_   4. Produces more cheese than any other country.

_S_   5. James Kraft, an American, introduced the process of cheese pasteurization.

_S_   6. High-protein cow's milk is the main ingredient in most cheeses.

_F_   7. If sour milk replaces sweet milk.

_S_   8. The flavor of cheese will be strong.

_S_   9. Cottage cheese is creamy.

_F_   10. Because cheese makers use a variety of methods.

B. Rewrite the fragments from numbers 1-10 above to make complete sentences. You may combine groups of words. If a group of words is already a sentence, write _sentence_ in the blank. *(Answers will vary.)*

1. *Sentence*

2. *European cheese making, a family tradition since the seventeenth century, is still popular.*

3. *Today the United States produces more cheese than any other country.*

4. *(See above.)*

5. *Sentence*

6. *Sentence*

7. *If sour milk replaces sweet milk, the flavor of the cheese will be strong.*

8. *Sentence*

9. *Sentence*

10. *Because cheese makers use a variety of methods, there are many different kinds of cheese available.*

A. Label each group of words S (sentence) or F (fragment).

___F___ 1. In almost every country around the world.

___S___ 2. People use the metric system for measuring.

___S___ 3. The metric system can be used for the measurement of weight, length, time, and temperature.

___F___ 4. Because it is extremely simple.

___F___ 5. Came up with the metric system in the 1790s.

___F___ 6. A team of talented French scientists.

___S___ 7. Seven base units make up all metric measurements.

___F___ 8. Part of what makes the metric system so simple.

___F___ 9. Even though the metric system is simple.

___S___ 10. Most Americans prefer the inch–pound system of measurement.

B. Rewrite the fragments from numbers 1-10 above to make complete sentences. You may combine groups of words. If a group of words is already a sentence, write *sentence* in the blank. *(Answers will vary.)*

1. *The metric system is used in almost every country around the world.*

2. *Sentence*

3. *Sentence*

4. *Many people like the metric system because it is extremely simple.*

5. *A team of talented French scientists came up with the metric system in the 1790s.*

6. *(See above.)*

7. *Sentence*

meters

grams

liters

Use part B if students need additional practice.

8. *These base units are part of what makes the metric system so simple.*

9. *Some people do not like to use metric measurements even though the metric system is so simple.*

10. *Sentence*

page 166

Compound sentences

page 291

Commas

page 301

Semicolons

Comma splice Joining 2 separate sentences w/ a comma (incorrect)

Recognizing Other Sentence Errors

A correct sentence must be a single sentence, not two or more sentences written as if they were one. These joined sentences are sentence errors. A **comma splice** consists of two sentences incorrectly joined by only a comma. One way to correct a comma splice is to change the incorrect comma to a period at the end of the first sentence and to capitalize the next word to form the beginning of a second sentence.

> **Wrong:** Charles Lindbergh flew across the Atlantic Ocean, his airplane was called the *Spirit of St. Louis.*

> **Right:** Charles Lindbergh flew across the Atlantic Ocean. His airplane was called the *Spirit of St. Louis.*

A **fused sentence** consists of two or more sentences incorrectly joined without any punctuation at all. You can correct a fused sentence by adding the missing punctuation at the end of the first sentence and capitalizing the first word of the second sentence.

> **Wrong:** His flight captured the world's attention the reporters gave Lindbergh the nickname "Lone Eagle."

> **Right:** His flight captured the world's attention. The reporters gave Lindbergh the nickname "Lone Eagle."

Fused sentence Joining 2 separate sentences w/ no punctuat (incorrect

---
IN SUMMARY

Comma splices and **fused sentences** are two or more sentences incorrectly written as if they were one sentence.

Correct these sentence errors by separating them into individual sentences.

Teaching Strategy:
Discussion

Some students may refer to both fused sentences and comma splices as *run-on sentences.* Explain to these students that there are two categories of errors: two sentences incorrectly joined with a comma and two sentences incorrectly joined with no punctuation at all. Ask students to volunteer examples of fragments, comma splices, and fused sentences. Ask other students to correct the examples.

Fragment - Incomplete sentence.

Missing either S or P Not a complete thought.

1-11 ⚾ PRACTICE THE SKILL

monday Do together (handwritten)

A. Label each group of words S (sentence), CS (comma splice), or FS (fused sentence).

___S___ 1. Tennis has changed greatly since the game's invention. *S*

___CS___ 2. The French played a game like tennis over seven hundred *CS*   *Correct way?* (handwritten)
years ago, the players hit the ball with their hands instead of
rackets.

___S___ 3. In the 1870s Major Walter Clopton Wingfield, an *S*
Englishman, developed modern tennis.

___FS___ 4. Wingfield played on grass courts the game became known *FS*
as lawn tennis.

___FS___ 5. The players used rackets they did not hit the ball with
their hands. *FS*

___CS___ 6. Mary Ewing Outerbridge brought lawn tennis
to the United States, she organized the first *CS*
American tennis court in New York.

___S___ 7. Today we rarely play tennis on grass. *S*

___CS___ 8. Most American tennis courts consist of asphalt or concrete,
carpet covers many indoor courts. *CS*

___FS___ 9. Table tennis is a miniature version of tennis a table replaces
the court. *FS*

___S___ 10. Tennis is a popular sport all over the world today. *S*

**B. Rewrite part A, changing the comma splices and fused
sentences to correct sentences. If a group of words is already a
sentence, write *sentence* in the blank.**

1. *Sentence* _____

_____

2. *The French played a game like tennis over seven hundred years ago.*

The players hit the ball with their hands instead of rackets.

3. *Sentence* _____

_____

4. *Wingfield played on grass courts. The game became known as lawn*

tennis.

Use part B if students need additional practice.

Sentences   **17**

5. *The players used rackets. They did not hit the ball with their hands.*

6. *Mary Ewing Outerbridge brought lawn tennis to the United States. She organized the first American tennis court in New York.*

7. *Sentence*

8. *Most American tennis courts consist of asphalt or concrete. Carpet covers many indoor courts.*

9. *Table tennis is a miniature version of tennis. A table replaces the court.*

10. *Sentence*

Monday
Independent

| 1-12 | REVIEW THE SKILL |

Rewrite the sentences to correct the fragments, comma splices, and fused sentences. Write *sentence* for a correct sentence.

1. Benjamin Franklin accomplished many remarkable things in his lifetime.

   Sentence

2. He started his career at age twelve, he worked in his brother's print shop.

   He started his career at age twelve. He worked in his brother's print shop.

3. Ten years later, Franklin owned his own print shop, he published newspapers and books.

   Ten years later, Franklin owned his own print shop. He published newspapers and books.

4. Although he was originally a printer.

   Although he was originally a printer, Franklin enjoyed scientific experiments too.

5. Franklin enjoyed scientific experiments too.

   Sentence _____

   _____

6. He developed many useful inventions he improved the efficiency of heating stoves.

   He developed many useful inventions. He improved the efficiency of

   heating stoves.

7. The colonial postal service.

   The colonial postal service owed its efficiency to Franklin's reforms.

   _____

8. Owed its efficiency to Franklin's reforms.

   (See above.) _____

   _____

9. He also established a fire department and a city police department.

   Sentence _____

   _____

10. Franklin started an academy the school became the University of Pennsylvania.

    Franklin started an academy. The school became the University of

    Pennsylvania.

1-13 PRACTICE THE SKILL

A. Label each group of words S (sentence), Frag (fragment), CS (comma splice), or FS (fused sentence).

____CS____ 1. Julia Ward Howe lived from 1819 to 1910, she was quite famous during her lifetime.

____S____ 2. She wrote, lectured, and crusaded in the antislavery and women's movements.

____FS____ 3. Her best-known writing is perhaps "The Battle Hymn of the Republic" she borrowed the tune from a popular song.

____F____ 4. The tune "John Brown's Body."

____FS____ 5. At a military encampment she wrote the song she later published it.

_____S_____ 6. After its publication in 1861, "The Battle Hymn of the Republic" was sung often by Union soldiers.

_____FS_____ 7. Howe wrote plays and poems she also edited an antislavery newspaper with her husband.

_____F_____ 8. In 1872 crusaded for a national Mother's Day.

_____S_____ 9. About voting rights for women, there were different views.

_____CS_____ 10. Howe was the first president of the New England Woman Suffrage Association, her influence as a writer for women's voting rights was great.

B. Rewrite part A, changing the fragments, comma splices, and fused sentences to correct sentences. If a group of words is already a sentence, write _sentence_ in the blank.

1. _Julia Ward Howe lived from 1819 to 1910. She was quite famous during her lifetime._

2. _Sentence_

3. _(See below.)_

4. _Her best-known writing is perhaps "The Battle Hymn of the Republic." She borrowed the tune from a popular song called "John Brown's Body."_

5. _At a military encampment she wrote the song. She later published it._

6. _Sentence_

7. _Howe wrote plays and poems. She also edited an antislavery newspaper with her husband._

8. _In 1872 Howe crusaded for a national Mother's Day._

9. _Sentence_

10. _Howe was the first president of the New England Woman Suffrage Association. Her influence as a writer for women's voting rights was great._

Evaluation

Use Test 1 or prepare your own test from unassigned practices, Chapter Review questions, or Concept Reinforcement questions.

≡Sliding Home

The dialogue in "The Drummer Boy of Shiloh" is realistic, much like our everyday speech. When we talk to our friends, we don't always speak in complete, logical sentences. Notice the fragments in the general's speech. "Won't be time once it all starts. . . . Even more of a fool. . . . There's your cheek, fell right off the tree from overhead." The general's meaning is clear to us, even though his sentences are not grammatically perfect. There is even a fragment in the narration: "Silence." Bradbury's choice to use only one word makes the "sentence" short and blunt, and it makes us "hear" the silence more powerfully.

- *What types of sentences (declarative, interrogative, imperative, exclamatory) does Bradbury use in the excerpt at the beginning of the chapter?*

- *Only one type of sentence is used in the first paragraph. What type is it? Why do you think the author uses so many short sentences in a row? Read the first paragraph out loud. Does it make you think of someone tossing and turning, trying to go to sleep?*

> **Genesis 1:1**
> *In the beginning God created the heaven and the earth.*
>
> **Acts 9:6**
> *And he trembling and astonished said, Lord, what wilt thou have me to do? And the Lord said unto him, Arise, and go into the city, and it shall be told thee what thou must do.*
>
> **Psalm 8:9**
> *O Lord our Lord, how excellent is thy name in all the earth!*

- *Which types of sentences are represented in the passages above?*

ESL: If ESL students question the reference to Joby's cheek falling off the tree, explain that Americans sometimes say that a young boy not yet old enough to shave has "peach fuzz" on his face (because the "fuzz" on a peach is like the fine hair on a young boy's face). The general is using a metaphor (Joby's face is a peach) to show how young he is.

- Declarative sentences and interrogative sentences

- Declarative sentences. Answers will vary. *(Short sentences create the impression of restlessness.)*

- Genesis 1:1
  Declarative

  Acts 9:6
  Answers will vary. *(Although the two sentences in the verse are declarative, some students may notice the interrogative and imperative clauses within the declarative sentences.)*

  Psalm 8:9
  Exclamatory

Enrichment: Speech Link

Divide the class into groups of four students each. Instruct each group to make up an appropriate skit. Each script should include only four sentences, one of each sentence type, or eight sentences, two of each sentence type. Allow each group to present its skit in front of the class.

One on One: Allow the student to invite other family members or friends to perform the skit with him. Present the skit before an audience of parents or neighbors.

Additional Resources

Students can read more about the lives of Hudson Taylor and John and Betty Stam in the following books available from BJU Press: *Hudson Taylor* by J. Hudson Taylor and *John and Betty Stam* by Kathleen White.

ESL: The phrasal verb *stand out* is an idiom in this sentence. You may need to explain its meaning to ESL students *(to be distinctive or prominent.)*

page 381
Reasons

Overview of Writing Process

Planning—Choosing a book and an approach

Drafting—Sketching out a book jacket; writing text

Revising—Making a final copy

Publishing—Displaying jackets in class

Objectives

Students will

1. state opinions about book jackets.
2. design book jackets.
3. present book jackets.

CREATING A BOOK JACKET

Man looketh on the outward appearance.
I Samuel 16:7

Years ago, the book jacket was a kind of dirt and dust protector. Now, book jackets serve as advertisements. An eye-catching picture or title or a favorite author's name makes you want to select one book above others. The information on the jacket influences you to reshelve the book or to buy it.

Your Turn

Design a book jacket for a favorite novel. Write material for the back cover and the inside flaps and illustrate the front cover.

Planning

Think about the books you have read recently. Which one was your favorite? What made it stand out above the others?

Identify your favorite part of the book. Did one chapter stand out? Or did the storyline make you want to keep reading? Perhaps one character became your favorite. Choose one thing to highlight in your review.

Consider your audience. Your purpose is to describe the book and to persuade someone else to read it. Write in a way that will appeal to your audience and answer questions someone considering this book might have.

Drafting

Write a short "review" of the book for the back cover. Pretend you are a critic and list your reasons for recommending the book. Make sure that your reasons are supported well, not simply based on preference.

Summarize the beginning of the story on the inside front flap. Here is an excerpt of a student summary of *The Cay* by Theodore Taylor:

> As *The Cay* begins, Phillip, an eleven-year-old American boy, is living on the island of Curaçao off the coast of Venezuela. His father is working for the Royal Dutch Shell company. During February of 1942 German submarines blow up some ships and an oil refinery nearby. Phillip's mother is frightened about what might happen if the family stays on the island. As Phillip and his mom leave to return to Virginia, the ship on which they are sailing sinks. Timothy, a really old West Indian man, rescues Phillip. Phillip becomes blind because of an injury from the explosion.

When summarizing, be careful not to give away the ending!

Ask "teaser" questions. Will Timothy and Phillip ever be rescued? How will Phillip and Timothy get along? Will Phillip ever get his sight back? Questions will make the reader want to find out more about the book.

Include a short biographical paragraph on the inside back flap. Find out something about the author's life. Theodore Taylor, author of *The Cay*, became interested in the Caribbean because he spent time there. That fact and other facts about him and his books will increase reader interest.

Draw a front-cover illustration. The illustration should represent the main idea of the book. Include both the title and the author's name.

Revising

Re-view the draft for ways to improve it. Does the cover convey the message of the book? Does the inside front flap make the reader want to read the story? Does the back flap include interesting facts about the author? Does the back cover include a review based on facts, not opinion?

Creating a Book Jacket
Lesson Support

Student Text
Chapter 18—pp. 353-54

Support Materials CD
Rubrics—p. 105

Scriptural Application

Discuss the popular saying "You can't judge a book by its cover." Whether we're judging books or people, most of us tend to come to conclusions without a thorough investigation. Therefore, we should learn how to represent what is on the inside in a simple, clear, and accurate way. Ask a student to read I Samuel 16:7 aloud. Remind the students that Christians must be aware of the effect their demeanor will have on the cause of Christ.

Introduction

Materials

• One jacketed book for each student

Hand out one jacketed book to each student, telling the students not to open the books but to study only the jackets. Then ask volunteers to tell why they would or would not want to read that book. Point out that they are evaluating the book based on its appearance.

Planning Strategies

Bring in several examples of good book jackets. Discuss the design and the text with the students. Draw attention to the kinds of information found on jackets.

Encourage students to bring the books that they choose to class. If a student is not familiar enough with any book to do this assignment, you might postpone his due date two weeks until he has read an appropriate

Let someone else look at your book jacket. Someone who has never read the book could check for interest level; someone who is familiar with the work could check for accuracy. Consider the suggestions as you revise.

Check your work for precision. Now is the time to find the best words for the context. The student who wrote about *The Cay* made the following changes to the first draft after examining it for precise words.

As Phillip and his mom leave to return to Virginia, the ship on
which they are sailing ~~sinks~~ is torpedoed and sunk. Timothy, ~~a really old~~ an elderly West Indian

man, rescues Phillip.

Proofread your book jacket for errors. If you run the spell checker on your computer, remember that it cannot catch certain errors. It will not notice if you write about someone who is a "close fried" (friend).

Publishing

Display your book jacket somewhere that others will see it. Perhaps the school librarian would be interested in your book jacket for an exhibit.

Add your book jacket to your portfolio. A well-done book jacket will be an example of your persuasive and informative writing skills.

Between Innings

Adopting Words

Many words we use every day in English come from other languages. When you order a *hamburger,* you acknowledge the German city of Hamburg, where the dish originated. When you say you want a *cookie,* you are using a word from Holland. Having *goulash* for supper? That is a Hungarian dish. And that "all-American" favorite *spaghetti* comes from Italy.

Even the names of many American places reflect other languages. *Tioga, Omaha, Susquehanna, Dakota,* and *Kansas* are Native American terms. What others can you think of? Other places have Spanish names: *Colorado, Los Angeles, Florida,* and *Nevada. New Orleans* comes from the French, and *Philadelphia* is Greek in origin. What about the name of your town or city?

You may also mention the origin of other familiar words:

- Umpire: Old French word *nonper* meaning "not paired." The umpire is the third person or the "not paired" person called upon to decide or rule between two contestants.

- School: Greek word that originally meant "leisure." In Ancient Greece, only a person with leisure time (someone wealthy enough not to have to work) could go to school.

Grand Slam: Writing Across the Curriculum

Cut a cartoon strip from a newspaper. Then cut the "bubbles" of words out and cut the frames apart. Glue the frames onto white paper, perhaps changing the order.

Into the blank spaces where the words had been, write your own script. This time, though, relate the script to something you have studied or experimented with in science class or in another class that you particularly like.

Try to make the script "match" the pictures and remember to add some humor too.

---

book. If students need help finding books, direct them to Chapter 18: Library Skills.

Drafting Strategy

Allow students to begin drafting their book jackets in class. Instruct them to complete the assignment for homework.

Revising Strategy

Challenge students to review their book jackets for qualities such as precise word choice and accurate sentence structure.

Publishing Strategy

Ask students to display their completed book jackets on their desks and to examine each others' book jackets. Allow students to tell which book jackets appeal to them and why. Collect the book jackets.

Evaluation

For help in grading this assignment, see "Grading Writing Assignments" (p. x) and Rubric 1 (Support Materials CD, p. 105).

Enrichment

Display some books from the 1800s. Discuss how publishers made books attractive before book jackets existed.

Writing Across the Curriculum

Instruct the students to try to empathize with the characters in the comic strip before they write script for the bubbles. Compile a list of several occupations from students' suggestions. *(teacher, coach, lawyer, taxi driver)* Instruct the students to choose an occupation from the list and to imagine what the life of someone in that occupation might be like.

CHAPTER 2

NOUNS

THE CAY
BY THEODORE TAYLOR

Objectives

Students will

1. define nouns in sentences as words that name persons, places, things, and ideas.

2. name the four forms of a noun: singular, singular possessive, plural, and plural possessive.

3. correctly spell singular and plural noun forms.

4. identify the correct formation for both singular and plural possessive nouns.

5. distinguish between common and proper nouns.

6. list the count and noncount characteristics of common nouns.

7. identify the correct forms for compound nouns.

Lesson Support

Student Text
Chapter Review 2—pp. 395-96

Support Materials CD
Warm-Ups—pp. 3-4
Concept Reinforcements—p. 55
Bulletin Boards—p. 205

1.) Warm-up (Nouns)

2.) In the morning, the air was crisp and the cay smelled fresh and clean. Timothy cooked a small fish, a pompano, that he'd speared at dawn down on the reef. Neither of us had felt so good or so clean since we had been aboard the *Hato*. And without discussing it, we both thought this might be the day an aircraft would swing up into the Devil's Mouth, if that's where we were.

The pompano, broiled over the low fire, tasted good. Of course, we were eating little but what came from the sea. Fish, langosta, mussels, or the eggs from sea urchins, those small, black round sea animals with sharp spines that attach themselves to the reefs.

Timothy had tried to make a stew from seaweed but it tasted bitter. Then he'd tried to boil some new sea-grape roots but they made us ill. The only thing that ever worked for him was sea-grape leaves, boiled first in sea water and then cooked in fresh water.

But above us, forty feet from the ground, Timothy said, was a feast. Big, fat green coconuts. When we'd landed, there were a few dried ones on the ground, but the meat in them was not very tasty. In a fresher one, there was still some milk, but it was rancid.

3.) Discussion ?'s

- *What names of things in this passage are not familiar to you?*

- *If you had to guess what these things are, what clues does this passage give you?*

- *Which names in the passage seem to have a Caribbean sound to them?*

- *Do you think you would like to eat with Timothy and the narrator?*

4.) Some of the names in this passage begin with capital letters. The capitals signal that these are names of specific things or places. *Hato* is the name of a ship. What other words in the passage lead you to believe that the *Hato* is a ship? *aboard*

5.) The list in the second paragraph gives many specific details. Writers use details like these to make you feel that you are a part of the scenes they are describing.

6.) Names of people, places, things, and ideas are called *nouns*. Nouns are just one of the parts of speech that good writers learn to use to advantage. After you finish this chapter, you will better understand how this writer used nouns to make us feel as if we were on the cay with Timothy and the narrator.

If a student questions the expression *Devil's Mouth*, explain that this name refers to a geographic feature of the book's setting.

Answers:

- Answers will vary but may include *cay, pompano, reef, Hato, langosta, mussels, sea urchins.*

- Answers will vary. *(Clues can be found in surrounding words.)*

- Answers will vary but may include *cay, pompano, Hato, langosta, mussels.*

- Answers will vary.

Hato - name of ship
Devil's Mouth - place
Timothy - boy's name

R

page 381
**Developing the
Supporting Sentences**

Nouns **25**

Literature Link

Read aloud (or ask a student to read aloud) the excerpt from *The Cay;* lead a discussion using the questions in the student text. Remind the students that we use nouns every day in our speech.

Nouns

The largest group of words in the English language is nouns; the next largest group is verbs, then adjectives, and then adverbs. There are thousands of words in each group. New words can be added to these classes by invention, by changing or combining other words, or by taking words from another language. In any complete sentence, it is the nouns, verbs, adjectives, and adverbs that carry most of the meaning in the sentence.

Nouns are words that name. Traditionally, nouns have been defined as the names of persons, places, things, and ideas.

Person: girl, Moira
Place: town, Boise
Thing: book, *Swiss Family Robinson*
Idea: emotion, happiness

2-1 PRACTICE THE SKILL

Underline the nouns.

1. Critics believe Edgar Allan Poe wrote a poem when a friend tragically died.

2. Poe chose to name his heroine after the legendary Helen of Troy.

3. Her circumstances led to the Trojan War.

4. In the poem, Poe alludes to Ulysses, who returned to his home after ten years of travel.

5. The themes of his poems often deal with death or terror.

6. "The Raven" is the most famous poem by Edgar Allan Poe.

7. The poem brought Poe his first taste of fame.

8. The structure of the poem is developed around questions asked by the speaker.

9. The death of a beautiful woman is the theme.

10. The raven repeats the same word at the end of several stanzas.

Students may underline *Helen* and *Troy* as two separate proper nouns or *Helen of Troy* as one proper noun. Either answer is acceptable.

8.)

Teaching Strategy: Induction

Write these sentences on the board or overhead transparency:

- Kellie bought a ___ for her ___.
- Dad's ___ heard several ___.
- We live in ___.
- Joe saw me at the ___.
- April gave ___ a gift.
- ___ is a good character quality.

Ask the students for words to complete the sentences. Ask them what the words in the blanks are naming. *(persons, places, things, or ideas)*

Scriptural Application

Materials

9.)
- "Swift Things Are Beautiful" by Elizabeth Coatsworth. (This poem may be found in *EXPLORATIONS IN LITERATURE for Christian Schools*, Second Edition, published by BJU Press.)

Read "Swift Things Are Beautiful" by Elizabeth Coatsworth. Instruct the students to identify the nouns in the poem.

Mention that all the nouns are examples of God's creation.

Fill in each blank with an appropriate noun. *(Answers will vary.)*

Dana	1. (person) and Denise worked at camp during the summer.
love	2. Denise's (idea) of water inspired her to be a lifeguard.
North Carolina	3. The camp was in (place).
games	4. The campers played many (thing).
woods	5. Out in the (place), Justin hid from the other team.
fear	6. Amy's (idea) of snakes affected her enjoyment.
Kirsten	7. (person) borrowed clothes from her sister.
messages	8. From camp, Todd sent (thing) to his best friend at home.
Texas	9. Ted wrote to his grandparents who live in (place).
Aaron	10. (person) was practicing for his swim test.

Begin [Day 2]

Forms of Nouns

Another way to define nouns is by how they change when they are used in different ways. In English most nouns have four forms: the **singular,** the **singular possessive,** the **plural,** and the **plural possessive.** Any word that can appear in these four forms is a noun.

singular

boy The singular form of the noun shows that just one person or thing is being named.

boy's The singular possessive form shows ownership by one person or thing. It usually modifies another noun.

plural

boys The plural shows that at least two persons or things are being named.

boys' The plural possessive form shows ownership by more than one person or thing. It usually modifies another noun.

STOP

 Learning Christianly

Nouns are important in language because naming is important in life. Read Genesis 1:3-5 and 2:19. What does the similarity between these two portions suggest about using language to name things?

 Learning Christianly

Mankind declares God's glory by being like Him in language. God made the world and then named much of it. But He also left much of it unnamed. He has seen fit to let mankind declare His glory by naming the rest. Adam's first task (as the being made in God's image and called to exercise dominion) was to name all the animals and birds, which God had left unnamed. Adam's skill and creativity in using language in this way declared God's glory. It demonstrated that God was able not only to create but also to create something that could then be remarkably creative. Remind your students that as they learn to use nouns skillfully, they are following in a long, rich tradition of God-glorifying work that extends all the way back to Adam. They are learning how to refer to parts of God's world skillfully with words. This ability is part of our task of declaring God's glory.

Teaching Strategy: Introduction

Make four columns labeled *singular, singular possessive, plural,* and *plural possessive* on the board or overhead transparency. Ask students to suggest nouns for the singular column. Then ask other students to fill in the plural column. Ask the students to describe the methods they used to form the plural nouns. Keep this list to use again when teaching possessive forms.

page 320

Plural nouns

Spelling the Plurals of Nouns

A singular noun indicates that there is only one person, place, thing, or idea. Plural nouns indicate that there are two or more persons, places, things, or ideas.

A) Regular plural formation

Pronunciation of Plurals (and Possessives)

English has three different pronunciations for its plural (and possessive) noun forms.

1. Plurals after *s, x, z, ch,* or *sh* sounds are pronounced /ez/.
   Examples: buses, boxes, quizzes, churches, dishes.
2. Plurals after *b, d, g, l, m, n, r, v, w,* or vowel sounds are pronounced /z/.
   Examples: dogs, dolls, cans, cows, arias.
3. Plurals after *f, k, p,* or *t* sounds are pronounced /s/.
   Examples: laughs, larks, shops, cots.

Add *s* to the singular form of most nouns to form the plural.

dog   dogs

Add *es* to singular nouns ending with *s, x, z, ch,* and *sh.*

dish   dishes

If the noun ends with a consonant followed by *y,* change the *y* to *i* and then add *es.*

city   cities

If the noun ends with a vowel followed by *y,* add only *s.*

monkey   monkeys

If the word ends in *f* or *fe,* consult your dictionary. For some nouns, add *s;* for others, change the *f* to *v* and add *es.*

chief   chiefs
wolf   wolves

If the word ends in *o,* consult your dictionary. For some nouns, add *s;* for others, add *es.*

piano   pianos
potato   potatoes

B) Irregular plural formation

Change the spelling.

man   men
goose   geese
mouse   mice

Change nothing.

deer   deer
Chinese   Chinese

Add *'s* to form the plurals of letters being discussed.

the *d*   the *d*'s

IN SUMMARY

Nouns name persons, places, things, and ideas.

Most nouns have four forms: **singular, singular possessive, plural,** and **plural possessive.**

Add *s* or *es* to most singular nouns to form the plural.

Some nouns have irregular forms for the plural.

 2-3   PRACTICE THE SKILL

Change the underlined nouns to the plural form. Write the answer in the blank.

_____mountains_____ 1. Black darkness cloaked the <u>mountain</u>.

trees, housetops 2. The wind tore the leaves from the <u>tree</u>, and raindrops hammered the <u>housetop</u>.

_____branches_____ 3. The <u>branch</u> of the tree hung low from the weight of the rain.

_____gutters_____ 4. Rain overflowed in the <u>gutter</u> of the old farmhouse.

_____skies_____ 5. The <u>sky</u> flashed lightning blue.

___flashes, z's____ 6. The lightning <u>flash</u> looked like a <u>z</u> in the sky.

crashes, valleys 7. Moments later, a <u>crash</u> of thunder rumbled through the <u>valley</u>.

___men, porches___ 8. The <u>man</u> ran quickly onto the <u>porch</u> to get out of the storm.

_____children_____ 9. After the rain the <u>child</u> went outside to play.

_____trout_____ 10. The day turned out to be perfect for fishing for <u>trout</u>.

Underline any error with plural forms of nouns. Rewrite the nouns correctly on the lines below the paragraph.

Minnesota is home to many wild <u>animalses</u>. The northern <u>forestes</u> are home to bears and <u>mooses</u>. Some of the most interesting creatures in the state are the <u>wolfs</u>. You can see smaller animals in Minnesota too. Beavers and <u>foxs</u> are abundant. Wildfowl, such as ducks and <u>turkies</u>, also live there. The state is famous for the <u>fishs</u> that live in its lakes. Some people fish all year long. Many people have <u>buildinges</u> called shanties to protect them from the cold. The <u>shantys</u> have holes in their floors that allow the fishermen to fish through <u>holeses</u> in the ice.

animals, forests, moose, wolves, foxes, turkeys, fish or fishes, buildings,

shanties, holes

page 112

Possessives

page 310

Apostrophe

Forming the Possessives of Nouns

Possessive nouns show ownership or belonging. They tell who or what owns a thing. All possessive nouns have apostrophes.

To form the singular possessive, add 's to the singular form of the noun (even if the noun already ends in s).

house	house's roof
Mr. Charles	Mr. Charles's car
child	child's toy
goose	goose's feathers

Traditionally, add only ' to the proper names *Jesus* and *Moses*.

Jesus   Jesus' disciples

To form the plural possessive, add ' or 's to the plural form of the noun. If a plural ends with s, add only ' to make it possessive.

houses	houses' foundations
the Bateses	the Bateses' vacation

If a plural does not end with s, add 's.

children	children's playground
geese	geese's pond

Teaching Strategy:
Discussion

Using the list of student suggestions from the activity described on page 27, fill in the singular possessive and plural possessive columns. Uncover each new example as you discuss it with the students. Ask students to explain how the possessive form is made.

Teaching Strategy:
Demonstration

Demonstrate this technique for forming the possessive of plural nouns. First, make the noun into its plural form. Then make the plural noun into its possessive form. Generally, add only the apostrophe to a plural noun that ends with s. *(toys* becomes *toys')* Add both the apostrophe and the s to a plural noun that does not end with s. *(children* becomes *children's)*

IN SUMMARY

To form the singular possessive, add 's to the singular form.
To form the plural possessive, add ' or 's to the plural form.

2-5 PRACTICE THE SKILL

Rewrite each phrase on the line beside it, changing each *of* phrase to a possessive noun form. *(Answers will vary.)*

1. the car of Mrs. Peterson _____ *Mrs. Peterson's car*

2. the collars of the dogs _____ *the dogs' collars*

3. the sister of Moses _____ *Moses' sister*

4. the food of the mice _____ *the mice's food*

5. the basketball of Angelo _____ *Angelo's basketball*

6. the suits of the men _____ *the men's suits*

7. the daughter of the Joneses _____ *the Joneses' daughter*

8. the passport of the tourist _____ *the tourist's passport*

9. the attention of the people _____ *the people's attention*

10. the color of the flowers _____ *the flowers' color*

Nouns 31

Rewrite each sentence, changing each underlined noun to its possessive form.

1. The <u>boy</u> hastily written lesson is illegible.

   The boy's hastily written lesson is illegible.

2. The <u>teacher</u> suggestion was to exert more effort.

   The teacher's suggestion was to exert more effort.

3. Mrs. Connelly complimented the <u>children</u> progress.

   Mrs. Connelly complimented the children's progress.

4. At the <u>teachers</u> meeting, the principal announced new policies.

   At the teachers' meeting, the principal announced new policies.

5. Our <u>choir</u> song won first place in interscholastic competition.

   Our choir's song won first place in interscholastic competition.

6. The <u>boys</u> choir and the <u>girls</u> choir will combine for a special concert.

   The boys' choir and the girls' choir will combine for a special concert.

7. In history class we heard the <u>president</u> speech.

   In history class we heard the president's speech.

8. In my book report I told a few facts about the <u>author</u> life.

   In my book report I told a few facts about the author's life.

9. In our book reports we are not to tell the <u>stories</u> endings.

   In our book reports we are not to tell the stories' endings.

10. In a science report Ted told about <u>sheep</u> aversion to fast-running water.

    In a science report Ted told about sheep's aversion to fast-running water.

Choosing Between Possessive and Plural

If you have trouble deciding whether a noun should be possessive or plural, try putting the noun into a prepositional phrase beginning with the word *of*. The *of* phrase, like the possessive form, shows ownership. The prepositional phrase may sound a little strange, but it will almost always make sense.

The *boys'* ride to the old barn took four hours.
The *ride of the boys* to the old barn took four hours.

Although the second sentence sounds wordy, it makes sense. The correct form of the noun is the plural possessive.

Usually the *of* phrase will not work when the plural form is needed. Sometimes you cannot substitute an *of* phrase for the noun without changing the meaning of the sentence.

Wrong: The ride of the boys their bicycles to the park.
Right: The boys ride their bicycles to the park.

The sentence with the *of* phrase does not make sense. The plural form, not the possessive form, is correct.

page 144
Prepositional phrases

IN SUMMARY

Use an *of* phrase to test whether the possessive form or the plural form of a noun is correct.

2-7   PRACTICE THE SKILL

Fill in each blank with the correct singular, singular possessive, plural, or plural possessive form of a word from the list below.

body   dolphin   fin   sound

_____dolphin__ S__   1. The __?__ is one of a group of mammals similar to the whale.

_____bodies__ P__   2. The __?__ of dolphins are shaped like torpedoes.

_____Dolphins__ P__   3. __?__ differ from porpoises in the shapes of their snouts and teeth.

_____bodies'__ PP__   4. Their __?__ abilities to slow the heart rate and collapse the lungs enable dolphins to dive deeply.

__PP P__
__Dolphins', fins__   5. __?__ flippers and __?__ balance and propel them through the ocean.

Nouns   **33**

body's SP   6. Scientists speculate that its _?_ blubber helps keep a dolphin afloat.

fins' PP   7. The two tail _?_ purposes are both propulsion and communication.

dolphin's SP   8. While underwater, a _?_ blowhole, located on the top of its head, remains closed.

sounds P   9. Dolphins are able to hear many _?_.

dolphin's SP   10. A _?_ built-in sonar system helps it locate and identify objects.

2·8 REVIEW THE SKILL

Using one of the words from the list, fill in the blank with the correct singular _(S)_, singular possessive _(SP)_, plural _(P)_, or plural possessive _(PP)_ form. Then use the abbreviations to tell which form you used.

bee   beekeeper   hive   honey

honey, S   1. The only source of _?_ is honeybees.

bee's, SP; bees', PP   2. Beeswax, another of the _?_ products, is an ingredient in chewing gum.

bees or hives, P   3. Some beekeepers are able to handle _?_ with their bare hands.

bees', PP   4. All worker _?_ hind legs have baskets that are used to carry pollen.

bee's, SP   5. A worker _?_ dance tells other bees where they can find nectar.

bees, P   6. Worker _?_ guard all of the hive's entrances against unwanted invaders.

beekeeper's, SP   7. If a _?_ movements around the hive are too quick, a bee is more likely to sting.

bees', PP   8. Many _?_ hives are transported cross-country in order to expose the bees to a variety of plants.

Honey's, SP   9. _?_ flavor varies according to the plant that supplied the nectar.

bee or hive, S   10. God's design in nature can be seen in the structure of the _?_.

2-9   USE THE SKILL

Underline any errors with plurals or possessives. Rewrite the words correctly on the lines below. Be prepared to explain your answers.

Andorra is one of the smallest country's in the world. (Notice that the country's name has two _rs_ in it.) Andorra is located between France and Spain. The Pyrenees Mountains surround Andorra's vallies.

For more than seven hundred years, two prince's, one from each of Andorra's neighbors, ruled Andorra. The peoples wishs for self-rule became reality in 1993 when they adopted their countries first constitution. This constitution limits the princes' power.

Today tourism is popular in Andorra, and many men and womans work in store's and hotel's. In the past, however, most Andorrans were farmers or shepherds. Many Andorran familys still live in their ancestors' farmhouses.

countries, r's, valleys, princes, people's, wishes, country's,

women, stores, hotels, families

End
Begin *Day 5*

STOP

Identifying Common and Proper Nouns

Whether singular or plural, possessive or not possessive, all nouns are either **common** or **proper.** Common nouns are general words for persons, places, or things. Proper nouns name specific people, places, or things. We capitalize proper nouns.

Recognizing Common and Proper Nouns

	Common	Proper
Persons	son	Randall
	pastor	Lloyd Harrison
	real estate agent	Pam Gossette
Places	park	Eder Park
	airport	O'Hare International Airport
	mountain	Mount McKinley
Things	flag	Old Glory
	magazine	_National Geographic_
	beagle	Snoopy

page 116

Proper adjectives

page 277

Capitalization

ESL: An ESL student whose native language does not use capitalization (such as Arabic) or uses capitalization more frequently than does English (such as German) may have difficulty differentiating between common and proper nouns. Emphasize to such students that English proper nouns are *always* capitalized but common nouns are capitalized only when they begin a sentence, are in a title, and so on.

Nouns   35

Enrichment

After discussing common and proper nouns, direct a differentiating activity. Divide the class into two groups. A member of Team One names a common noun, and a member of Team Two names a corresponding proper noun. If Team Two correctly names a proper noun, it gains one point. If Team Two cannot name a proper noun, Team One gains a point only if it can name a proper noun. After five minutes, reverse the teams' roles. Emphasize the fact that proper nouns are capitalized. If Team One needs some suggestions, begin

with this list: river (Mississippi), business (Eastman Kodak), holiday (Christmas), governor, car, street, religion, country, month.

Enrichment

The meanings of Bible names are listed in many Bible dictionaries and reference Bibles. Allow students to investigate the meanings of sets of names in Scripture, noting carefully the way a name sometimes reflects the character of the person. Remind the students that events in a person's life might result in his name being changed, as in the cases of Abram and Jacob.

IN SUMMARY

Common nouns are general words for persons, places, things, and ideas. Common nouns are not generally capitalized.

Proper nouns are specific words for persons, places, things, and ideas. Proper nouns must be capitalized.

2-10 **PRACTICE THE SKILL**

Underline the nouns in the sentences below. Label each noun C (common) or P (proper).

1. Jason flew on a plane to France.
   (P) (C) (P)

2. His vacation to this new country was exciting.
   (C) (C)

3. Jason left his family at the LaGuardia International Airport.
   (P) (C) (P)

4. The plane stopped in Paris.
   (C) (P)

5. In this city, people can see the Louvre.
   (C) (C) (P)

6. Jason walked down the Champs-Elysees.
   (P) (P)

7. Cafes are located along this street.
   (C) (C)

8. The Duponts took him to see Notre Dame, the famous cathedral.
   (P) (P) (C)

9. Then the family rode the metro back to their chalet.
   (C) (C) (C)

10. Jason traveled to Normandy on a train.
    (P) (P) (C)

2-11 **REVIEW THE SKILL**

Replace each common noun in parentheses by writing a proper noun in the blank. *(Answers will vary.)*

_____Patrice_____ 1. (girl) is in the seventh grade.

Calvary Academy 2. She attends (school).

_____Fridley_____ 3. The school is located in (city).

_____Dennis_____ 4. (boy), her older brother, attends the same school.

Columbia Heights 5. They live nearby in (another city).

Thursday	6. On (weekday) her history class took a field trip.
Sibley House	7. They visited (historic site).
Henry Sibley	8. There, the students learned about (historical figure).
Minnesota	9. That person was an important figure in the history of (state).
Miss Gray	10. (teacher) and the students enjoyed their trip.

Day 6

STOP

Identifying Count and Noncount Nouns

So far you have studied three pairs of noun characteristics: singular and plural, possessive and nonpossessive, and common and proper. In addition to these characteristics, common nouns (and only common nouns) are also **count** and **noncount.** Normally we make distinctions between count and noncount nouns automatically.

Count nouns, unlike noncount nouns, can be made plural to show _how many_. Changing a singular count noun to plural changes the number but not the meaning of the word. We can speak of _a book, one book,_ or _two books._ Count nouns can be singular or plural in form. You can test a singular noun to see whether it is a count noun by putting either the word _a_ or the word _one_ in front of it. When a count noun is plural, it can have a number word other than _one_ before it.

> A _book_ lay on the desk.
> One _book_ lay on the desk.
> Two _books_ lay on the desk.

Noncount nouns are always singular, never plural, in form. Noncount nouns will not take _a_ or _one_ before them.

Wrong: The pitcher is for _a milk._
Right: The pitcher is for _milk._
Wrong: The glass would not hold _milks._
Right: The glass would not hold much _milk._

[handwritten notes in margin: Count nouns can be made plural to show how many. Test with "a" or "one" before it.

Noncount nouns are always singular in form. Can't use "a" or "one" before it.]

> Noncount nouns are sometimes called mass nouns.

[handwritten: "a" or "one"]

Count and Noncount Nouns

1. Use _many_ with plural count nouns and _much_ with noncount nouns.
   We ate _many_ rolls and _much_ rice at dinner last night.
2. Use _a few_ with plural count nouns and _a little_ with noncount nouns.
   We ate _a few_ biscuits with _a little_ gravy.
3. Do not put an _s_ on the end of a noncount noun.
   Wrong: We ate many rices for dinner.
   They have many knowledges.
   Right: We ate a lot of rice for dinner.
   They have much knowledge.

ESL: Learning count and non-count nouns is essential for ESL students. Knowing when to use articles (_a, an,_ and _the_) requires a knowledge of count and noncount nouns.

Teaching Strategy: Demonstration

Illustrate the difference between count and noncount nouns by bringing to class a stack of books and several glasses of water. Elicit from the students that we refer to the one group of objects as _books_ but we do not refer to the other group as _waters._ Ask the students to explain why _water_ is classified as noncount. (_It cannot be counted._)

[handwritten: books is count cuz it can be counted]

[handwritten: water is non count because it cannot be counted]

Teaching Strategy: Discussion

If a student mentions the exception _still waters_ from Psalm 23, explain that _still waters_ is a poetic way of saying _calm streams._ The word _water_ is generally non-count except in some idioms.

Remind the students that proper nouns cannot be distinguished as count or non-count. Although we might occasionally speak of the "four Bobs in the class," proper nouns are not usually counted.

Count nouns can be made plural to show how many.
Noncount nouns are always singular in form.

2-12 PRACTICE THE SKILL

Label each underlined noun CO (count) or N (noncount).

_N_ 1. Did the glass hold much <u>cola</u>? *N*

_CO_ 2. Did you wear your <u>socks</u> today? *CO*

_N_ 3. Can you bring me the <u>water</u>? *N*

_N_ 4. The aspirin gave me some <u>relief</u> for my headache. *N*

_CO_ 5. Do you like my new <u>coat</u>? *CO*

_CO_ 6. My mom bought me matching <u>mittens</u> to wear also. *CO*

_CO_ 7. It's fun to go shopping with my <u>mom</u>. *CO*

_CO_ 8. Occasionally, we leave the stores with many <u>bags</u>. *CO*

_N_ 9. After driving around town so much, we have to refill the car with <u>gas</u>. *N*

_N_ 10. At the end of the day, we are out of <u>cash</u>. *N*

2-13 REVIEW THE SKILL

Label each underlined noun CO (count) or N (noncount).

_CO_ 1. Dolley Madison was a prominent citizen of Washington, D.C., under two different <u>presidents</u>. *CO*

_CO_ 2. Because his wife had died, President Thomas Jefferson asked Dolley to act as official White House <u>hostess</u>. *CO*

_CO_ 3. Later, her <u>husband</u> became president of the United States. *CO*

_N_ 4. She is famous today for her <u>courage</u> during the War of 1812 when the British invaded the city and threatened to burn the White House. *N*

_N_ 5. Dolley refused to flee until she arranged for the <u>safety</u> of important state papers and a historic painting of George Washington.

_CO_ 6. Lucy Hayes, the <u>wife</u> of President Rutherford B. Hayes, was also a remarkable woman.

_CO_ 7. She graduated from Wesleyan Female College in Ohio during a time when many women did not attend a <u>college</u>.

_CO_ 8. Lucy was the first president's wife to earn a college <u>degree</u>.

_N_ 9. She believed <u>slavery</u> and alcohol were ruining the country and became famous for her opposition to them.

_N_ 10. In fact, critics nicknamed her "Lemonade Lucy" because she served <u>lemonade</u> instead of alcohol in the White House.

Identifying Compound Nouns

Some nouns have been formed by combining two words. These nouns are called **compound nouns.** The meaning of a compound word is often a special combination of the meanings of the two original words.

> Compound nouns in English have their main stress (loudest syllable) in the first part of the compound: <u>high</u>chair, <u>bas</u>ketball, <u>red</u>head, <u>son</u>-in-law. However, when an adjective modifies a noun, the noun has the main stress: a high <u>chair</u>, a red <u>head</u>.

book + mark = bookmark

son + in + law = son-in-law

thunder + bolt = thunderbolt

red + head = redhead

Notice the different ways that compound nouns are written. Some are written as one word; others are hyphenated. Because the hyphen has been omitted from many compound nouns in modern spelling, you must often check a dictionary for spellings.

IN SUMMARY

Compound nouns are made by joining two or more words or by hyphenating two or more words.

Teaching Strategy: Discussion

If a student asks about words such as *high school,* explain that some compounds are written as separate words. Do not include open compounds on quizzes or tests.

2-14 PRACTICE THE SKILL

Underline each compound noun.

1. <u>Yellowstone</u> is the oldest national park in America and a popular vacation spot.

2. Many families enjoy the <u>campgrounds</u> and the famous geysers.

3. The park is known for its abundance of <u>wildlife</u> too.

4. <u>Wildflowers</u> such as fringed gentian and mountain <u>bluebell</u> cover the meadows during the summer.

5. But in the winter, heavy snow covers the park; in fact, three of the park's five entrances are closed because of the <u>snowfall</u>.

6. Another famous <u>campsite</u> is the Grand Canyon.

7. Many people have seen minor <u>rockslides</u> at the Grand Canyon.

8. The <u>pathway</u> into the Grand Canyon is very narrow in some places.

9. One of the <u>highlights</u> of the hike is to see the massive stone formations from the bottom.

10. The Grand Canyon is one of the biggest <u>outspreads</u> of rock in the United States.

2-15 REVIEW THE SKILL

Underline each compound noun.

1. The <u>thunderstorm</u> was finally over, and Alison and Katy decided to go for a hike.

2. They borrowed <u>backpacks</u> from their <u>great-uncle</u>.

3. Alison and Katy set off down the <u>footpath</u>.

4. Yesterday, the <u>riverbed</u> had been almost dry.

5. Now the trickle of water made a beautiful <u>waterfall</u>.

6. Once they reached the <u>mountaintop</u>, Alison and Katy decided to turn around.

7. The <u>thunderstorm</u> returned with heavier <u>rainfall</u>.

8. The massive amount of rain began to form its own <u>watercourse</u>.

9. The <u>raindrops</u> were so large they looked almost like <u>hailstones</u>.

10. Alison and Katy found shelter at the <u>campground</u>.

2-16 USE THE SKILL

A. Label the underlined nouns *C* (common) or *P* (proper).

B. Label each underlined common noun *CO* (count) or *N* (non-count).

C. Correct any incorrect spelling of plurals or any incorrect possessives by writing the correct word above the error.

       ^PLois Lenski grew up in a small ^POhio town in the early 1900s. After col-
lege, she moved to New York and then to ^PLondon to study art. She soon
was writing and illustrating bookes *(books)*. Many of Loises' *(Lois's)* ^{C,CO}books tell about
childs *(children)* growing up in small towns across the ^PUnited States,
reflecting her ^{C,N}fondness for her own childhood. Her ^{C,CO}illustrations help

to tell the story by depicting the people and places her words describe.

Her book *Strawberry Girl* won the 1946 ^PNewbery Medal, an award
for an outstanding ^{C,CO}contribution to childrens *(children's)* ^{C,N}literature. ^PLois Lenski
also wrote storyes *(stories)* for very young readers. One of her books is a
frontier ^{C,CO}tale about Cowboy Small, who carries his bedroll and dishs *(dishes)*
tied to his ^{C,CO}saddle. He and the other cowboies *(cowboys)* use their lassos to rope
calfs *(calves)*. They eat their lunches at the chuckwagon where the cook serves them
^{C,N}beef, red beans, and ^{C,N}coffee. Lois Lenski wrote or illustrated approximately
one hundred books in her ^{C,CO}career.

STOP

Include this on Test 2

A. Rewrite the paragraph, changing the underlined words to the correct possessive forms or plural forms.

B. Correct any fragments, comma splices, or fused sentences. There are five errors of this type. *(Answers will vary.)*

Daniel Boone was born in Pennsylvania his <u>family</u> move to North Carolina happened in 1750. As an adult he devoted his life to exploring and settling <u>Americas</u> <u>frontier</u>. A wagon driver, John Findley. Told Daniel Boone a story about a hunter's paradise. There were many <u>buffalo</u> as well as <u>deer</u> and <u>turkey</u>. Boone traveled over the Appalachian Mountains through rugged wilderness, he reached the unexplored area of Kentucky. His path is now called the Cumberland Gap. His knowledge of the Indians saved many <u>settlers</u> <u>life</u>. Two years later on a return trip to North Carolina. The Indians attacked a group of settlers after they left against <u>Boones</u> <u>wish</u>.

Daniel Boone was born in Pennsylvania. His <u>family's</u> move to North Carolina happened in 1750. As an adult he devoted his life to exploring and settling <u>America's frontiers</u>. A wagon driver, John Findley, told Daniel Boone a story about a hunter's paradise. There were many buffalo/buffalos/ buffaloes as well as deer and turkeys. Boone traveled over the Appalachian Mountains through rugged wilderness. He reached the unexplored area of Kentucky. His path is now called the Cumberland Gap. His knowledge of the Indians saved many <u>settlers' lives</u>. Two years later on a return trip to North Carolina, the Indians attacked a group of settlers after they left against <u>Boone's wishes</u>.

☰SLIDING HOME

The more specific a writer's nouns are, the sharper and clearer the picture in the reader's mind will be. For example, the noun *fish* in the second paragraph of *The Cay* excerpt is general; there are thousands of kinds of fish. But *langosta, mussels,* and *sea urchins* each name a specific type of sea creature. Can you see why it is important for a writer to be as precise as possible?

- *Can you find any compound nouns in the excerpt?*

- *What nouns would you change to make this passage be set in Alaska rather than the Caribbean?*

page 386

Precise words

- Yes.
- Answers will vary but may include *pompano, langosta, mussels, coconuts.*

> *I Kings 7:47-51*
>
> *47 And Solomon left all the vessels unweighed, because they were exceeding many: neither was the weight of the brass found out.*
>
> *48 And Solomon made all the vessels that pertained unto the house of the Lord: the altar of gold, and the table of gold, whereupon the shewbread was,*
>
> *49 And the candlesticks of pure gold, five on the right side, and five on the left, before the oracle, with the flowers, and the lamps, and the tongs of gold,*
>
> *50 And the bowls, and the snuffers, and the basons, and the spoons, and the censers of pure gold; and the hinges of gold, both for the doors of the inner house, the most holy place, and for the doors of the house, to wit, of the temple.*
>
> *51 So was ended all the work that king Solomon made for the house of the Lord. And Solomon brought in the things which David his father had dedicated; even the silver, and the gold, and the vessels, did he put among the treasures of the house of the Lord.*

- *How many different nouns are in this passage? How many can you classify?*

- Thirty-one. (*Solomon, vessels, weight, brass, house, Lord, altar, gold, table, shewbread, candlesticks, side, oracle, flowers, lamps, tongs, bowls, snuffers, basons, spoons, censers, hinges, doors, holy place, temple, work, things, David, father, silver, treasures*) All thirty-one nouns can be classified into noun categories such as singular/plural, count/noncount, and common/proper.

Nouns 43

Literature Link

Use the Sliding Home activity as a closure activity for the section on compound nouns.

Enrichment: Speech Link

Instruct the students to write a three- or four-sentence narrative passage. Direct the students to identify the nouns in the passage and to label each noun as NI (new information) or OI (old information). New information (NI) is information that has not been mentioned before in the piece. Old information (OI) is information that the reader already knows. OI is best de-

fined as the "old news." In the example below, NI is in bold print and OI is underlined.

Mom bought **Bob** a new **jacket**.
Mom bought **Sally** new **boots**.
Sally needs a new **coat** too.

This technique identifies the most important information in the sentences. Young performers have a tendency to make all text important; such overemphasis often confuses the audience. When the students perform the passages in class, they should emphasize the NI and de-emphasize the OI.

Scriptural Application

Read I Kings 7:47-51 aloud. Use the questions in the student text for discussion.

Overview of Writing Process

Planning—Observing

Drafting—Writing the entries

Revising—(Not appropriate to assignment)

Publishing—Reading entry to class

Objectives

Students will

1. observe an object over a period of time.

2. describe the object in journal entries.

3. read entries from their journals to the class.

Learning Christianly

Adam named his wife, Eve, with a poem (Gen. 2:23). In fact, most modern versions indicate that verse 23 is a poem by setting it off in poetic form. That Adam would write a poem suggests that in calling us to exercise dominion over the earth with language, God is not calling us simply to use language accurately. Part of glorifying God with language is glorifying Him with beautiful, creative speech. It is instructive to note that before Adam reaches the end of his first day, he makes use of poetry to fulfill his God-given calling.

Learning Christianly

Genesis 2:20-24 records the climax of Adam's naming of God's creatures. How does Adam name this final creature? What does this manner of naming indicate about how humans should use language?

DESCRIBING FROM OBSERVATION

And they brought up an evil report of the land . . . saying, The land, through which we have gone to search it, is a land that eateth up the inhabitants thereof; and all the people that we saw in it are men of great stature. . . . And all the congregation lifted up their voice, and cried; and the people wept that night.
Numbers 13:32; 14:1

Observation journals—sometimes called field notes—are used by writers of many professions. Scientists, teachers, and artists all use field notes when they record their observations of persons, objects, or places. Writers must look closely at a subject and take notes on what they see. Some famous observation journals record such events as the fall of the Berlin Wall or the sinking of the *Titanic*; others may tell about everyday happenings such as the student sitting in the bus seat in front of you or a lady feeding the ducks.

Your observation journal, because it will record *things*, will no doubt be filled with many nouns. Use a variety of specific nouns as you write so that your reader can envision what you describe.

Your Turn

Watch something or someone over a period of time; record and describe your observations in a journal. One of the following may be a possibility for the subject of your journal.

- A growing thing (tree, plant, flower)—Observe the growing thing for two weeks, at different times of the day, in different lights, in different types of weather. Record any changes, such as leaves falling or withering, buds forming, petals opening and closing, and so on.

- The moon—Watch the moon for a period of two weeks, every night if possible. Describe how the moon looks each night or describe how the sky looks if the moon is not visible one night.

- A baby—Watch a baby or a toddler for a prolonged period of time (at least an hour) and keep a log of your observations. Record how the child reacts to his physical surroundings, to people he comes in contact with, and to problems he encounters.

Planning

Brainstorm with friends for ideas. Questions may help to get the ideas flowing. Ask members of your brainstorming group about the places they like to go or the strangest things they have ever seen. Consider having each person start with the statement "You won't believe what I saw yesterday/last week. I saw. . . ." This discussion should give you some starter ideas of where to go or whom to go to for some good observation.

Decide on something to observe. The ideas for observation mentioned above are merely a starting point. You will want to use the brainstorming session or some other method for coming up with an idea to make your decision. Below is a list of ideas that one student came up with by writing

---

Describing from Observation

Lesson Support

Support Materials CD
Rubrics—p. 106

Scriptural Application

Ask a student to read Numbers 13:32 and 14:1 aloud and then lead a discussion about the events described in those verses. When the Israelites sent twelve men to spy out Canaan, the results were surprising. Ten described the land as dangerous, but two described it as a wonderful gift from God. All of the spies were using the same skills of describing from observation, and all had observed the same land. But in the end, two very different reports were given. This biblical account demonstrates that there is more to describing from observation than the mechanics of planning, drafting, revising, and publishing. For an observation to be valid (and therefore truly useful), it must be made from the proper perspective. We cannot do a good job of representing the reality we see unless we are looking at that reality with the right as-sumptions in mind. Remind the students that their assumptions about reality will come through in their writing. Just as the two good spies did, Christian students should describe their observations in a way that demonstrates their belief that God is good and His Word is always true.

Teaching Strategy

Ask the students to name the characteristics of a good observer. *(Answers may vary but should include such qualities as patience, focus, and eye for detail.)* Then ask students to name some kinds of people just the next thing that came to his mind—a sort of word association technique:

local pond
scum/algae
fish
water lilies
fishing
ducks
* watching people feed the ducks

When the student thought of people feeding ducks, she decided to visit a nearby pond and observe people in action. Try to vary your observations as much as possible—different times of day, different situations, different angles, and so on. This will give a well-developed picture of your subject.

Take all of your senses with you. The tendency may be to write only what you see. (This is an *observation* journal after all.) Remember to include smells, sensations, tastes, sounds, and sights in your journal. Taylor uses several of the senses in *The Cay*. Notice on page 25 his sentences that describe the smell of the air; the taste of seaweed, sea-grape leaves, and coconuts; the feel of finally being clean; and the sight of the sea urchins. Try thinking about the thing you are describing using a sense not ordinarily associated with that subject, for example, the smell of a penny or the taste of the wind. Be prepared to include some of these types of observation in your journal entry.

pages 375-77
Chapter 20

Drafting

Write in complete sentences. This will help you to be as specific as possible as you write. Remember that your journal will be read by others, so you want your reader to be able to understand exactly what you mean—short, choppy phrases or single words, although fine for your own use, may be difficult for a reader to decipher.

Take special care with the nouns and verbs you select. Make sure that they are precise and strong. The following excerpt from an observation journal shows how the right nouns and verbs make an entry come alive.

page 381
Developing the supporting sentences

> A lady sits by the lake in a floppy hat, eating something and throwing pieces of bread to the ducks. Two children, a girl and a boy, play hide-and-seek in the trees. On a park bench a teenage boy wears a denim jacket, listening to headphones. A young man and woman walk slowly around the lake, talking. The woman gestures often with her arms, and her laugh comes across the water. Several yards behind them a mother pushes a stroller. A tiny, long-haired dog walks beside her, pausing now and then to sniff at something in the grass.

Choose a title. After you have written your journal entries, decide on a title that encompasses the whole work. The title should let a reader know what the group of entries is about and should make the reader want to read on. The writer of the observation by the lake might have titled her work "Lakeside Wanderers" or "At Carisbrooke Pond."

---

who need to be good observers. *(Answers may include coaches, scientists, doctors, artists, engineers, police officers, and rangers.)*

Introduction

Challenge students to use all of their senses as they record ideas for an observation journal. Allow two or three minutes for the students to observe something from where they are currently sitting. Ask for volunteers to give observations that they have made and write them for display. *(Some of the observations may be complete sentences, and others may be only words or phrases.)* Use these observations to write for display a four- or five-sentence observation. Draw the students' attention to words that indicate *taste, smell, sound,* and *sensation.*

Planning Strategies

Give a sketchy description of something that is familiar to the students. (For example, a flag of the United States might be described as a rectangular piece of cloth with two color fields.) Ask the students whether they can identify the object that you have described. Give additional descriptive clues until the object is identified. Discuss the importance of describing accurately.

Direct students to choose something or someone that they can observe over a period of time and to write three entries for an observation journal. Lead them to see that journal writing it is more personal and generally shorter than academic writing.

Encourage the students to focus their observation entries on all five senses. Tell them to ask themselves what details reveal

Check for complete sentences. If you were rushed when you wrote your observations, you may have needed to use your own version of shorthand or to write in incomplete sentences in portions of your journal. As you revise, be sure to eliminate these fragments from your writing.

Revise your entry before publishing. The student who wrote about the people at the lake made the following changes to the entry. Notice how much stronger the new words are. (The newer words are printed in italics.) Specific nouns like *hot dog* and *pines* and vibrant verbs like *slouches* and *trots* show rather than tell about your topic.

> A lady sits by the lake in a floppy hat, eating *a hot dog* and throwing pieces of *a bun* to the ducks. Two children, a girl and a boy, play hide-and-seek in the *pines*. On a park bench a teenage boy *slouches deep into* his denim jacket, listening to headphones. A young man and woman walk slowly around the lake, talking. The woman gestures often with her arms, and her laugh echoes across the water. Several yards behind them a mother pushes a stroller. A tiny, long-haired dog *trots* beside her, pausing now and then to sniff at something in the grass.

Proofread your journal. Look at the grammar, usage, and punctuation as well as the capitalization and spelling in each entry. Try reading the entries aloud—your ear might help you hear an error that your eyes might miss.

Stage a public reading. Encourage class members to read portions of their journals aloud. Allow for commentary from others who have visited the place or who know the person being described.

Illustrate and bind the observation journals. Display the book in the classroom. Include several blank pages for comments.

Post the entries on the class webpage. If you post your journal, try to take a photograph of the person or place to post with it. Then add to the journal as you continue your observations. Encourage feedback from site visitors by including a link to your e-mail address.

Mail the observation journal. The person you described or someone who knows the place you observed would probably enjoy reading your journal. Send him a copy of your journal or give him the address of your website.

---

the most important part of their observations. For example, suggest that they might focus one entry on the smell of the surroundings and another on the sounds associated with the observation.

Drafting Strategies

Encourage the students to use complete sentences with specific details for their entries. Remind them that their observation journal will be read by others; therefore, each description should be exact.

Direct the students to look at the paragraph on p. 46 for examples of specific nouns. Encourage the students to be precise in their writing and to use a variety of sentence structures.

Revising Strategies

Ask students to evaluate their own observations for focus, clear descriptions, and a sense of purpose. Direct the students to mark the passages where they have succeeded. Then encourage the students to revise the remaining passages.

Peer Response

If time allows, match each student with a partner to participate in peer response. Tell each student to read his partner's entries and to answer these questions:

- Can I see the person, place, or object being described?
- Does the writer reveal how he feels about the subject?
- What details do you particularly like? dislike?
- Is the organization of the entry clear?

HISTORY of the
ENGLISH LANGUAGE

The United States of America is just a little over two hundred years old. But America's common language, English, is much older. Ancient people in Europe and Asia spoke a language that we now call Indo-European. Some believe that the Indo-European language, called a *parent language,* was spoken as early as 3000 B.C. It was from this ancient language that English was born.

People who spoke the Indo-European language spread out into different parts of the world. As groups moved farther and farther away and interacted with people who spoke other languages, the Indo-European language changed. One of these groups moved into northern and western Europe; these people developed the *Germanic* languages.

Around A.D. 450, three of the Germanic tribes sailed across the North Sea and settled in Britain. They were the Angles, the Saxons, and the Jutes. The language they spoke in Britain until A.D. 1100 is now called Old English or *Anglo-Saxon,* after the two largest tribes. The largest tribe gave its name to the country ("Angle-land") and to the language ("Angle-ish"). Can you see how we got our word *English?*

Inform the students that some Old English literature still exists. *Beowulf* (the first recorded piece of literature in English) was probably written around A.D. 725.

Direct each writer to use his partner's comments as a guide during revision. Then encourage the students to proofread their observation entries before submitting them.

Publishing Strategy
Invite each student to read his best journal entry to the class. Encourage each student to bring a photograph of the object he observed to display at the time of his presentation.

Evaluation
For help in grading this assignment, see "Grading Writing Assignments" (p. x) and Rubric 2 (Support Materials CD, p. 106).

Enrichment
Challenge students to observe a single object and then to describe it from several different perspectives (as viewed by a scientist, an artist, a nurse, etc.).

Scriptural Application
Read Psalm 19:1-2 aloud. Remind the students that God shows Himself to us not only through the world of nature but also through His working in everyday events. Only by an observant recognition of His hand in our lives can we know His personal care for us and express our thanks.

Enrichment
Obtain copies of journals kept by Puritans such as Samuel Sewall, Anne Bradstreet, Mary Rowlandson, and William Bradford. Invite students to read these writings as examples of people who intently observed the Lord's dealings in the everyday events of their lives.

VERBS

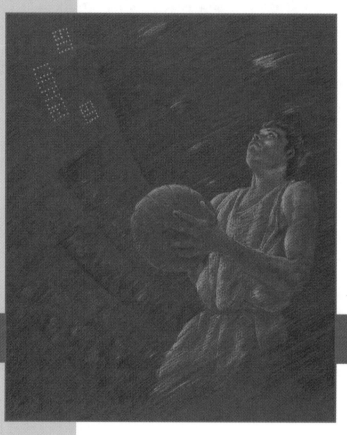

FOUL SHOT
BY EDWIN A. HOEY

Objectives

Students will

1. identify verbs as showing action or state of being.

2. distinguish between transitive and intransitive verbs.

3. label transitive verbs and their direct and indirect objects.

4. identify linking verbs.

5. distinguish between predicate nouns and predicate adjectives.

6. distinguish between transitive verbs and linking verbs.

7. identify and distinguish between auxiliaries, main verbs, and complete verbs.

8. identify the three principal parts of verbs.

9. use the present, past, and future tenses correctly.

10. use the present perfect, past perfect, and future perfect tenses correctly.

11. compose sentences using the tenses correctly.

Lesson Support

Student Text
Chapter Review 3—pp. 397-99

Teacher's Edition
Diagram Answers—pp. 445-46

Support Materials CD
Warm-Ups—pp. 5-7
ESL Helps—p. 44
Concept Reinforcements—pp. 56-58
Bulletin Boards—p. 206

With two 60's stuck on the scoreboard
And two seconds hanging on the clock,
The solemn boy in the center of eyes,
Squeezed by silence,
Seeks out the line with his feet,
Soothes his hands along his uniform,
Gently drums the ball against the floor,
Then measures the waiting net,
Raises the ball on his right hand,
Balances it with his left,
Calms it with fingertips,
Breathes,
Crouches,
Waits,
And then through a stretching of stillness,
Nudges it upward.
The ball
Slides up and out,
Lands,
Leans,
Wobbles,
Wavers,
Hesitates,
Exasperates,
Plays it coy
Until every face begs with unsounding screams—

And then

     And then

         And then,

Right before ROAR-UP,
Dives down and through.

Verbs   **49**

Literature Link

Read "Foul Shot" and discuss the questions on page 50 with the students.

- *Hoey's poem breaks down into many smaller actions the single act of a boy shooting a free throw—drums the ball, raises it, balances it on his hand, and so on. What effect does naming all of these minor actions have on the poem?*

- *How do you feel throughout most of the poem?*

Hoey's poem describes only a brief moment in time. But notice how Hoey out the moment by mentioning small details of action: the player "soothes his hands along his uniform," "drums the ball against the floor," "measures the waiting net," "raises the ball," "calms it with fingertips," and so on. The details slow the pace of the poem. They make us hold our breath. They build anticipation, capitalizing on the feeling of suspense that builds inside all of us as we wait for a climax: will the ball go through the net or not? Slowing the pace of the poem is like replaying a shot in slow motion: it draws out the waiting so that the moment of triumph is even more exhilarating.

Action words like *seeks, drums, measures,* and *raises* are called *verbs.* Hoey uses many action verbs in his poem because the scene he is describing is an active one. But not every verb in our language expresses action. In this chapter, you will learn more about action verbs and other types of verbs.

Verbs

Probably there is no word in a sentence more important than the verb. Verbs give life to sentences, and they connect with other words in important ways. For example, in the clause "The player dribbled the ball," *dribbled* not only describes the action but also tells two other things: what the player did and what was done to the ball. Understanding verbs—both the types and the various forms they can take—will help you use them correctly.

Recognizing Verbs

A **verb** shows action or tells state of being. In other words, a verb can tell what someone or something does or is. A verb that shows state of being is often a form of the word *be (am, is, are, was, were, be, being, been).*

> Harley *ran* down the court. *(action)*
> He *threw* the ball. *(action)*
> His shot *was* good. *(state of being)*
> Mr. Chavez *is* the coach. *(state of being)*

As you have learned, a verb acts as the main word in the predicate in any sentence. Therefore, it is important that you know how to find verbs in sentences. All verbs appear in similar forms. Nearly every verb can have *s* or *ing* added to it without changing the meaning: *play, plays, playing.* Any word that will fit into the following test frames can be a verb.

He It } ____ s	He It } is ____ ing
He plays.	He is playing.
He thinks.	He is thinking.
It rolls.	It is rolling.

IN SUMMARY

A verb shows action or state of being.
Almost any verb will fit in the verb test frame.

3·1 PRACTICE THE SKILL

Underline each verb.

1. The black-footed ferret <u>is</u> one of the rarest mammals in North America.

2. The ferret <u>grows</u> up to two feet long.

3. A domestic ferret <u>weighs</u> more than a black-footed ferret.

4. A domestic ferret <u>is looking</u> at me with its red eyes.

5. The ferret <u>is hunting</u> underground by scent and sound.

page 184

**Special forms
of the verb *be***

page 5

**Finding subjects
and predicates**

page 320

Spelling rules

If you ask your students to write out the words they try in the test frame, remember that some verbs require spelling adjustments when a suffix is added. See Chapter 16 for these rules.

Teaching Strategy:
Induction

Write a sentence like the following on the board or overhead transparency: *We talk.* Read the sentence aloud and underline *talk;* then erase *talk* but leave the line. Divide the class into three groups and choose a student to be the recorder for each group. Allow thirty seconds for the students to list as many words as they can think of to replace *talk.*

When the time is up, determine which team has the most verbs that no other group has. Use the test frames on page 51 to elimi-nate any words in the lists that are not verbs. Point out to the students that all the words left in the list are verbs.

One on One: Take the role of one of the teams for this activity. The student can take the role of the other team.

6. Ferrets <u>chase</u> prairie dogs.

7. They also <u>catch</u> rabbits.

8. That tame ferret <u>is wearing</u> a muzzle.

9. The muzzle <u>prevents</u> the death of the prey.

10. Some people <u>confuse</u> ferrets and weasels.

3-2 ⚾ REVIEW THE SKILL

Supply the missing verbs. Use a different verb in each blank.
(Answers will vary.)

_____ have _____ 1. Tomorrow Gary will _?_ an operation on his knee.

_____ is _____ 2. He _?_ nervous about the procedure.

_____ prayed _____ 3. His church _?_ for him last night.

_____ injured _____ 4. He _?_ his knee in a soccer game last week.

_____ kicking _____ 5. He was _?_ the ball when another player slid into him.

_____ limping _____ 6. He has been _?_ ever since then.

_____ begin _____ 7. The surgery will _?_ at 9:00 A.M.

_____ wait _____ 8. Gary's parents will _?_ in the lobby during the operation.

_____ asked _____ 9. Gary _?_ his friends to visit him later.

_____ cares _____ 10. Everybody _?_ about him.

② Transitive and Intransitive Verbs

Transitive Verbs and Direct Objects

Just as a sentence fragment needs additional information to make it a complete sentence, a verb may need a receiver for its action in order to express a complete thought. This receiver is called a **direct object** (DO). A verb that needs a direct object is a **transitive verb** (TrV). A direct object is a noun or pronoun that receives the action of the verb.

Dmitri baked a cake.
Dmitri baked *what? (a cake)*

In the sentence above, *cake* is the direct object of the action verb *baked*. *Cake* follows the verb, receives the action of the verb, and answers the question "whom or what?" about the verb. To identify the direct object, first find the subject and the verb; then ask "whom or what?" The direct object is compound if more than one word answers the question "whom or what?"

Dmitri baked a *cake* and a *pie*.

Sentences that contain these elements follow the pattern **S-TrV-DO.** Look at the diagram for this sentence:

Dmitri baked a cake.

| Dmitri | baked | cake |

Transitive comes from the Latin word *transire,* "to go over or across." The action of a transitive verb goes across to a receiver.

Intransitive Verbs

Some verbs do not need objects to express a complete thought. These verbs are **intransitive** (InV). An intransitive verb is a verb that needs nothing to complete it. It does not send its action toward anyone or anything. The sentence pattern is **S-InV.**

Dmitri baked in the kitchen.

In this example, the words *in the kitchen* follow the verb *baked,* but they do not answer the question "what?" about the verb. *Kitchen* is not a direct object because it is not receiving the action of being baked. *Baked* is an intransitive verb in this sentence. Look at the diagram for this sentence:

Dmitri baked in the kitchen.

| Dmitri | baked |

Transitive Verbs and Indirect Objects

Sometimes a sentence with a transitive verb and a direct object may include another word that tells who or what was affected by the verb's action on the direct object. This word is called an **indirect object** (IO).

page 247
Trpublesome verbs

Verbs **53**

Teaching Strategy: Introduction

Discuss the etymology of *transitive,* "to go over or across." What does the prefix *in* mean in the following words: *inactive, incapable, inoperable, inaccurate, inconsistent? (not)* What then does *intransitive* mean? *(not transitive)*

Teaching Strategy: Induction and Discussion

Divide the class into two teams. Give one team the phrase "Water engulfed" and give the other team the phrase "I saw." Ask the teams to come up with simple finishers to these starters. After one minute, tell the students to stop writing and to look at their answers. What do the answers have in common? What kinds of words did they use to finish the sentences? Lead the students to some general conclusions.

Compare the students' conclusions with the information on transitive verbs and direct objects on page 53. Remind students of the relationship between direct objects and verbs and of the question direct objects answer, "whom or what?"

Ask the students how the two phrases used by the teams are different from the phrase *The boy ran.* Look at the information on page 53 to compare ideas and discuss intransitive verbs.

Read pages 53-54 and discuss the relationship between verbs, direct objects, and indirect objects. Remind students of the questions indirect objects answer, "to whom" or "for whom?"

One on One: Ask the student to list some finishers for both starters. Examine the lists with the student to come up with rules about the answers. Then complete the activity.

7ᵗʰ

An indirect object is a noun or pronoun that tells *to whom* or *for whom* the subject does something. It always comes after the verb but before the direct object.

Dmitri baked Katya a cake.
Dmitri baked a cake *for whom? (Katya)*

In the example, *Katya* is the indirect object. The noun *Katya* tells us for whom Dmitri baked a cake. To identify the indirect object, find the simple subject, the verb, and the direct object; then ask, "To whom or for whom was the action done?" The next example contains a compound indirect object.

Dmitri baked Katya and Angela a cake.

Sentences with both a direct object and an indirect object follow the pattern **S-TrV-IO-DO.** The diagram for this pattern is similar to the diagram for S-TrV-DO. Look at the diagram for this sentence:

Dmitri baked Katya a cake.

| Dmitri | baked | cake |
| | | Katya |

IN SUMMARY

A **transitive verb** needs a direct object to receive its action.

An **intransitive verb** does not need a direct object to receive its action.

A **direct object** is a noun or pronoun that receives the action of a transitive verb.

An **indirect object** is a noun or pronoun that tells to whom or for whom the verb's action was done.

3-3 PRACTICE THE SKILL

Label the sentence patterns *S-InV, S-TrV-DO,* or *S-TrV-IO-DO.* Above each word of the sentence pattern, write its label.

     S   TrV   DO
1. The banker called the police.
     S   InV
2. Many policemen arrived quickly.
     S   TrV   IO   DO
3. The captain showed his men the plans.
     S   TrV   DO
4. He unfolded a map.
     S   TrV   IO   DO
5. He told the policemen their orders.
     S   InV
6. The men ran to their positions.

Reinforcement

Emphasize the differences between transitive and intransitive verbs by giving students the opportunity to use the same verbs in both ways: *wrote, drive, sang, leaned, eat.*

Ask students to think of any verbs which are always transitive *(take, complete)* or always intransitive *(arrive, come).*

Evaluation

If you have assigned sentence diagramming with Practice the Skill 3-3, check answers on page 445.

1.) banker | called | police

2.) policemen | arrived

3.) captain | showed | plans
        \ men

Diagram

(handwritten top right:) 7th

(handwritten right margin:)
DO: Ask whom or what about the verb?

IO: Ask to/for whom?

    S   TrV   DO
7. They surprised the thieves.

    S   TrV   IO   DO
8. The thieves gave the police the stolen funds.

    S   TrV   DO
9. The police arrested the thieves.

          S   TrV   IO   DO
10. Then the police handed the happy banker his money.

 3·4   REVIEW THE SKILL

Label the sentence patterns *S-InV*, *S-TrV-DO*, or *S-TrV-IO-DO*. Above each word of the sentence pattern, write its label.

  S   TrV   DO
1. Belshazzar gave a great feast. *gave what? Feast To whom? ✗*

    S   InV
2. Many lords came to the palace. *what came? LORDS, so no DO.*

   S   TrV   IO   DO
3. The servants brought them golden vessels. *Brought what? vessels / To whom? them IO* DO

        S   TrV   IO   DO
4. Mysterious fingers wrote Belshazzar a message. *wrote what? message·DO / To whom? Belsh IO*

   S   TrV   DO
5. The message frightened him. *Frightened who? him·DO*

  S   TrV   IO   DO
6. Belshazzar offered his wise men fine clothes. *offered what? clothes / To whom? men IO*

   S   TrV   IO   DO
7. The queen gave the king a suggestion. *gave what? suggestion / To whom? king IO* DO

   S   TrV   DO
8. Belshazzar promised a reward. *promised what? reward DO*

   S   TrV   DO
9. Daniel supplied Belshazzar the interpretation. *supplied what? interpretation / To whom? Belsh IO* DO

   S   InV
10. Belshazzar died during the night. *who died? Belsh (sub., so no DO)*

(handwritten circled:) 3

Linking Verbs, Predicate Nouns, and Predicate Adjectives

A "being" verb usually acts in a sentence as a **linking verb.** A linking verb links the subject with a word that renames or describes the subject. It functions almost like an equal sign.

   David (was a) shepherd. ** ← put on board*
   David = shepherd.

The word *shepherd* renames the subject *David*. The simple predicate *was* acts as a linking verb because it links *David* to *shepherd*.

If the word that follows the linking verb is a noun or a pronoun, it is called a **predicate noun.** A predicate noun renames the subject.

   Tom is the goalie. *→ renames subject*
   (S LV PN)

In the example, *goalie* is a predicate noun. You recognize *Tom* as the subject. *Tom* and the *goalie* are the same person. *Goalie* follows the verb and renames *Tom*.

page 192
Predicate noun

Predicate nouns are sometimes called predicate nominatives. Both predicate nouns and predicate adjectives are sometimes called subject (or subjective) complements.

(handwritten right margin:)
Being verb → linking verb
          ↓
subject → renaming word
David = shepherd
was links:
David → shepherd
subject   renaming word

Verbs   **55**

Enrichment: Speech Link

Lights, Camera, Action Verbs!

Before the lesson, write action verbs (enough for each student) on slips of paper and put the slips into a hat or a bowl. Divide the class into two teams. Instruct each team member to draw one slip from the hat. Give teams three minutes to act out as many verbs as possible. Award one point for each correct guess. The team with the most points wins. Possible verbs include *juggle, slap, laugh, shop, blush, huddle, dive, brush, sing, vacuum, hop, cry, dig, sew, fold, manicure, bat, break,* *eat, handcuff, swim, read, fish, fly, climb, pray,* and *write.*

One on One: Instruct the student to prepare a list of ten action verbs while you do the same. Do not look at each other's list. Ask him to act out the verbs as you try to guess them. Then reverse roles.

Teaching Strategy: Introduction

Review the definition of a verb (shows action or state of being) and discuss the second half of that definition. What does *state of being* mean? (Students will probably come up with an answer involving what something *is*.) Elicit a list of *be* verbs from the students.

page 102

Adjectives

This sentence follows the pattern **S-LV-PN.**

If the word that follows a linking verb is an adjective, it is called a **predicate adjective.** A predicate adjective usually describes the subject.

Tom is tall. — Adj

In this example, *tall* is a predicate adjective. If you try putting *tall* in front of *Tom (tall Tom)*, you can see that *tall* describes *Tom,* but it does not rename him. This sentence follows the pattern **S-LV-PA.** Both S-LV-PN and S-LV-PA can contain compounds.

Tom is the goalie and the team captain.
Tom is tall and thin.

The patterns S-LV-PN and S-LV-PA are diagrammed the same way. Look at the diagram for this sentence.

Tom is the goalie.

| Tom | is \ goalie |

Now look at the diagram for this sentence.

Tom is tall.

| Tom | is \ tall |

IN SUMMARY

A **linking verb** links the subject of a sentence to a word that renames or describes the subject.

A **predicate noun** is a noun in the complete predicate that follows a linking verb and renames the subject.

A **predicate adjective** is an adjective in the complete predicate that follows a linking verb and describes the subject.

3-5   **PRACTICE THE SKILL**

Underline each linking verb. Label the sentence patterns *S-LV-PN* or *S-LV-PA*. Above each word of the sentence pattern, write its label.

     S   LV   PN
1. James Naismith was a creative gym teacher.
     S LV   PA
2. In 1891 he was responsible for the invention of a new game.
     S   S LV   PA
3. He and his boss were eager for an indoor team sport for the winter.
     S   LV   PN
4. The legacy of that desire is basketball.
     S   LV   PN
5. Two peach baskets attached to balcony railings were the first hoops.

Teaching Strategy

Combination with Chapter 5: Adjectives—

Mention to students the adjective test frame *(The _____ thing is very _____.)* and the questions adjectives answer— "which one?" "what kind?" "how many?" and "whose?" Most students will be familiar with these terms already.

Evaluation

If you have assigned sentence diagramming with Practice the Skill 3-5, check answers on page 445.

7th

            S   LV   PN

6. The first ball was a soccer ball.

            S   LV   PN

7. The first players were members of Naismith's gym class.

      S   LV   PA

8. The sport was popular then.

          S   LV   PA

9. But its popularity is even greater now.

                   S   S   LV

10. Both neighborhood kids and professional athletes are

    PA

    enthusiastic about Naismith's creation.

 3-6 REVIEW THE SKILL

Underline each linking verb. Label the sentence patterns _S-LV-PN_ or S-LV-PA. Above each word of the sentence pattern, write its label.

                S   LV   PN

1. The United States Marine Corps is a separate military branch within
the Department of the Navy.

      S   LV   PA

2. Marines were unique from the beginning in their dual operations on
land and sea.

            S   LV   PN

3. The commandant is the top officer of the corps.

     S LV   PN

4. He is a member of the Joint Chiefs of Staff.

      S   LV   PN

5. "Boots" are new recruits.

        S   LV   PA

6. Their instruction is rigorous.

       S LV   PN

7. The result is highly disciplined soldiers.

      S LV   PN

8. Marines are the first troops in battle in most major conflicts.

      S LV PA   PA

9. The corps is capable and courageous in its conduct.

       S   LV   PA

10. The Marines are indispensable to the military system.

    As you may have noticed, forms of the verb _be_ often function as linking verbs. Certain other words can act as either linking verbs or action verbs, depending on the sentences they are in. These words include _become, stay, remain, grow, seem, appear, smell, sound, feel, taste,_ and _look_. Remember that these words are not always linking verbs. To determine whether a verb is a linking verb, you must see how that verb is used in a particular sentence.

    Halley's Comet _appears_ bright. (linking)
    Halley's Comet _appears_ every 77 years. (intransitive)
    The horn _sounded_ loud. (linking)
    I _sounded_ the horn. (transitive)
    This chocolate _tastes_ delicious. (linking)
    He _tastes_ the chocolate. (transitive)

 Learning Christianly

One of the most fascinating uses of a linking verb in the Bible is found in Exodus 3. Here God calls Moses to lead His people. Moses responds by asking what God's name is. God answers, "I AM THAT I AM" (v. 14). This statement is very difficult to translate. Some scholars have suggested the following translation: "I am I AM." In other words, God is telling Moses that His name is I AM. If this translation is correct, the sentence is a good example of the pattern S-LV-PN. What is fascinating is that the predicate noun in this sentence also has a subject and a linking verb. But this predicate noun does not have its own predicate adjective or noun. What do you think God meant to communicate through the S-LV pattern of this PN in Exodus 3:14?

 Learning Christianly

By calling Himself I AM, God chooses a name for Himself that emphasizes His infinity. It is as if God is saying, "Moses, do not be afraid. I am the One Who is ____. And, Moses, don't even try to fill in that blank because it can't be done without unduly limiting Me. Whatever you need for Me to be in the coming weeks and months, I will most certainly be because I am I AM ___." The purpose of any name is to communicate individual identity by expressing the limits of that person's character or personality. God, however, chooses a name that conveys His individual identity by reminding mankind of His limitlessness.

Teaching Strategy: Discussion

Review the material on pages 55-56, emphasizing that a linking verb can function as an equal sign. Discuss the sentence patterns _S-LV-PN_ and _S-LV-PA_.

Explain that _be_ verbs are not the only words that act as linking verbs. Just as there are verbs which can be transitive or intransitive depending on context, there are verbs which can be action (transitive or intransitive) or linking depending on context.

Write this sentence on the board or overhead transparency: _The blanket is soft._ Underline _is;_ then ask students to substitute other non-_be_ verbs without changing the basic meaning of the sentence _(seemed, appeared, felt, looked)_. Point out that each new verb is replacing _is_ in the original sentence. Explain that a verb that can be replaced by a form of _be_ functions as a linking verb.

Teaching Strategy: Discussion

After the students finish Practice the Skill 3-5, discuss the answers. Use the chart on page 58 to make sure students understand the difference between _PN_ and _PA_: the first is a noun or pronoun, and the other is an adjective.

Remember to distinguish between nouns used as predicate nouns and nouns used as direct objects. A predicate noun renames the subject and follows a linking verb. It is "equal to" the subject.

Landon is a fisherman. S-V-PN → follows LV + renames subject
Landon = fisherman.

A direct object does not rename the subject; it is a receiver of the verb's action. The verb before a direct object is always a transitive verb.

Devin ate the cake. S-TrV-DO → follows TrV + does not rename subject
Devin ate *what? (the cake)*

No verb can be both a transitive verb and a linking verb at the same time in the same sentence.

	Part of speech	Position in sentence	Function
Direct Object	Noun or pronoun	Follows a transitive verb	Receives the action of the verb. Answers "S + V + whom/what?" Does not normally rename the subject.
Indirect Object	Noun or pronoun	Follows a transitive verb but comes before the direct object	Tells who or what was affected by the verb's action. Answers "S + V + to/for whom/what?" + DO
Predicate Noun	Noun or pronoun	Follows a linking verb	Renames (in other words, is another name for) the subject. We can usually put an equal sign between the S and the PN.
Predicate Adjective	Adjective	Follows a linking verb	Describes the subject.

IN SUMMARY

Some verbs can be either transitive verbs or linking verbs; however, no verb can be both action and linking at the same time in the same sentence.

Scriptural Application

Discuss the King James Version's use of the word *wax* as a linking verb. What linking verbs could be substituted for the word *wax* in the following verses? (*grow, become,* etc.)

Exodus 32:10—wax hot
Leviticus 25:47—wax rich
I Samuel 3:2—wax dim
Psalms 102:26—wax old
Isaiah 29:22—wax pale
Matthew 24:12—wax cold
II Timothy 3:13—wax worse

Read Exodus 32:1-14. Why has the wrath of the Lord waxed hot in these verses? *(because of the wickedness of the people in building and worshiping a golden calf)* How does Moses plead for the people? What is God's response to Moses' plea? How is God merciful to us every day?

Scriptural Application

Every day we use the basic patterns for sentences, which show God's order and design in language. Even though the basic patterns are always the same, we can use them to express any idea we may have.

TODAY

3-7 ⚾ PRACTICE THE SKILL

Underline each verb. In the blank, identify each *linking* verb.

                                  S   TrV   DD
_____ 1. Andre goes to Calvary High School.   *to what*

                                  S LV   PN
___linking___ 2. He is a freshman. = *renames subject*

                                  S LV   PA
___linking___ 3. He appears tall for his age.

                                  S   TrV   IO   DO
_____ 4. Andre gives the team his best effort at each   *gives what? to whom?*
                     soccer game.

                                       S   LV   PA
___linking___ 5. His junior varsity squad remains undefeated.

                                  S   IAV
_____ 6. His sister participated in the band last year.

                                  S   TrV   DO
_____ 7. LaTasha played the flute.

                                       S LV   PN
___linking___ 8. This year she is an excellent cheerleader.

                                  S   TrV   DO
_____ 9. Their parents come to all of their games.

                                  S   TrV   DO
_____ 10. They support Calvary High loyally.

Friday

3-8 ⚾ PRACTICE THE SKILL

**Underline each linking verb. Label the sentence patterns *S-LV-PN* or
S-LV-PA. Above each word of the sentence pattern, write its label.**

         S   LV   PN
1. The first notable work of English literature is *Beowulf*.

         S   LV   PA
2. The author remains unknown to this day.

         S   LV   PN
3. The language of the poem is Old English.

          S   LV   PA   PA
4. In battle, Beowulf seems strong and courageous.

          S   LV   PN
5. Beowulf's opponent was Grendel.

          S   LV   PA
6. Grendel's roar sounded ferocious.

    S   LV   PA
7. He looked extremely fierce.

    S   LV   PA
8. He appeared much stronger than Beowulf.

                  S   LV   PN
9. After the battle, Beowulf became a hero.

          S   LV   PA
10. The Danish people were thankful for Beowulf's help.

Reinforcement

After the students complete Practice the
Skill 3-7, discuss the answers. Which sentences without linking verbs contain
transitive verbs and which contain intransitive verbs?

Enrichment

Materials
• Newspapers

Bring in a newspaper and ask students to
identify the verbs used in the headlines as
transitive, intransitive, or linking. Some
headlines may not be complete sentences.

Evaluation

If you have assigned sentence diagramming with Practice the Skill 3-7 or 3-8,
check answers on pages 445-46.

(handwritten: Warm- up for Monday 9-16-19)

Underline each verb. Label the sentence patterns *S-InV, S-TrV-DO, S-TrV-IO-DO, S-LV-PN,* or *S-LV-PA.* Above each word of the sentence pattern, write its label.

1. The Mitchells are missionaries to the Philippines.
   <small>S   LV   PN</small>
2. They became quite busy with the local church in the area.
   <small>S   LV   PA</small>
3. Mila attends their church.
   <small>S   TrV   DO</small>
4. She comes faithfully each Sunday.
   <small>S   InV</small>
5. Mila sang a solo.
   <small>S   TrV   DO</small>
6. Her voice echoed throughout the sanctuary.
   <small>S   InV</small>
7. It sounded beautiful.
   <small>S   LV   PA</small>
8. Her parents bought her a new dress for the occasion.
   <small>S   TrV   IO   DO</small>
9. Mila's friend came with her.
   <small>S   InV</small>
10. He gave Mila a corsage.
    <small>S   TrV   IO   DO</small>

(handwritten left margin: DO: Asks; whom? what? IO: Asks: To whom? For whom?)

(handwritten right margin: Have students change InV into TrV.)

Auxiliaries

(handwritten: ← comes from Latin root which means "help")

Auxiliaries, sometimes called *helping verbs,* are words that help the **main verb** in a sentence to express special meaning. The following are common auxiliaries.

- am, is, are, was, were, be, being, been
- have, has, had
- do, does, did
- will, would, shall, should, can, could, may, might, must

An auxiliary and a main verb together form a complete verb. A complete verb may consist of the main verb alone (if there are no auxiliaries) or one or more auxiliaries along with the main verb.

Billy Sunday once *played* baseball for the Chicago White Sox.
By 1896 he *had become* a preacher of the gospel.
Our Sunday school class *will be studying* his life this week.

Be sure to include the complete verb when you diagram a sentence that uses auxiliaries.

class	will be studying

*(handwritten left margin: helping verbs PPT Aux. + Main Verb = Complete Verb * Sometimes, main verb is the complete verb.)*

Another grammar system splits the part of speech this textbook calls verbs into two separate parts of speech, verbs and auxiliaries, because an auxiliary cannot stand alone as the predicate in a clause.

The words in the first three bulleted groups (except *being* and *been*) can stand alone as main verbs in a sentence. The last group acts only as auxiliaries.

The last group contains *will, shall,* and the **modal auxiliaries.** Modal auxiliaries do not change form to show tense. Instead, they express the speaker's mood: ability, possibility, obligation, necessity, and so forth.

Teaching Strategy: Introduction

Discuss the etymology of *auxiliary* with the students. Many churches have a "Ladies Auxiliary" group. Ask students to speculate about what that term means.

Teaching Strategy: Induction

Write the following sentences on the board or overhead transparency:

- Are you entering the track and field competition?
- Which events do you enjoy most?
- Do you like the 100m dash?
- Many fine athletes have excelled in that event.
- Some have not run other events but chose to concentrate on that one instead.

Ask the students what kind of words go in the blanks. *(helping verbs or auxiliaries)* Instruct the students to fill in the blanks and compare their answers with the list on page 60. Ask them what other auxiliaries would fit in the blanks.

After the students complete Review the Skill 3-9, discuss the answers. Ask how many of the intransitive verbs can be made transitive. *(1—echoed)*

(handwritten: #6 echoed words sounds confusion)

Some auxiliaries can be used alone as main verbs. You have already learned that *be* can act as a linking verb. *Have* and *do* can also act alone as main verbs. These three auxiliaries and all their forms are listed at the beginning of this section.

They *are learning* more every week. *(auxiliary + main)*
They *are* young. *(main)*
They *have remembered* to take their books home. *(auxiliary + main)*
They *have* their tickets. *(main)*
He *does forget* his books sometimes. *(auxiliary + main)*
He *does* it frequently. *(main)*

ETYMOLOGY *Auxiliary* comes from the Latin word *auxilium*, meaning "help."

IN SUMMARY

Auxiliaries and **main verbs** together form complete verbs.

3-10 PRACTICE THE SKILL

Underline each complete verb. Write each auxiliary verb in the blank.

_____ *has* _____ 1. Mexico City has been the capital of Mexico since 1821.

_____ *will* _____ 2. People will fill the downtown of Mexico City all day.

no aux.
have=main verb 3. José and Elena Hernandez have a house on the outskirts of Mexico City.

_____ *can* _____ 4. They can walk to church on Sundays.

_____ *must* _____ 5. José's friend must travel downtown each day.

No aux. 6. Many wealthy people live along the Paseo de la Reforma.

_____ *may be* _____ 7. The College of Mexico may be found in downtown Mexico City.

_____ _____ 8. Mountains surround the city.

_____ *is* _____ 9. Soccer is played by people of all ages.

_____ *have* _____ 10. José and Elena have bought tickets for the final soccer game of the season.

Verbs **61**

Teaching Strategy: Introduction

Combination with Chapter 9: Subject-Verb Agreement
On the board or overhead transparency write the following sentences with blanks for the verbs:

- Now I __ ready.
- Now she __ ready.
- Now they __ ready.
- Yesterday he __ ready.
- Yesterday they __ ready.
- Tomorrow I will __ ready.

- She is __ patient, waiting for us to be ready.
- She has __ ready for two hours.

Ask the students to volunteer the correct verb for each blank. Point out to the students that they already know and use all of the various forms of the verb *be*.

Enrichment
Write sentences containing the helping verbs *should have, could have,* and *would have* on the board or overhead transparency and ask students to read the sentences aloud. (Be sure the auxiliary and main verb appear together in the sentences.) Then read the sentences aloud yourself, emphasizing the verbs as "could've" or "coulda." Point out that the slurred pronunciation sounds like a verb and a preposition—"could of." Ask what problems this could create for a listener not familiar with English.

3-11 REVIEW THE SKILL

Underline each complete verb. Write the auxiliaries in the blanks.

_____	1. Some of the men of Cameroon <u>hunt</u> pythons.
must	2. The hunters <u>must be</u> smart and courageous.
will	3. The pythons <u>will hide</u> in old animal holes.
must	4. The hunters <u>must crawl</u> through narrow tunnels after the snakes.
have	5. Some hunters <u>have encountered</u> snakes as long as twenty feet.
_____	6. The hunter <u>grabs</u> the snake behind its head and <u>pulls</u> it slowly out of the hole.
are	7. The hunter's friends <u>are waiting</u> for him outside the hole.
might	8. The python <u>might try</u> an escape or an attack.
must	9. The men <u>must kill</u> the snake quickly.
_is, is_	10. The meat of the snake <u>is eaten,</u> and the skin of the snake <u>is preserved.</u>

Principal Parts of Verbs

Every verb has three basic forms. These basic forms are called the principal parts of the verb. The first principal part is called the **present.** The second principal part is called the **past.** The third principal part is called the **past participle.** The past participle is used with some form of the auxiliary *have.* As you study tenses, you will learn how to use these parts.

For most verbs the second and third principal parts are just alike, usually ending in *ed.* We call these verbs regular verbs. Irregular verbs form their past and past participle in some other way.

page 340

Pronouncing the word

	Present	Past	Past Participle
Regular	work	worked	(have) worked
Irregular	set	set	(have) set
	stand	stood	(have) stood
	take	took	(have) taken

Learning the principal parts of irregular verbs is necessary in order to avoid mistakes in usage. You can find the principal parts of a verb in any

62   Chapter 3

Notice the three categories of irregular verbs in the chart:

1. All three principal parts are alike *(set).*

2. The second and third principal parts are alike *(stand).*

3. All three principal parts are different *(take).*

Teaching Strategy: Discussion

Discuss the information and charts on pages 62-63. Emphasize to students that knowing the principal parts helps them to use verbs correctly. Be sure to point out that the third principal part is used only with a form of *have.* (*Note:* The chart on page 63 features irregular verbs. Regular verbs, for which the second and third principal parts are identical, are included only if the verb is often misused.)

standard dictionary. The principal parts are usually given right after the pronunciation of the word. The principal parts for some troublesome verbs are given below.

ESL: Show ESL students how to look up past tense and past participle in the dictionary (look up present tense to find the other forms of the verbs). A good ESL dictionary should have information on tense, count/noncount status, and several other items.

Present	Past	Past Participle
bring	brought	brought
burst	burst	burst
choose	chose	chosen
climb	climbed	climbed
come	came	come
do	did	done
drag	dragged	dragged
draw	drew	drawn
drink	drank	drunk
drive	drove	driven
drown	drowned	drowned
eat	ate	eaten
fall	fell	fallen
get	got	gotten, got
give	gave	given
go	went	gone
grow	grew	grown
lay	laid	laid
lie	lay	lain
ride	rode	ridden
ring	rang	rung
rise	rose	risen
run	ran	run
see	saw	seen
set	set	set
shrink	shrank, shrunk	shrunk, shrunken
sing	sang, sung	sung
sit	sat	sat
slay	slew	slain
sneak	sneaked	sneaked
speak	spoke	spoken
steal	stole	stolen
swim	swam	swum
take	took	taken
throw	threw	thrown

IN SUMMARY

All verbs have three principal parts: **present, past, past participle.**

The past participle is always used with a form of the auxiliary *have*.

3-12 PRACTICE THE SKILL

Underline the correct verb form in parentheses. Be prepared to explain your answers.

1. Joshua had *(went, gone)* to spy out the land with eleven other men.

2. Of the twelve, only he and Caleb *(chose, chosen)* to take the land God had promised.

3. The Israelites wandered for forty years because they did not obey what the Lord had *(spoke, spoken)*.

4. Because of their disobedience, they *(fell, fallen)* into wickedness.

5. They *(broke, broken)* God's law, but God was merciful to them.

6. While they wandered in the wilderness, the children of Israel *(saw, seen)* the Lord provide for them.

7. Because Joshua and Caleb had *(did, done)* what God had told them, they were allowed to cross the Jordan; but other men their age who had not believed were not permitted to cross.

8. Joshua *(took, taken)* the children of Israel to Jericho.

9. When God destroyed Jericho, His people *(knew, known)* His power.

10. Joshua *(wrote, written)* the events of Jericho's destruction in Joshua 6.

 check answers

3-13 REVIEW THE SKILL

Underline the correct verb form in parentheses.

1. Jim had *(open, opened)* a letter his friend had written.

2. The wind *(blown, blew)* Jim's letter away.

3. Before he could reach it, it *(fell, fallen)* into the fountain.

4. He had *(took, taken)* a rest at a small café in Madrid.

5. After ordering a pastry, he had *(drank, drunk)* a glass of mineral water.

6. Then he had opened his letter and had *(threw, thrown)* the envelope into the trash can.

7. His letter landed in the fountain; everyone at the café *(saw, seen)* it.

8. Jim thought no one there *(spoke, spoken)* English.

9. But one old man finally *(broke, broken)* the silence.

10. "Well, that *(did, done)* it, my boy."

Reinforcement

After the students complete Practice the Skill 3-12, discuss the answers, naming the principal part used. Remind students to use the chart on page 63 to check their answers.

Simple Tenses

Tense tells a verb's time: present, past, or future. Without tense we could not separate in conversation what happened yesterday from what is happening today and what will happen tomorrow. We form all the tenses from the three principal parts of the verb.

The simple tenses are the present, the past, and the future. A verb in one of the first two tenses is a one-word verb. A verb in the future tense includes the auxiliary *will* or *shall*.

ETYMOLOGY *Tense* comes from the Latin word *tempus,* meaning "time."

Present Tense

The present tense of a verb comes from the first principal part of that verb. With some verbs, the present tense tells present time—that the action or state of being is occurring right now.

God *sees* you.
He *knows* the truth.

With action verbs, the present tense tells what is done as habit or usual practice.

My brother and I *ride* our bikes in the park every day.

When a singular noun or *it, he,* or *she* is the subject of the sentence, we add *s* or *es* to the first principal part.

My *brother* rides his bike on the trail.
He rides his bike on the trail.

For a plural subject, the verb never takes the added *s*. The following sentences show the differences between singular and plural forms of a present-tense verb.

Singular	Plural
I *ride* my bike to the bridge.	We *ride* our bikes to the bridge.
You *ride* your bike to the bridge.	You *ride* your bikes to the bridge.
He *rides* his bike to the bridge.	They *ride* their bikes to the bridge.

Past Tense

The second principal part is the form used for the past tense. The past tense expresses an action that has already occurred.

Scott *opened* the door.
Kylee *typed* her book report yesterday.

page 183

Subject-Verb agreement

The chart showing the three principal parts for irregular verbs (pp. 62-63) shows each verb in its plural form. The singular form ending in *s* is not included. Remind the students that the first principal part of each verb has a singular and a plural form.

Teaching Strategy:
Induction

Write these sentences on the board or overhead transparency:

- I __ every day.
- I __ yesterday.
- I __ tomorrow.

Ask the students to fill in the blanks with a variety of verbs. *(eat, sleep, walk, read)* Ask them what is different about the verbs they put into the third sentence. *(They require two words.)* Point out that they already know how to form three of the six tenses they will learn: present, past, and future.

Future Tense

The auxiliary *will* or *shall* and the first principal part combine to form the future tense of a verb. (The first principal part is the same one used for the present tense.) The future tense refers to events that have not yet occurred. It is made the same way for every verb.

Sid *will open* the presents after we sing to him.
You and my sister *will ride* your bicycles to meet us.

When you identify a verb in the future tense, be sure to include both the auxiliary *will* or *shall* and the first principal part.

IN SUMMARY

The **present tense** of a verb comes from its first principal part.
Use the present tense to express an action that is occurring now or occurs habitually.
The **past tense** of a verb is its second principal part.
Use the past tense to express an action that has already occurred.
The **future tense** of a verb is the auxiliary *will* or *shall* and the verb's first principal part.
Use the future tense to express action that has yet to occur.

3-14   PRACTICE THE SKILL

Fill in each blank with the given verb in the tense indicated.

_____will enjoy_____ 1. Juwan _?_ this book about the lives of missionaries in China. *(enjoy, future)*

_____are_____ 2. Some missionaries in China _?_ well known by Christians. *(be, present)*

_____slew_____ 3. The Communist forces _?_ John and Betty Stam in 1934. *(slay, past)*

_____brought_____ 4. Their deaths _?_ many Chinese to salvation. *(bring, past)*

_____read_____ 5. Many people still _?_ about the Stams' effect on China. *(read, present)*

_____stood_____ 6. The Stams _?_ strong for God. *(stand, past)*

_____rang_____ 7. Their story _?_ throughout China and the United States. *(ring, past)*

Scriptural Application

Read Hebrews 13:8, "Jesus Christ [is] the same yesterday, and to day, and for ever." Point out that verbs change depending on whether they refer to the past, present, or future, but God and His Word never change.

_____marveled_____ 8. The Chinese _?_ at their faith in God. *(marvel, past)*

_____empowers_____ 9. God _?_ His children. *(empower, present)*

_____will glorify_____ 10. They _?_ God with their lives. *(glorify, future)*

3·15 PRACTICE THE SKILL

Fill in each blank with the given verb in the tense indicated.

_____struggle_____ 1. Even some missionaries _?_ spiritually while growing up. *(struggle, present)*

_____doubted_____ 2. At one point during college, Isobel Miller _?_ God's existence. *(doubt, past)*

_____gave_____ 3. God made Himself real to her, and she _?_ Him control of her life. *(give, past)*

_____marries_____ 4. On November 4, 1929, she _?_ John Kuhn. *(marry, present)*

_____will go_____ 5. After the ceremony they _?_ to France for their honeymoon. *(go, future)*

_____spent_____ 6. Before the wedding, John _?_ time in Chengchiang. *(spend, past)*

_____recognizes_____ 7. He still _?_ the need for Christians there. *(recognize, present)*

_____sought_____ 8. John and Isobel _?_ the Lord's will for their lives. *(seek, past)*

_____will come_____ 9. They _?_ back to Chengchiang after their honeymoon. *(come, future)*

_____will minister_____ 10. They _?_ there for nearly a year until they transfer to Tali. *(minister, future)*

Rewrite each underlined verb, changing it to the tense in parentheses.

wrote   1. Thomas Jefferson <u>will write</u> the first draft of the Declaration of Independence. _(past)_

blame   2. The colonists <u>blamed</u> the British government for many infringements on their freedom. _(present)_

state   3. Our Founding Fathers <u>will state</u> their rights in this document. _(present)_

will require   4. The Stamp Act <u>required</u> the colonists to pay taxes on newspapers and other items. _(future)_

repealed   5. The British government <u>will repeal</u> the act because of protests. _(past)_

will reject   6. King George III <u>rejects</u> the appeal of the colonists. _(future)_

will memorize   7. In history classes, many students <u>memorize</u> parts of the Declaration of Independence. _(future)_

follows   8. The writing of the Bill of Rights <u>followed</u> the writing of the Declaration of Independence. _(present)_

copied   9. Someone <u>copies</u> the declaration on parchment. _(past)_

signed   10. All fifty-six members of Congress <u>sign</u> the document on August 2, 1776. _(past)_

Perfect Tenses

    The **perfect tenses** express actions that are completed, or perfected. The perfect tenses include the present perfect, the past perfect, and the future perfect. So far, we have studied two of the three principal parts. We have learned how to form the present and future tenses from the first principal part, and we have learned that the second principal part is the same as the past tense.

Teaching Strategy

Combination with Chapter 9: Subject-Verb Agreement

If your students have particular trouble with subject-verb agreement, you may wish to discuss pages 183-84 in Chapter 9 before beginning this lesson.

Teaching Strategy: Introduction

Ask students to find the word _perfect_ in a dictionary. Guide the students in a discussion of how _perfect_ can mean _complete._ What does it mean when something is

completed? What time frame do all of the perfect tenses convey? _(past)_

Teaching Strategy: Discussion

Review principal parts and point out that today's lesson will deal with the third principal part only. Stress that perfect tense verbs take their tense name from the form of _have_ used. Write the words _have_ or _has, had,_ and _will have_ on the board. Use the chart on page 69 to discuss the names of the present perfect, past perfect, and future perfect tenses.

Teaching Strategy: Induction

Write the following sentences on the board or overhead transparency:

- Susan wore her red shoes today.
- Susan has worn her red shoes every day this week.
- Josh brought a visitor to class yesterday.
- Josh has brought a visitor to class.

Ask students to explain the differences between the meanings of these sentences. Guide the students to see that in the first

The third principal part is the past participle. The three perfect tenses use this principal part along with some form of the auxiliary verb *have*. The present perfect, the past perfect, and the future perfect are named for the simple tense of *have* used to form them.

Tense	Auxiliary
Present Perfect	*have* or *has*
Past Perfect	*had*
Future Perfect	*will have* (or *shall have*)

Present Perfect Tense

The present perfect tense expresses action completed during the present time period, often up to the present moment. This tense is made by combining the present tense of the auxiliary *have* and the past participle of the main verb.

Present perfect tense = *have* or *has* + past participle

Scott *has opened* the door for the girls every day this week.
Kylee *has typed* all of her book reports for her English class.
The boys *have opened* the door for the girls every day this week.
They *have typed* all of their book reports for English class.

IN SUMMARY

The three **perfect tenses** use forms of the auxiliary *have* and the past participle of the main verb.

Use the **present perfect tense** to express action completed during the present time period, often up to the present moment.

3-17 PRACTICE THE SKILL

Fill in each blank with the given verb in the present perfect tense.

has visited   1. Susannah Thompson _?_ the Olneys. *(visit)*

have gone   2. They _?_ to the New Park Street Chapel. *(go)*

has asked   3. Charles Spurgeon _?_ Susannah a poignant question. *(ask)*

have chosen   4. They _?_ a small, simple wedding ceremony. *(choose)*

has traveled   5. Mrs. Spurgeon has not gone with her husband, but Spurgeon _?_ to many places. *(travel)*

---

sentence Susan completed the action of the verb in a past time period; in the second sentence Susan's action, although still in the past, has continued up to the present. Likewise, in the third sentence, Josh brought his visitor in the past; in the last sentence, the present perfect tense suggests that Josh's visitor may be sitting there at the time. The present perfect tense is more specific than the past tense; the other words in the sentence help make the meaning clear, but they are not necessary because the verb tense itself conveys the message. (*Note:* This is a difficult concept, even for adults. The more examples you can provide, the better.)

<u>has written</u> 6. Charles _?_ Susannah many letters. *(write)*

<u>has begun</u> 7. Susannah _?_ a book fund for poor men in the ministry. *(begin)*

<u>has sent</u> 8. God _?_ many needed donations. *(send)*

<u>has occupied</u> 9. Susannah _?_ her time with this needed work. *(occupy)*

<u>has had</u> 10. She _?_ her own ministry there in Great Britain. *(has)*

3·18 **REVIEW THE SKILL**

Fill in each blank with the given verb in the present perfect tense.

<u>has written</u> 1. Washington Irving _?_ a story about Rip Van Winkle. *(write)*

<u>has been</u> 2. Rip always _?_ helpful in the neighborhood. *(be)*

<u>has tried</u> 3. However, he _?_ to avoid work at home whenever possible. *(try)*

<u>have climbed</u> 4. To get away one fine day, Rip and his dog _?_ into the mountains to hunt squirrels. *(climb)*

<u>has asked</u> 5. A strange little man _?_ for Rip's help to carry a large keg. *(ask)*

<u>has led</u> 6. The man _?_ Rip into a hollow where a group is playing ninepins. *(lead)*

<u>has drunk</u> 7. Rip _?_ much from the keg during the game. *(drink)*

<u>has slept</u> 8. He _?_ for twenty years. *(sleep)*

<u>have been</u> 9. The townspeople _?_ surprised to see him again. *(be)*

<u>has enjoyed</u> 10. Rip _?_ his new life in the village. *(enjoy)*

Scriptural Application

Read James 1:4, "But let patience have her perfect work, that ye may be perfect and entire, wanting nothing." Discuss the Bible's use of the word *perfect* in light of the discussion of perfect tenses. How does *perfect* mean *complete* in this verse?

Evaluation

Because sentences containing perfect tenses often require dependent clauses in their construction, no exercises in this lesson are suitable for diagramming at this grade level.

Additional Resources

Students can learn more about the lives of John and Isobel Kuhn, John and Betty Stam, and Charles H. Spurgeon in the following books and video available from BJU Press:

By Searching by Isobel Kuhn
C. H. Spurgeon Tonight (video)
Charles Spurgeon by Kathy Triggs
Isobel Kuhn by Lois Hoadley Dick
John and Betty Stam by Kathleen White
Nothing Daunted: The Story of Isobel Kuhn by Gloria Repp

Past Perfect Tense

The past perfect tense expresses an action completed before some past time or event. The past perfect tense is formed using *had* (the past tense of the auxiliary *have*) along with the past participle of the verb.

Past perfect tense = *had* + past participle

When we talk about something that happened before a certain time or before something else happened, we use the past perfect tense.

The Vikings *had discovered* America before Columbus arrived.
Before the Pilgrims established Plymouth Colony, colonists *had settled* at Jamestown.

IN SUMMARY

Use the **past perfect tense** to express action completed before some past time or event.

3-19 **PRACTICE THE SKILL**

Underline each simple predicate. In the blank to the left, identify the tense of the simple predicate as past or past perfect.

past perfect	1. Mutual mistrust <u>had affected</u> the relationship between the white people and Indians for years.
past	2. The last battle between the Indians and the settlers <u>occurred</u> at Wounded Knee Creek.
past perfect	3. Several Indian tribes <u>had lived</u> in the area between the Missouri River and the Rocky Mountains.
past	4. Eventually, the white settlers <u>forced</u> treaties on the various Indian tribes.
past	5. The treaties <u>gave</u> the Indian land to the settlers.
past perfect	6. Soon the Indians <u>had moved</u> onto reservations.
past perfect	7. Ranchers <u>had moved</u> into the Plains area.
past	8. Texas <u>became</u> a cattle empire.
past	9. The westward expansion of the railroads <u>contributed</u> to the rise of the cattle industry.
past	10. Ranches and the railroad <u>spread</u> quickly from Texas into Colorado, Oregon, and Wyoming.

Teaching Strategy:
Induction

Instruct the students to think of an event that happened last week. Ask a volunteer to share his example with the class. *("Last week I went to the dentist.")* Then ask him what happened before his dental visit that caused him to have to make the appointment. *("Before I went to the dentist, I had chipped my tooth.")* Help students to see that the chipped tooth occurred *before* the trip to the dentist.

Students may ask whether using two simple past tense verbs would also be correct.

("Before I went to the dentist, I chipped my tooth.") Both sentences are correct. The use of the past perfect is primarily for precision.

Using a term such as "paster than past" may help students differentiate between past and past perfect. Note that apart from the use of other contextual clues such as *before* or *by the time that,* past perfect is the only means of indicating that a past event occurred before another event in the past.

3-20 REVIEW THE SKILL

Fill in each blank with the given verb in the tense indicated.

_____sailed_____ 1. Christopher Columbus _?_ across the Atlantic Ocean. *(sail, past)*

_____had traveled_____ 2. Many of the European explorers _?_ as far as Africa. *(travel, past perfect)*

_____had worked_____ 3. Christopher _?_ together with his brothers. *(work, past perfect)*

_____persuaded_____ 4. His father _?_ him to work in business. *(persuade, past)*

_____married_____ 5. Columbus _?_ Felipa Perestrello Moniz in 1479. *(marry, past)*

_____had mistaken_____ 6. When he had planned his trip, Columbus _?_ the location of Japan. *(mistake, past perfect)*

_____had proposed_____ 7. By 1483 Columbus _?_ his plan to King John II of Portugal. *(propose, past perfect)*

_____sought_____ 8. He _?_ the gold, silk, and spices of the East Indies. *(seek, past)*

_____rejected_____ 9. King John II _?_ Columbus's plan. *(reject, past)*

_____had approved_____ 10. Finally, by 1492 Spanish monarchs _?_ his plan. *(approve, past perfect)*

Future Perfect Tense

The future tense of *have (will have* or *shall have)* and the past participle of a verb make the future perfect tense. This tense tells about an action that will be done before a future time or event.

Future perfect tense = *will* (or *shall) have* + past participle

> By the time Tristan visits next year, I *will have moved* to Illinois.
> Dad *will have closed* the store when I get there after soccer practice.

We do not use this tense very often, but there are times when only the future perfect tense will say exactly what we mean.

Teaching Strategy: Demonstration

Write this sentence fragment on the board or overhead transparency: *By the end of this class we will have . . .* Tell students to finish the sentence with such phrases as *discussed three new tenses* or *completed one exercise.* Tell the students that they have just used the future perfect tense.

Use the material on page 72 to discuss the meaning and uses of the future perfect tense. Remind students that this is the least-used tense of the six.

ESL Strategy

Many ESL students have difficulty knowing when to use perfect tenses. Refer to ESL Helps page 44 (Support Materials CD) to explain the perfect tenses more fully.

Enrichment

Bake a batch of cookies to use as a follow-up discussion of tenses. As you and the students eat the cookies, ask students to describe the experience. *("Our teacher has baked four dozen cookies," or "By the end of class today, I will have consumed ten cookies!" or "I eat cookies every day after school.")*

Use the **future perfect tense** to express action that will be completed before a future time or event.

 3-21 PRACTICE THE SKILL

A. Underline each complete verb.

B. Label the auxiliaries *aux.*

C. Write in the blank the tense of each complete verb: *present, past, future, present perfect, past perfect,* or *future perfect.*

_____ past _____ 1. The Spanish <u>invaded</u> the Aztec Empire in Mexico in 1521.

_____ past perfect _____
Aux.
2. By 1821 the Mexicans <u>had gained</u> their independence from Spain.

_____ present perfect _____
Aux.
3. The population <u>has increased</u> for years.

_____ present _____ 4. Pablo and his parents <u>live</u> with his grandparents in Tampico.

_____ present _____ 5. He <u>goes</u> to the school in town.

_____ present perfect _____
Aux.
6. For a year he <u>has studied</u> about the Aztecs.

_____ future _____
Aux.
7. His sister <u>will start</u> school next year.

_____ future perfect _____
Aux. Aux.
8. On May 2 their Aunt Dina <u>will have taught</u> at their school for five years.

_____ past perfect _____
Aux.
9. Pablo <u>had walked</u> to school every day.

_____ future _____
Aux.
10. Aunt Dina <u>will drive</u> him to school next year.

Fill in each blank with the given verb in the tense indicated.

will have introduced 1. By the end of each two-year session, Congress _?_ over ten thousand bills. (*introduce, future perfect*)

have held 2. A bill is not passed until both houses _?_ committee and floor debates on it. (*hold, present perfect*)

will have debated 3. Perhaps Congress _?_ all the bills by the end of its session. (*debate, future perfect*)

had filibustered 4. Some people _?_ in opposition to the bill. (*filibuster, past perfect*)

have supported 5. Often special interest groups _?_ the bills. (*support, present perfect*)

will have held 6. Some committees _?_ meetings to discuss specific issues. (*hold, future perfect*)

had decided 7. Sometimes before a bill passed, the president _?_ to veto it. (*decide, past perfect*)

discusses 8. Because of the veto, Congress _?_ the bill again. (*discuss, present*)

became 9. Later, the bill _?_ law after it had received a two-thirds majority. (*become, past*)

will propose 10. Congressional members _?_ other bills next session. (*propose, future*)

Remember that the main verb in all three perfect tenses is identical—the third principal part. Therefore, you must look at the auxiliary forms to determine the tense.

3-23 USE THE SKILL

Write a sentence using the tense indicated. Use verbs other than *be* verbs wherever possible. *(Answers will vary.)*

1. Describe your neighbor's shoes. *(present)*

_____

_____

2. Tell about the most memorable gift you ever gave someone. *(present perfect)*

_____

_____

3. Describe how your appearance will have changed fifty years from now. *(future perfect)*

_____

_____

4. Write a sentence about cars of the future. *(future)*

_____

_____

5. Tell about the last thing that made you sad. *(past perfect)*

_____

_____

6. Write a sentence about your hobby. *(present)*

_____

_____

7. Describe your favorite family vacation. *(present perfect)*

_____

_____

8. Tell about a job you would like to have in twenty-five years. *(future perfect)*

_____

_____

End

Learning Christianly

Think for a moment about the people in your family and your friends. What do you think of when you think of each person? What is it that makes each person unique? Now try to pick a verb for each person that matches that person well. For instance, you might choose the verb *think* in relation to your dad and the verb *laugh* in relation to your best friend. In the Bible God is often called names that are verbs. Read the following passages: Job 19:25; Psalm 40:17; Romans 11:26. What do these verb names reveal about God?

Learning Christianly

People are often distinctive because of the ways they act. What you are like inside determines what you will do and how you will act. Once you notice the way people act, you can tell a lot about what they are like on the inside. Many of God's names reveal that He is an active God. Furthermore, He interacts with the people He has made in wonderful, unexpected ways. Even though God is all-powerful and holy, some of His verb names also communicate other important truths about Him. Through these three verses and others, we understand that God loves people and desires to do good for them.

Enrichment

After the students complete Use the Skill 3-23, ask students to share their favorite sentences orally.

9. Write a sentence about what major you hope to have in college. *(future)*

_____

_____

10. Describe your most recent birthday. *(past perfect)*

_____

_____

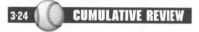

3-24 CUMULATIVE REVIEW

Locate and correct the fifteen errors in the paragraph: fused sentences, comma splices, fragments, noun plurals, and verb principal parts. Use the lines below to write the paragraph correctly. *(Some answers will vary.)*

Some people moved west for quick riches some moved west for a new beginning. Along the trail. Many people and cattles died from diseases or starvation. Indians occasionally waylaid the travelers. Sometimes the Indians and the travelers fighted. Large groups emigrated across the land and settled in the West. The Gold Rush in the 1840s. Enticed many mans to California. Often mans leaved their families and comed out West alone. Some familys moved. Not many womans had came initially. Some towns had only one woman some towns had none. As towns grew. More women came to the West.

Some people moved west for quick riches. Some moved west for a new

beginning. Along the trail many people and cattle died from diseases or

starvation. Indians occasionally waylaid the travelers. Sometimes the

Indians and the travelers fought. Large groups emigrated across the land

and settled in the West. The Gold Rush in the 1840s enticed many men to

California. Often men left their families and came out West alone. Some

families moved. Not many women had come initially. Some towns had

only one woman, and some towns had none. As towns grew, more women

came to the West.

_____

≡SLIDING HOME

Read the poem at the beginning of the chapter again. Notice the variety of verbs that Hoey uses in describing the action of the ball after it leaves the basketball player's hands. The ball *slides, lands, leans, wobbles, wavers, hesitates, exasperates, plays,* and finally *dives.* Does it seem to you as though the ball takes on a personality all its own at this point? How do these creative verbs enhance the picture of this scene in your mind?

- *Which verbs in "Foul Shot" surprise you the most? Which please you the most?*

- *What verbs might Hoey have used at the end of the poem if the ball had not gone through the net?*

page 386
Precise words

- Answers will vary but may include *nudge, waivers, exasperates, dives.*
- Answers will vary but may include *rolls off, falls away, pops out.*

> **Proverbs 30:25-27**
>
> **25 The ants are a people not strong, yet they prepare their meat in the summer;**
>
> **26 The conies are but a feeble folk, yet make they their houses in the rocks;**
>
> **27 The locusts have no king, yet go they forth all of them by bands.**

- *How many action verbs are in this passage? How many linking verbs?*

- *Why do you think there are more of one kind than the other?*

- Four action verbs; two linking verbs.
- Answers will vary. (Action verbs are more descriptive.)

PERSUADING AN AUDIENCE

And he reasoned in the synagogue every sabbath, and persuaded the Jews and the Greeks.

Acts 18:4

Every time you hear a radio announcement about a school concert or a new restaurant that is opening, read in the newspaper about a clothing sale, or look at a billboard telling about a vacation resort, you are seeing or hearing a kind of persuasion.

Advertising tries to persuade you to do something or to buy something. Have you ever thought about how advertising works? Good ads target a specific audience and thrust forward one message to that audience. Incorporating strong verbs helps convey the message to the target audience.

By following a few rules you can become an effective advertiser. A good advertisement should contain the *what,* the *when,* and the *where.* The *what* tells about the product, place, or event; the *when* gives the time, if needed, or the date a new product will be available; the *where* explains at what place the event will be held or the product can be found.

page 378
Determining purpose

Overview of Writing Process

Planning—Selecting the topic and audience

Drafting—Brainstorming and composing

Revising—Reviewing with a checklist

Publishing—Presenting the ad in class

Objectives
Students will
1. analyze ads.
2. write ads.

Literature Link
Discuss the Sliding Home questions on page 77.

Reinforcement
Read the questions following the Bible verses on page 77. Once students have identified action and linking verbs, ask them which action verbs are transitive and which are intransitive.

Persuading an Audience
Lesson Support

Support Materials CD
Writing Worksheets—p. 93
Rubrics—p. 107

Scriptural Application
Read Acts 18:4 aloud and lead a discussion about Paul. Paul was skilled at persuasion, and he did not keep this skill to himself. He knew that people need more than information; they also need information presented in a persuasive way.

Explain to the students that cultivating the skill of persuasion enables Christians to be prepared servants of God.

Introduction
Materials
- Three print ads for different brands of the same product

Pass the advertisements around the class without comment. When everyone has seen all three ads, ask the students to choose the one they like best. Lead a short discussion of their reasons in favor of that particular ad.

Perhaps an announcement will need a *how* in it. That is a section to explain, for example, how to get to a meeting, how to sign up for a contest, or how to get tickets for a play. If there is a *how* part in an advertisement, it should be simple and orderly.

Not all ads are visual; some must rely on the imagination for images. For example, compare the following two radio ads:

Canine Gourmet is now on sale at your local grocer's. The most delicious dog food available. Isn't your dog worth it?

[Sound of silverware on fine china; light barking in background]

Gruff voice: I say, Muffie, what's that you're eating?

Lighter "poodle" voice: Canine Gourmet. My human just got it for me at the market. Want to try it?

The second ad makes more use of the special advantages of radio. Some people may think that a radio ad, because it does not have a picture, is more limiting than a television or magazine ad. But consider how much harder it would be for film to portray the effect of rich dogs eating in a fancy restaurant. Radio ads can often do far more adventurous advertising at far less cost.

Your Turn

Write a radio announcement designed to persuade someone to try a product, use a service, or attend an event.

Planning

Choose a product, service, or event to highlight. Think of what is going on in your school or community. Is there an upcoming fitness run or craft show that would interest someone in your audience? Have you discovered a product that you really enjoy? Or do you have a service to offer, such as doing yard work or walking dogs?

Decide on a target audience. Once you have chosen what to advertise, you must think about *who* would be interested in your product/service/event. Will you target families? the elderly? young people? Think about who will be buying or using your product.

Write a statement of the message you want to project. What is the purpose of your ad? The purpose of the Canine Gourmet ad is to sell dog food. Will the audience remember the poodle's voice or the name of the dog food? The most memorable part of any advertisement really should be the event, the product, or the service being advertised. But sometimes the "gimmick" of the ad can overpower the message. Although many people may talk about an entertaining advertisement, it is useless if they cannot remember the purpose.

Decide on your approach. In a short radio announcement, a good opening is crucial. It gets the listeners' attention. Notice the difference between the following announcements.

page 378

Considering audience

Teaching Strategy

Discuss the effectiveness of several current advertisements. Ask the students these questions: *Which ads stay with you? Why do ads stay with you?* Share any particular ads that were effective in persuading you to purchase a product, visit a location, or participate in an event.

Planning Strategies

Lead a brainstorming session. Ask the students to list or to invent products, events, or services they might like to write ads for. Display the suggestions for discussion.

Distribute a copy of Writing Worksheet 3 to each student. Allow time for the students to complete the first three sections in class.

Drafting Strategies

Encourage students to use persuasive language, to create clear mental pictures, and to invent catchy slogans as they write their ads. Remind students that they must get the audience's attention before they will be able to "sell" their products.

Remind students that the claims they make for their products must be reasonable and attainable. Overly exaggerated claims hamper the effectiveness of an ad.

Revising Strategies

Provide an opportunity for students to review their ads and to identify any trite expressions or overused words. Then direct the students to replace these with more effective choices. Encourage students to evaluate the vocabulary of their ads in relation to the target audience.

Next Friday at seven-thirty in the auditorium on Rodeville Road, the choirs and band of Emmanuel Christian High School will present a free concert. Everyone is invited to attend.

At this joyous season of Christmas, the students of Emmanuel Christian High School invite you to "The Lord Is Come," a concert of Christmas music performed by the choirs and band in the Emmanuel Christian Church Auditorium. The concert will be presented on Friday, December 18, at 7:30 P.M. Emmanuel Christian School is located at 9345 Rodeville Road in Cheyenne. Admission is free.

Which is more effective in its opening?

Write a rough draft. The message of your advertisement should be short, appealing, and simple. Identify your product, the *what* of your ad. Then include the *when, where,* and *how* if these are applicable. As you write your ad, use action verbs to convey your message and choose words that fit your target audience. Since many radio advertisements are thirty seconds or shorter, make every word count toward your purpose.

Revising

Examine your ad to see that you have a single message and that the message comes through in the ad. You do not want to overload the listener with too much information that is not relevant to your main message. Radio advertisements are usually no longer than sixty seconds and some are as short as fifteen seconds; therefore, you must focus on your main idea. Use strong verbs that convey the message you are trying to get across to your audience.

Proofread for correctness. Check for errors in grammar and mechanics. Your credibility as an advertiser is diminished if your ad contains grammatical errors. Remember, however, that ad writers sometimes use fragments for emphasis or appeal.

Ask a peer to read your ad. Does the ad get the reader's attention? Does the ad persuade him to do what you wanted? Ask the reader to tell you what is most appealing about the ad. What is most effective about the ad?

Publishing

Make an audio recording of your ad. Ask your classmates to assume the parts of speakers in your advertisement. Play the recording of your ad for the class or another group.

Exchange ads with classmates and read the ads to the class. You may be interested in hearing how others orally interpret the words and phrases in your ad.

Include the script in your writing folder. Writing a radio advertisement is a different type of writing assignment from many that you do. Adding this to your folder will provide another sample of your writing.

Divide the class into groups of three or four students each. Direct each student to exchange his ad with someone else in his group. Allow time for each student to read the ad that he has received to the group. Explain to the students that listening to someone else's oral interpretation of an ad can help the writer determine whether the ad is successful and persuasive.

Publishing Strategy

Peer Response

Allow each student to present his ad to the class. After each presentation, ask the class to determine who they think the target audience is. Briefly discuss how well the ad targets the audience. Collect the ads after everyone has presented his ad.

Evaluation

For help in grading this assignment, see "Grading Writing Assignments" (p. x) and Rubric 3 (Support Materials CD, p. 107).

Enrichment

Encourage students to collect examples of advertisements and to analyze them for audience and effectiveness.

Scriptural Application

Review the story of Shadrach, Meshach, and Abednego in Daniel 3. Point out their well-chosen words as they declared their faith in God. Lead the students to see how the lives of these young men were a persuasive testimony to the king.

Inspector Jameson's current case had brought him to the lavishly decorated Brindle Antiques. A soft tone sounded as he and Officer Bell crossed the threshold. Attractive pieces of furniture of various styles were carefully and interestingly arranged throughout the store. Inspector Jameson stopped to run his hand along the top of a beautiful chest. Officer Bell took the opportunity to pop a peppermint candy into his mouth. Jameson studied the chest. Its feet were worn and several nicks showed along the bottom of one side. Yet the piece had character in spite of use, and Mrs. Jameson would certainly like it.

"May I help you, sir?" A young woman stood beside Jameson.

"Oh, thank you. Not just now. I'm waiting for someone." She nodded and went to another customer.

Soon a man came to him. "Good morning, Inspector. I'm Hector Montgomery. I understand you need to determine the authenticity of these furnishings."

"Dr. Montgomery, thank you for meeting us. I got your name from this brochure from another store. Yes, we need your expertise."

"Glad to help if I can," said Dr. Montgomery.

"There is strong suspicion of fraud here, and personally I am quite curious about the methods you use to determine the age of furniture. Have you come to any conclusions yet?" asked Inspector Jameson.

"Well, let me show you what I have found and satisfy your curiosity about my procedures. Step over to this hutch. It's a good example of my findings. This one is advertised as an authentic 1860s Irish pine hutch. Notice the overall color, or patina, of the wood. The color is consistent and the general style and size of this hutch are typical of pine pieces from the 1860s."

Officer Bell, whose curiosity was not as keen as Inspector Jameson's when it came to furniture, had wandered over to an ostentatious hat stand, an odd-looking Victorian relic. He absent-mindedly turned over the price tag. When the tag's figure registered in his mind, he gasped, lodging the peppermint in his throat. He coughed and lurched forward, becoming entangled

Critical Thinking

Discuss the meaning of *fraud. (a deception deliberately practiced to secure unfair or unlawful gain)* Ask the students for examples of possible fraudulent advertising for a grocery store. *(claiming that fruit is fresher than it is, mislabeling places of origin on foods, tampering with expiration dates)*

Discuss what the Bible says about fraud in Psalm 10:4-7. Ask the students for biblical examples of people who committed fraud. *(Saul, Ananias and Sapphira, the serpent in the Garden of Eden)*

Bring in an antique object or a reproduction (or a photograph if neither is available). Ask the students how they would determine whether the object is genuine. Explain that there are experts who specialize in determining whether old-looking objects are really old or just reproductions.

After the students read the story, point out Officer Bell's observation that repaired antiques and reproductions are not illegal unless the object is advertised as being genuine.

with the hat stand. Inspector Jameson and Dr. Montgomery watched in amazement. It appeared to the onlookers as though Officer Bell were waltzing with the hat stand while gasping admiration. The encounter was soon over as the peppermint dislodged and the stand righted itself. Officer Bell straightened his uniform and dutifully returned to Inspector Jameson's side.

Dr. Montgomery continued. "Now look at the drawers. See how the runners are worn smooth and have a concave appearance from being pulled in and out? That indicates years of use. The hardware is all original also. There are no telltale signs of previous hardware on the drawer back. The key works and shows real signs of age and use."

"So you believe this hutch to be a genuine antique?" asked the Inspector.

"The lesson is not quite over, Inspector Jameson! Notice one last item. The glass in the hutch doors . . ."

Jameson put his hand behind one pane of glass. "It seems wavy to me," said Jameson.

"Yes," said Montgomery, "old glass is wavy. Perhaps you've noticed this in old houses?" Officer Bell joined the conversation. He had suddenly become very interested in furniture.

"Has this fellow found genuine but damaged antiques and repaired them to sell at first quality prices? That is not illegal unless the furniture is advertised as completely original," said Officer Bell.

"Well," said Montgomery, "I think Inspector Jameson can answer that now."

Jameson ran his hand behind all the panes in the hutch. Near the top he stopped and looked at Montgomery. "Fraud." Montgomery nodded.

"Yes, Inspector. The case, wood, hardware, patina, and wear are original 1860s. This glass pane is not. The discrepancy could be an honest mistake, except that I myself appraised this piece for the owner and pointed out this discrepancy. There is no doubt that the owner of this store is practicing fraud."

Officer Bell was astonished. "'How did you know, Inspector?"

"Why, my old friend, it was clear as a bell!"

1. What did Jameson mean when he said that the answer "was clear as a bell"?

2. From looking at the brochure, why do you think Jameson felt he could trust Dr. Montgomery?

3. If Officer Bell wants to find out more about the hat stand he encountered, which evening of the week should he keep open?

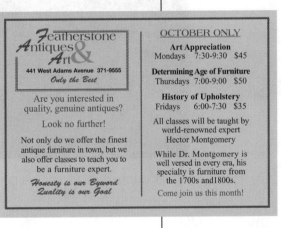

- Jameson's answer is a pun. He knows that the hutch is not a genuine antique because one glass pane is clear, not wavy like the original glass panes.

- He is a world-famous antiques expert. He works for a store that values honesty.

- Thursday night

Verbs   81

PRONOUNS

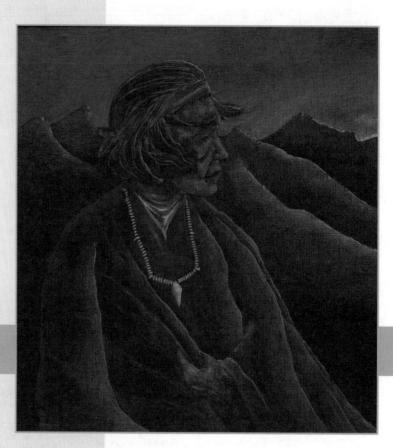

CHIEF COCHISE

Lesson Support

Student Text
    Chapter Review 4—pp. 401-2

Teacher's Edition
    Diagram Answers—p. 446

Support Materials CD
    Warm-Ups—pp. 9-10
    Concept Reinforcements—pp. 59-60

Excerpt from a speech at a conference where Cochise was told the Apaches would be sent to a reservation

I have no father or mother. I am alone in the world. Nobody cares about Cochise. That is why I do not care to live and want the rocks to fall and cover me up. If I had a father and mother like you, I would be with them and they with me.

When I was going around the world, everybody was asking for Cochise. Now he is here. You see him and hear him. Are you glad? If so, say so. Speak, Americans and Mexicans. I do not want to hide anything from you nor have you hide anything from me. I will not lie to you. Do not lie to me.

I want to live in these mountains. I do not want to go to Tularosa. That is a long way off. The flies on those mountains eat out the eyes of the horses. The bad spirits live there. I have drunk of these waters, and they have cooled me. I do not want to leave this place.

- *To whom is Cochise speaking?*

- *What words would you use to describe the way Cochise is feeling as he delivers this speech?*

- *When Cochise makes this speech, he is a prisoner. What request is he making of his captors?*

- *How is the way Cochise refers to himself in the third sentence different from the way he refers to himself in the first two sentences? Can you find other places where he uses this technique?*

Cochise is pleading that he not be sent to a reservation at Tularosa, New Mexico. Sometimes he uses *I* and *me;* sometimes he calls himself *Cochise.* When he speaks using *I* and *me,* he seems strong and independent. But when he calls himself *Cochise,* he seems to be speaking of someone else for whom he has much pity. His manner of speaking had a great effect on his audience. General Oliver Howard petitioned the United States government to let Cochise stay on his own land. Cochise was granted that right.

Words like *I, me, you, they,* and *that* are used in this passage as *pronouns.* They take the place of the nouns *Cochise, Americans and Mexicans, father and mother,* and *Tularosa.* Cochise also uses the words *nobody, everybody,* and *anything,* which are also pronouns.

Point out that the reference to "bad spirits" reflects the beliefs of Cochise and other Native Americans throughout history who did not accept Christ as Savior. It does not reflect the beliefs of Bible-believing Christians.

- Cochise is speaking to United States lawmakers, the people who will decide where he will live.
- Answers will vary. *(alone, desperate, confident something will be done)*
- He is asking that he not be sent to the reservation at Tularosa.
- He refers to himself in the third person (Cochise). He uses this technique again in the first part of the second paragraph.

Pronouns   **83**

Literature Link

Read the excerpt aloud as the students read silently. As you read, replace each *I* and *me* with the proper noun *Cochise.* Ask the students to respond to the difference between your reading and their silent reading. The students may say that the repetition of *Cochise* makes the reading cumbersome or that the repetition distracted them from the content and meaning of the passage.

Pronouns and Antecedents

Pronouns are words that substitute for nouns. Using pronouns simplifies our writing and speaking. Usually, repeating the same nouns over and over makes writing awkward and wordy.

> When *Sven* was riding *Sven's* bicycle home from school, *Sven* saw a wallet on the sidewalk.
> When Sven was riding his bicycle home from school, he saw a wallet on the sidewalk.

Pro means "in place of." What does *pronoun* mean?

page 197
Pronoun-Antecedent agreement

page 209
Pronoun reference

The noun that a pronoun refers to is called the **antecedent**. In the example, *Sven* is the antecedent of *his* and *he*. The antecedent usually appears before the pronouns that refer to it. The antecedent may even appear in a previous sentence. Occasionally an antecedent will appear after the pronoun.

> *Sven* stopped *his* bicycle.
> *Sven* picked up the *wallet*. *He* opened *it* curiously.
> As soon as *he* saw *it*, *Sven* recognized the owner's *name*.

IN SUMMARY

A **pronoun** is a noun substitute. An **antecedent** is the noun that a pronoun refers to.

4-1 PRACTICE THE SKILL

Underline the pronouns. Write each pronoun and its antecedent on the line below the sentence.

1. Keesha, have you read about Mark Twain? His real name was Samuel Clemens.

   you, Keesha; his, Mark Twain

2. He took that pen name from the river term for "two fathoms deep."

   He, Clemens

3. Clemens is remembered best for his humorous writings, for they captured people's imaginations.

   his, Clemens; they, writings

4. Clemens's life produced its share of sadness, though.

   its, life

5. Clemens and his wife, Olivia, had three daughters in their family: Susy, Clara, and Jean.

   his, Clemens; their, Clemens and his wife, Olivia

Teaching Strategy: Induction

Write the "Sven" example sentences from page 84 on the board or overhead transparency. Show the students that "Sven's" and "Sven" are the antecedents and that "his" and "he" are the pronoun replacements. Ask them to draw some conclusion from the example. Lead them to discover these facts:

1. The antecedent is *usually* a noun.
2. The antecedent usually comes *before* the pronoun replacement.

3. It is often easier to find the pronoun first in the sentence and then to find the antecedent.
4. The antecedent may not be in the same sentence as its pronoun replacement.

6. When Susy died from spinal meningitis in 1896, <u>they</u> were devastated.

they, Clemens and his wife, Olivia

7. Even before <u>her</u> death, though, Clemens had been having financial troubles.

her, Susy

8. <u>He</u> had to spend several years working <u>his</u> way out of debt.

He, Clemens; his, Clemens

9. Olivia died in 1904, and <u>her</u> youngest daughter followed <u>her</u> mother to the grave only five years later.

her, Olivia; her, youngest daughter

10. These disappointments certainly affected Clemens, and <u>they</u> probably contributed to the pessimism of <u>his</u> later writings.

they, disappointments; his, Clemens

 4-2 REVIEW THE SKILL

Underline each pronoun. Write its antecedent in the blank.

_____Moses_____ 1. Jochebed, the mother of Moses, put <u>him</u> in a basket.

_____Miriam_____ 2. Miriam watched <u>her</u> brother in the river.

____brother or Moses____ 3. <u>He</u> floated in a small basket.

____brother or Moses____ 4. <u>His</u> mother had made the basket.

_____basket_____ 5. <u>It</u> was made of bulrushes and waterproofed.

___Pharaoh's daughter___ 6. Pharaoh's daughter sent <u>her</u> maids to get the basket.

____basket, maids____ 7. When the maids opened <u>it</u>, <u>they</u> saw Moses.

_____Moses_____ 8. Miriam brought Moses' mother to care for <u>him</u>.

_____Moses_____ 9. Pharaoh's daughter named <u>him</u>.

_____Israelites_____ 10. Moses loved the Israelites and <u>their</u> God.

Personal Pronouns

The pronouns we most frequently use are the **personal pronouns**. All personal pronouns have four characteristics: **person**, **number**, **gender**, and **case**. Refer to the chart as you study these four characteristics.

Singular

	Subjective Case	Objective Case	Possessive Case
First Person	I	me	my, mine
Second Person	you	you	your, yours
Third Person			
neuter	it	it	its
masculine	he	him	his
feminine	she	her	her, hers

Plural

	Subjective Case	Objective Case	Possessive Case
First Person	we	us	our, ours
Second Person	you	you	your, yours
Third Person	they	them	their, theirs

Person tells whether the personal pronoun refers to the speaker, the person spoken to, or the person spoken of.

First person is the person speaking: *I* am here.
Second person is the person spoken to: *You* are here.
Third person is the person spoken of: *He* is here.

Number tells whether the personal pronoun is singular or plural.

Singular: *He* is here.
Plural: *They* are here.

Gender tells whether the personal pronoun is masculine, feminine, or neuter. A difference of gender is shown only with the third-person singular pronouns.

Masculine: *He* is here.
Feminine: *She* is here.
Neuter: *It* is here.

Case tells how the personal pronoun is being used in a sentence. The three cases of personal pronouns are subjective, objective, and possessive. Later you will study how these three cases are used correctly. For now, notice the case forms for the third-person singular masculine pronoun.

Subjective: *He* is the pastor.
Objective: The congregation likes *him*.
Possessive: *His* sermons teach us God's Word.

page 112
Possessives

page 209
Pronoun case

page 217
Courtesy order

Teaching Strategy: Discussion

Prepare a transparency of the personal pronoun chart and display it on an overhead projector. Cover and uncover different sections of the personal pronoun chart as you discuss the characteristics of personal pronouns.

Teaching Strategy

See student text page 86 for the definition and examples of gender. In the English language, only nouns that are obviously masculine are called masculine nouns *(John, Harry, Ramal)*, and only nouns that are obviously feminine are called feminine nouns *(Sue, Sally, Joan)*. Therefore, the majority of English nouns are neuter *(desk, chair, car)*.

If a student questions this rule, explain that some English idioms are exceptions. For example, names of ships and countries are sometimes considered to be feminine.

ESL Strategy

If you have an ESL student, be aware that many foreign languages assign masculine or feminine characteristics to words that are neuter in English.

Personal pronouns reflect **person** (first, second, third), **number** (singular, plural), **gender** (masculine, feminine, neuter), and **case** (subjective, objective, possessive).

4-3 PRACTICE THE SKILL

Replace each underlined word with an appropriate pronoun.

She   1. <u>Diana</u> read the story about David and Goliath.

Her   2. <u>Diana's</u> teacher asked her to read the story.

_He_   3. <u>Mr. Reynolds</u> is the Bible teacher.

_It_   4. <u>The story</u> is found in I Samuel 17.

him   5. Goliath challenged <u>David</u> to fight.

his   6. David accepted <u>Goliath's</u> challenge.

his   7. Saul offered <u>Saul's</u> armor to David.

them   8. David collected five stones; he put one of <u>the stones</u> in his sling.

_he_   9. <u>David</u> used the sling, and the stone that David threw hit Goliath.

They   10. <u>The Israelites</u> praised David.

Learning Christianly

Subjects like writing and grammar can be difficult to learn and even more difficult to master. Why should we spend so much time learning to excel in these areas? Read Genesis 1:27-28. These verses explain that since God made humans in His image, they are able to be like Him in some ways and to act like Him in some ways. In light of these verses, how can refining your writing and grammar skills allow you to act more like God?

Learning Christianly

Each thing that God does is both beautiful and purposeful. He does all things well (Mark 7:37). When a student strives to act like God in an area of life, he is giving a testimony to God's incomparable glory. Unsaved people need to hear and see a testimony that tells them that God is both great and good. Refining writing and grammar skills allows your student to act more like God for two reasons. First, this process results in each student's having a skill that has been made excellent and that is impressive in itself because it demonstrates sacrifice. Everything that God does is excellent, and in using a skill made excellent, your students are acting like Him. Second, refining these skills allows a student to understand even more the practical value that writing and grammar can offer. The more a person learns about these subjects, the more he will realize how useful they are. Since God Himself works things together for good (Rom. 8:28), we can act like Him when we use things such as writing and grammar for others' good.

Enrichment

Materials

- Prepare index cards for personal pronoun characteristics. Place the characteristics on one side of the card and the pronoun on the other side of the card. Each card should include these characteristics: person, case, and number. *(first, subjective, singular)* You should have twenty-four cards if you use all the possible combinations.

Use the index cards for a class competition. Divide the class into two teams. Two students, one from each team, compete against each other. Read the description of the pronoun from the card. The first student to call out the correct pronoun earns one point for his team.

One on One: Use the index cards as flash cards or allow your student to quiz himself with the index cards.

Replace each underlined word or phrase with an appropriate pronoun.

___It___ 1. The story of Elijah and the prophets of Baal should encourage every Christian.

___Its___ 2. The story's description of how God worked in and through Elijah gives hope to others.

___them___ 3. Elijah challenged the prophets of Baal to a contest to determine who served the true God.

___they___ 4. Elijah would offer a bullock on an altar, and the prophets of Baal would do the same thing.

___He___ 5. The God that sent fire down to consume the sacrifice would be acknowledged to be the true God.

___their___ 6. The prophets of Baal spent hours trying to get Baal to listen to the prophets' cries, but Baal remained silent.

___his___ 7. When it was Elijah's turn, Elijah ordered that twelve barrels of water be poured over the sacrifice and wood.

___him___ 8. Immediately after Elijah prayed, God responded to Elijah with fire that consumed not only the sacrifice but also everything in and around the altar, even the water.

___she___ 9. Surprisingly, Elijah fled after this great victory because Queen Jezebel threatened to kill him.

___her___ 10. Yet God did not allow Jezebel's threats to ruin Elijah's service but showed Elijah that there was still work to be done and people to help do it.

Demonstrative Pronouns

The **demonstrative pronouns** *this, these, that,* and *those* point out objects, persons, places, or ideas. These pronouns may function as subjects, predicate nouns, direct objects, indirect objects, and objects of prepositions. Use *this* (singular) or *these* (plural) for objects that are near and *that* (singular) or *those* (plural) for objects that are far away.

The words known as demonstrative pronouns can also be used as demonstrative adjectives. Although this textbook does not teach the term *demonstrative adjective,* an example of demonstrative words used as adjectives can be found in Chapter 5.

Teaching Strategy: Induction

Write the following sentences on the board or overhead transparency:

- I bought ___. *(this)* (Hold and point to one book.)
- I have read ___. *(these)* (Hold and point to two books.)
- Please lend me ___. *(that)* (Point to a book on a student's desk.)
- Please put ___ on the desk. *(those)* (Point to books that are on a student's desk that is farther away from you.)

Ask the students to fill in each blank with the correct demonstrative pronoun as you act out the directions. Ask the students to explain their answers.

Subject:	*These* are mine.
Predicate Noun:	His favorite cookies are *those*.
Direct Object:	I gave her *that*.
Indirect Object:	She gave *this* more attention.
Object of Preposition:	She has three of *these*.

Interrogative Pronouns

The five **interrogative** pronouns are often used to ask questions.

Which of us will enter the battle?
What does the Lord require of you?
Who is on the Lord's side?
Whom shall I send?
Whose are the commands?

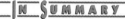

IN SUMMARY

Demonstrative pronouns point out objects, persons, places, or ideas; they can be used any way a noun can be used in a sentence.

Interrogative pronouns are generally used to ask questions.

 4-5 PRACTICE THE SKILL

Underline the demonstrative and interrogative pronouns. Label each underlined pronoun *Dem* (demonstrative) or *Inter* (interrogative).

Dem   1. Please take <u>that</u> to Mika.

Inter   2. <u>Which</u> do you mean?

Dem   3. <u>This</u> is the one.

Inter   4. <u>Who</u> gets the item?

Dem   5. We choose <u>these</u>.

Inter   6. <u>What</u> do you want?

Dem   7. I prefer <u>those</u>.

Inter   8. <u>Whom</u> shall I choose?

Inter   9. <u>Who</u> handles problems well?

Dem 10. <u>That</u> stumps many people.

page 215

Who and **whom**

page 217

Whose and **who's**

ESL: Refer to ESL Helps page 43 (Support Materials CD) for more information about inverted order in interrogative sentences.

Teaching Strategy:
Introduction

Ask a student to find and read aloud the definition of *interrogate* in a dictionary. Ask the students what they think interrogative pronouns are used for. *(Interrogative pronouns ask questions.)*

A. Label each underlined pronoun *Per* (personal), *Dem* (demonstrative), or *Inter* (interrogative).

B. Write the antecedent of each personal and each demonstrative pronoun.

_____Inter_____ 1. <u>Who</u> was Jacques Cousteau?

Per, Jacques Cousteau 2. <u>He</u> was a well-known French oceanographer.

_____Inter_____ 3. <u>What</u> made Cousteau famous?

Per, Jacques Cousteau 4. The Aqua-Lung was invented by <u>him</u>.

Dem, Aqua-Lung 5. <u>This</u> is a breathing device used to allow divers to move freely in the ocean.

Per, Aqua-Lung (device) 6. <u>It</u> was an important piece of equipment for Cousteau and his sons.

Per, Cousteau and sons 7. <u>Their</u> research ship was named *Calypso*.

Per, Calypso 8. <u>It</u> became famous as Cousteau's reputation grew.

Dem, reputation 9. <u>That</u> allowed Cousteau to produce television programs.

Dem, programs 10. <u>These</u> emphasized marine conservation and dramatized ocean exploration.

Reflexive and Intensive Pronouns

Reflexive pronouns and **intensive pronouns** are made from pronoun forms with *self* or *selves* added. Only certain pronoun forms can become reflexive or intensive.

Singular	
First Person	myself
Second Person	yourself
Third Person	
neuter	itself
masculine	himself
feminine	herself
Plural	
First Person	ourselves
Second Person	yourselves
Third Person	themselves

Reflexive pronouns are used as direct objects, indirect objects, and objects of prepositions. They always refer to the same person or thing as the subject. Therefore, the subject is the antecedent. Reflexive pronouns are the only direct objects that refer to the subject.

page 219

Reflexive and Intensive pronouns

Direct Object:	The parrot bit *itself.*
Indirect Object:	Joey asked *himself* a question.
Object of Preposition:	We looked for *ourselves* in the picture.

Intensive pronouns do not function as part of a sentence pattern. Instead, they emphasize a noun or a pronoun already used in the sentence. The antecedent is the word that the intensive pronoun emphasizes. Because intensive pronouns are not part of the sentence pattern, they can be removed without changing the basic meaning of the sentence.

We met the author *himself.*
We *ourselves* met the author.

IN SUMMARY

Reflexive pronouns are used as direct objects, indirect objects, and objects of prepositions; they always refer to the subject.

Intensive pronouns emphasize a noun or a pronoun already in the sentence, but they do not function as part of the sentence pattern.

Remind the students that an intensive pronoun can always be returned to the position immediately following the noun that it is intensifying; a reflexive pronoun cannot be moved. Intensive pronouns function as appositives, which are introduced in grade 9.

Teaching Strategy: Introduction

To introduce reflexive and intensive pronouns, hold a mirror before a student and ask him what he sees. If the student does not answer "myself," hold the mirror before other students until someone answers "myself." Reply, "He sees himself." Ask the students whether that person is in the mirror. Someone will reply, "No, it is his reflection." Stress that the mirror reflects the person who sees it.

Explain that reflexive pronouns, like a reflection in a mirror, reflect the subject of a sentence and cannot serve as the subject themselves.

Teaching Strategy: Discussion

Use the example sentences on page 93 to point out that reflexive pronouns appear in the sentence patterns that have a direct object, an indirect object, or an object of the preposition.

Remind the students that only a reflexive pronoun can be a direct object that refers to the subject.

If a student questions the use of reflexive pronouns as objects only, explain that only rarely does a reflexive pronoun act as a predicate noun. *(He wasn't himself today.)*

Teaching Strategy: Discussion and Demonstration

Prepare a transparency of the chart on page 91. Cover the bottom half of the chart for this discussion.

Explain that pronouns ending in *self* and *selves* are not always reflexive pronouns; they can have a different function in a

Label the sentence patterns *S-InV, S-TrV-DO, S-TrV-IO-DO, S-LV-PN,* or *S-LV-PA.* In the blank, label the underlined pronouns *Int* (intensive) or *Ref* (reflexive).

____Int____ 1. Samuel Wesley <u>himself</u> was Samuel Westley originally.
          S   LV   PN

____Ref____ 2. Wesley gave <u>himself</u> the new name during his years at Oxford.
          S   TrV   IO   DO

____Ref____ 3. Wesley's father and grandfather made names for <u>themselves</u> as
                  S   S   TrV   DO

        Nonconformist ministers.

____Int____ 4. Wesley <u>himself</u> returned to the established church and
          S   InV

        contributed to its defense with his writing and speaking.
     InV

____Int____ 5. Ironically, Wesley's name is <u>itself</u> famous because of his sons'
                          S   LV   PA

        work with the new Methodist movement.

____Int____ 6. Susanna Wesley was a remarkable woman <u>herself</u>.
          S   LV   PN

____Ref____ 7. From a family of twenty-five children, she could read Greek
                                         S   TrV   DO

        and Hebrew for <u>herself</u> by the age of thirteen.
           DO

____Ref____ 8. Her faith spoke for <u>itself</u> in the lives her many children led.
          S   InV

____Ref____ 9. They provided <u>themselves</u> entertainment on many occasions.
          S   TrV   IO   DO

____Int____ 10. Susanna <u>herself</u> talked with each child for an hour every week.
           S   InV

Label the sentence patterns *S-InV, S-TrV-DO, S-TrV-IO-DO, S-LV-PN,* or *S-LV-PA.* In the blank, label the underlined pronouns *Int* (intensive) or *Ref* (reflexive).

____Ref____ 1. Harriet Tubman made a name for <u>herself</u> as a leader of the
          S   TrV   DO

        Underground Railroad.

____Int____ 2. The Railroad <u>itself</u> owed much of its success to Tubman.
           S   TrV DO

---

sentence: to emphasize, or intensify, a noun or pronoun that is part of the sentence pattern. Review the information about intensive pronouns on page 91.

Review the example sentences for intensive pronouns on page 91. Explain that an intensive pronoun usually (but not always) immediately follows the noun that it emphasizes. Use the three sample sentences on the transparency to demonstrate that an intensive pronoun can be removed without changing the meaning of the sentence.

S TrV IO DO
_____Ref_____ 3. In fact, Tubman earned <u>herself</u> the nickname Moses for

her efforts.

S LV PN
_____Int_____ 4. Tubman <u>herself</u> was a slave from birth.

S LV PN
_____Int_____ 5. Her husband had been a slave <u>himself</u> but was free by the time

of their marriage.

S InV
_____Ref_____ 6. Tubman escaped to Philadelphia by <u>herself</u> in 1849.

S TrV DO
_____Ref_____ 7. After her own escape, Tubman gave <u>herself</u> to the work of the

Underground Railroad.

S TrV DO
_____Ref_____ 8. About three hundred slaves owed <u>themselves</u> and their

DO
freedom to Tubman's nineteen trips on their behalf.

S InV S
_____Int_____ 9. Several rewards for her arrest appeared, but the hunters

TrV DO
<u>themselves</u> never could catch Tubman.

S TrV IO DO
_____Ref_____ 10. In later years, Tubman assigned <u>herself</u> the job of caring for

the elderly, the needy, and the uneducated.

Indefinite Pronouns

Unlike personal pronouns, **indefinite pronouns** do not always refer to specific persons or things. These pronouns usually do not have clear antecedents.

Some Common Indefinite Pronouns			
anybody	everybody	nobody	somebody
anyone	everyone	no one	someone
anything	everything	nothing	something
all	both	many	none

Indefinite pronouns can be used as subjects, predicate nouns, direct objects, indirect objects, or objects of prepositions.

Subject:	*Everyone* has a favorite meal.
Predicate Noun:	My mother's cooking is really *something*.
Direct Object:	She can make *anything*.
Indirect Object:	She tells *nobody* her secret recipes.
Object of Preposition:	The meals are a pleasant surprise for *all*.

page 186

Subject-Verb agreement

page 200

Pronoun-Antecedent agreement

Teaching Strategy:
Discussion

Discuss the information about indefinite pronouns on page 93.

Indefinite pronouns do not refer to specific persons or things.
Indefinite pronouns usually do not have antecedents.

4-9 PRACTICE THE SKILL

Underline the indefinite pronouns.

1. Brenda has invited <u>everyone</u> to the picnic.

2. May we bring <u>anything</u>?

3. <u>Somebody</u> will want salad.

4. <u>No one</u> offered us cake.

5. Is <u>anyone</u> bringing <u>anything</u> for a tablecloth?

6. Is <u>everybody</u> coming at noon?

7. <u>Some</u> will be late.

8. Is <u>everything</u> ready?

9. <u>Someone</u> dropped the hamburgers.

10. The work for the picnic will be <u>nothing</u>.

4-10 REVIEW THE SKILL

Underline the indefinite pronouns.

1. Does <u>anyone</u> play the trumpet?

2. Probably <u>everybody</u> has at least heard a trumpet.

3. It is a popular instrument for <u>many</u> in bands and orchestras.

4. <u>Anybody</u> can see that trumpeters push down valves.

5. Mouth movement is not as obvious to <u>everyone</u>.

6. <u>Both</u> are important, though, for making music.

7. Musicians started playing <u>something</u> like a trumpet around 1200 B.C.

8. But <u>none</u> of the original trumpets had valves to help create different notes.

9. Mouth position and breath support were <u>everything</u>.

10. Today's trumpet is definitely easier to play, but <u>no one</u> would deny that it still requires much hard work.

Evaluation

If you have assigned sentence diagramming with Practice the Skill 4-9, check answers on page 446.

Underline the pronouns. Label each pronoun above the word: *P* (personal), *Dem* (demonstrative), *Inter* (interrogative), *Ref* (reflexive), *Int* (intensive), or *Ind* (indefinite).

Phillis Wheatley came to America on a slave ship when <u>she</u> *(P)* was about eight years old. A wealthy merchant named John Wheatley bought <u>her</u> *(P)* as a slave for <u>his</u> *(P)* wife. Although most slaves were uneducated, <u>both</u> *(Ind)* of the Wheatleys recognized that Phillis was intelligent, and Phillis proved <u>that</u> *(Dem)* by learning to read and write. <u>She</u> *(P)* also studied geography, history, and Latin; at age fourteen Phillis taught <u>herself</u> *(Ref)* to write poems. <u>Many</u> *(Ind)* of <u>these</u> *(Dem)* were published in Phillis's book *Poems on Various Subjects: Religious and Moral.* <u>It</u> *(P)* was published in England in 1773. The poems <u>themselves</u> *(Int)* discussed Phillis's deep religious convictions. Phillis also wrote about life as a slave. <u>Who</u> *(Inter)* could better write about <u>this</u> *(Dem)*? Almost <u>everything</u> *(Ind)* Phillis wrote was deeply personal. As a young woman, Phillis was freed, and <u>she</u> *(P)* married John Peters. Although <u>she</u> *(P)* died almost unknown, <u>everyone</u> *(Ind)* reading Phillis's work today recognizes <u>her</u> *(P)* important contribution to American poetry. <u>She</u> *(P)* was the first important black poet of the New World.

Underline each pronoun. Fill in the blank with the type of pronoun:
demonstrative, indefinite, intensive, interrogative, **or** *reflexive.*

1. <u>Who</u> joined the League of Nations?

   _____ *interrogative* _____

2. The absence of the United States was a surprise to <u>all</u>.

   _____ *indefinite* _____

3. <u>This</u> baffled the proponents of the League.

   _____ *demonstrative* _____

4. <u>What</u> barred the United States from joining <u>this</u>?

   _____ *interrogative, demonstrative* _____

5. <u>Whom</u> was the League protecting?

   _____ *interrogative* _____

6. The League maintained safety and protection for <u>itself</u>.

   _____ *reflexive* _____

7. However, not <u>everyone</u> was concerned for other nations.

   _____ *indefinite* _____

8. <u>Many</u> of the nations defeated <u>themselves</u> and the purpose of the League.

   _____ *indefinite, reflexive* _____

9. <u>This</u> was proved when France <u>itself</u> would not aid Ethiopia.

   _____ *demonstrative, intensive* _____

10. In the end, <u>no one</u> helped <u>anyone</u> for the fear of <u>everyone</u>.

    _____ *indefinite, indefinite, indefinite* _____

Locate and correct the ten errors in the paragraph: fragments, comma splices, noun plurals, singular and plural noun possessives, verb forms (for example, *had wrote*), and spellings of verb forms. Use the lines below to write the paragraph correctly.

One of the most docile and timid creatures of the sea is the manatee. Sometimes called a sea cow. There are three species of manatees, the types of manatees are Caribbean, Amazon, and African. Another name for manatees is "Sirenia." Because of their resemblance to mermaids or sirens. The legend of the mermaid probably originated when sailors had seed some dugongs in the Red Sea. Dugong's are similar to manatees. Most manatees lives in tropical areas. Manatees are the largest of all plant-eating animals that live their entire lives in the water, a manatees diet might consist of a hundred pounds of water plants in a day! Female manatees take good care of their young. A mother plays with her baby and sometimes carrys it on her back. Manatees's lives are generally solitary, but occasionally they will come together in a group. This occurs in winter in places where the water is unusually warm.

One of the most docile and timid creatures of the sea is the manatee, sometimes called a sea cow. There are three species of manatees; the types of manatees are Caribbean, Amazon, and African. Another name for manatees is "Sirenia," because of their resemblance to mermaids or sirens. The legend of the mermaid probably originated when sailors had seen some dugongs in the Red Sea. Dugongs are similar to manatees. Most manatees live in tropical areas. Manatees are the largest of all plant-eating animals that live their entire lives in the water. A manatee's diet might consist of a hundred pounds of water plants in a day! Female manatees take good care of their young. A mother plays with her baby and sometimes carries it on her back. Manatees' lives are generally solitary, but occasionally they will come together in a group. This occurs in winter in places where the water is unusually warm.

Try reading the passage from Cochise's speech again, substituting nouns for each pronoun. Do you see how valuable pronouns are in making writing clearer and more concise?

- *What is the personal pronoun Cochise uses most frequently in the last paragraph?*

- *How does the use of* I *make the ending stronger?*

> **Isaiah 14:13-15**
>
> **13 For thou hast said in thine heart, I will ascend into heaven, I will exalt my throne above the stars of God: I will sit also upon the mount of the congregation, in the sides of the north:**
>
> **14 I will ascend above the heights of the clouds; I will be like the most High.**
>
> **15 Yet thou shalt be brought down to hell, to the sides of the pit.**

- *To whom does the pronoun* I *refer? What does this pronoun reveal about its antecedent?*

WRITING TO A PEN PAL

The elder unto the wellbeloved Gaius, whom I love in the truth. Beloved, I wish above all things that thou mayest prosper and be in health, even as thy soul prospereth.

III John 1-2

Notice how Cochise introduced himself through his speech. He made it very personal by his numerous references to *I*. How would you introduce yourself through a letter to someone who had never seen you before?

Your Turn

Imagine that you have been assigned a pen pal in another state and that this person knows nothing about you. Write a letter introducing yourself.

Planning

Make a list of the things that you want your pen pal to know about you. Take a few minutes and write down what you like, what you like to do, and where you like to go. Be sure to include things that make you *you*. Do not try to organize the ideas yet but be as specific as possible.

Group related ideas. After you complete your list, use colored pens to mark similar items. For example, you could mark items about your parents, brothers, sisters, pets, house, and room with the same color and then list them under the category *family*. Continue to mark and categorize your ideas until you have organized all of them.

Drafting

Write the salutation. Begin with a friendly salutation. Since you know the name of your pen pal, be sure to include his or her name.

page 376
Ask yourself questions

- The pronoun *I*
- It personalizes the problem, letting his audience see a real person affected by the laws.

- The personal pronoun *I* refers to Satan. The pronoun reveals that its antecedent is proud and wants praise for himself.

Overview of Writing Process

Planning—Listing important items to include; choosing a pen pal profile

Drafting—Writing the letter on notebook paper

Revising—Proofreading and correcting the letter and copying the corrected letter onto stationery

Publishing—Displaying letters in the classroom

Objectives

Students will

1. choose a profile for a pen pal.

2. compose a letter.

Literature Link

Ask students to volunteer answers to the Sliding Home questions on page 98.

Scriptural Application

Ask the students to think about how many times they say *I* or *me* in their conversations. Then read Isaiah 14:13-15 on page 98. The *I* in this passage refers to Satan, or Lucifer (see verse 12). The pronoun reveals Satan's proud belief that he will one day be "above the stars of God." Warn the students against a proud spirit and an emphasis on self.

Writing to a Pen Pal

Lesson Support

Support Materials CD

Writing Worksheets—p. 94
Rubrics—p. 108
Bulletin Boards—p. 206

Scriptural Application

Read III John 1-2 aloud and then share the following information with the students. The apostles knew that letters from a friend can be encouraging and edifying. In fact, much of the New Testament is com-posed of letters the apostles wrote to friends or to churches. For the Christian, exchanging letters with a pen pan can be a similarly rich experience. It allows him to profit from someone living in a different area of the world. More importantly, how-ever, it allows him to edify and encourage someone he rarely sees.

Teaching Strategy

Direct the students to read the sample letter in the textbook. Discuss what makes a good letter. *(humor, personal details, awareness of the reader's interests, etc.)*

Determine the order of your ideas. What do you want your pen pal to know first? next? last? When you have decided, you are ready to begin writing your letter.

Choose your words carefully. Remember that your reader has only your words; the reader cannot see your face or hear your voice. Be sure that you give your pen pal honest details about yourself.

Write well-organized paragraphs. Begin each paragraph with a topic sentence that presents the main idea of that paragraph. Adapt the categories that you used to organize your list of ideas. Remember, though, that your letter should not be simply a list. Add details and bits of humor. Let your personality shine through. Use personal pronouns as you write.

Write the closing. The closing should be friendly and appropriate, such as *Your friend* or *Sincerely.* Be sure to sign your name legibly too.

Revising

Question yourself about your letter. Are all the words spelled correctly? Are the ideas within the paragraphs arranged in a logical way? Have you presented an accurate picture of yourself? Did you include an appropriate salutation and closing? Are the paragraphs indented neatly?

Write a clean copy of your letter. Use your best penmanship for the final copy of your letter. A handwritten letter is more personal than a letter generated from a word processor. Remember that this letter is your pen pal's first impression of you. You want to make a positive impression.

Publishing

Prepare your letter for mailing. Fold your letter carefully and insert it into an appropriately sized envelope. Write the complete address for your pen pal on the front of the envelope. Be sure to include your return address in the upper left corner of the envelope.

Create a memory book. If you establish a writing relationship with a pen pal, save the letters that you receive from your pen pal and preserve them in an album. Read through previous letters before you write a new letter.

page 386

Precise words

Dear Pen Pal,

My name is Angelique Randall, and I am twelve years old. I am in seventh grade at Trinity Christian School. My dad is the science teacher at the school, and my mom works part-time in the school office. I have three younger brothers and one little sister. My sister, Meghan, is my favorite person to play with. She is only three years old, and since I'm the oldest of us kids, I get to be Meghan's baby sitter lots of times.

I like to do a lot of different things. I play volleyball for our school team. We had our first game last night and won. I am still learning the overhand serve, but I'm getting better at it. I also love little kids. I help my mom teach the kindergarten Sunday school class at our church. Just last week, she taught me how to bake cinnamon rolls. I think that's going to become one of my favorite things to do, because I love to eat them!

I think my favorite subject at school is science, maybe because I have such a great teacher. A lot of kids ask me if I want to be a science teacher when I grow up, like my dad. I'm not sure what I want to do yet. I love to study about weather and storms and things like that, so I think it would be fun to be a meteorologist. But I'll just have to wait and see. Whatever else I do, I know I want to be a mom, because I think kids are so much fun.

Please write soon and tell me all about yourself. I can't wait to hear from you.

Your friend,
Angelique

P.S. I'm sending you my school picture from sixth grade. My hair is longer now, and I have braces.

P.S. is an abbreviation for the term *post script,* which means "to write after." P.S. introduces an additional message after the main part of a letter.

Planning Strategies

Distribute a copy of Writing Worksheet 4 to each student. Tell each student to choose a name, a home state, and an age for his pen pal from the lists.

Allow the students to list items about themselves that they want to include in their letters. Suggest that they read their journals for ideas to include.

Drafting Strategy

Encourage each student to research the state where his pen pal lives in order to formulate meaningful questions.

Instruct students to draft their letters on notebook paper and then to proofread their letters and correct any errors.

Revising Strategy

Direct each student to copy his corrected letter onto stationery of his choice.

Publishing Strategy

Display the letters on a bulletin board.

Evaluation

For help in grading this assignment, see "Grading Writing Assignments" (p. x) and Rubric 4 (Support Materials CD, p. 108).

Enrichment

Invite the parents of each student to write a response to their child's letter, posing as his pen pal.

Scriptural Application

Read II Corinthians 3:2. Ask students what metaphor is being used in the verse. *(People are called an "epistle.")* Remind students that a Christian life is like a letter. When others "read" someone's letter by observing his behavior and listening to his speech, they should clearly see Christ.

Chapter Goals

Students will

1. acquire an understanding of adjectives in comparison; of other parts of speech acting as adjectives; and of articles, possessive adjectives, and common and proper adjectives.

2. use adjectives correctly in oral and written sentences.

ADJECTIVES

THE SPECKLED BAND
BY SIR ARTHUR CONAN DOYLE

Objectives

Students will

1. define an adjective.

2. summarize the questions that an adjective answers.

3. identify the word being modified by an adjective.

4. use adjectives to show comparison with both regular and irregular adjectives.

5. differentiate between nouns and pronouns functioning as adjectives and those functioning as nouns and pronouns.

6. identify articles.

7. form singular and plural possessives correctly.

8. differentiate between possessives functioning as adjectives and possessives functioning as independent possessives.

9. identify and distinguish common and proper adjectives.

Lesson Support

Student Text
Chapter Review 5—pp. 403-4

Teacher's Edition
Diagram Answers—p. 447

Support Materials CD
Warm-Ups—pp. 11-12
ESL Helps—pp. 45-46
Concept Reinforcements—pp. 61-62
Bulletin Boards—p. 207

It was a singular sight which met our eyes. On the table stood a dark lantern with the shutter half open, throwing a brilliant light upon the iron safe, the door of which was ajar. Beside the table, on the wooden chair, sat Dr. Grimesby Roylott, clad in a long gray dressing gown, his bare ankles protruding beneath, and his feet thrust into red heelless Turkish slippers. Across his lap lay the short stock with the long lash which we had noticed during the day. His chin was cocked upward and his eyes were fixed in a dreadful rigid stare at the corner of the ceiling. Round his brow he had a peculiar yellow band, with brownish speckles, which seemed to be bound tightly round his head. As we entered he made neither sound nor motion.

"The band! The speckled band!" whispered Holmes.

I took a step forward. In an instant his strange headgear began to move, and there reared itself from among his hair the squat diamond-shaped head and puffed neck of a loathsome serpent.

- *How do you think the author wants the reader to feel as he reads this passage?*

- *What details add to the suspense of the scene?*

- *Could you draw a picture of the room? Of the way the doctor is dressed?*

You would probably be able to draw this scene because the author describes it meticulously. He uses words like *wooden, gray, heelless, dreadful, brownish,* and *diamond-shaped.* These words appeal to the senses. Suppose Doyle had told us only that the doctor wore slippers. There are many kinds of slippers. But Doyle uses descriptive words to narrow our choices. These are "red heelless Turkish slippers." Without the words *red, heelless,* and *Turkish,* we might imagine that he wore pink bunny slippers.

Descriptive words that sharpen our understanding of nouns are called *adjectives.* As you study this chapter, you may be surprised to find how many adjectives you use all the time.

- Answers will vary. (fearful, anticipating the outcome, eager to read more)
- Answers will vary. (the dark lantern with the shutter half open, the safe door open, Dr. Roylott's eyes fixed in the rigid stare)
- Answers will vary. (The vivid details make it easy to draw a picture of the room or the doctor.)

Adjectives   **101**

Literature Link

Read and discuss the excerpt from "The Speckled Band" by Sir Arthur Conan Doyle.

page 56
Predicate adjectives

page 144
Prepositional phrases

page 233
Adjective or Adverb?

Adjectives

A **modifier** is a word that tells more about another word. It describes the other word. Modifiers help us say exactly what we mean. Without modifiers many of our sentences would be dull. Modifiers enrich the meanings of our nouns and verbs.

As we use modifiers in our writing, we should remember that the modifiers alone cannot get our ideas across. The basic sentence parts are always the most important words of our sentences. We must begin with strong nouns and verbs. Then we add modifiers to make the meanings of these words clearer.

Adjectives are words that modify nouns. In other words, an adjective gives details that make the noun's meaning clearer. Adjectives tell *what kind, which one, how many,* or *whose* about the nouns they modify.

What kind?   The *weary* hiker trudged through the *dark* forest.

Which one?   Would *this* trail lead him home?

How many?   He checked the map for the *third* time.

Whose?   *His* compass would help.

In these sentences adjectives give details about the hiker, the forest, the trail, the time, and the compass. The adjectives *weary, dark, this, third,* and *his* help us create a picture.

Most adjectives come just before the nouns they modify. Other adjectives come after a linking verb; these adjectives are called predicate adjectives. A predicate adjective always describes the subject of the sentence.

The long, dusty trail was *steep.*

To determine whether a word is an adjective, ask if it answers any of the adjective questions. You can also use the adjective test frame. Any word that will fit into the frame may be used as an adjective. Some adjectives will fit the test frame, but some will not. Remember, if a word modifies a noun it is an adjective.

The _____ thing (or person) is very _____ .

The *bright* thing is very *bright.*

The *tall* person is very *tall.*

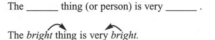

Adjectives modify nouns and tell what kind, which one, how many, or whose. Many adjectives will fit the adjective test frame.

Teaching Strategy

Combination with Chapter 12: Adjective and Adverb Usage

If students become confused about modifier differences during the course of the chapter, see the section "Adjective or Adverb?" on page 233.

Teaching Strategy: Induction

Materials
- Unusual object or food item

Bring an unusual object to class and display it prominently. (Or bring a food item for each student to taste.) Ask students to describe the object with one word. Write the individual one-word answers on the board or overhead transparency.

For example, suppose you have brought a *didjeridoo* (an Australian musical instrument) to class. The students might say that it is *long, narrow, wooden, an Aborigine's, noisy,* and *music.* (Write *musical,* underline `al,* and say you'll talk about this later.) After writing these responses on the board, you might prompt the students by asking,

"How many didjeridoos have you seen before?" If the answer is that this is the first, add *first* or *one* to the adjective list.

Next ask the adjective questions on page 102 about the words listed on the board. You may want to mention that numbers are often, but not always, adjectives answering "how many?" Note that *music* does not answer one of the questions, but *musical* does.

Next try the listed adjectives in a test frame written on the board or overhead transparency:

Underline the adjectives. Draw an arrow from each adjective to the noun it modifies.

1. Many people enjoy golf.

2. Historically, the British royalty played this sport.

3. Queen Mary of Scotland was an avid golfer.

4. The sport became popular in America.

5. People made the early clubs from wood.

6. American golfers changed to steel clubs.

7. Initially, golfers used leather balls.

8. The leather balls became soggy in the rain.

9. Someone designed a solid, dimpled ball.

10. That cheap little ball changed the game.

5-2 REVIEW THE SKILL

Underline the adjectives.

1. Thomas Alva Edison was a famous inventor.

2. He married Mary Stillwell, and they had three children.

3. After Mary's death, he married the daughter of a wealthy industrialist.

4. Thomas Edison spent his early years in Milan, Ohio.

5. In later years, he became nearly deaf.

6. Despite physical problems, Edison masterminded many new inventions.

7. In 1886 he moved to an improved laboratory in West Orange, New Jersey.

8. Edison invented the cylindrical phonograph.

9. His inventions introduced new concepts to several other industries also.

10. Edison's inventions brought him worldwide honor.

Adjectives   **103**

The ___ thing is very ___. *(long, narrow, noisy, musical)* (Remember: Although any word that fits the frame may be an adjective, not all adjectives fit the frame. Adjectives that answer "what kind?" fit the frame. Adjectives that answer "which one?" "how many?" and "whose?" do not.)

Teaching Strategy: Induction

Use the test frame bulletin board for an additional inductive activity for adjectives.

Reinforcement

Materials
• Pictures

Divide the class into teams and give each team a picture you have chosen. (Landscapes work well for this activity.) Tell each team to choose a fast writer as its recorder. Ask students to think of as many adjectives to describe the picture as they can in thirty seconds; the recorder will write them on paper. When the time is up, students trade pictures and begin the listing process again. When each team has

had every picture, read the answers aloud and cross out any words that are not adjectives or that another team has listed. The winning team will have the most adjectives unused by any other team.

One on One: Display a picture for you and your student. Instruct your student to list in one minute as many adjectives as possible to describe the picture. You do the same. Compare your lists to see who has the most original adjectives in his list.

5-3 USE THE SKILL

Write descriptive sentences using the instructions below. Check for adjectives in your sentences. *(Answers will vary.)*

1. Describe an invention of your own.

   _____

   _____

2. Tell about a fantastic sports play you have witnessed.

   _____

   _____

3. Write an interesting fact about a book you have enjoyed recently.

   _____

   _____

4. Use words to show what your brother's, sister's, or parents' (or your own!) hair looks like in the morning.

   _____

   _____

5. Describe what your toothpaste tastes like.

   _____

   _____

6. Proverbs 17:22 says, "A merry heart doeth good like a medicine." Whom do you know who has a merry heart? Describe that person.

   _____

   _____

7. Write specifics about a pet you would like to own someday.

   _____

   _____

8. Tell about your favorite flower, tree, or plant.

   _____

   _____

Learning Christianly

Adjectives are a valuable reminder of the privilege of being created in the image of God. They reflect the awareness that humans have, as well as their creativity and sometimes even their sense of humor. In a sense, then, adjectives are a way of celebrating the privilege of being human and being like the Creator in some ways. Only humans in God's creation have the ability to recognize all of the categories in God's creation, and they should use adjectives responsibly in describing the world in a Christian way.

Learning Christianly

Adjectives are a grammatical way of separating things into categories. Some things are tall and others are short. Some are green and others are red. Have you ever realized that animals and plants don't have the ability to recognize the categories to the extent that humans do? Since God has made humans to be distinctive in their awareness of His creation, why are words like adjectives so valuable?

Teaching Strategy

After the students have completed Practice the Skill 5-1, instruct them to check their answers against the definition of an adjective first and then to see how many fit the test frame.

9. The Bible has much to say about friends. Briefly describe one of your friends.

_____

_____

10. If you could come up with a new soda product, what would it taste like? Write a one-sentence advertisement for your soda.

_____

_____

Comparing with Adjectives

Most adjectives answer the question "what kind?" and come just before the nouns they modify. These are adjectives that can show comparison. They have **comparative** and **superlative** forms in addition to the stem, or **positive,** form. The comparative form compares two people or things; the superlative form compares three or more people or things. For most adjectives the comparative form is the stem + *er.* The superlative form for most of the common adjectives is the stem + *est.* For adjectives that would sound awkward with *er* or *est,* we use the words *more* and *most* before the adjectives.

Positive	Comparative	Superlative
cool	cooler	coolest
weary	wearier	weariest
beautiful	more beautiful	most beautiful

Jon is tall, but Stephen is taller. Eric is the tallest boy in the class.

February is a popular month for weddings, but summer months are more popular. In fact, June is the most popular month for weddings.

Irregular adjectives do not follow these simple rules for forming the comparative and superlative. Rather than simply adding *er* and *est* or *more* and *most,* irregular adjectives may have entirely different forms to show comparison.

Positive	Comparative	Superlative
good	better	best
well	better	best
bad	worse	worst
many	more	most
little	less	least

Adjectives that can be compared will always fit into the test frame. But be sure to use the stem form of the word when using the test frame.

page 237

Comparisons

Teaching Strategy: Induction

Using the list of adjectives generated by the inductive activity, list the words that answer the question "what kind?" in one column and label it *positive.* Form two other columns and label them *comparative* and *superlative.* Ask questions to help students complete the chart. *(If I had an instrument that extended beyond this one, it would be a <u>longer</u> instrument. A didjeridoo that continued out the door and down the hall would be the <u>longest</u> instrument of the three.)* Help the students to see that the positive degree describes one object, the comparative degree compares two objects, and the superlative degree compares three or more objects. Using adjectives in context with the nouns they modify will help the students to cement the idea of the noun's function in their minds.

Discuss the material on page 105 about irregular adjectives.

Wrong: The *loudest* thing is very *loudest.*
Right: The *loud* thing is very *loud.*

As you can see, using the superlative form of the adjective in the test frame results in an illogical sentence.

IN SUMMARY

Regular adjectives show comparison by adding *er* and *est* or *more* and *most* to the stem form of the adjective.

Irregular adjectives may have entirely different forms to show comparison.

5-4   PRACTICE THE SKILL

Fill in each blank with the correct form of the adjective.

_____greatest_____ 1. Many Bible scholars consider Martin Luther the _?_ reformer. *(great, superlative)*

_____most famous_____ 2. Martin Luther's _?_ work was his Ninety-five Theses. *(famous, superlative)*

_____earlier_____ 3. His _?_ years were spent in Mansfeld, Saxony. *(early, comparative)*

_____harshest_____ 4. Luther's _?_ criticism came from the religious leaders of the day. *(harsh, superlative)*

_____most helpful_____ 5. His wife Katie was the _?_ person in his life. *(helpful, superlative)*

_____sudden_____ 6. The _?_ death of Martin and Katie's daughter Magdalena grieved them. *(sudden, positive)*

_____worse_____ 7. Martin's health became _?_ after her death. *(bad, comparative)*

_____sharpest_____ 8. His writings were _?_ during his bouts of pain. *(sharp, superlative)*

_____greatest_____ 9. Martin's death in 1546 caused Katie's _?_ sorrow. *(great, superlative)*

_____dangerous_____ 10. After Martin's death, Katie and her children began a _?_ flight from Wittenberg. *(dangerous, positive)*

Scriptural Application

Use this introduction to adjectives to discuss God's glory as displayed in the vastness of language. God has given us a myriad of ways to express ourselves verbally.

Additional Resources

Students can learn more about Martin Luther from these materials available from BJU Press.

- *The Triumph of Truth: A Life of Martin Luther* by J. H. Merle D'Aubigné, edited by Mark Sidwell
- *Martin Luther* by Mike Fearon
- *Martin Luther* (video)
- *Where Luther Walked* (video)

Fill in each blank with the correct form of the adjective in parentheses.

_____best_____ 1. John Stallworth was one of the _?_ wide receivers in the NFL. *(good, superlative)*

_____clumsier_____ 2. However, in school he was _?_ than his friends. *(clumsy, comparative)*

_____larger_____ 3. His _?_ size gave him an edge over his opponents. *(large, comparative)*

_____worst_____ 4. He broke his foot and leg in his _?_ season. *(bad, superlative)*

_____highest_____ 5. John had the _?_ Super Bowl average yards per catch. *(high, superlative)*

_____most sensational_____ 6. His reception over his opponent's back was one of the _?_ plays ever. *(sensational, superlative)*

_____more popular_____ 7. On the Steelers' team, John Stallworth played with the _?_ Lynn Swann. *(popular, comparative)*

_____quicker_____ 8. Many times it was questioned who was _?_ . *(quick, comparative)*

_____most different_____ 9. The characteristic that was _?_ was their catching style: Stallworth used his hands while Swann used his body. *(different, superlative)*

_____best_____ 10. Some people believe that Stallworth and Swann were the _?_ receiver pair in the NFL. *(good, superlative)*

More Adjectives

Sometimes other parts of speech act like adjectives. For instance, some nouns and pronouns function as adjectives when they modify another noun. Nouns and pronouns functioning as adjectives will not fit the adjective test frame. Remember that these words are adjectives only when they modify nouns. If these words are functioning as subjects or objects, they are not adjectives.

page 291

Commas in a series

Adjective: Robert Louis Stevenson wrote *this* book.

           S   LV   **PN**

Pronoun: *This* is my favorite book.

Adjective: *Treasure Island* is an *adventure* story.

   S   TrV   **DO**

Noun: It describes the *adventures* of Jim Hawkins.

Do not be confused by nouns that function as adjectives. A noun that functions as an adjective always comes right before the noun that it modifies and after any other adjectives that may be there. When you see a word that may be either a noun or an adjective, determine how the word is functioning in the sentence.

S   TrV   **DO**
He polished the brass.

S   TrV   **DO**
He polished the large brass bell.

In the first example *brass* is a noun because it functions as the direct object of the transitive verb *polished*. *Brass* is the main noun in the phrase *the brass*. In the second example *brass* is an adjective because it modifies the noun *bell*. *Brass* is not the main noun. The complete phrase is *the large brass bell*.

To diagram an adjective, write it on a slanted line beneath the word it modifies. Look at the diagram for this sentence:

He polished the large brass bell.

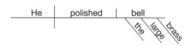

Teaching Strategy: Introduction

Make a list of nouns that become adjectives with the addition of a suffix. *(fish/fishy, book/bookish, beauty/beautiful, grace/gracious)* Ask students these questions about the nouns: What endings make these nouns adjectives? Which endings seem most common? Could any of the words have more than one possible ending? *(beautiful/beauteous, graceful/gracious)*

Announce that today the class will be looking at nouns that act as adjectives with no additional endings to change them.

Teaching Strategy

Combination with Chapter 15: Punctuation

If a student has trouble correctly punctuating items in a series, remind him that for a comma to be correct in a series of adjectives before a noun, he should be able to reverse the order of the adjectives or say *and* in the place of the comma without changing the meaning.

Teaching Strategy: Induction

Write these sentences on the board or overhead transparency: The new dog was active. We bought a dog collar for Rover. Underline the word *dog* in both sentences. Ask what the function of *dog* is in both sentences. (In the first sentence, *dog* is a noun; in the second it is an adjective.) It may be important to emphasize function in the sentence to your students. A word's part of speech in isolation may be different from its use in the sentence.

To the left of the number tell whether the italicized word is an adjective, noun, or pronoun.

adjective 1. Francis Marion was a *farm* boy from South Carolina.

noun 2. His first experience with *war* was a skirmish with the Cherokee Indians in 1761.

noun 3. In 1775, Marion left his parents' *farm* and joined the Revolutionary War effort.

adjective 4. He defended Charleston, South Carolina, from a *British* attack.

noun 5. By the time the *British* had captured Charleston in 1780, Marion had left the city.

adjective 6. But his *war* experience was not over.

adjective 7. Marion soon formed a small band of fighters to run *surprise* attacks on the British.

adjective 8. *These* attacks frustrated British troops, who spent much time chasing Marion through the swamplands of northeastern South Carolina.

pronoun 9. The British had never seen fighters like *these!*

noun 10. Attacks by *surprise* were Marion's specialty and earned him the nickname "Swamp Fox."

Repeat the activity with these sentences:

- My grandfather worked on the <u>photograph</u> album for the family reunion.
- I snapped a <u>photograph</u> of my cousin.

- The food at the <u>missions</u> banquet was delicious.
- Our church sends a large portion of our offerings to <u>missions.</u>

- My father carries <u>coffee</u> in a travel mug.
- The mug's shape keeps the <u>coffee</u> mug from tipping over.

- Jesus called <u>twelve</u> disciples to follow Him.
- The <u>twelve</u> were with Him in the upper room.

Instruct the students to notice which underlined words are nouns and which are adjectives. Can they spot any pattern? Guide the students to see that when the word is used as an adjective, it comes before the noun it modifies.

To the left of the number tell whether the italicized word is an adjective, noun, or pronoun.

noun   1. You have no doubt heard of *mistletoe.*

adjective   2. However, many people have never seen the *mistletoe* plant.

adjective   3. The plant is actually a parasite that grows on *tree* branches.

pronoun   4. *This* sometimes damages the host trees.

noun   5. One variety of mistletoe grows primarily on the apple *tree.*

noun   6. Mistletoe has oblong green leaves and white berries. Birds find the mistletoe *berry* quite tasty.

adjective   7. When the bird eats the berry, *berry* seeds stick to his beak, and he carries the seeds to his next perch.

adjective   8. In *this* way, the mistletoe plant is spread to other trees.

adjective   9. The mistletoe plant plays a role in *Christmas* tradition.

noun   10. At *Christmas,* a person caught under the mistletoe gets a kiss!

Articles

The most common adjectives are the **articles** *a, an,* and *the. The* is a **definite article** because it points to specific things. *A* and *an* are **indefinite articles** because they point to nonspecific things.

> Today we will plant *a* flower in our garden. (any flower)
> My favorite flower is *the* rose. (a specific flower)

page 251
Troublesome words

> Use *a* before a consonant (*b, c, d, f, g,* etc.): What *a* beautiful day! Before a vowel, *a* changes to *an* (vowels: *a, e, i,o, u*): He gave *an* apple to his teacher.

IN SUMMARY

Some nouns and pronouns can also function as adjectives.
The **articles** *a, an,* and *the* are the most common adjectives.

5-8   PRACTICE THE SKILL

Underline the articles.

1. Christians should develop a strong daily prayer life.

2. The God of heaven desires daily prayers.

3. For some people, prayer is a last resort.

4. Intercessory prayer benefits the welfare of others.

5. Jesus is the heavenly intercessor.

6. God hears a sincere request.

7. An immediate answer does not always come.

8. The infinite plans of God outweigh finite human ones.

9. We must offer an earnest, heartfelt request.

10. Godly, fervent prayers produce the result of closeness to God.

Teaching Strategy: Discussion

Discuss the information on page 111 about articles. Remind the students of any articles they named in the introductory inductive activity at the beginning of the chapter. *(an Aborigine's)*

ESL Strategy

For further explanation of articles, use ESL Helps pages 45-46 (Support Materials CD).

Evaluation

If you have assigned sentence diagramming with Practice the Skill 5-8, check answers on page 447.

Enrichment: Speech Link

Materials

• *Favorite Poems Old and New* selected by Helen Ferris (This anthology is available from BJU Press.)

Group Interpretation

Divide the class into small groups. Provide each group with a copy of a poem that uses descriptive adjectives. *("The Months" by Christina Rossetti, "Dogs and Weather" by Winifred Welles, and "At the Aquarium" by Max Eastman work well for this activity.)* Tell the students that good speakers have a mental picture of what they are talking about; they are not merely quoting or reading words. Instruct each group to identify the adjectives in the poem. Remind the groups that adjectives modify nouns and pronouns, answer

Underline the articles. Draw an arrow from each to the noun it modifies.

The hedgehog is a small nocturnal animal with a pointed nose and stiff spines covering its back. The spines of the hedgehog do not come out as easily as do the quills of the porcupine, an alarmingly prickly creature that is often confused with the hedgehog. When a hedgehog is threatened, it rolls itself into a ball. This protects the underpart of its body, which has no spines. This action is one of the few defenses of the timid hedgehog.

Hedgehogs also exhibit an unexplained behavior. First, they produce a foamy saliva. Then they spread the sticky foam all over their bodies. Scientists believe this froth may have a cooling effect on the hedgehog, but they are not sure. Hedgehogs have an average life span of three or four years, with some animals living to be as old as six years.

Possessives

A **possessive** is a noun form or pronoun form that shows ownership. Possessives usually function as adjectives. A possessive that functions as an adjective answers the question "whose?" about the noun it modifies.

page 30
Forming possessives

page 86
Possessive pronouns

Possessive Pronouns		
Person	**Singular**	**Plural**
first	my, mine	our, ours
second	your, yours	your, yours
third	its, his,	their, theirs
	her, hers	

A possessive noun usually signals that another noun will follow in the sentence.

Connie's bicycle is new.

---

specific questions, and may fit in the test frame on page 102. Encourage groups to explore the meanings of the adjectives in the poem and the way they add life to the nouns and pronouns. Some students might benefit from drawing pictures of what the poem makes them see. Allow each group to perform a portion of the poem, keeping in mind the pictures they have talked about.

Teaching Strategy: Introduction

Announce that today the class will continue to study nouns that function as adjectives and also pronouns that function as adjectives. Again stress the importance of focusing on a word's function within the sentence.

Teaching Strategy: Induction

Write the following sentence on the board or overhead transparency: *The bicycle is new.* Ask students to identify the parts of

the sentence that they already know. *(Bicycle is a noun and the subject of the sentence; new is an adjective and the predicate adjective in the sentence; is is the linking verb; the is an adjective.)* Erase the opening *The* and write *Connie's* in its place. Ask them to identify *Connie's* function in the sentence. (Although by itself *Connie* is a noun, *Connie's* is an adjective because it modifies a noun.) Tell them that this type of adjective is also called a *possessive* because it shows possession.

The possessive noun *Connie's* modifies the noun *bicycle* to tell us who owns the bicycle. Possessive nouns usually act as adjectives rather than as nouns. Possessive pronouns act like possessive nouns and can take the place of possessive nouns.

Connie's bicycle is new.

Her bicycle is new.

The possessive pronoun *her* replaces the possessive noun *Connie's*. The possessive pronoun modifies the noun *bicycle* and shows ownership. To diagram a possessive noun or pronoun used as an adjective, follow the diagram for any other adjective:

Connie's bicycle is new.

```
  bicycle   |  is  \  new
   \
  Connie's
```

Sometimes an entire phrase (a group of words) shows possession. A possessive phrase consists of a possessive noun modified by at least one other adjective.

Her brother's old bicycle has a new seat.

In this example, the word *brother's* is not the complete possessive. The possessive phrase *her brother's* tell us exactly who owns the bicycle. Possessive pronouns can also replace an entire possessive phrase.

Her brother's old bicycle has a new seat.

His old bicycle has a new seat.

The possessive pronoun *his* replaces the possessive phrase *her brother's*. The possessive pronoun is an adjective because it modifies the noun *bicycle*. A possessive phrase is diagrammed slightly differently than other adjectives are diagrammed. The adjective that precedes the possessive word is attached to the possessive itself rather than to the main noun:

Her brother's old bicycle has a new seat.

```
  bicycle   |  has  |  seat
   \                  \  \
  brother's          a   new
   \
  old
   \
  Her
```

Sometimes a possessive noun or pronoun can replace more than just a noun or a possessive phrase. A possessive noun or pronoun can also replace an entire phrase.

Her brother's old bicycle has a new seat.
His has a new seat.

Adjectives   113

If students question the diagram for a possessive phrase, explain that the adjectives before the possessive modify the possessive itself. The possessive then modifies the main noun. Use this example for further explanation: *the old dog's new collar.* The adjectives *the* and *old* modify the possessive *dog's;* the adjectives *dog's* and *new* modify the noun *collar.* The diagram would look like this:

```
  collar
   \  \
 dog's  new
  \ \
 the old
```

Replace *Connie's* with *Mark's,* the *teacher's,* and the *boys'* and point out that all of these modify bicycle and are adjectives. Now replace *Connie's* with *her* and ask what the function of the word is. By now, students should understand that as long as the word modifies the noun following it, it is an adjective.

Using the same sentence, erase the noun but leave the possessive. *(Mark's is new.)* Ask what the function of Mark's is. *(Without the noun,* Mark's *stands alone as the subject.)* Explain that this is called an *independent possessive* and that it is used chiefly in speaking and not in formal writing.

Learning Christianly

Learning Christianly

In this example, the possessive pronoun *his* does not modify any noun in the sentence. Instead, the word *his* replaces the entire phrase *her brother's old bicycle.* When a possessive acts in place of a noun or a noun and its adjectives, it is called an **independent possessive.** Independent possessives are not adjectives because they do not modify nouns. An independent possessive replaces the noun and all of its modifiers.

> *Jill's birthday* was last week.
> *Jill's* was last week.

In the first sentence, the possessive noun *Jill's* is an adjective. It modifies the noun *birthday.* In the second example, *Jill's* does not modify any other noun. It is an independent possessive functioning as the subject of the sentence.

> She opened *my gift.*
> She opened *mine.*

The possessive pronoun *my* is an adjective because it modifies the noun *gift* and shows ownership. The possessive pronoun *mine* is an independent possessive. It does not modify any noun in the sentence. Instead, *mine* replaces the phrase *my gift* and acts as the direct object in the sentence.

Because independent possessives replace other nouns or pronouns, they should be diagrammed according to the function of the word or phrase they replace. Look at the diagram for this sentence:

His has a new seat.

Now look at the diagram for this sentence:

She opened mine.

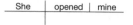

In Summary

Possessives are nouns and pronouns that show ownership and signal that a noun will follow.

Independent possessives are not adjectives; they replace nouns and function as nouns.

Literature Link

Instruct the students to look again at the excerpt from "The Speckled Band." Challenge the students to find the possessive pronouns in the passage.

A. Label the sentence patterns *S-InV, S-TrV-DO, S-TrV-IO-DO, S-LV-PN,* or *S-LV-PA.*

B. Underline each possessive noun or pronoun functioning as an adjective twice and the other adjectives once.

C. Draw an arrow from each adjective to the noun it modifies.

D. Circle any independent possessives.

1. Williamsburg is one of the colonists' beautiful cities.

2. The Virginia Colony chose Williamsburg as its capital.

3. Virginia's highest court met twice during the year.

4. A session attracted many Virginian families.

5. The sessions became a favorite social event of theirs.

6. Also, the American colonies' first mental institution opened here.

7. Today, Williamsburg's businesses benefit from many tourists.

8. Their shops exhibit many of the original craftsmen's trades.

9. One notable colonial shop is the blacksmith's shop.

10. His was a useful service.

ESL: ESL students will have a much easier time *identifying* articles than using them. Refer to ESL Helps page 45 of the Support Materials CD for more information about articles.

Virginia is part of the proper name *Virginia Colony.*

A. Underline each possessive noun or pronoun functioning as an adjective twice and any other adjectives once.

B. Draw an arrow from each adjective to the noun it modifies.

C. Circle the independent possessives.

1. A young Katie von Bora married the distinguished Martin Luther in 1525.

2. Martin's father supported their marriage.

3. Katie gave Martin's hectic household order.

4. The busy Martin benefited from Katie's constant encouragement and faithful prayers.

5. God blessed the Luthers with a baby son early in their marriage.

6. Their daughter died from a mysterious disease.

7. His wife helped strengthen Luther in his downcast state.

Adjectives   115

8. <u>His</u> grief was more <u>intense</u> than hers

9. Later, Duke George desired <u>Luther's</u> death.

10. Theirs was not <u>an easy</u> life.

Proper Adjectives

page 35
Common and Proper nouns

page 277
Proper adjectives

You have already learned that nouns can be common or proper. Adjectives can also be **common** or **proper**. Proper adjectives are adjectives that are made from proper nouns.

Last night we ate dinner at a Chinese restaurant.
Charles Dickens wrote his stories during the Victorian era in England.

In the first example *Chinese* is a proper adjective made from the proper noun *China*. In the second example the proper adjective *Victorian* is made from the proper noun *Victoria*.

Adjectives cannot be made plural in English.
Wrong: Some Indians chiefs were extremely brave.
Right: Some Indian chiefs were extremely brave.

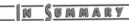

IN SUMMARY

Proper adjectives are adjectives made from proper nouns.

5-12 PRACTICE THE SKILL

Underline the proper adjectives.

1. Yes, let's go to the mall and get some <u>Chinese</u> food.

2. How does a <u>Mexican</u> enchilada sound?

3. Have you ever tried <u>Cajun</u> food?

4. <u>Italian</u> pasta appeals more to me.

5. I could order <u>French</u> bread with it.

6. My friend Anne prefers <u>Thai</u> beef salad.

7. Suzanne enjoys an <u>Indian</u> dish called chicken curry.

8. The <u>Japanese</u> restaurant also serves other <u>Oriental</u> foods.

9. A <u>Hong Kong</u> fried rice dish is a favorite with many diners.

10. For children, a good old <u>American</u> cheeseburger is always a possibility.

116

Because of their function, this text calls proper nouns that do not change form when modifying ("a June day") proper adjectives.

Teaching Strategy: Introduction

Remind students of common and proper nouns studied in Chapter 2 and of your discussion of nouns' being made into adjectives. Ask them what kind of adjectives they think proper nouns make. *(proper adjectives)* List students' examples on the board.

Enrichment

Materials
• Newspapers or magazines

Ask students to make a list of vivid adjectives (or cut words from newspapers/magazines). Tell them to find adjectives of all types studied. *(descriptive, adjectives formed from other parts of speech, articles, possessives, and proper adjectives)* Direct students to put their adjectives into sentences. Have students cut pictures from magazines or draw their own pictures to illustrate the adjective in the sentences they

have chosen. Display the finished pieces in the classroom.

Underline each proper adjective.

1. Have you seen the Renaissance furniture at the mall? We studied the Renaissance in history.

2. The Spanish style exhibited a Moorish influence through the intricate geometric designs.

3. I prefer the Gothic style of furniture for my living room.

4. If you like rococo furniture, then you may also like the Chippendale style of furniture.

5. Biedermeier furniture presents an informal style that many like too. This furniture was named for Gottlieb Biedermeier, an imaginary person.

6. Far Eastern influences can be seen in the pine Scandinavian furniture.

7. Some of the handpainted pieces are often mistaken for the Pennsylvania Dutch furniture of the 1920s.

8. My mother enjoys many different styles of furniture. She has a beautiful Queen Anne desk in her study.

9. Plain Shaker rockers line the front porch of our home.

10. Her favorite piece is a Hepplewhite chair designed by George Hepplewhite.

 REVIEW THE SKILL

A. Underline the adjectives.
B. Draw an arrow from each adjective to the noun it modifies.
C. Label each predicate adjective *PA*. Circle any independent possessives.

1. On the North American continent there are approximately seven hundred types of poisonous plants.

2. Some of these plants are extremely toxic.

3. Some mushrooms are deadly.

4. The berries from many forest plants can cause severe illness.

5. Perhaps the most infamous poisonous shrub is poison ivy.

117

6. This plant is part of the cashew family.

7. Its tissues discharge an acidlike oil that irritates human skin.

8. Yours will probably feel as though it is on fire if you come in contact with the plant.

9. This oil causes a painful rash.

10. However, the ugly eruptions themselves are not infectious. *PA*

5-15 CUMULATIVE REVIEW

A. Locate and correct the ten errors in the paragraph: fragments, comma splices, fused sentences, noun plurals, singular and plural noun possessives, verb forms (e.g., *had throwed*), and spellings of verb forms. Use the lines below to write the paragraph correctly.

B. Improve the paragraph by replacing each underlined noun with a more precise noun. *(Answers will vary.)*

Colorado has been called "The Centennial State." Because it becomed a state on the hundredth anniversary of the Declaration of Independence. The capital of Colorado is Denver two earlier territorial capitals were Colorado City and Golden. The building in Denver has a gold-plated dome. Some other things also represent Colorado. Colorados state flag is as colorful as the state itself. The red *C* symbolizes a Spanish word for red, *colorado*. The gold ball represents Colorado's gold production, the blue and white stripes represent blue skys and mountain snow. The state bird is the lark bunting, and the state flower is the Rocky Mountain columbine. Recognized for its symmetrical blue and white petals. Colorado is also known for the quality of it's mountain-growed food. The Rocky Ford cantaloupe is popular throughout the entire United States. Above all else, Colorado has been knowed for its great beauty. It well deserves its recognition as a paradise of the Rocky Mountains.

Colorado has been called "The Centennial State" because it became a

state on the hundredth anniversary of the Declaration of Independence.

The capital of Colorado is Denver. Two earlier territorial capitals were

Colorado City and Golden. The capitol in Denver has a gold-plated dome.

Some other symbols also represent Colorado. Colorado's state flag is as

colorful as the state itself. The red C symbolizes a Spanish word for red,

colorado. The gold ball represents Colorado's gold production; the blue and

white stripes represent blue skies and mountain snow. The state bird is

the lark bunting, and the state flower is the Rocky Mountain columbine,

recognized for its symmetrical blue and white petals. Colorado is also

known for the quality of its mountain-grown fruit. The Rocky Ford can-

taloupe is popular throughout the entire United States. Above all else,

Colorado has been known for its great beauty. It well deserves its recogni-

tion as a paradise of the Rocky Mountains.

120 Chapter 5

- Answers will vary. *(There is less tension.)*
- Answers will vary.

- The adjectives give a detailed description of the king's palace.
- Without the adjectives the passage is not as descriptive.

≡SLIDING HOME

Good writers choose their adjectives carefully, using only those they really need. You can think of adjectives as the salt of writing. A little seasoning goes a long way.

- *Read the last paragraph of "The Speckled Band" excerpt without the adjectives. How is the scene different? Has it lost some tension?*

- *Try replacing the adjectives with some that will make the snake a garter snake. Does the scene now seem funny instead of scary?*

> *Esther 1:3-6*
>
> *3 In the third year of his reign, he made a feast unto all his princes and his servants; the power of Persia and Media, the nobles and princes of the provinces, being before him:*
>
> *4 When he shewed the riches of his glorious kingdom and the honour of his excellent majesty many days, even an hundred and fourscore days.*
>
> *5 And when these days were expired, the king made a feast unto all the people that were present in Shushan the palace, both unto great and small, seven days, in the court of the garden of the king's palace;*
>
> *6 Where were white, green, and blue, hangings, fastened with cords of fine linen and purple to silver rings and pillars of marble: the beds were of gold and silver, upon a pavement of red, and blue, and white, and black, marble.*

- *What do the adjectives do for this description?*

- *Read the passage without the adjectives. How does it change?*

Literature Link

Read and discuss the Sliding Home questions on page 120.

Creating a Poem from Prose

Lesson Support

Support Materials CD
Writing Worksheets—p. 95
Rubrics—p. 109

Scriptural Application

Ask a student to read Proverbs 25:11 aloud. Then share the following information with the students. In his poem "Essay on Criticism," Alexander Pope explains that a good poem should communicate

CREATING A POEM FROM PROSE

A word fitly spoken is like apples of gold in pictures of silver.
Proverbs 25:11

What is the difference between poetry and prose? Prose is what you read in the newspaper, in a textbook, and in your favorite adventure novel. Prose is very much like conversation, although it is usually more formal than everyday speech. Prose also lacks metrical structure. Poetry, on the other hand, could be compared to music. A poem is arranged in lines, has qualities of sound, and compresses ideas into fewer words than prose. Metered poetry has a set pattern of stresses and nonstresses in its rhythm. Remember, however, that a poem does not have to rhyme. One type of poem, a "found" poem, uses descriptive words and phrases adapted from a prose text.

Your Turn

Write a "found poem" based on a descriptive prose selection.

Planning

Choose a prose selection. As you consider what to select, keep in mind that your text should be a particularly descriptive passage that brings specific pictures, or images, to your mind or inspires a certain emotion inside you. The text of your poem should come directly from the prose text of something else. Look for an appropriate passage in a novel, in a letter, in a newspaper or a magazine, on a billboard, or in an advertisement. Be sure to have a copy of the text for your use as you work.

One student chose to use a portion of a letter written to him by his grandfather.

> I often thought about Abraham and Job when I was your age. Those stories used to bother me. Really. I wondered why Abraham should have to live through those agonies of climbing the hill with his son, expecting to have to kill him when they reached the top. I wondered why Job would be required to lose everything, not knowing that all would be restored—and not all restored even then, but replaced.
>
> Later I thought that the ordeals of Abraham and Job made them stronger, better. Then I thought—who wants to be that strong and good? Then I thought—if God in omniscience already knew how Job and Abraham would respond, why did He test them so? And then, finally, it appeared that God was not showing Himself how they would respond—but rather He was showing them. Aha.

Read the selection several times. After you have become familiar with the prose selection by reading it silently, try reading it aloud to discover where a speaker would pause in reading the words.

Use slash marks to indicate the natural breaks in thought. Read the selection aloud again and divide each paragraph into its natural phrases. Think about how to break the lines to make the most of the text's natural rhythm and to emphasize its most important ideas. Consider using a highlighter to mark selected words, phrases, and sentences that contain vivid and clear descriptions. Be sure that your selected descriptions portray a clear picture for the reader.

Overview of Writing Process

Planning—Choosing a prose passage

Drafting—Dividing paragraphs into natural phrases; breaking lines for poem

Revising—Rereading piece with line breaks; creating a title

Publishing—Making a final copy

Objectives

Students will

1. find a piece of prose to frame as a found poem.

2. arrange the prose passage into a poem.

---

something that "oft was thought but ne'er so well expressed." Poetry gives us the opportunity to appeal to the beauty and power of language to communicate forcefully and briefly. In poetry each word is important and can produce an effect as pleasing as a golden apple in a silver picture.

Introduction

Direct the students' attention to page 121 to identify the differences between poetry and prose. Ask a student to tell where he thinks poetry comes from. After a brief discussion, explain that not all poetry begins as poetry.

Scriptural Application

Ask the students for their thoughts about the grandfather's responses to the questions about Abraham and Job. *(Answers will vary.)* Remind students that nothing happens by accident. Ask them to recall times when they have seen the wisdom of God revealed after an event was over. Conclude the discussion by reading Romans 8:28 aloud.

Teaching Strategy

Distribute a copy of Writing Worksheet 5 to each student. Discuss the examples and point out the steps of creating a found poem.

Planning Strategies

Direct the students to read the grandfather's letter on page 121 of the text. Ask the students why the grandson used the letter for his found poem. *(Answers will vary but may include the following: Because the student had expressed concern about Abraham to his grandfather, he*

Notice how the student used slashes to indicate the natural breaks.

I often thought about Abraham and Job when I was your age. / Those stories used to bother me. / Really. / I wondered why Abraham should have to live through those agonies / of climbing the hill with his son, / expecting to have to kill him when they reached the top. / I wondered why Job would be required to lose everything, / not knowing that all would be restored— / and not all restored even then, / but replaced.

Later I thought that the ordeals of Abraham and Job made them stronger, / better. Then I thought / —who wants to be that strong and good? / Then I thought— / if God in omniscience already knew how Job and Abraham would respond, / why did He test them so? / And then, / finally, / it appeared that God was not showing Himself how they would respond— / but rather He was showing them. / Aha.

Drafting

Edit the prose selection. Look at the portions of the text that you have marked. Delete any words and phrases that you decide are unnecessary.

Evaluate sentence breaks. You may want to alter these breaks. Keep in mind the text's natural rhythm and emphasize its most important ideas. Remember that your poem does not have to rhyme.

Arrange the lines of your poem. Using the slash marks, determine which ideas to put into each line. You may incorporate a few phrases into a single line. Other phrases are important enough to stand alone, each on its own line. Use a variety of line lengths to emphasize the descriptive portions.

Write your found poem. Write a rough draft of your poem without stopping to fix errors. Use your marks to guide you as you write out each line.

Abraham and Job.
Those stories used to bother me.
Really.
I wondered why Abraham
should have to live through
those agonies
of climbing the hill with his son,
expecting to have to kill him
when they reached the top.
I wondered why Job
would be required to lose everything,
not knowing that all would be restored—
and not all restored even then,
but replaced.
Later I thought that the ordeals
of Abraham and Job
made them stronger, better.
Then I thought—but who wants to be
that strong and good?
Then I thought—if God in omniscience
already knew how Job and Abraham would respond,
why did He test them so?
And then, finally,
it appeared that God was not showing Himself
how they would respond—
but rather He was showing them.
Aha.

already had an interest in the subject. Because the letter was so well written, he decided to use the letter for his assignment). Instruct each student to find a short piece of prose (about two paragraphs) to make into a poem and to record the bibliographical information for the selection.

As an alternative to finding a prose selection, allow students to write prose accounts of events that seemed small to them at first but later proved to be significant. The prose account must be at least two paragraphs.

Ask two or three volunteers to read their prose selections aloud and to explain why they chose as they did.

Direct the students' attention to page 122 in the text. Discuss the way in which the grandson divided the ideas in his grandfather's letter. Ask students to identify short divisions that show emphasis. *(Really, but replaced, And then, finally, Aha)* Then instruct the students to make slash marks throughout their prose pieces, indicating where natural pauses occur in the reading.

Drafting Strategy

Encourage the students to mark specific ideas or words and phrases to emphasize. Then instruct them to write out the prose in poetic lines, following the examples in the text and giving the important words or phrases their own lines. Emphasize to the students the importance of being selective in their choice of words and phrases.

Revising Strategies

Ask a volunteer to read the found poem on page 122 aloud to the class. Challenge each student to read his found poem aloud to himself several times. Encourage the

Re-examine your poem to be sure that the arrangement emphasizes the important ideas. Notice that the most important idea of the example poem comes last: God tested Abraham and Job, not to show *Himself* how they would respond but to show *them* how they would respond. The poem progresses as a series of thoughts, put into the form of questions, and finally leads to this conclusion. Ending a poem immediately after the most important idea is one of the best ways to emphasize that idea. Readers tend to remember best what was said at the end, not at the beginning, of a poem. Including the word *Aha,* a surprising word of discovery, immediately draws our attention to what was said right before it to make sure we have made the same discovery as the speaker in the poem. If necessary, rearrange the line breaks in your poem so that the most important ideas are easy for the reader to find.

Proofread for correctness. Remember that when you create a found poem, you may drop words from the text but you may not add your own words to the text. Once you have determined that you have not added any words of your own, check for correct grammar, spelling, and punctuation.

Make a final, error-free copy of your found poem. Include an appropriate title for your found poem. Write or type the poem according to standard manuscript form, with correct margins and spacing.

page 382

Organizing sentences

Post your poem on a poetry bulletin board. Choose a title for the poem and display them together on the bulletin board. You may wish to post not only your found poem but also the text from which you created your poem.

Present your poem orally. Read through your poem several times before you present it for the class. Include the title of the poem when you read it.

---

students to focus on precision and conciseness as they read.

Remind students that they cannot add words to the original. Challenge them to double-check the words of their found poem.

Publishing Strategy

Divide the class into groups of three or four students. Allow each student to read his found poem for the group. Encourage the students to share their responses.

Scriptural Application

Remind students that Christians are in a sense "found poems." By Christ's working, their lives become more beautiful than they ever could be without His authorship.

Evaluation

For help in grading this assignment, see "Grading Writing Assignments" (p. x) and Rubric 5 (Support Materials CD, p. 109).

Enrichment

Direct the students to bring a favorite possession to class. Allow time for the stu-

dents to write descriptions of their possessions. Then ask a volunteer to read his description for the class. Instruct the students to listen carefully for intonation and pauses as the volunteer reads aloud. Then display the description and lead the students in "finding" a poem in it.

Enrichment

Publish an anthology of the students' found poems.

Officer Bell searched through the coupon section of the Yellow Pages. "A unit 10 x 8 x 12—just what I need, and Compact Storage company has an address on my side of town too. I'll just give them a call at lunch." He sighed in relief and circled the telephone number printed on the coupon. "Why I ever bought that hat stand! What was I thinking? A Victorian hat stand and me in an apartment. I'll take it to Grandmother Bell next summer; then this mistake will be over. What would Inspector Jameson think if he knew I bought that thing. I hope the storage unit is tall enough!"

Officer Bell reviewed Inspector Jameson's instructions for the day. "Earlier this year counterfeiters began flooding the area with products produced in Mexico bearing fake name-brand logos. I want a list of all the local flea markets in the area. We'll visit each market during the next few weeks and interview each manager. We must find the vendors. Most of them are honest and will help lead us to the source of these fakes. Have the list ready by tomorrow morning." Officer Bell began combing through the Yellow Pages compiling a list of flea markets the counterfeiters might try to misuse.

However, lunchtime found him on the phone with Compact Storage working out the details of delivery, lease, insurance, and size. "That seemed simple enough," he thought. "Saved me a trip too, calling ahead like that. One trip this afternoon and one trip next summer—very neat. It's done."

Delivery of the hat stand was accomplished as smoothly as the phone call. The manager even offered to help him secure the hat stand in a storage unit.

"Not a scratch; thank you for your help, Mr. Boyd. The job was a lot easier with two doing it," said Officer Bell as he also placed a bowling ball bag inside the unit. It was an old ball he didn't use, and it was forever in his way in the bottom of the closet. "Getting more value for my dollar storing it here with the hat stand," he thought.

He noticed Mr. Boyd staring at the unlikely match, hat stand with bowling ball. "They're an odd pair. The hat stand is for my Grandmother. The ball's just here to be out of the way," Bell explained.

"Oh, don't mind my looking," said Mr. Boyd. "I'm just naturally curious. I've seen odder things than that. A woman once wanted to store her husband's snake while he was away. She couldn't stand the thing and didn't want it in the house while he was gone. I told her it wouldn't be right. Snake or no, it's a living creature and shouldn't be shut up like that. Now your hat stand isn't as odd as that! One guy had a windmill from Texas that he had taken apart and brought here! Can you believe that? Officer, I'm a curious man in a curious business! But that was years ago. The oddest thing lately has been a guy who comes every Monday. He takes out a dozen boxes and puts them in his truck. But I never see him put any boxes in. Surely he must. But then I just work days."

Bell asked, "What's in the boxes?"

"I don't know. The labels are in Spanish. So, here's your key, sir."

Critical Thinking

Ask the students to name some types of advertising. *(newspaper, television, direct mail, radio, magazine, billboards, window displays, key chains, automobile windshield flyers, telephone directories)*

Ask the students how many of these types named they saw on the way to school this morning. Were the ads effective? What does the fact that the students remember the advertisement say about its effectiveness?

Ask the students how they have used the yellow pages in the telephone book. Ask a volunteer to relate his experiences. Was the product or service easy to find? Did he prefer the ads with pictures, larger type, or color?

Bring a telephone book (yellow pages) to class and have the students look up the first entry under "Swimming Pools." Have any of the opening advertisers manipulated the names of their companies in order to get the first entry? *(e.g., AAA First Class Pools, Aabstract Pools) (Note: Check beforehand for objectionable en-* tries or interesting examples of spelling manipulation.) Would a company's having the first entry influence you to call that company first?

Officer Bell was still reliving the conversation when he arrived at work the next morning. He told Inspector Jameson every detail about the odd people Mr. Boyd had met.

"What were you doing at Compact Storage?" asked the Inspector.

His own mistake took Officer Bell completely by surprise. "Oh, I just stored some stuff that was in my way. You know, small apartment and all. It's just temporary till summer."

"Those are odd stories, Bell. Tell me—where is Compact Storage?"

"On Trail Drive. It was the only one near my place."

"Really," said Jameson. "Where are the others?"

Bell flopped open the Yellow Pages. "Here. You can see for yourself. They're all in the busier sections than the one I use."

The Inspector studied the ads. "Aha," he said. "Your storage unit may be close, but it certainly isn't the safest!

"I have a new theory. It's a good thing you have a small apartment. Otherwise we could have spent weeks trying to solve the counterfeit case. Let's go visit your hat stand, Bell!"

"How did you know I bought the hat stand? Oh never mind; how did you come up with a new theory on the counterfeit case?"

1. *Supposing Officer Bell did not know the names of all the streets in town, how else could he have known all the other storage units were across town from him?*

2. *What details in Bell's recounting of his visit to Compact Storage alerted Jameson to a possible link with the counterfeiter?*

3. *What do you think Jameson noticed about the ads that made him say it was not the safest storage?*

4. *How do you think the lack of safety helped Jameson form a new theory?*

- All of the other storage units have telephone numbers that begin with *667*. The telephone number for Compact Storage begins with *991*, indicating that it is probably located in another part of town.

- When Bell said the boxes had Spanish labels on the boxes, Jameson became curious. Bell also reported that a man takes the boxes out during the day but that Mr. Boyd (who works only during the day) never sees who puts the boxes in (presumably at night).

- When he saw that Compact Storage had easy access and little security, he was suspicious.

- It would be convenient for a person doing illegal things to choose storage away from more trafficked areas.

CHAPTER 6

Chapter Goals

Students will

1. understand the function of an adverb in a sentence.

2. learn comparative forms of adverbs.

3. learn that *not* functions in a verb phrase to make it negative.

4. understand that some adverbs do not have comparative forms.

ADVERBS

THOSE WINTER SUNDAYS
BY ROBERT HAYDEN

Objectives

Students will

1. identify the purpose, function, and general position of adverbs in a sentence.

2. locate adverbs by certain "adverb questions" and by their relationship to verbs, adjectives, or other adverbs in the sentence.

3. name *not* as an adverb that functions in a verb phrase to make the sentence negative.

4. correctly spell the positive, comparative, and superlative forms of adverbs.

5. use the correct positive, comparative, or superlative forms of adverbs to give more precise information about the words they modify.

6. identify adverbs that do not change form.

7. identify adverbs showing comparison by irregular forms.

Lesson Support

Student Text
Chapter Review 6—pp. 405-6

Teacher's Edition
Diagram Answers—pp. 447-48

Support Materials CD
Warm-Ups—pp. 13-14
Teaching Helps—p. 35
Concept Reinforcements—p. 63
Bulletin Boards—p. 207

Sundays too my father got up early
and put his clothes on in the blueblack cold,
then with cracked hands that ached
from labor in the weekday weather made
banked fires blaze. No one ever thanked him.

I'd wake and hear the cold splintering, breaking.
When the rooms were warm, he'd call,
and slowly I would rise and dress,
fearing the chronic angers of that house,

Speaking indifferently to him,
who had driven out the cold
and polished my good shoes as well.
What did I know, what did I know
of love's austere and lonely offices?

- *Who is the speaker in this poem?*

- *What word in the second stanza tells you that the speaker did not like to get up in the morning?*

- *What word in the last stanza reveals how the speaker, as a teenager, viewed his father?*

- *How old do you think the speaker is at the time he recalls this memory? How has his view of his father changed since his youth?*

- the child of the man described in the poem

- *slowly*

- *indifferently*

- Answers will vary. *(The speaker is probably an adult now. The speaker no longer regards the father as a harsh man.)*

The speaker in this poem is looking back on his younger days at home. He seems a bit ashamed of his behavior. He says he spoke indifferently to his father; he says he responded slowly when his father called. He seems to have been more concerned with his own comfort than with the sacrifices his father was making for him. Words like *indifferently* and *slowly* help to show that the writer is now sorry for how he spoke and responded to his father.

Just as adjectives sharpen our focus on nouns, adverbs add information to verbs and other words. In this chapter you will learn that we can recognize adverbs by asking certain questions.

Literature Link

Read "Those Winter Sundays" and discuss
the questions on page 127.

An alternative grammar system divides the part of speech traditionally known as adverb into two: adverbs and qualifiers.

Adverbs

- usually modify verbs.
- have positive, comparative, and superlative forms.
- answer the questions "when?" "where?" or "how?"

Qualifiers

- usually modify adjectives or other adverbs.
- do not show comparison.
- answer the question "to what extent?"
- are sometimes called *intensifiers* because they either strengthen or weaken the meaning of the adjective or adverb they modify.

ESL: Note that different languages put the negation in different places in the sentence. If students have a problem with using *not*, here are a few rules to help them.

1. If there is an auxiliary in the sentence, put the *not* after the first auxiliary.
   Russ <u>will come</u> soon.
   Russ <u>will</u> not <u>come</u> soon.

2. If there is a *be* verb in the sentence, put the *not* after the *be* verb.
   Yoichi <u>is</u> wealthy.
   Yoichi <u>is</u> not wealthy.

3. If there is no auxiliary and no *be* verb, add some form of the word *do*. Put the *not* between *do* and the verb.
   Tami <u>likes</u> candy.
   Tami <u>does</u> not <u>like</u> candy.
   Tami <u>ate</u> three pieces.
   Tami <u>did</u> not <u>eat</u> three pieces.

page 146

Prepositional phrases

page 149

Preposition or Adverb?

page 237

Double negatives

page 310

Apostrophes

Adverbs

Adverbs are words that modify verbs, adjectives, or other adverbs. Adverbs that modify verbs tell *when, where,* or *how* about the verbs they modify. Adverbs that modify adjectives and other adverbs tell *to what extent.* They strengthen or weaken the meaning of the words they modify.

ETYMOLOGY

Adverb comes from the latin *ad-* (additional) and *verbum* (word). *Adverb* literally means "additional word."

When?	The soccer team is at Locke Park *now.*
Where?	They practice *there.*
How?	Mr. Schmidt coaches them *well.*
To what extent?	Their schedule is *somewhat* full already.
	The goalie watches the ball *very* carefully.

Even though *not* does not answer any of the common adverb questions, we do consider it to be an adverb. It is used to make a sentence negative.

Raoul is *not* playing today.
He did *not* quit the team.
He can*not* play soccer with a broken leg.
The other players have*n't* heard the news.

6-1 PRACTICE THE SKILL

Underline the adverbs in the following sentences.

1. One of the <u>most</u> attractive qualities a person can have is a spirit of gratefulness.

2. Numerous people, including parents, doctors, and teachers, have <u>unselfishly</u> contributed to our lives.

3. We <u>often</u> do <u>not</u> give them the credit they deserve.

4. One of the <u>very</u> best rewards a person can receive is gratitude.

5. You may have worked exceptionally <u>hard</u> and been disappointed because you received no word of appreciation.

6. Can you think of some people who have especially <u>helped</u> you to succeed?

7. You should send a thank-you note and <u>sincerely</u> thank them.

8. You would be <u>quite</u> surprised at their reaction.

9. Have you said "Thank you" to your parents <u>lately</u>?

10. Scripture <u>specifically</u> reminds us, "In every thing give thanks" (I Thess. 5:18).

Teaching Strategy:
   Introduction

Prepare an overhead transparency from Teaching Helps page 35 (Support Materials CD). Display it to the students and point out the questions that adverbs answer and the positions in which adverbs can appear in a sentence.

Scriptural Application

Explain that modifiers enhance or change the meaning of sentences. Read some examples from Scripture [emphasis ours]:

Exodus 20:15—"Thou shalt *not* steal."
Luke 23:43—"*To day* shalt thou be with me in paradise."

Underline the ten adverbs in the following paragraph.

The men stood in a tight huddle and <u>painfully</u> raised their hands to shield the brightness from their eyes. The sun shone <u>relentlessly</u> on the men's <u>excessively</u> white skin. All ten of them looked <u>anxiously</u> down the dusty road to see Him. The Man and His followers were <u>quickly</u> approaching. They all had heard of this Man and how He <u>liberally</u> healed diseases such as leprosy. <u>Soon</u> they stood before Him. He spoke few words. The ten men watched the decaying flesh on their hands <u>gradually</u> transform into <u>exceptionally</u> smooth and healthy skin. <u>Only</u> one man returned to give thanks to Jesus, who had healed him.

Positions of Adverbs

You have already learned that adjectives usually come just before the nouns they modify. Adverbs that modify adjectives or other adverbs also come just before the words that they modify.

The bread tasted *quite* good.

She ate it *too* quickly.

Adverbs that modify verbs, however, can appear many different places in the sentence.

After the verb: They will eat *now*.

After the verb and direct object: They will eat the bread *now*.

After the auxiliary verb: They will *now* eat the bread.

Before the complete verb: They *now* will eat the bread.

At the beginning of the sentence: *Now* they will eat the bread.

Adverbs   **129**

Notice that the adverb sometimes appears between parts of the complete verb. For example, if an adverb appears after an auxiliary verb, the adverb is interrupting the complete verb. The complete verb is the auxiliary verb and the main verb; the adverb that appears between them is not part of the complete verb.

The diagram format for adverbs is similar to the format for adjectives. Be sure to attach the adverb line to the word it modifies. Look at the diagram for this sentence.

She ate it quickly.

IN SUMMARY

Adverbs modify verbs, adjectives, or other adverbs.

Adverbs tell *when, where, how,* or *to what extent* about the words they modify.

Most adverbs can appear in many different places in the sentence.

6-3 PRACTICE THE SKILL

A. **Underline the adverbs.**
B. **Draw an arrow from each adverb to the word it modifies.**
C. **Label each modified word *V* (verb), *Adj* (adjective), or *Adv* (adverb).**

___V___ 1. Daily Duane reads his Bible.

Adv, V 2. Duane nearly always finishes his devotions before breakfast.

___V___ 3. Proverbs is usually Duane's choice for study.

__Adj__ 4. Duane likes the exceptionally beautiful language of Proverbs.

___V___ 5. He studies the verses carefully.

___V___ 6. Duane also memorizes many Proverbs passages.

__Adj__ 7. The verses seem easily applicable to his daily life.

___V___ 8. Regularly Duane offers a friend help in a study of Proverbs.

__Adj__ 9. His study of Proverbs is almost complete.

___V___ 10. He does not neglect other parts of the Bible.

Evaluation

If you have assigned sentence diagramming with Practice the Skill 6-3, check answers on pages 447-48.

6·4 ⚾ REVIEW THE SKILL

A. Underline the adverbs.

B. Draw an arrow from each adverb to the word it modifies.

C. Label each modified word *V* (verb), *Adj* (adjective), or *Adv* (adverb).

V, Adv   1. The Sargasso Sea lies <u>somewhat</u> <u>east</u> of the North American continent.

Adj   2. It is <u>most</u> notable for its seaweed surface.

V   3. Christopher Columbus <u>first</u> <u>scientifically</u> described the surface in 1492.

V   4. The Sargasso Sea <u>often</u> appears in legends of ships lost at sea.

Adv, V   5. <u>Only</u> <u>recently</u> have scientists discovered several interesting facts about the Sargasso Sea.

V   6. The seaweed <u>somehow</u> floats by its own air sacs.

V   7. These small air sacs appear <u>strategically</u> on the leaves' undersides.

V   8. The water of the Sargasso Sea is <u>not</u> typical.

Adj   9. It is <u>extremely</u> clear with a high salt content.

V   10. The temperature <u>sometimes</u> reaches 83°F.

North America

Atlantic Ocean

Sargasso Sea

South America

Adverbs   **131**

PRACTICE THE SKILL

6-5

Fill in each blank with an adverb that answers the question in parentheses. *(Answers will vary.)*

_____mechanically_____ 1. The soldiers _?_ marched in their formations. *(how?)*

_____immediately_____ 2. Their sergeant commanded them to halt _?_. *(when?)*

_____nearly_____ 3. His orders could be heard by _?_ all the base. *(to what extent?)*

_____sarcastically_____ 4. One general commented _?_ that the sergeant must be having a good day. *(how?)*

_____now_____ 5. Colonel Villiers commanded that the soldiers return _?_! *(when?)*

_____left, right_____ 6. March _?_! File _?_! *(where?)*

_____Finally_____ 7. _?_ the drill was finished. *(when?)*

_____directly_____ 8. Anthony marched _?_ to the barracks and fell into his bed. *(where?)*

_____fully_____ 9. He had rarely felt so _?_ exhausted! *(to what extent?)*

_____not_____ 10. He could _?_ keep his eyes open for long. *(negative)*

Fill in each blank with an adverb that answers the question at the end of the sentence. *(Answers will vary.)*

_____Yesterday_____ 1. _?_ I rode in a hot-air balloon for the first time. *(when?)*

_____very_____ 2. The experience was _?_ exciting! *(to what extent?)*

_____not_____ 3. I did _?_ know what to expect. *(negative)*

_____carefully_____ 4. The pilot _?_ filled the balloon with hot air. *(how?)*

_____quickly_____ 5. The balloon _?_ rose into the air. *(how?)*

_____below_____ 6. We watched the people _?_ . *(where?)*

_____above_____ 7. The crowd watched the balloon flying high _?_ . *(where?)*

_____next_____ 8. The pilot opened the vent _?_ . *(when?)*

_____very_____ 9. We descended _?_ gently. *(to what extent?)*

_____never_____ 10. I will _?_ forget the adventure. *(negative)*

page 233

Adjective or Adverb?

page 237

Comparisons

Comparing with Adverbs

Like adjectives, many adverbs have **comparative** and **superlative** forms; the comparative form is used for two people or things, and the superlative form is used for three or more people or things. These forms are made by adding *er* and *est* to some adverbs or by using *more* and *most* with others. Irregular adverbs form comparative and superlative in other ways. A reliable dictionary will give you the comparative and the superlative forms of any irregular adverb.

	Positive	Comparative	Superlative
Regular			
	fast	faster	fastest
	early	earlier	earliest
	fairly	more fairly	most fairly
	neatly	more neatly	most neatly
Irregular			
	well	better	best
	badly	worse	worst

Javier runs <u>faster</u> than Greg, but Ivan runs the <u>fastest</u> of all on the track team.

Tomatoes grow <u>well</u> in my garden, but Brussels sprouts grow even <u>better</u>.

Many common adverbs, especially those that modify adjectives or other adverbs, do not have comparative or superlative forms. To make comparisons with these (among others) would not make sense: *not, daily, now, almost, here, very, really, somewhat, almost,* and *too.*

IN SUMMARY

Regular adverbs show comparison by adding *er* and *est* or *more* and *most* to the stem form of the adverb.

Irregular adverbs have different forms to show comparison.

Some adverbs cannot be compared.

Teaching Strategy: Induction

Ask a student to describe the way he does something. His description should include an adverb. *(I run quickly.)* Ask another student to compare an action to the first student's action. *(I run more quickly than my teammate.)* Then ask a third student to compare his action to those of the first two students. *(I run most quickly of all the competitors.)*

Ask student volunteers to describe the changes in the form of the adverb. Lead them to the conclusion that the adverb uses *er* or *more* for comparing two items and *est* or *most* for comparing three or more items. Inform the students that they have just used adverbs in their positive, comparative, and superlative forms.

Teaching Strategy: Discussion

Explain that only regular adverbs show comparison by adding *er* or *est* or *more* or *most* to the stem form of the adverb. Give an example of an irregular adverb form to demonstrate how it shows comparison differently. *(badly, worse, worst)*

Make three columns labeled *positive, comparative,* and *superlative* on the board or overhead. Fill in the positive column with students' suggestions. Then fill in the other columns as students offer the correct comparative or superlative form for each positive form.

Fill in each blank with the correct form of the adverb in parentheses. Some adverbs may need two words to make the comparative or superlative form.

most seriously   1. The seventh grade class took their science experiments _?_ . *(seriously, superlative)*

best   2. They built model rockets to see whose would fly _?_ . *(well, superlative)*

strictly   3. Rules were _?_ enforced to ensure a safe launch. *(strictly, positive)*

more enthusiastically   4. At first, the science teacher talked _?_ than did the students. *(enthusiastically, comparative)*

earlier   5. Once construction started, however, the students arrived at school _?_ than usual and worked on their rockets. *(early, comparative)*

fastest, farthest   6. Prizes were to be given to those whose rockets flew _?_ and _?_ . *(fast, superlative; far, superlative)*

excitedly   7. After a lot of preparation, everyone watched _?_ as the students approached the launch pads. *(excitedly, positive)*

more quickly   8. Josie's model rocket climbed _?_ into the sky than she had expected. *(quickly, comparative)*

higher   9. However, Fritz's soared _?_ and stayed up longer than hers did. *(high, comparative)*

most slowly   10. Fiona's rocket floated to earth _?_ because it had the largest and most elaborate parachute. *(slowly, superlative)*

Scriptural Application

The Christian walk is full of choices. Someone's spiritual choices reflect the kind of Christian he is ("By their fruits ye shall know them," Matthew 7:20). In the same way, our writing will be judged and known by our word choices. To be appropriately creative, exciting, interesting, and informative takes skill and practice.

Fill in each blank with the correct form of the adverb in parentheses.

more slowly   1. Generally, people believe that turtles travel _?_ than any other animal. *(slowly, comparative)*

more quickly   2. However, some turtles can move _?_ than you would think. *(quickly, comparative)*

most rapidly   3. Sea turtles swim the _?_ of all of the turtle species. *(rapidly, superlative)*

fastest   4. The green turtle is the _?_ of all the sea turtles, reaching speeds of twenty miles per hour. *(fast, superlative)*

better   5. That turtle swims _?_ than we humans do. *(well, comparative)*

longer   6. Turtles live _?_ than most animals. Some can live over one hundred years. *(long, comparative)*

greatly   7. Turtle markings differ _?_. Shells can be black, brown, green, yellow, orange, or red. *(greatly, positive)*

most aggressively   8. Of all turtles, snapping turtles strike the _?_ at strangers. *(aggressively, superlative)*

frequently   9. Some people eat turtles _?_ and use their shells for ornamentation. *(frequently, positive)*

more frequently   10. Young people _?_ keep turtles as pets than older people do. *(frequently, comparative)*

6-9 USE THE SKILL

Insert at least one adverb into each sentence. Try to use a variety of adverbs. *(Answers will vary.)*

1. The beautiful city of Tokyo, Japan, was founded in 1457 by a mighty Japanese warrior.

   The extremely beautiful city of Tokyo, Japan, was founded in 1457 by

   a mighty Japanese warrior.

2. This lovely city is the Japanese capital and is the center of Japan's important commerce.

   This quite lovely city is the Japanese capital and is presently the center

   of Japan's most important commerce.

3. Conditions in Tokyo are crowded.

   Conditions in Tokyo are now crowded.

4. At the center of the city proper lies the gorgeous Imperial Palace, which is surrounded by ornate parks.

   At the center of the city proper lies the gorgeous Imperial Palace, which

   is completely surrounded by fairly ornate parks.

5. Many of the crowded streets in Tokyo do not have names; instead, sections of the city, called wards, are named.

   Many of the highly crowded streets in Tokyo do not even have names;

   instead, sections of the city, usually called wards, are named.

6. Over eight million people live in Tokyo, and there is a serious housing shortage.

   Over eight million people live in Tokyo, and there really is a fairly

   serious housing shortage.

7. Since World War II, Tokyo's economy has been strong, and electrical machinery and publishing has played an active role.

   Since World War II, Tokyo's economy has generally been strong, and

   electrical machinery and publishing has played an active role.

Learning Christianly

Insert several different adverbs into the following sentence: "The knight rescued the damsel." How do the different adverbs change your view of the knight? If you're trying to be more than a little creative, you're probably discovering that adverbs can have a significant impact on how we view the people and events presented in a sentence. What does the importance of adverbs in language suggest about the importance of how we do what we do in life?

Learning Christianly

We tend to think of a person's character as being revealed almost entirely by what he *does*. But the importance of adverbs in writing should remind us that *how* a person does something can be just as revealing as the action itself. God is most interested in what we are rather than in what we do. And what a person *is* often is best revealed by the "adverbs" in his life rather than just by his "verbs." For example, consider the following verse: "Let the word of Christ dwell in you richly" (Col. 3:16). The test of whether a person is truly devoted to Jesus Christ is not whether he lets the Bible's statements simply "dwell" in his mind. A Christian shows himself to be what he should be when the adverb "richly" can honestly be applied to the verb "dwell."

Adverbs **137**

Teaching Strategy: Group Activity

Divide the class into ten small groups. Assign each group one question from Use the Skill 6-9. Each group should list several possible adverbs for their assigned sentence. As the groups read their lists, notice how one group's answers will stimulate other groups to think of even more responses.

One on One: Direct your student to become an "adverb detective." Instruct him to read the sentences from Use the Skill 6-9 to several people, asking each person to supply an adverb for each sentence. He should encourage those he interviews to be creative with their responses.

8. At the respected Tokyo Stock Exchange, enthusiastic members trade large numbers of valuable stocks.

   At the highly respected Tokyo Stock Exchange, enthusiastic members

   quickly trade large numbers of valuable stocks.

9. Tokyo has twice been destroyed: by earthquake in 1923 and by fearful bomb raids during World War II.

   Tokyo has twice been destroyed: once by earthquake in 1923 and

   again by fearful bomb raids during World War II.

10. Modern Tokyo features both the old and the new Japan. Visitors to this diverse city may see residents in traditional kimonos side by side with those in Western dress.

    Modern Tokyo features both the old and the new Japan. Visitors

    to this diverse city may actually see residents there in traditional

    kimonos side by side with those in typically western dress.

A. Locate and correct the ten errors in the paragraphs: fragments, comma splices, fused sentences, noun plurals, singular and plural noun possessives, verb forms (e.g., *had wrote*), and spellings of verb forms.

B. Add a descriptive adjective or adverb where you see a caret (^).

Are you traveling to Hong Kong? You might visit the Kansu Street Jade Market. Full of ^ jade ornaments and ^ jewelry. Several different types of jade exist. Emperor's jade is ^ expensive, it is deep green in color. Mutton fat jades' color is white, and mauve jade is light purple. Other jade color's are yellow, brown, and orange.

Australian jade and soapstone look like jade, but they are much ^ common. They are softer and ^ valuable than true jade, wise jade buyers will avoided these ^ stones. Sometimes salesmans trick buyers. They dye cheap stones then they sell buyers these impostors. Occasionally, careless tourists have took home worthless jade. You should stay away from false jade! On your trip to Hong Kong.

Hong Kong

Are you traveling to Hong Kong? You might visit the Kansu Street Jade Market. It is full of beautiful jade ornaments and expensive jewelry. Several different types of jade exist.. Emperor's jade is very expensive; it is deep green in color. Mutton fat jade's color is white, and mauve jade is light purple. Other jade colors are yellow, brown, and orange.

Australian jade and soapstone look like jade, but they are much more common. They are softer and less valuable than true jade. Wise jade buyers will avoid these cheap stones. Sometimes salesmen trick buyers. They dye cheap stones. Then they sell buyers these impostors. Occasionally, careless tourists have taken home worthless jade. You should stay away from false jade on your trip to Hong Kong!

Adverbs   **139**

Evaluation

To evaluate the students' understanding of the material, ask them questions that will stimulate critical thinking. *(Can you compare an adjective with an adverb? How are adjectives and adverbs alike? How are they different?)*

Enrichment

Materials

• 4" x 6" cards with the adverb questions (one question per card): "How?" "When?" "Where?" "To what extent?"

Adverb Headlines

On the board or overhead transparency, write this sentence: *The policeman spoke about safety.* Ask students to select an adverb question card. The student should change the sentence to answer the adverb question on his card. For example, a student who draws "When?" should add an adverb that answers that question. *(Today the policeman spoke about safety.)* As the game progresses, ask students to draw more than one card. For example, a student who draws "How?" and "When?" should add two adverbs to the sentence.

(Today the policeman spoke forcefully about safety.) You may want to use a new sentence after several turns.

Literature Link

Ask a student to read aloud "Those Winter Sundays" on page 131. Discuss the Sliding Home questions on page 140.

=SLIDING HOME

If adjectives are the salt of writing, adverbs are the pepper. Most good writers use even fewer adverbs than adjectives. So the ones they choose must be exactly right.

- *Hayden included two adverbs in the poem's first line. Try reading the line, leaving them out. What meaning do they add? Do you think they make the first line stronger?*

- *Can you think of any "austere and lonely offices" that your parents perform for you? When was the last time you thanked them?*

> **I Samuel 18:14-15**
>
> *14 And David behaved himself wisely in all his ways; and the Lord was with him.*
>
> *15 Wherefore when Saul saw that he behaved himself very wisely, he was afraid of him.*

- *What adverb is used twice? How is it different the second time?*

- *What adverb would describe how you behave yourself?*

REPORTING A FAMILY TRADITION

Honour thy father and mother; (which is the first commandment with promise;) That it may be well with thee, and thou mayest live long on the earth.
Ephesians 6:2-3

Whether it means eating popcorn on Saturday or trimming a tree each Christmas, your family has traditions, special activities to celebrate special moments. Look at this example of a student report about family tradition.

My family has a special way of celebrating the first day of school every fall. When school gets out at noon on the first day, Mom meets us with a big picnic basket and drives to our favorite park. It has a creek with lots of smooth stones sticking out of the water. While Mom organizes the food, my brother and I have races crossing the creek on the rocks. Last year he tried to jump too far and landed in the creek. He was so surprised that he just sat there in the water. I thought Mom would be mad but she just laughed.

After our creek race, we sit on the blanket and have our lunch. Mom always makes special sandwiches on thick, crusty bread. My brother and I can always eat at least two. We drink lemonade out of brightly colored plastic cups. But the best part is dessert. Every year Mom tries out a new cheesecake recipe. Last year's was the best ever. It was chocolate with cherries on top.

After lunch is over, Mom takes out a notebook and asks us what our favorite thing about the past summer was. When we tell her, she writes it down. Then she reads us what we said in the past about the other summers. It's a neat way to remember things.

**Sidebar (left column):**

- Answers will vary. *(The adverbs tell the reader that the father got up early every day of the week. They make the line stronger.)*
- Answers will vary. *(making meals, washing clothes, fixing broken things)*

- *wisely;* the second time *very* modifies *wisely.*
- Answers will vary.

Overview of Writing Process

Planning—Choosing a family tradition to write about

Drafting—Writing the report

Revising—Reviewing with a checklist

Publishing—Displaying reports and photos in the classroom

Objectives

Students will

1. recognize meaningful family traditions and choose one to report.

2. write a report describing that tradition.

Reporting a Family Tradition

Lesson Support

Support Materials CD

Writing Worksheets—p. 96
Rubrics—p. 110

Scriptural Application

Read Ephesians 6:2-3 aloud and discuss the concept of honoring parents. Any childhood includes both good and bad memories, and it is up to each of us to choose which memories that we will hold dear. Part of honoring our parents is not only respecting them in their presence but also choosing to dwell on positive memories—like a pleasant family tradition—that can help us to cherish them.

Introduction

Ask a student to read the sample report on page 140 aloud. Discuss the family traditions your students celebrate, such as traditions kept at Christmas or on birthdays.

Planning Strategies

Instruct students to make a list of at least five family traditions. Then ask them to review their lists, choosing a report topic based on these criteria:

- Which tradition is unique to my family?

- Which tradition holds the most pleasant memories for me?

- Which tradition is most interesting to me?

- Which tradition would be most interesting for others to read about?

Your Turn

Write a report about a special tradition that is unique to your family.

Planning

Choose a tradition that is unique to your family. List the ways that your family spends birthdays, vacations, and holidays. Considering what you know about other families, choose one of your family's unique traditions.

Determine the details that the reader will need to know. Whom does this tradition include? When and where does it take place? Why does your family keep it? Use descriptive words that appeal to your reader's senses.

Organize the facts in chronological order. Analyze the facts that you have compiled and group them to represent a clear time sequence.

Drafting

Begin your report. The first sentence should indicate who participates in the family tradition, what the tradition is, and when it takes place.

Write your report. Record the details that explain your family tradition clearly. Use a new paragraph to indicate another aspect of the tradition.

Revising

Evaluate your report for word choice and correctness. Be sure that you used specific words to give vivid details. Eliminate any unnecessary exaggerations. Correct any errors of grammar, spelling, or punctuation.

Prepare a clean copy of your report. Include necessary changes.

Publishing

Deliver a speech. Read your report to the class if your teacher allows.

Post your report on a bulletin board. Include family photographs.

HISTORY of the ENGLISH LANGUAGE

"Angle-ish" was different from the English we speak today. Over the centuries "Angle-ish" changed and developed as it was influenced by many other languages.

In A.D. 597, a group of Roman monks came to England as missionaries. They brought many religious words with them, such as *disciple* and *nun*. Later, daring seamen from the north, called Vikings, invaded England. They brought words such as *reindeer* and *window* to the language.

France took over the government of England for a time. Because the French were in power, French became the language of the upper class. Many English people peppered their sentences with French words and phrases to be fashionable. Even today words like *government, pastor,* and *captain* reflect the French influence on the English language.

Adverbs   **141**

Encourage students to use lists or clusters to organize details about their tradition.

Drafting Strategy

Tell the students that their opening sentence should include any background information that would aid the reader in understanding the family tradition. Allow students to begin drafting during class.

Revising Strategy

Distribute a copy of Writing Worksheet 6 to each student. Encourage students to check their reports against the checklist, reviewing their reports for chronological progression of ideas and clarity of explanation. Remind them to incorporate any changes or additions before they prepare the final draft.

Publishing Strategy

Challenge students to submit their reports to a local newspaper or magazine.

Scriptural Application

Ask a volunteer to read Exodus 20:3-11 aloud. Point out that God designed at least one tradition that He commands us to keep: setting aside one day of the week as a special day for remembering the Lord.

Encourage students to honor the Lord by reflecting on God's goodness to them.

Evaluation

For help in grading this assignment, see "Grading Writing Assignments" (p. x) and Rubric 6 (Support Materials CD, p. 110).

Enrichment

Encourage each student to "borrow" a tradition from a fellow student and to try it with his own family. Later, allow the students to report their experiences with borrowed traditions.

PREPOSITIONS, CONJUNCTIONS, & INTERJECTIONS

PSALM 70

Make haste, O God, to deliver me; make haste to help me, O Lord.

2 Let them be ashamed and confounded that seek after my soul: let them be turned backward, and put to confusion, that desire my hurt.

3 Let them be turned back for a reward of their shame that say, Aha, aha.

4 Let all those that seek thee rejoice and be glad in thee: and let such as love thy salvation say continually, Let God be magnified.

5 But I am poor and needy: make haste unto me, O God, thou art my help and my deliverer; O Lord, make no tarrying.

- *What do you think "Aha, aha" in verse 3 means? Has anyone ever said something like this to you? How did he mean it?*

- *What is David's response?*

- *How can you tell that David wants an answer very soon?*

In this psalm, David is asking the Lord to deliver him from those who seek after his soul, who mock him. We can see the earnestness in his request by the way he says "O God" rather than "God" and "O Lord" rather than "Lord," and by the way he describes himself. He says that there are those who seek after his soul and that he is poor and needy.

When the letter *O* is used as a word, it is called an *interjection.* Interjections usually show strong feeling. In this chapter you will learn about interjections, prepositions, and conjunctions.

- Answers will vary. *(Those who say "Aha, Aha" have a mocking attitude.)*

- Answers will vary. *(David responds that they should be ashamed.)*

- David says, "make haste" and "make no tarrying."

Literature Link

Look at Psalm 70 on page 143. Allow the students to work in groups to answer the discussion questions.

Prepositions

A **preposition** is a word that shows the relationship between its object and another word in the sentence. An **object of the preposition** is the noun or pronoun that follows the preposition. All prepositions have objects.

Preposition (pre + position) literally means something "placed in front of."

The baseball *on* the box is a gift.
The baseball *under* the box is a gift.
The baseball *in* the box is a gift.
The baseball *behind* the box is a gift.
The baseball *outside* the box is a gift.

In each of these sentences, a preposition links the subject *baseball* to *box,* the object of the preposition. The preposition shows how the baseball is related to the box. Notice that the relationship between the baseball and the box changes whenever the preposition changes.

Commonly Used Prepositions

about	behind	except	on	to
above	below	for	onto	toward
across	beside	from	out	under
after	between	in	outside	until
against	beyond	inside	over	upon
among	but	into	past	with
around	by	like	since	within
at	down	near	through	without
before	during	of	throughout	

page 191

Agreement

Prepositional Phrases

A preposition and its object together form a **prepositional phrase.** If the object has any modifiers, they are also part of the prepositional phrase. The object itself is the simple object of the preposition. The object and its modifiers together are the complete object of the preposition.

The baseball *with the red stitches* is a gift *from my favorite uncle.*

This example contains two prepositional phrases. Each prepositional phrase consists of a preposition followed by a noun and its modifiers. The preposition *with* links the complete object of the preposition *the red stitches* to the subject *baseball.* The preposition *from* shows the relationship between its object *my favorite uncle* and the predicate noun *gift.*

Teaching Strategy: Induction

Guide the students to see how important prepositions are in many sentences. Write these sentences on the board or overhead transparency:

• The top the mountain we could see the prairie the distance.
• We could see the crooked course a river the prairie.
• Several squirrels scampered the trunk a tree.

Ask the students to add whatever words are necessary to complete the sentences. Write the students' sentences on the board or overhead transparency and underline the words they have added. *(At the top of the mountain we could see the prairie in the distance.)* Ask what important part of speech comes after the underlined words. *(Nouns)* Now ask how these underlined words have helped the sentence. *(The nouns that had seemed unconnected to the rest of the sentence are now connected.)* Ask students to suggest other prepositions, and point out how a preposition can affect the meaning of a sentence. (Do not erase the three sentences; use them again later when teaching the prepositional phrase.)

Teaching Strategy: Induction

Ask the students whether they know a prefix that means "before." Write *prefix* on the board as a clue. Underline *pre.* Ask the students where *pre* is in the word *preposition.* (at the beginning) Instruct a student volunteer to underline each prepositional phrase in the example sentences from the previous activity and to put a second line

Sometimes a prepositional phrase may contain a compound object. In the prepositional phrase *of David and Goliath,* both *David* and *Goliath* are objects of the preposition *of.*

The story *of David and Goliath* appears in I Samuel 17.

page 33
Choosing between Possessive and Plural

IN SUMMARY

A **preposition** relates its object to another word in the sentence.

The **object of a preposition** is the noun or pronoun that follows the preposition.

A **prepositional phrase** consists of the preposition and the complete object of the preposition.

7-1 PRACTICE THE SKILL

A. Place parentheses around each prepositional phrase.

B. Label each preposition *P.*

C. Label each object of the preposition *OP.*

1. Ronald Reagan's birthplace is (near Chicago, Illinois.)
   P   *OP*

2. (On March 4, 1952,) Reagan married Nancy Davis.
   P   *OP*

3. California elected him (to the governor's office.)
   P   *OP*

4. The 1980 election pitted Reagan (against President Carter)
   P   *OP*

5. The race (among the Republican candidates) was close.
   P   *OP*

6. Ronald Reagan finished well everywhere (except Iowa and Michigan.)
   P   *OP*   *OP*

7. He split the votes (in the Michigan primary) (with George Bush.)
   P   *OP*   *P*   *OP*

8. George Bush campaigned (until May 26, 1980.)
   P   *OP*

9. Finally, the Republicans chose Reagan (for their nominee.)
   P   *OP*

10. George Bush became Reagan's vice presidential nominee (in the 1980
    P

    presidential campaign.)
    OP

---

under each preposition. Ask what similarity the students see in the word order of all the phrases. *(The preposition comes before the noun or pronoun object.)*

Lead the students to discover that the position of the preposition in relation to its object is always the same. Emphasize that every preposition has a noun or pronoun as an object. Now the students can compose the word *preposition* from its two parts. Guide them to the conclusion that the name is appropriate because a preposition has a position before its object.

Teaching Strategy: Discussion

Direct the students' attention to the definitions of *preposition, object of the preposition,* and *prepositional phrase* on page 144. Point out the etymology on page 144. The prepositions that students learn first usually tell location.

A. Place parentheses around each prepositional phrase.
B. Label the object of the preposition *OP*.
C. Label the sentence patterns *S-InV, S-TrV-DO,* or *S-TrV-IO-DO.*

1. (In the sixteenth century)French immigrant workers greatly advanced the art(of papier-mâché.)

2. This art casts paper strips(onto a mold.)

3. Some people place petroleum jelly(underneath the strips.)

4. The artist should tear the paper(along its grain.)

5. Smaller pieces (against the mold)form better.

6. (For variety,) you may use different-colored paper.

7. (Across the first layer) you should place the second layer.

8. Each layer(of strips)covers the previous layer.

9. Each piece must lie smoothly(upon the mold)

10. Otherwise, air may stay(beneath the layers.)

Functions of Prepositional Phrases

One use of prepositional phrases is to modify nouns. These prepositional phrases are called adjectival prepositional phrases because they function like adjectives. These phrases add information about the nouns they modify.

page 102
Adjectives

Naaman was a captain *of the host.*

The prophet *of God* taught Naaman a lesson *in obedience.*

page 128
Adverbs

In the first example the prepositional phrase *of the host* tells more about the noun *captain.* In the second example the prepositional phrase *of God* describes *prophet,* and *in obedience* describes *lesson.* Notice that the prepositional phrases in these examples come right after the nouns they modify. A prepositional phrase that modifies a noun normally comes just after the noun.

Another use of prepositional phrases is to modify verbs. These prepositional phrases are called adverbial prepositional phrases because they are functioning like adverbs. These phrases add information about the verbs they modify.

Adverbial prepositional phrases answer adverb questions. However, only adverbial prepositional phrases that modify adjectives and other adverbs answer "to what extent?" This text discusses only adverbial prepositional phrases that modify verbs.

146   Chapter 7

Teaching Strategy: Induction

Write this sentence on the board or overhead transparency: *The beauty of a rainbow ended the day.* Ask a volunteer to underline the prepositional phrase. *(of a rainbow)* Ask these questions: What word does the phrase modify? *(beauty)* What part of speech is the word *beauty? (noun)* Instruct the student to draw an arrow from the underlined phrase to the word that the phrase modifies. Remind the students that the phrase works as a unit. Point out that

some phrases act as adjectives telling *what kind, which one, how many,* or *whose.*

Write this sentence on the board or overhead transparency: *We will play baseball today.* Ask the students which word in the sentence is an adverb. *(today)* Ask them what an adverb does in a sentence. *(tells when, where,* or how *about the word it modifies)* Write another sentence replacing the adverb with an adverbial prepositional phrase: *We will play baseball after school.* Point out that the phrase answers the same question that the adverb answers—*when.*

Enrichment

Ask a student to read the two sentences about Naaman on page 146. Instruct the students to turn to II Kings 5 for the entire story. Ask the students to locate prepositional phrases and the words they modify.

Refer to the verses on page 160. Discuss the two questions with the passage from II Timothy.

At the airport we waited *inside the terminal.*

The airplane coasted *to a smooth stop at 6:45.*

Both examples contain two prepositional phrases. In the first example, *at the airport* and *inside the terminal* both modify the verb *waited.* They tell *where* about the verb. They are both adverbial prepositional phrases. In the second example, *to a smooth stop* tells *how* about the verb *coasted. At 6:45* tells *when* about the verb *coasted.* Because both phrases modify the verb, both are adverbial prepositional phrases.

A prepositional phrase that is acting like an adverb can appear in different places in the sentence.

After the verb: We met *at the gate.*
After the direct object: I met my father *at the gate.*
At the beginning
of the sentence: *At the gate* I met my father.

Sometimes adjectival prepositional phrases and adverbial prepositional phrases occur in the same sentence.

He carried his suitcase *to the trunk of our car.*

In this example the prepositional phrase *to the trunk* modifies the verb *carried;* therefore, it is an adverbial prepositional phrase. The prepositional phrase *of our car* modifies the noun *trunk.* It is an adjectival prepositional phrase. Notice that one prepositional phrase can modify the object of another prepositional phrase.

A prepositional phrase is always diagrammed under the word it modifies. Look at the diagram for this sentence:

He carried his suitcase to the trunk of our car.

```
He | carried | suitcase
        |           his
       to   trunk
        the   of  car
                    our
```

IN SUMMARY

Prepositional phrases can be used like adjectives to modify nouns or like adverbs to modify verbs.

Scriptural Application

God is a God of order. Point out to the students that the placement of the parts of speech shows order in our language. For example, an adjectival prepositional phrase comes after the noun it modifies.

Reinforcement

Ask each student to locate three objects in the classroom. Then instruct the students to write sentences with those objects in prepositional phrases. Tell them to underline the prepositional phrases. *(I am sitting in my chair.)*

Evaluation

Evaluate your students' understanding by asking them to use prepositional phrases in sentences (oral or written).

Enrichment

Tell the students to look at the night sky with its constellations and then to describe in a few sentences the placement of one constellation in relation to another. Ask the students to share their descriptions in class the next day.

7-3 PRACTICE THE SKILL

Place parentheses around each prepositional phrase. Draw an arrow from each prepositional phrase to the word it modifies.

1. Many people admire the work (of Benjamin West.)

2. Benjamin West lived (in a Quaker community) (in Swarthmore, Pennsylvania.)

3. His first paintbrushes came (from the hairs) (of the family cat.)

4. King George III (of England) commissioned West.

5. Benjamin West became the history painter (for King George III.)

6. West's paintings were commissioned (for the new chapel) (in Windsor Castle.)

7. West had divided the Bible (into four dispensations.)

8. (Without instruction) (from the king,) he could not work quickly.

9. (During years) (of work,) West's frustration grew.

10. Finally, the king abandoned his plans (for the paintings.)

Evaluation

If you have assigned sentence diagramming with Practice the Skill 7-3, check answers on page 448.

Additional Resources

After the students have completed Practice the Skill 7-3, you may want to show the students some art work by Benjamin West in the video *Symbols in Religious Art* available from BJU Press.

Enrichment: Speech Link

Materials

- "Catalogue" by Rosalie Moore (This poem is available in *EXPLORATIONS IN LITERATURE for Christian Schools,* Second Edition, published by BJU Press.)

Divide the class into small groups. Supply each group with a poem or a cutting of a poem that contains prepositional phrases. Allow each group a few minutes to identify the prepositional phrases. Then allow each group to perform a choral reading of its poem.

One on One: Instruct your student to identify the prepositional phrases in a short poem. Then allow him to read the poem for family members or neighbors.

A. Underline each adjectival prepositional phrase with one line.

B. Underline each adverbial prepositional phrase with two lines.

C. Draw an arrow from each prepositional phrase to the word it modifies.

"Well, Arby, this is a big day for you."

"Yes sir," I said. "I'm a little scared about the speech." No one in our family had ever given a speech at a graduation ceremony. Later I practiced my speech on my mom four times. When we got to school, the parents went into the auditorium, and we went to our classroom. I was sure that I would go blank right up in front of the whole entire world. I would stumble. I would crash. I would get a little piece of dust under my contact. I marched in with the other students. The principal said a bunch of good things about the school. Then it was time for my speech. I walked behind the pulpit and stood up on a little step. I could feel my hands shaking, and I stuffed them into my pockets. Then I saw Mr. Watson sitting in the back row.

Selected passages from *Arby Jenkins* by Sharon Hambrick (BJU Press, 1996).

Preposition or Adverb?

Some words used as prepositions can also be used as adverbs. To determine whether a word in a sentence is a preposition or an adverb, look for an object of the preposition.

The runner ran *down* the road.
The runner fell *down*.

In the first sentence, *down* is a preposition. It is followed by the object *road*. In the second sentence, *down* is an adverb that tells where the runner fell. It has no object. A word is not a preposition if it does not have an object.

page 128

Adverbs

Teaching Strategy: Discussion

Read the paragraphs about words that can be used as prepositions or as adverbs. Explain that if there is no object, the word cannot be a preposition. Instruct the students to write sentences with *up* as a preposition and *up* as an adverb. Discuss the information on page 149.

ESL Strategy

For further explanation of prepositions, use ESL Helps pages 47-48 (Support Materials CD).

Reinforcement

Use the bulletin board on page 208 of the Support Materials CD as an interactive teaching tool. Ask various students to read the sentence aloud, each time using a different preposition. Discuss the ways in which the sentence's meaning changes as a result.

Reinforcement

Instruct each student to draw a floor plan of his bedroom and to write an explanation of where the objects are located. Ask a volunteer to read his description. Let other students identify prepositional phrases in the student's writing.

Enrichment

Instruct the students to pretend they are about to run a race and tell them to write about the race. When they finish, ask them to locate any adverbs and prepositional phrases in their writing.

Some words used as prepositions can also be used as adverbs.

A preposition is followed by an object; an adverb does not have an object.

7-5   PRACTICE THE SKILL

Label each italicized word *Prep* (preposition) or *Adv* (adverb).

__Adv___   1. As they grow *up*, many people cherish their teddy bears.

__Prep__   2. A cartoonist named the first teddy bear *after* President Theodore (Teddy) Roosevelt.

__Adv___   3. Roosevelt's fame grew as the story spread *around*.

__Prep__   4. *From* that point, teddy bears increased in popularity.

__Prep__   5. Another bear well known *to* many children is Paddington.

__Prep__   6. Paddington's adventures amuse children *of* many ages.

__Adv___   7. One time Paddington dressed *up* for the opera.

__Adv___   8. Another time, for his birthday, he put a magic show *on*.

__Prep__   9. *During* their lifetimes, most children love many bears.

__Prep__ 10. Many people love their bears even *beyond* their childhood years.

Reinforcement

To help students understand how prepositions show relationships, direct one student to sit in a chair at the front of the room. Ask another student to stand in the front with his pencil. Ask the standing student to place the pencil in different locations relative to the student in the chair. *(beside, over, under)* Ask another student to describe in a sentence the pencil's location. *(The pencil is <u>over his head</u>.)*

One on One: Place a pencil in different locations relative to another object, such as a box of tissues. Instruct your student to describe in a sentence the pencil's location. *(The pencil is <u>beside</u> the box.)*

Label each underlined word *Prep* (preposition) or *Adv* (adverb).

Adv 1. The time drew <u>near</u> for the announcement of the winner.

Adv 2. A private citizen had never traveled into space <u>before</u>.

Prep 3. NASA chose Christa McAuliffe as the first teacher <u>in</u> space.

Adv 4. She was glad not to be left <u>behind</u> when the mission started.

Prep 5. Christa had grown close <u>to</u> the other nine candidates.

Prep 6. In the weeks <u>after</u> her selection, Christa sat for many interviews and publicity shots.

Prep 7. She spent hours training <u>with</u> the other astronauts.

Prep 8. Finally, they were prepared <u>for</u> their mission.

Adv 9. Tragically, the shuttle exploded in flight while the spectators watched <u>below</u>.

Prep 10. <u>Despite</u> the tragedy, the memory of Christa McAuliffe inspires courage.

Conjunctions

A **conjunction** is a connecting word that joins words or groups of words in a sentence. A **coordinating conjunction** joins sentence parts of the same type. The parts of a sentence joined by a coordinating conjunction make up a **compound part** of the sentence. Some commonly used coordinating conjunctions in English are *and, but, or, nor,* and *yet.*

page 8
Compound subjects and predicates

Conjunction comes from the Latin prefix *con-,* meaning "together," and the Latin verb *jungere,* meaning "to join."

ETYMOLOGY

Coordinating comes from our word *coordination. Coordination* is from the Latin prefix *co-,* meaning "same," and the Latin noun *ordinatio,* meaning "arrangement." In English, words joined by a coordinating conjunction have the same basic function.

ETYMOLOGY

Teaching Strategy:
Demonstration

Write these two sentences on the board or overhead transparency:

- Adrianne ____ Ashley walked into the classroom.
- Adrianne had been sick, ____ Ashley felt fine.

Ask the students for words that fit into the blanks. *(and, but)* Tell the students that these words are conjunctions. Ask the students what the words have joined. *(nouns, complete sentences)*

Literature Link

Instruct the students to read Psalm 70 on page 143. Ask them to locate the coordinating conjunctions. *(and, but)*

Teaching Strategy:
Participation

Direct the students to compose a few sentences about some people or objects in the room using coordinating conjunctions. Encourage them to use several different coordinating conjunctions. Let several students share their sentences with the class.

Joining Words

A coordinating conjunction may join single words of the same function within a sentence.

Compound subject

Jeff and *Kim* memorized the verses.

Compound predicate

Jeff *memorized* and *recited* Psalm 103.

Compound direct object

He will memorize *Romans 12* or *James 1* next.

Compound predicate noun

Kim's favorite passages are *Psalm 103*, *Proverbs 3*, and *I Corinthians 13*.

Compound adjective

The *eleventh* and *twelfth* verses of Psalm 103 are Jeff's favorites.

Compound adverb

He recited them *quickly* but *correctly*.

In each sentence the words joined by the coordinating conjunction have the same function. For example, in the first sentence *Jeff* and *Kim* are both subjects. Together *Jeff* and *Kim* form the compound subject. Coordinating conjunctions must join words that share the same function in the sentence.

Joining Phrases

A coordinating conjunction can also join phrases.

Compound complete subject

A group of oceanographers and *a team of salvagers* recovered an ancient ship.

Compound complete predicate

A violent storm *sank the ship* and *killed the crew*.

Compound prepositional phrases

The old wooden ship *with a full crew* and *under Henry VIII's flag* had been part of the war fleet.

Compound complete predicate noun

Some observers at the recovery were *Prince Charles of England* and *other officials of the British government*.

Remember that coordinating conjunctions join only those phrases that share the same function.

A compound part is always diagrammed in the same general way that a similar single part would be diagrammed. The line is split into two lines, and the parts of the compound are written on the lines. The conjunction is written on a broken line joining the two lines. Look at the diagram for this sentence:

Jeff and Kim memorized the verses.

When diagramming a compound part made of phrases, be sure to include all parts of the phrase on the correct line. Now look at the diagram for this sentence:

A violent storm sank the ship and killed the crew.

page 166

Compound sentences

page 291

Commas in a series

IN SUMMARY

A **conjunction** is a connecting word that joins words or groups of words in a sentence.

A **coordinating conjunction** joins sentence parts of the same type.

The parts of a sentence joined by a coordinating conjunction make up a **compound part** of the sentence.

7-7 PRACTICE THE SKILL

A. Circle each coordinating conjunction.
B. Underline the words or phrases that the conjunction joins.
C. Label each underlined compound part *S* (subject), *V* (verb), *Pred* (complete predicate), *DO* (direct object), *IO* (indirect object), *PN* (predicate noun), *PA* (predicate adjective), *Adj* (adjective), *Adv* (adverb), or *OP* (object of the preposition).

Pred 1. Joseph Haydn played the violin (and) sang at an early age.

_PA_ 2. He was alone (and) independent at age eight.

_PN_ 3. After his time in a church choir, Haydn was a musician (and) teacher in Vienna.

_OP_ 4. In 1761 Haydn became the composer for Prince Nicholas Esterhazy (and) his court.

Prepositions, Conjunctions, Interjections **153**

_DO_ 5. Haydn left the <u>court</u> (and) his <u>job</u> after the Prince's death.

_S_ 6. <u>Symphonies</u>, <u>string quartets</u>, (and) <u>sonatas</u> are Haydn's most famous works.

_V_ 7. People rarely <u>perform</u> (or) <u>mention</u> Haydn's operas.

_PN_ 8. On a trip through Germany, Ludwig von Beethoven became Haydn's <u>friend</u> (and) <u>pupil</u>.

Adj 9. Haydn probably wrote not <u>104</u> (but) <u>108</u> symphonies.

Adv 10. Haydn traveled <u>often</u> (yet) <u>unwillingly</u> away from his Austrian home.

7-8 REVIEW THE SKILL

A. Circle each coordinating conjunction.

B. Underline the words or phrases that the conjunction joins.

C. Label the underlined words or word groups **S** (subject), **V** (verb), **Pred** (complete predicate), **DO** (direct object), **IO** (indirect object), **PN** (predicate noun), **PA** (predicate adjective), **Adj** (adjective), **Adv** (adverb), or **OP** (object of the preposition).

1. In the 1800s physicians practiced <u>medicine</u> (and) <u>pharmacy</u> in the same building.
   $\overset{DO}{}$ $\overset{DO}{}$

2. Some tasty (yet) ineffective medicines became quite popular.
   $\overset{Adj}{}$ $\overset{Adj}{}$

3. The products available at Old Corner Drug Store in Waco, Texas, included <u>medicines</u>, <u>foodstuffs</u>, (and) <u>flavored carbonated beverages</u>.
   $\overset{DO}{}$ $\overset{DO}{}$ $\overset{DO}{}$

4. Pharmacist Charles C. Alderton of the Old Corner Drug Store <u>mixed</u> (but) did not <u>name</u> the first Dr Pepper drink in 1885.
   $\overset{V}{}$ $\overset{V}{}$

5. Named by the drugstore's owner, the new drink made its national debut at the 1904 World's Fair along with <u>the hot dog bun</u> (and) <u>the ice-cream cone</u>.
   $\overset{OP}{}$ $\overset{OP}{}$

6. The original Dr Pepper tasted <u>spicy</u> (or) <u>tangy</u> (but) not <u>sour</u>.
   $\overset{PA}{}$ $\overset{PA}{}$ $\overset{PA}{}$

7. After Dr Pepper's invention, <u>Coca-Cola</u> (and) <u>Pepsi Cola</u> entered the carbonated beverage market.
   $\overset{S}{}$ $\overset{S}{}$

8. The Pepsi Cola Company <u>acquired national distribution rights for Dr Pepper</u> (and) <u>increased competition with the Coca-Cola Company</u>.
   $\overset{Pred}{}$ $\overset{Pred}{}$

9. <u>In 1939</u> Dr Pepper scientists <u>removed the caffeine</u> (and) <u>added vitamin B-1 to the drink</u>.
   $\overset{Pred}{}$ $\overset{Pred}{}$

10. Because consumers did not like the bad-tasting product, they <u>quickly</u> (and) <u>loudly</u> mandated a return to the original formula.
    $\overset{Adv}{}$ $\overset{Adv}{}$

Interjections

Interjections are words that indicate emotion, agreement or disagreement, greeting, politeness, and hesitation or beginning. Many interjections show strong feeling.

From the Latin *interjicere,* meaning "to throw between," we get our English word *interjection.*

Emotion:	*Wow!* We're finally at the top.
Agreement:	*Yes,* we climbed one hundred steps.
Greeting:	*Hello!* When did you arrive?
Politeness:	I enjoyed the view. *Thank you.*
Hesitation:	*Well,* you can come back anytime.

Interjections can stand alone, punctuated as sentences; or they can appear along with a regular sentence in which they have no real part. Unlike prepositions and conjunctions, interjections do not show relationships between other words in the sentence. They do not function as subjects, predicates, objects, or modifiers. Because an interjection has no grammatical function, it can be omitted from a sentence without changing the meaning much—except, of course, that the emotion would be lost.

> Oh, no!
> Sorry, I didn't see you there.

Some words used as interjections can also be used as other parts of speech.

Verb:	Your visit will *please* her.
Interjection:	Leave your dog outside, *please.*
Adjective:	She allows *no* dogs in her house.
Interjection:	*No,* she will not make an exception for your dog.

In the first set of examples, the word *please* first functions as a transitive verb. *Please* is an interjection expressing politeness in the next sentence. In the second set of examples, the word *no* first functions as an adjective modifying the noun *dogs.* In the last sentence, the word *no* does not have a grammatical function. It is an interjection expressing disagreement. To decide whether a word is an interjection or another part of speech, determine whether it has a grammatical function in the sentence.

Because interjections do not function as parts of the sentence, they are diagrammed on a separate line above the sentence. Look at the diagram for this sentence:

Yes, we climbed the steps.

page 287

Punctuation

An alternative grammar system uses the term *isolate* for this group of words and the term *interjection* only for those isolates that show strong emotion.

Some interjections are phrasal rather than single words (*you know, sure thing, good job,* etc.).

Teaching Strategy: Introduction

Discuss the etymology of *interjection* on page 155.

Literature Link

Instruct the students to locate the interjections in Psalm 70 on page 143. (*O; Aha, aha*) Ask the students to compose a sentence using an interjection.

Teaching Strategy: Demonstration

Point out that the use of a comma, a period, or an exclamation point gives a clue as to the feeling expressed by the interjection. For example, an exclamation point usually indicates more emotion than either a comma or a period. Write these sentences on the board or overhead transparency to illustrate the differences:

- Oh, please, let's go.
- Oh, please. Let's go.
- Oh, please! Let's go!

An **interjection** is a word that stands alone, not modifying other
words nor working as part of the sentence pattern.

Interjections show emotion, agreement or disagreement, greeting,
politeness, and hesitation or beginning.

Some words used as interjections can also be used as other parts
of speech.

7-9 PRACTICE THE SKILL

Underline the interjections in the following sentences.

1. Would you please tell Laurie that she needs to come to the office right away?

2. Yes, I will tell her as quickly as possible.

3. Tell Stephen that he needs to come too. Thank you.

4. Uh-oh! I think they are in trouble.

5. No, Mr. Conrad just wants to ask them about the winter banquet.

6. How was the meeting? Good!

7. I didn't think the meeting would take that long. Sorry.

8. Well, I know meetings can take a long time.

9. Hey, is our banquet going to be fun?

10. That sounds great. Wow!

7-10 USE THE SKILL

Fill in each blank with a conjunction or a preposition. *(Answers will vary.)*

The story of Queen Esther __and__ her cousin Mordecai is evidence
__of__ God's care for His people. Because Vashti would not appear
__before__ King Ahasuerus, the king was angered __and__ decreed that she
be banished __from__ the royal palace. Many candidates were brought
__before__ the king to replace Vashti, __but__ the king preferred Esther
__above__ all of the others. Soon after Esther was made queen, the king

Learning Christianly

God created everything to be good (Gen. 1:31). Like everything else He made, God created language both for His glory and for our good. Profanity contradicts both of these purposes. The verb *profane* itself means "to put to an improper or unworthy use." Using profane words is using words for an improper purpose—often to express disgust with something that God has allowed to happen. When someone uses profanity, he is insulting God for allowing something to happen, instead of declaring His glory. In addition, he is also keeping those around him from being able to see God's glory. Interjections are a wonderful part of language but, like anything else, they should be used "to the glory of God."

Learning Christianly

Have you ever heard someone curse or swear? Some interjections like this are called profanity, and the Bible prohibits us from using them (Eph. 4:29). Read I Corinthians 10:31. Why is using interjections like profanity a misuse of language?

Scriptural Application

Read the passages with conjunctions and interjections on page 160. Ask the students to use a concordance to locate other verses about wisdom from the book of Proverbs.

Evaluation

Instruct the students to write a sentence using an interjection in response to a situation you assign, such as an unfamiliar food or a surprise party. Ask students to share their sentences with the class.

promoted Haman __to__ a high rank in the kingdom; __but__ Haman was an evil man. Because Mordecai refused to bow __to__ Haman, Haman wanted to destroy Mordecai __and__ his people, the Jews. Neither Haman __nor__ the king knew that Queen Esther was also a Jew. After three days of fasting, Esther came __into__ the king's court __and__ requested an audience __with__ him and with Haman. __During__ the banquet that Esther had prepared, the queen told Ahasuerus about the plan to destroy all Jews. She requested that her life be spared. The king was furious __with__ the man who dared try to kill his queen. Soon it was revealed that Haman was the man, __and__ Haman was hanged __on__ the gallows that he had prepared for Mordecai.

 REVIEW THE SKILL

Underline the interjections and conjunctions in the following sentences. Label each underlined word *Conj* (conjunction) or *Inter* (interjection).

__Inter__ 1. <u>Hey</u>, did you read about Dave Dravecky?

__Conj__ 2. Dave played for the San Diego Padres <u>and</u> the San Francisco Giants.

__Inter__ 3. <u>Wow</u>! He played on both teams!

__Inter__ 4. Would you <u>please</u> lend me the book about him?

__Conj__ 5. His story is realistic <u>yet</u> amazing.

__Conj__ 6. Dravecky had cancer surgery <u>and</u> lost most of his deltoid muscle.

__Conj__ 7. He endured a vigorous <u>but</u> surprisingly short rehabilitation.

__Inter__ 8. <u>Yes,</u> his recovery astounded everyone.

__Conj__ 9. His quick comeback to baseball surprised his doctors <u>and</u> his teammates.

__Inter__ 10. Did you enjoy his story? <u>Good</u>!

Evaluation

If you have assigned sentence diagramming with Review the Skill 7-11, check answers on page 449.

Enrichment: Speech Link

Assign one student in the class a specific situation such as "You just received an F on a test" or "You wrecked your dad's riding lawn mower." The student should then try to tell everyone what has happened using appropriate interjections. Students asking and answering questions must also include interjections in their sentences. Here is an example:

Situation: John is a bank teller, and he has just been robbed.

Teacher: John has a problem, and we have to figure out what that problem is. We may ask John questions; however, each question must include an interjection.

Student: Would you, please, tell us whether you are a man or a woman?

John: Well, I am a man.

Student: Hey, are you an old man?

John: No, that has nothing to do with my problem.

A. Label each underlined word *Adv* (adverb), *Prep* (preposition), *Conj* (conjunction), or *Inter* (interjection).
B. Draw an arrow from each adverb to the word it modifies.
C. Place parentheses around each prepositional phrase.
D. Label each prepositional phrase *Adj P* (adjectival phrase) or *Adv P* (adverbial phrase).

The <u>highly</u> unusual Mexican jumping bean is named (<u>for</u> its fast popping movements.) The bean is <u>actually</u> a seed (<u>from</u> a shrub) found (<u>in</u> Mexico.)
<u>Oh</u>, it is not really the bean that is jumping! A caterpillar lives <u>inside</u>, <u>and</u>

its movements cause the bean's jumping. The caterpillar grabs the bean's inner walls (<u>with</u> its tiny legs) and snaps its body. <u>Presto</u>! The bean pops! The caterpillar hollows the inside (<u>of</u> the seed,) <u>but</u> the outside remains a hard shell. The seed's jumping helps scare <u>away</u> birds <u>or</u> animals that would eat the seed. (<u>After</u> several months,) the caterpillar cuts an escape hatch (<u>for</u> itself,) <u>yet</u> it cannot <u>quite</u> leave the bean. <u>First</u>, it must spin a cocoon. Then it changes (<u>into</u> a moth.) The moth <u>very</u> <u>soon</u> emerges (<u>through</u> the lid) it cut earlier.

Complete each sentence by giving a word whose part of speech is indicated. *(Answers will vary.)*

_____Hey_____ , have you _____ever_____ heard Beethoven's *Ninth*
   Interjection   *adverb*

Symphony? It is a(n) _____beautiful_____ _____composition_____ ! From an early age,
             adjective   *noun*

Beethoven showed signs of becoming a(n) _____talented_____ musician. He
                              adjective

played both the violin _____and_____ the piano and wrote many pieces for
              conjunction

piano and strings. Beethoven's only opera _____is_____ *Fidelio*, which is
                           verb

_____not_____ performed _____often_____ . Unfortunately, Beethoven had a
  adverb   *adverb*

difficult family life. His mother died when Beethoven was _____only_____
                                 adverb

seventeen. As a result of several visits to Vienna, Beethoven _____moved_____
                                       verb

there permanently. _____In_____ his twenties, Beethoven began to lose his
           Preposition

hearing. Soon he became almost _____completely_____ deaf, _____but_____ this
                   adverb   *conjunction*

did not keep him from writing music. In fact, _____during_____ the last years
                           preposition

of his life, it is reported that in order to compose he removed the legs from

his piano. This allowed him to feel the vibrations from the instrument.

_____Wow_____ , Beethoven _____really_____ overcame a lot to become an
  Interjection   *adverb*

accomplished musician.

SLIDING HOME

Notice in Psalm 70 that David says "O God" and "O Lord" in the first verse and the last verse. He opens and closes his prayer with the same intensity. In his request, he uses conjunctions to heighten the emotion: "be ashamed and confounded," "turned backward, and put to confusion," and "poor and needy." In each phrase, the words after the conjunction build onto the meaning of the first word. For example, David wants his enemies not only to be embarrassed but also to be defeated (one meaning of *confounded*).

- *Notice the prepositional phrase in verse 4 of this psalm. What question does the phrase answer? Why is the object of the preposition so important?*

- *How many conjunctions can you find in this psalm? Find the two conjunctions in verse 5. Compare the sets of words that they link. What important contrast exists between the words linked by the first conjunction and the words linked by the second?*

Prepositions

II Timothy 3:16-17

16 All scripture is given by inspiration of God, and is profitable for doctrine, for reproof, for correction, for instruction in righteousness:

17 That the man of God may be perfect, throughly furnished unto all good works.

- *How many prepositions are used in this passage?*

- *How do all of the objects of the preposition for relate to profitable?*

Conjunctions

Revelation 5:11-12

11 And I beheld, and I heard the voice of many angels round about the throne and the beasts and the elders: and the number of them was ten thousand times ten thousand, and thousands of thousands;

12 Saying with a loud voice, Worthy is the Lamb that was slain to receive power, and riches, and wisdom, and strength, and honour, and glory, and blessing.

- *Read verse 12 without the ands. Read it with the ands. Why do you think the second reading is more powerful?*

Interjections

Proverbs 24:5

A wise man is strong; yea, a man of knowledge increaseth strength.

- *What is the interjection in this verse?*

- *How does the interjection add a special emphasis to the point this verse is making?*

Left margin notes:

- The prepositional phrase answers the question "In whom should the Christian's gladness be based?" The object of the preposition identifies God as the source of a Christian's joy and gladness.

- Seven conjunctions; *poor and needy* and *my help and my deliverer* (Students will note that there are actually three conjunctions in verse 5; however, *but* functions in effect to join two independent clauses, a concept not covered in this chapter and therefore avoided for this activity); the first set is the need and the second set is the way to satisfy that need.

Prepositions
- Nine prepositions
- They all modify *profitable*.

Conjunctions
- Answers will vary. *(Repeating the word* and *creates the impression of many voices praising the Lamb. The repetition also conveys the speaker's sense of wonder.)*

Interjections
- *yea*
- The interjection breaks the reader's focus and makes him refocus on the words that follow.

Describing a Process

Lesson Support

Support Materials CD
Writing Worksheets—p. 97
Rubrics—p. 111

Scriptural Application

Ask a volunteer to read Nehemiah 8:8 aloud. Explain to the students that this verse reminds us of the importance of learning to be thorough in our explanations. Being able to read the Bible is important, but it is even more valuable to be able to explain its meaning to others in detail. By describing a process, one may acquire the skill of knowing how to give thorough explanations.

Introduction

Materials
- A copy of two recipes for the same food for each student, one recipe more thorough than the other

Give each student a copy of both recipes. Instruct the students to read the shorter one silently. Ask them what kinds of questions they have. Then instruct them to read the longer (more complete) recipe. Ask them which of their questions were answered in the second reading. Invite students to comment about which recipe they think is more effective.

Planning Strategy

Instruct students to pay particular attention to the chronological order of the steps for their process. Advise them to be careful not to omit a step in the process.

Drafting Strategy

Remind students to define any unfamiliar terms that might be a part of their process. In addition, tell students to consider in-

DESCRIBING A PROCESS

So they read in the book in the law of God distinctly, and gave the sense, and
caused them to understand the reading.

Nehemiah 8:8

Have you ever studied the instructions for something and still been confused? If so, you understand the importance of *thoroughness*. A thorough writer gives complete information and answers all the reader's questions.

Your Turn

Write a paragraph explaining how to make something.

Planning

Choose your process. Decide on a topic that interests you, preferably something that you have experience doing.

Identify your audience. Consider what your audience knows about the process already and what information the audience will need to know.

Organize your information. List each necessary item. Then list the steps of the process in the correct order. Take notes as you perform the process.

page 382

Organizing sentences

Drafting

Write your draft. First, name the process and tell why it is important. Then name the necessary materials and explain each step of the process. To conclude, congratulate your reader on completing the process.

Anticipate difficulties. Tell the reader what might be done to make the process easier. Mention options in case the process does not work.

Use smooth transitions. Transition words such as first, next, then, after, while, and last help the reader follow the sequence of the steps.

Revising

Ask a peer to read your paragraph. A reader can detect problems that you have missed. Encourage your peer to comment on weaknesses.

Revise for correction. Make changes that clarify the steps in the process. Identify and correct any errors in grammar, punctuation, and spelling.

Make a clean copy with changes and corrections. Here is one example:

Gelatin is a delicious and easy-to-prepare dessert. Before you begin, gather a saucepan, a measuring cup, a three-ounce package of gelatin, a gelatin mold, and two cups of water. To begin, pour one cup of water into the saucepan. Turn the stove to high and wait for the water to boil. When bubbles form on the water, pour three ounces of gelatin into the water. Turn the stove off and remove the pan. Stir the mixture until the gelatin dissolves. When you can see no more powder, pour one cup of cold water into the mixture. Finally, pour the mixture into the mold and place it in the refrigerator. When the gelatin is firm, it is ready.

Publishing

Make a visual recording of the process. Demonstrate the process while you explain it orally. Contribute your recording to the school library.

Demonstrate your process for the class. On the day of your presentation, remember to bring the items necessary to complete the entire process.

You may wish to use students' compositions in a class activity. Challenge a student to make a sandwich following a classmate's directions. Are the directions clear and accurate? Is the student able to make the sandwich successfully?

ESL: Be aware that your foreign students may never have made a peanut butter sandwich (or any kind of sandwich).

Overview of Writing Process

Planning—Making an outline

Drafting—Writing the paragraph

Revising—Testing instructions; rewriting for clarity after "publishing"

Publishing—Showing to classmates; handing in to teacher

Objectives

Students will

1. make an outline for a process paragraph.

2. write a process paragraph.

3. test the paragraph's clarity with a classmate.

---

cluding reasons why someone needs to know their particular process.

Revising Strategy

Peer Response

Distribute a copy of Writing Worksheet 7 to each student. Ask each student to trade papers and materials with a partner and to do the project his partner has described as the partner observes. Allow each student to use the worksheet to evaluate his paragraph and then to revise it.

Publishing Strategy

Remind each student to bring the materials needed to perform the process he describes on the day his paragraph is due. Provide time for students to read their process paragraphs as they work through their processes for the class. Encourage students to tell of any problems they encountered as they followed the steps of the process.

Scriptural Application

Read II Timothy 3:16-17. Remind students that God is a God of order and that His

Word gives us instructions that are always clear enough to follow.

Evaluation

For help in grading this assignment, see "Grading Writing Assignments" (p. x) and Rubric 7 (Support Materials CD, p. 111).

Enrichment

Ask students to name types of writing in which too many details would be inappropriate. *(poetry, descriptive paragraphs in a story or novel, etc.)* Present a few poems or prose excerpts to use as examples.

CLAUSE STRUCTURE

THE SON FROM AMERICA
BY ISAAC BASHEVIS SINGER

The village of Lentshin was tiny—a sandy marketplace where the peasants of the area met once a week. It was surrounded by little huts with thatched roofs or shingles green with moss. The chimneys looked like pots. Between the huts there were fields, where the owners planted vegetables or pastured their goats.

In the smallest of these huts lived old Berl, a man in his eighties, and his wife, who was called Berlcha (wife of Berl). Old Berl was one of the Jews who had been driven from their villages in Russia and settled in Poland. In Lentshin, they mocked the mistakes he made while praying aloud. He spoke with a sharp "r." He was short, broad-shouldered, and had a small white beard, and summer and winter he wore a sheepskin hat, a padded cotton jacket, and stout boots. He walked slowly, shuffling his feet. He had a half acre of field, a cow, a goat, and chickens.

The couple had a son, Samuel, who had gone to America forty years ago. It was said in Lentshin that he became a millionaire there. Every month, the Lentshin letter carrier brought old Berl a money order and a letter that no one could read because many of the words were English. How much money Samuel sent his parents remained a secret. Three times a year, Berl and his wife went on foot to Zakroczym and cashed the money orders there. But they never seemed to use the money. What for? The garden, the cow, and the goat provided most of their needs. Besides, Berlcha sold chickens and eggs, and from these there was enough to buy flour for bread.

- *Are Berl and Berlcha rich or poor? What do you think they think "rich" is?*

- *Do you think the story is told by a person who lives in Lentshin or America?*

- *Why do you think Berl's son wrote his parents in English?*

This story reads as though it were told in the village of Lentshin. For one thing, we see the letters arriving rather than being sent. Another clue is the simple way in which the story is told. The words are plain, and the sentences are short. This style gives the reader the feeling of listening to someone who is not a native English speaker.

In this chapter, you will learn different ways sentences are put together.

- Answers will vary. *(They think "rich" is helping others and doing something with their life instead of letting everything be done for them.)*
- Lentshin
- Answers will vary. *(He wanted his parents to learn English words; he was gone for forty years and forgot some of his native language; he was showing off his education.)*

Literature Link

Discuss the excerpt from "The Son from America" and the accompanying questions with the students.

Phrases

A **phrase** is a group of words that does not contain both a subject and a predicate. You have learned already about verb phrases, possessive phrases, and prepositional phrases. Every sentence includes phrases.

<u>Miss Chen's class</u> <u>is reading</u> <u>a biography</u> <u>about William Carey</u>.

The example above has four phrases underlined. *Miss Chen's class* is a phrase that functions as the complete subject of the sentence. The simple predicate of the example is the verb phrase *is reading.* Another phrase, *a biography,* acts as the direct object. *About William Carey* is an adjectival prepositional phrase that modifies the simple direct object. Some of these phrases include words that could be subjects; one is a simple predicate; but no phrase includes both a subject and a predicate.

Clauses

A **clause** is a group of words that has both a subject and a predicate working together (a subject-predicate pair). There are two kinds of clauses. An **independent clause** can stand alone as a sentence; it expresses a complete thought. A **dependent clause** is unable to stand alone as a sentence; it contains an introductory or connecting word that makes it express an incomplete thought. The word that makes the clause dependent is called a subordinating word. A dependent clause actually relies on the independent clause for its complete meaning. Dependent clauses that are left to stand alone are sentence fragments.

page 5

Finding subjects
and predicates

              S   TrV   DO
Independent: William Carey obeyed God's Word.

                         S   TrV   DO
Dependent: Although the English preachers rejected Carey's idea

page 13

Recognizing fragments

The first example is labeled *independent* because it contains a subject-predicate pair and expresses a complete thought. The second example also contains a subject-predicate pair. However, it is a dependent clause because the subordinating word *although* leaves unanswered questions. It does not express a complete thought. It cannot stand alone as a sentence. The chart below lists some common subordinating words.

Common Subordinating Words		
after	if	though
although	since	unless
as	so	until
as if	so that	when
because	than	where
before	that	while

Teaching Strategy: Introduction

On the board or overhead transparency, write these phrases: *in the words, a smart student,* and *is seen.* Ask the students these questions: What are these? *(phrases)* Are they sentences? *(no)* Why are they not sentences? *(no subject and predicate to make a complete thought)*

Write these groups of words on the board or overhead transparency: *When he saw me at the store* and *I was on an errand for Mom.* Ask the students these questions: Are both of these groups of words sentences? *(no)* Why? *(The first one cannot stand alone as a complete thought; it leaves the reader or listener hanging.)* Do both of these have subjects and predicates? *(yes)* What word makes the first example different from the second example? *(The word* when *makes the group of words an incomplete thought.)* How can you make these two groups of words into one sentence? *(Join the two: When he saw me at the store, I was on an errand for Mom.)*

Teaching Strategy: Discussion

Discuss the differences among phrases, independent clauses, and dependent clauses. Explain that a phrase is a group of words working together; it has no sentence pattern. An independent clause expresses a complete thought, has a sentence pattern, and may stand alone as a sentence. Although a dependent clause also has a sentence pattern, the dependent clause cannot stand alone as a sentence.

A **phrase** is a group of words that does not contain both a subject and a predicate.

A **clause** is a group of words that contains both a subject and a predicate.

An **independent clause** can stand alone as a sentence.

A **dependent clause** contains a subordinating word that makes it unable to stand alone as a sentence.

8·1 PRACTICE THE SKILL

Label each underlined group of words _P_ (phrase), _IC_ (independent clause), or _DC_ (dependent clause).

__DC__ 1. The planet Mars is approximately 78,840,000 miles farther from the sun <u>than is Earth</u>.

__DC__ 2. <u>Although Mars is more than 34,000,000 miles from Earth</u>, it is Earth's second closest planet.

__IC__ 3. <u>Mars orbits the sun</u> approximately every 687 days.

__P__ 4. <u>At 4,223 miles in diameter</u>, Mars is only slightly larger than half of Earth's size.

__DC__ 5. Mars travels in an elliptical pattern <u>as it orbits the sun</u>.

__IC__ 6. Because of this tilt, <u>the sun heats the northern and southern halves differently</u>.

__P__ 7. <u>Rarely above the freezing point</u>, Mars's climate is colder than that of Earth.

__DC__ 8. <u>Since Mars's surface apparently has polar caps</u>, some scientists believe that Mars contains water.

__P__ 9. A reddish mineral called limonite is responsible <u>for Mars's surface color</u>.

__IC__ 10. Because scientists are fascinated with the question of life on this planet, <u>space probes have explored Mars</u>.

Clause Structure   **165**

Reinforcement

Pass out short newspaper or magazine articles. Instruct the students to locate phrases, independent clauses, and dependent clauses. Ask the students to share their finds with the class and to tell whether the words that they have found are a phrase, an independent clause, or a dependent clause. Do not expect the students to find all the phrases or clauses in the article.

Additional Resources

Students can read more about William Carey in the following books available from BJU Press.

- *William Carey: Father of Modern Missions* by Basil Miller.
- *William Carey: Missionary Pioneer* by Kellsye M. Finnie.

Label each underlined group of words *P* (phrase), *IC* (independent clause), or *DC* (dependent clause).

DC   1. The barracuda lives in saltwater seas, <u>where it is known for its destructive nature.</u>

P   2. The fish feeds <u>on both other fish and people.</u>

P   3. <u>Its extremely sharp teeth and aggressive habits</u> have earned the barracuda the title "tiger of the sea."

DC   4. <u>Although there are twenty-one species of barracuda,</u> the great barracuda is the largest.

IC   5. <u>This species can grow to be six feet long!</u>

P   6. The great barracuda lives in the Atlantic Ocean <u>with at least five other species.</u>

IC   7. <u>Two other species live in the waters around Hawaii;</u> one species lives off the Pacific coast of the United States.

DC   8. <u>Because barracuda most often live in shallow water,</u> they can be a menace to swimmers.

IC   9. <u>Barracuda can also swim</u> far out into the ocean.

IC   10. Interestingly, <u>this fierce animal resembles the common freshwater pike.</u>

Simple Sentences

A **simple sentence** consists of one independent clause. All of the sentences you have studied so far in this book have been simple sentences. A simple sentence has only one subject and one predicate. However, either the subject or the predicate or both may be compound. All four of the examples are simple sentences even though some of them have compound parts.

> William Carey obeyed God's Word.
> He and his supporters formed England's first missionary society.
> Carey traveled to India and ministered there.
> Carey and his helpers learned the language and translated the Bible.

Compound Sentences

A **compound sentence** consists of two or more independent clauses. In other words, it is made of two or more simple sentences joined together by punctuation and sometimes a conjunction. Notice how the two simple sentences can be joined to form a compound sentence.

Teaching Strategy: Participation

Point out the examples of simple sentences on page 166. Remind the students that simple sentences may have compound parts. Instruct the students to write simple sentences about what they observe in the classroom. Encourage them to use compound parts. Ask a few students to share their sentences with the class.

ETYMOLOGY Compound comes from the Latin *companere,* meaning "to put together."

Simple: The English preachers rejected his idea.
$\overset{\text{S}}{}$ $\overset{\text{TrV}}{}$ $\overset{\text{DO}}{}$

Simple: Carey obeyed God's Word.
$\overset{\text{S}}{}$ $\overset{\text{TrV}}{}$ $\overset{\text{DO}}{}$

Compound: The English preachers rejected his idea, but Carey
obeyed God's Word.

A compound sentence is always made up of at least two subject-predicate pairs. In addition, a compound sentence may have compound parts within it.

The missionary society supported William Carey, and he went to India.

Carey learned the language; he and his helpers translated the Bible.

These sentences are not incorrect sentences because they are joined correctly. Diagram a compound sentence in the same way that you would diagram two simple sentences; then join the two diagrams with a vertical dotted line (with a platform in the middle) from the verb of the first sentence to the verb of the second sentence.

Look at the diagram for this sentence: The missionary society supported William Carey, and he went to India.

IN SUMMARY

A **simple sentence** consists of one independent clause.

A **compound sentence** consists of two or more independent clauses.

page 16

Comma splices

page 151

Conjunctions

page 291

Commas in a series

You may want to point out to your students that a comma followed by a conjunction is often (but not always) a clue for spotting compound sentences.

Teaching Strategy: Discussion

Discuss the etymology of the word *compound.* Ask the students these questions: When two sentence patterns are joined together, what kind of sentence is formed? *(compound)* Do the sentences that are joined have to be the same sentence pattern? *(no)* If the students answer incorrectly, ask them to label this example: I was his friend, but he had known me only for a brief time. *(First pattern: I [S], was [LV], friend [PN]; second pattern: he [S], had known [TrV], me [DO])*

Evaluation

Evaluate the simple sentences students wrote based on their observation of the classroom. Do they understand simple sentences? Are they getting simple sentences with compound parts confused with compound sentences?

8-3 PRACTICE THE SKILL

Label the sentences S (simple) or Cd (compound).

S   1. Frozen foods stay fresh for long periods of time.

Cd   2. Many cooks buy food in bulk and freeze part of it for later, or they make and freeze whole meals.

S, S   3. Today, companies freeze a variety of food products. These products include pizza, juices, and vegetables.

S   4. In 1925 Clarence Birdseye first quick-froze vegetables and fish.

Cd   5. The Postum Company bought Birdseye's patents, and the company began a frozen-food division in 1929.

S   6. However, Birdseye's vision for frozen foods did not become a reality until the 1950s.

Cd   7. In the 1950s freezers were more available to the average consumer; therefore, frozen food was used more widely in the home.

Cd   8. Presently, most companies use liquid nitrogen for the quick-freeze process, but this method is expensive.

S   9. For safety, frozen food must be handled properly at home.

Cd   10. Food poisoning can develop; cooks must cook the food quickly.

8-4 REVIEW THE SKILL

Label each sentence S (simple) or Cd (compound).

S   1. The psalms are poems of prayer and praise.

Cd   2. Asaph wrote ten psalms, and Solomon wrote Psalm 72 and Psalm 127.

S   3. The sons of Korah contributed Psalm 84, Psalm 85, and Psalm 87.

Cd   4. Moses wrote Psalm 90, but none of the others are his poetry.

Cd   5. David wrote Psalm 18; II Samuel 22 also includes this song of praise.

Evaluation

If you have assigned sentence diagramming with Practice the Skill 8-3, check the answers on pages 449-50.

Enrichment

Ask the students to read a portion of Scripture, such as the story of Jonah. Instruct them to write a summary of the story in their own words. Then instruct them to find the simple and compound sentences in their summary.

___S___ 6. The psalms are of various lengths and about various topics.

___S___ 6. The psalms are of various lengths and about various topics.

___Cd___ 7. Psalm 117 is the shortest psalm in the Bible; Psalm 119 is the longest.

___S___ 8. The sections of Psalm 119 correspond to the letters of the ancient Hebrew alphabet.

___Cd___ 9. Children often memorize Psalm 23, yet adults love this psalm too.

___Cd___ 10. Many Christians choose a favorite psalm, but all the psalms give the readers a sense of God's wisdom, power, and love.

Complex Sentences

Like a compound sentence, a complex sentence consists of at least two clauses. However, a compound sentence contains two or more independent clauses whereas a **complex sentence** contains one independent clause and one or more dependent clauses.

> **S   TrV   DO   S   TrV   DO**
> After the preachers rejected his idea, Carey explained his beliefs in a pamphlet.

The example is a complex sentence because it contains one independent clause *(Carey explained his beliefs in a pamphlet)* and one dependent clause *(After the preachers rejected his idea).* Both clauses contain a subject and a predicate; the dependent clause also contains the subordinating word *after.*

Compound or Complex?

To determine whether a sentence is compound or complex, first find all the subjects and all the predicates. Then match the subjects to the predicates. Now you have found the clauses. Next, look for any subordinating words. If a clause contains a subordinating word, the clause is dependent. If it does not contain a subordinating word, the clause is independent. Now count the number of dependent and independent clauses in your sentence. If there are two independent clauses, the sentence is compound. If there are one or more dependent clauses and only one independent clause, the sentence is complex.

> **   S   TrV   DO**
> **Compound:** The English preachers rejected his idea, but
> **   S   TrV   DO**
> Carey obeyed God's Word.

> **   S   TrV**
> **Complex:** Although the English preachers rejected his
> **   DO   S   TrV   DO**
> idea, Carey obeyed God's Word.

This textbook introduces the concept of complex sentences. Because complex sentences include dependent clauses that function as part of the sentence pattern or as modifiers, students are not shown how to diagram complex sentences at this grade level.

Teaching Strategy: Introduction

Use the term *sentence-idea* with the students for an idea or thought that can conveniently be expressed in a simple sentence. Explain that we can join sentence-ideas in various ways. We can join them on an equal basis, making compound sentences. We can also join them on an unequal basis, making a complex sentence. The ideas that are less important we place in a dependent clause. Discuss the second Sliding Home question on page 174.

Teaching Strategy: Participation

Write on the board or an overhead transparency these groups of two sentences:

- An early pencil was similar to a painter's brush. The pencil consisted of fine pieces of hair.

- The word *pencil* means "a painter's brush." This word developed from the Latin word *penicillus.*

Ask the students to combine each group into one sentence. Elicit as many different combinations as possible.

Identify the complex sentences from the sentence combinations the students composed. Point out the logical difference between compound sentences and complex sentences. A compound sentence shows an equal relationship between two ideas; a complex sentence shows an unequal relationship between two ideas.

Notice that the example labeled *compound* has two independent clauses joined by a comma and a coordinating conjunction. The example labeled *complex* has a dependent clause introduced by a subordinating word, and it has an independent clause. There is no coordinating conjunction joining the two clauses. The dependent clause may appear before the independent clause, after the independent clause, or within the independent clause.

Before: *Because Carey understood God's command,* he became a missionary to India.

After: The preachers realized their mistake *when they read Carey's pamphlet.*

Within: Carey's actions *while he was on the mission field* influenced many people.

page 295

Commas to separate

I̲N̲ S̲U̲M̲M̲A̲R̲Y̲

A **complex sentence** consists of one independent clause with at least one dependent clause.

8-5 PRACTICE THE SKILL

A. Label the sentence patterns of all clauses as *S-InV, S-TrV-DO, S-TrV-IO-DO, S-LV-PN,* or *S-LV-PA.*

B. Place parentheses around any dependent clauses.

C. Label each sentence *S* (simple), *Cd* (compound), or *Cx* (complex).

_____S_____ 1. In the early 1800s mail delivery to California from east of the
        Mississippi River could take several weeks.

_____Cx_____ 2. Two Missouri businessmen devised a plan for faster mail
        service(after they realized the need.)

_____Cd_____ 3. The men bought four hundred horses and hired approximately
        eighty riders; this new business was the pony express.

_____Cd_____ 4. The express riders carried the mail for approximately two
        hundred miles a day, and they could deliver a letter to the
        West Coast in about ten days.

Reinforcement

Prepare a list of simple sentences. Challenge your students to complete each sentence starter with a humorous dependent clause. Here are a few examples to get you started: I saw Paul *(when he was in the hall.)* This is the dog *(that we found in the smog.)* Did you see the desk *(while it was at rest?)*

Evaluation

Evaluate the students' understanding of simple, compound, and complex sentences by asking them to write sentences of each type on a topic you assign. Ask them to identify the dependent clauses and the subordinating words that they have used.

Enrichment: Speech Link

Divide the class into small groups and assign each group an object (teapot, camera, Bible, etc.). Direct each group to write a description of the object, using no more than three simple, compound, or complex sentences. Each group will read its description to the class two times. After the first reading the class will identify simple, compound, and complex sentences. After the second reading the class will try to identify the object of the description. *(This person wears a lab coat and helps other people. [a simple sentence, a doctor or a pharmacist])*

One on One: Instruct your student to write descriptions of objects in the house or car. Allow him to read the descriptions to family members or neighbors to see whether they can guess what objects are being described. Ask your student to identify the types of sentences in his descriptions.

<u>Cx</u> 5. (Although a rider traveled about seventy-five miles in a day,)
a horse traveled about ten to fifteen miles at a time.

<u>S</u> 6. The horses needed time for rest and preparation for the next
trip.

<u>Cx</u> 7. The fastest trip between Missouri and California occurred
(when the express carried copies of a speech by President
Abraham Lincoln.)

<u>Cd</u> 8. During its two-year history the pony express continued day
and night, and riders traveled in all kinds of weather.

<u>S</u> 9. Most riders carried both guns and knives for protection
against attack.

<u>Cx</u> 10. (Until the telegraph opened in October 1861,) the pony express
was the quickest method of message delivery.

 8-6 REVIEW THE SKILL

Place parentheses around each dependent clause. Label each sentence S (simple), Cd (compound), or Cx (complex).

<u>S</u> 1. During World War II, a group of Native Americans played an
important role in the Pacific arena.

<u>Cx</u> 2. These Navajos received special training (so that they could
serve their country.)

<u>Cd</u> 3. The code name for the Navajos was *Dineh* or "The People";
the *Dineh* coded and decoded critical messages between
Marine Corps divisions.

<u>Cd</u> 4. The code included regular Navajo words and some made-up
words using Navajo terms; for example, *Daghailchiih*, or
"Mustache Smeller," became the code name for Adolf Hitler.

<u>Cx</u> 5. (Although many Navajos volunteered for duty in 1939,) the
marines did not recruit them as Code Talkers until 1942.

<u>Cx</u> 6. At first some people believed that the Navajo code was too
easy (because the Code Talkers could decode so quickly.)

Enrichment

Write these four related sentences on the
board or overhead transparency and number them:

1. Roberto threw the ball.
2. Michelle caught a fast ball.
3. Everyone watched the game.
4. Everyone cheered.

Assign two or three of the sentences to
each student. Instruct some students to
combine their sentences to make new simple sentences and other students to make
compound or complex sentences.

Allow the students to identify their new
sentences as simple, compound, or complex. Ask them also to distinguish independent clauses from dependent clauses.
Be aware that some students may create
compound-complex sentences, which they
have not yet studied.

Learning Christianly

Different versions punctuate these sentences differently. The KJV presents these verses as consisting of only three sentences. Each of these three sentences is a complex sentence. If you take the time to try to diagram them, you learn that these sentences are very complex. Other translations attempt to simplify this difficult clause structure by inserting more periods. If we want to understand God's Word, we must take time to learn about the complexities of clause structure. Simple sentences are the simplest way to communicate, but God has chosen to convey much of His mind through sentences that are far from simple.

Learning Christianly

When writing for younger audiences, we often have to adjust our style. Normally, we like to use many compound and complex sentences. But children who are just learning to read find those types of sentence difficult to follow. For them to understand us, we should break up our compound and complex sentences into simple sentences. Learning this skill is very valuable for all writing. If a first grader can understand what you have written, certainly anyone who can read will understand you too. But perhaps you now have a troubling question facing you: "If the clearest sentence is a simple sentence, why bother learning about the other sentence types?" There are many good answers to that question, and one of the best answers concerns the nature of the Christian Scriptures. Read Ephesians 1:3-14 and see how many simple sentences you find.

8-7 USE THE SKILL

Combine each pair of sentences, using the word in parentheses.
(Answers will vary.)

1. Weather prediction has been attempted for thousands of years. People want to know the weather ahead of time. *(because)*

   Weather prediction has been attempted for thousands of years

   because people want to know the weather ahead of time.

2. Weather forecasting existed many years ago. Prediction was based on the locations of the stars. *(when)*

   Weather forecasting existed many years ago when prediction was

   based on the locations of the stars.

3. Both the rain gauge and the weathervane had been invented by 50 B.C. Weather prediction was still unreliable. *(while)*

   While weather prediction was still unreliable, both the rain gauge and

   the weathervane had been invented by 50 B.C.

4. Scientists realized the importance of air pressure in weather forecasting. Many scientific inventions followed. *(after)*

   After scientists realized the importance of air pressure in weather

   forecasting, many scientific inventions followed.

5. Weather knowledge in the early 1800s could not be transmitted effectively. Storm reports usually arrived after the storm itself. *(since)*

   Since weather knowledge in the early 1800s could not be transmitted

   effectively, storm reports usually arrived after the storm itself.

6. Satellites take pictures of the earth. Meteorological centers receive these pictures. *(after)*

   After satellites take pictures of the earth, meteorological centers

   receive these pictures.

7. The stations transmit information to centers. Weather forecasts are prepared. *(where)*

   The stations transmit information to centers where weather

   forecasts are prepared.

8. The weather patterns follow the rules of physics. Mathematical calculations can help to predict the weather. *(because)*

   Because weather patterns follow the rules of physics, mathematical

   calculations can help to predict the weather.

9. The first successful computer-assisted weather forecast occurred in 1950. Scientists have improved the computer formulas for forecasting. *(since)*

   Since the first successful computer-assisted weather forecast occurred in

   1950, scientists have improved the computer formulas for forecasting.

10. Bjerknes developed an explanation for weather changes. His theory improved the accuracy of forecasting. *(when)*

   When Bjerknes developed an explanation for weather changes, his

   theory improved the accuracy of forecasting.

8-8 CUMULATIVE REVIEW

A. Label each underlined word *N* (noun), *P* (pronoun), *V* (verb), *Adj* (adjective), *Adv* (adverb), *Prep* (preposition), *Conj* (conjunction), or *Inter* (interjection).

B. Draw an arrow from each adjective or adverb to the word it modifies.

Have <u>you</u> ever been <u>out</u> <u>on</u> a lake and heard a <u>low</u>, haunting sound? You <u>probably</u> heard one of the <u>most</u> <u>interesting</u> birds in North America, <u>the</u> loon. Unfortunately, this <u>beautiful</u> bird <u>is</u> not as commonly seen as it once may have been. Are there any loons in Alaska? <u>Yes</u>, all <u>five</u> species of loons are present in Alaska. People like to watch the <u>loons</u> on lakes, <u>and</u> <u>most</u>

Reinforcement

After the students complete Use the Skill 8-7, ask them to compose compound and complex sentences about a topic of their choice. Refer them to the chart of subordinating words on page 164.

Enrichment

Divide the class into groups. Ask each group to take part of the excerpt from "The Son from America" and write it all in simple and compound sentences. Ask one member from each group to read what the group has written. Discuss how eliminat-

ing complex sentences changes the effect of the story.

One on One: Assign your student one section of the excerpt from "The Son from America." Instruct him to rewrite the section all in simple and compound sentences. Read the section aloud to him and ask him to discuss how eliminating complex sentences changes the effect of the story.

Scriptural Application

Use the information on page 174 about Proverbs 25:21-22 as a devotional and a teaching tool.

consider them *an important* part of the *Alaskan* wilderness. Some people mistake cormorants *or* other diving birds for loons. The five species living in Alaska *are* Common, Yellow-billed, Red-throated, Pacific, and Arctic. *Which* is most famous for its call? It is the Common loon. The Yellow-billed loon is *larger* than the Common. It is the largest of all North American diving birds. *One* who engages in loon watching must observe *them carefully*. If one gets too close, a loon may become *very nervous*. It will run and splash across the surface of the lake. *This* is called the "penguin dance." If one wants to hear the *eerie* calls of the loons, the best time is in the summer. Loons are usually quiet *in* winter.

≡Sliding Home

Isaac Bashevis Singer carefully uses simple, compound, and complex sentences in his story. When the idea is simple, the structure is simple: "The chimneys looked like pots." When the idea is more difficult, the structure is too: "Every month, the Lentshin letter carrier brought old Berl a money order and a letter that no one could read because many of the words were English." However, Singer uses more simple sentences than any other kind, perhaps to help us remember the simple life of Berl and Berlcha.

- *Look at paragraph two; find the fifth sentence. What kind of sentence structure does Singer use?*

- *What type of sentence structure does the first sentence in the passage have? Do you think it should be broken into two separate sentences rather than left as one? Why or why not?*

- *Find several examples of simple sentences.*

- *Look at the beginnings of the sentences. Do they all begin with subjects? Do you think that they should? How does a varied sentence structure make the passage better?*

> **Proverbs 25:21-22**
>
> *21 If thine enemy be hungry, give him bread to eat; and if he be thirsty, give him water to drink:*
>
> *22 For thou shalt heap coals of fire upon his head, and the Lord shall reward thee.*

- *What are the two dependent clauses in verse 21? What is the subject of the two independent clauses in this verse?*

- *How are the two parts in verse 21 alike in structure?*

Margin notes (left column):

- Compound
- Complex. Answers will vary. *(No. The details in the complex sentence create a picture of the village as a unified whole.)*
- Answers will vary. *(First paragraph: sentences two and three. Second paragraph: sentences four, six, and seven. Third paragraph: sentences five, six, and eight)*
- No. Answers will vary. *(The varied sentence structure supports the characterization. Singer uses one type of sentence structure for the villagers and another type of sentence structure for the American.)*

- *If thine enemy be hungry,* and *if he be thirsty.* The subject is understood *you* because the sentences are imperative sentences.
- They both include a dependent clause followed by an independent clause.

DRAMATIZING A SCENE

> I was in the Spirit on the Lord's day, and heard behind me a great voice, as of a trumpet, saying, I am Alpha and Omega, the first and the last: and, What thou seest, write in a book, and send it unto the seven churches. . . . And when I saw him, I fell at his feet as dead.
>
> *Revelation 1:10-11, 17*

Have you ever seen a play performed on stage? Many plays consist of several acts, each act having several scenes. There are many ways to define the term *scene*. In a general sense, a scene is simply a short section of a play, usually taking place in one location with one set of characters. When the location changes or new characters enter the action or a new idea is introduced, a new scene begins.

Your Turn

Choose a passage from a Bible account or from a book or a story that you like. Then write a dramatic scene for a play based on the excerpt that you chose. Put in stage directions wherever you can to keep the scene from becoming too still.

Planning

Choose a passage to adapt. Keep in mind that the text you choose should include some kind of conflict. Conflict in literature (including drama) is any kind of problem or disagreement. Sometimes the conflict is between two or more characters who have opposing views on an issue. Sometimes the conflict is within one character who must choose between two contrary courses of belief or action. Another type of conflict sets a character against a force greater than himself or herself; that force might be God or some manifestation of creation, such as nature.

One student was assigned by his teacher to select a passage from the book of Esther and to adapt it as a scene from a play. After reading the entire book, Tony chose a section that he found especially interesting and dramatic—the first ten verses of the sixth chapter of Esther. What is the conflict in this passage?

Determine your purpose. What lesson or message do you want your reader to learn from your scene? In his dramatic scene, Tony strives to reveal the character of both the king and Haman. To determine your purpose, read your passage several times. In addition to your text, you may need to read several verses or pages before and after your selection in order to get a more complete picture of the entire story. Tony read his chosen text several times; he also read previous verses that revealed more of Haman's character.

Develop your characters. At this point you need to identify the characters in your scene. Tony chose to develop two major characters: the king and Haman. Although the servant appears prominently at the beginning of the scene, the conflict of the scene does not involve him.

King	Haman	Servant
endured sleeplessness	angry	obedient
disturbed by injustice	sought to destroy Jews	
uninformed about his country's affairs	deceitful	
easily influenced	self-centered	

Overview of Writing Process

Planning—Choosing a work or part of a work to dramatize

Drafting—Setting the scene; roughing out the scene; reading dialogue aloud

Revising—Writing out the final draft; adjusting lines and descriptions

Publishing—Getting a partner's assessment

Objectives
Students will

1. select a work or part of a work to dramatize.
2. create a play scene from the selected piece.
3. critique a classmate's work.

Dramatizing a Scene

Lesson Support

Support Materials CD
Writing Worksheets—p. 98
Rubrics—p. 112

Scriptural Application

Ask a volunteer to read Revelation 1:10-11 and 17 aloud. Lead a discussion about Revelation 1. In this passage the apostle John describes the intense drama of his encounter with the glorified Christ. He could have simply reported the details of this experience, but instead he appealed to the power of drama to recreate the experience for his readers. Learning the skill of dramatizing a scene can have a powerful effect on the people your students will seek to influence.

Scriptural Application

For several days prior to this lesson, encourage students to read the Book of Esther. Use a class discussion of the book's events as an introduction to writing a dramatic scene.

Introduction

Ask the students whether any have been in a play. Allow a few minutes of discussion about their experiences. Draw the discussion toward the lines of dialogue they had to memorize. Lead students to think about how a playwright writes lines for plays.

Teaching Strategy

Ask students to name some of the reasons Tony had to keep returning to his source, the Book of Esther. *(to make sure he was true to the narrative; to decide what he would include; to get ideas for setting up a scene)*

What kind of interaction do your characters have with each other? What part do they play in the scene? What do the characters need to do in the scene? Write a brief character sketch for each of the characters, describing both inward and outward characteristics.

Plan your scene. The text that you have chosen may provide descriptions that will help you plan your scene. These descriptions may be the physical appearance of the characters and the surroundings or the inner thinking of the characters. Tony chose to set the whole scene in the king's chamber because the Scripture says that the king could not sleep. The Bible does not describe the king's chamber, but Tony imagined that it would be grand and regal, with a lot of rich fabrics and gold and silver.

But this was not enough. In his first plan Tony did not include the part about Haman being there to ask the king to put Mordecai to death. After Tony thought about his ideas, he decided to include Haman talking to himself outside the door to the king's chamber. He decided to divide the stage so that one part would be the chamber and the other part would be the court outside the chamber.

Drafting

Designate a block of time to write. Your scene will flow more smoothly if you are able to write your first draft of the entire scene in one sitting. Do not be concerned at this point about errors. You will have the opportunity to evaluate your writing at a later time and to revise and proofread as necessary.

Develop the scene. Now you are ready to begin writing your scene. Begin by including any stage notes that will help set the scene. Tony's first stage note describes the physical appearance of the stage.

> [The scene opens in the king's chamber. There is a big pile of silk pillows and comforters where the king has been trying to get to sleep. There is a gold chair with footstool in the room. The king is sitting in the chair. There is a curtain that divides the king's room from the court. There are a pillar and a bench on that side of the stage.]

Begin writing your scene. After he wrote a stage note that helped him to imagine the setting for his scene, Tony began to write. Because he based his scene on a passage from the Bible, he used the information from the Book of Esther as his guide. In fact, Tony used the Bible's words as closely as he could.

Include dialogue between the characters to move the scene along. If necessary, use your characters' dialogue to give any background information that the audience might need to understand the scene better. At the beginning of Tony's scene, the servant reads from the book of records of the chronicles that tells of a plot to kill the king. The dialogue between the king and his servant reveals that nothing has been done for Mordecai, the man who warned the king of the plot.

Scriptural Application

Draw a parallel between a play script and God's plan for the students' lives. Just as a playwright has a plan for his play and wants the actors to see that plan and help to get his message across, so God has a plan and wants Christians to follow Him in the parts He gives to them. We can rest in the confidence that God will bring about a happy ending.

Planning Strategies

Read the selected verses from Esther with the class. Ask students to compare the scene Tony wrote to the Book of Esther. Ask them what Tony omitted and what he added. *(He added lines of dialogue and descriptions of settings; he omitted some action and details.)*

Direct each student to select a passage to adapt for this assignment. Tell the students that they may choose a Bible passage or a part of some book or story to dramatize, following the example in the text for length and format. If several students select related passages, consider encouraging them to write their individual scenes as part of a larger play.

Scriptural Application

Point out that Bible characters were real people, not merely characters in stories. What we read in the Bible really happened, and the things that God did for people centuries ago He is able to do for us too. James 5:17 reminds us that Elijah was a person just like us and struggled just as we do. Yet because of God's involvement in his life, he was able to experience wonderful things.

If your dramatic scene comes from a Scripture passage, make the characters' words as close to the words of Scripture as possible. Compare Esther 6:2 with the servant's speech and Esther 6:9 with Haman's speech.

Esther 6:2	And it was found written, that Modecai had told of Bigthana and Teresh, two of the king's chamberlains, the keepers of the door, who sought to lay hand on the king Ahasuerus.
Servant	On the first day of the month, Bigthana and Teresh, two of the king's chamberlains, the keepers of the door, sought to lay hands on King Ahasuerus.
Esther 6:9	And let this apparel and horse be delivered to the hand of one of the king's most noble princes, that they may array the man withal whom the king delighteth to honour, and bring him on horseback through the street of the city, and proclaim before him, Thus shall it be done to the man whom the king delighteth to honour.
Haman	And let this apparel and horse be delivered to the hand of one of the king's most noble princes, that they may array the man withal whom the king delighteth to honor, and bring him on horseback through the streets of the city, and proclaim before him, "Thus shall it be done to the man whom the king delighteth to honor."

Indicate action through dialogue and stage notes. In a play both the dialogue and the characters' actions reveal the characters' motives and inner thoughts. Read the stage notes that Tony wrote to describe the actions and reactions of Haman. Which reveal to you more about Haman—the action or his dialogue?

[The scene opens in the king's chamber. There is a big pile of silk pillows and comforters where the king has been trying to get to sleep. There is a gold chair with footstool in the room. The king is sitting in the chair. There is a curtain that divides the king's room from the court. There are a pillar and a bench on that side of the stage.]

King:	Servant, come here.
Servant:	Your Majesty?
King:	I cannot sleep. Bring me the book of records of the chronicles and read them to me.
Servant:	[to the audience] If that don't put him to sleep, nothin' will! [turning to another servant] Go quickly and bring the book. [The other servant leaves, and the first servant turns to the king.] Do you wish anything to eat or drink, your Majesty?
King:	No, I want only to hear the book read.

Planning Strategies

Instruct each student to determine the purpose he wishes to accomplish with his scene. Then discuss the importance of determining a target audience and writing for that audience. Remind the students that young children may take words and actions literally. Teens, on the other hand, understand implications and abstract references more easily.

Instruct the students to choose the characters for their dramatic scenes. Draw their attention to the table on page 175. Then direct students to read their passages again.

Encourage them to record any ideas that they think of that will help them to develop their characters.

Encourage the students to read their passages several times as they begin to plan their scenes. Point out the discussion on pages 175-76 and the decisions that Tony made as he worked on his scene from Esther.

Drafting Strategies

Encourage the students to plan ahead so that they can write their first drafts in one sitting. Emphasize the importance of continuity with each scene. Explain that a scene should demonstrate sequential action—one thing following another. Draw the students' attention to Tony's scene and ask them to identify the sequential action *(king upset that nothing had been done for Mordecai; summoning of Haman; king's sending Haman to honor Mordecai)*

Discuss the importance of conflict in a scene. Explain that conflict occurs when something or someone stands in the way of a character's achieving his goal. (If necessary, review the information about conflict from page 175.) Then ask the students

[The other servant returns with book. The first servant starts to read.]

Servant: On the first day of the month, Bigthana and Teresh, two of the king's chamberlains, the keepers of the door, sought to lay hands on the king Ahasuerus.

King: Yes. I quite remember that incident. Those wicked men! But they have been punished. Read on.

Servant: The man who warned the king was Mordecai.

King: Ah, yes, Mordecai. A faithful man. What honor and dignity has been done to Mordecai for this?

Servant: [scanning over the page and then looking up] There is nothing done for him.

King: What? Nothing? This is wrong, I must think of something. Who is in the court? Go and see if any of my nobles are in the court.

[The king and the servant stay still. The lights go down on them. Haman comes into the court and begins to walk back and forth, talking to himself.]

Haman: That old Mordecai! I will not rest until he gets what he deserves! How he ruins my life! Surely the king will let me hang him!

[The lights come up on the other side of the stage, and the servant and the king begin to move again.]

King: Go, I say, and send me in a noble.

[The servant bows and goes out through the curtain. He sees Haman. He turns back in to the king.]

Servant: Behold, Haman standeth in the court.

King: Let him come in.

[The servant goes out into the court. Haman steps up to him.]

Servant: Lord Haman.

Haman: What is it?

Servant: The king wants you to go in and talk to him.

Haman: [Pushing past the servant, he goes to the king.] Your Majesty, you wanted to see me?

King: Yes. What shall be done unto the man whom the king delighteth to honor?

Haman: [smiling very big and sticking out his chest] Well, your Majesty, if it were up to me, I would say this. For the man whom the king

---

to identify the conflict in Tony's scene. *(conflict between Haman and Mordecai)* Ask them to identify what stands in Haman's way. *(the king's orders)*

Remind students that writing a dramatic scene is a method of storytelling. Encourage them to reveal their characters through dialogue and interaction with other characters. If the students are adapting passage from the Bible, remind them to make their dialogue as similar to the original as possible. Remind the students to use stage notes to indicate settings or actions that cannot be revealed through di-

alogue but warn them not to rely too heavily on stage notes. The dialogue in the scene should be the primary means of communicating to the actors and the audience.

Revising Strategies

Direct the students to evaluate their own dramatic scenes. Are there at least two characters in the scene? Does the dialogue move? Is there something that happens in the scene—an issue to be resolved? Are the word choices exact and clear?

Peer Response

Distribute a copy of Writing Worksheet 8 to each student. Ask each student to exchange dramatic scenes with a partner. Tell the students to read the scenes first and then to fill in the questionnaire. If time allows, let students read and respond to more than one dramatic scene.

Instruct the students to resolve any problems they discovered while evaluating their scenes by revising thoroughly. Remind them to incorporate useful suggestions from their peers as they revise.

delighteth to honor, let the royal apparel be brought which the king used to wear, and the horse that the king rides upon, and the crown royal which is set upon his head.

[The king nods. He gets up and goes to sit on the bed.]

Haman: And let this apparel and horse be delivered to the hand of one of the king's most noble princes, that they may array the man withal whom the king delighteth to honor, and bring him on horseback through the streets of the city, and proclaim before him, "Thus shall it be done to the man whom the king delighteth to honor."

King: Make haste, and take the apparel and the horse, as thou has said, and do even so to Mordecai the Jew, that sitteth at the king's gate. Let nothing fail of all that thou has said.

[Haman turns away from the king with a very sick look on his face. He starts to leave.]

King: That was a very good idea you had. I think I can sleep well now! [He lies down.]

Haman: Yes, your Majesty.

[Haman goes out into the court. He stamps his foot and shakes his fist. When the servant comes up to him, he pushes him out of the way and leaves the stage in a huff. Lights go out.]

Revising

Read through your scene out loud. As you read, ask yourself some questions. Does your scene flow smoothly? Does your scene reveal the conflict and the solution? Does the dialogue sound like real conversation? Are your characters convincing? If the answer to any of these questions is *no,* try to think of a solution to the problem.

Ask someone else to read your scene. Does your reader hesitate at any particular point in the scene? Does your reader misinterpret any part of the scene? When the reader has finished reading the scene, ask the reader to suggest changes that would make the scene more effective.

Make revisions for clarity. Implement the changes that you have determined will improve your scene.

Proofread your scene. Check for correctness of format, grammar, spelling, usage, and mechanics.

Publishing

Present your scene to your class or family and friends. In preparation for the presentation of your scene, invite interested friends to audition for the speaking parts. In addition to the speakers, you will also need people to work as a prop manager and a stage director.

Record your scene. Use a camera to record the performance while you present your scene to an audience. The recording could be a part of a permanent collection for your school, your class, or your family.

Publishing Strategy

Ask students to volunteer their dramatic scene for use in a vacation Bible school program or a Sunday school class. Encourage students to be willing to help perform the dramatic scene.

Scriptural Application

Ask a volunteer to read John 2:13-15 aloud. Lead a discussion about the drama involved in this passage. Call the students' attention to the fact that this event is recorded in each of the gospels.

Evaluation

For help in grading this assignment, see "Grading Writing Assignments" (p. x) and Rubric 8 (Support Materials CD, p. 112).

Enrichment

If several students have taken parts of one book of the Bible for their scenes, suggest that they put the scenes into one longer play.

Grand Slam: Writing Across the Curriculum

During World War II, both sides used codes to keep communications secret—and both sides kept cracking the other side's codes. Then the Allies turned for help to the Navajo people. Known as Code Talkers, these soldiers used their native language to form a code that baffled the enemy. For example, the Navajo word for "owls" meant *bombers;* the Navajo word for "eggs" meant *bombs.* Nazi intelligence never cracked the Navajo code.

Try your hand at designing a code for secret communication. A code can be simple or complex. A simple code reverses the alphabet:

A B C D E F G H I J K L M N O P Q R S T U V W X Y Z
Z Y X W V U T S R Q P O N M L K J I H G F E D C B A

In this code, "Meet me for lunch" reads like this: "Nvvg nv uli ofmxs." You can also use symbols or numbers to replace letters.

After you have a code, choose your message. Write it in code and give the coded message to someone else to decipher or translate.

Only in English

Between Innings

Some things we say to each other would not make sense in any other language. We call these things *idioms.* You know what it means to have a frog in your throat. But translate that directly into French, and a French person might rush to save your life. To say the same thing, a French person would say he had *un chat à la gorge,* which means "a cat in the throat." Which do you think is a more accurate description of the problem?

In Germany, the English idiom "to chew someone out" is *jemandem den Kopf waschen.* Literally translated, the phrase means "to wash someone's head." If you think that phrase sounds funny, imagine how ours sounds to a German.

Challenge the students to write sentences using creative idioms. Have the students exchange papers and rewrite other students' idioms to make them understandable to everyone.

Writing Across the Curriculum

Communications in code, or secret writing, is known as cryptology. The word *cryptology* is derived from the Greek words *kryptos,* which means "hidden," and *logos,* which means "word."

Priests in ancient cultures often kept religious rituals secret from the lower classes to protect their own higher social position. Many religious rituals were written in secret codes.

Julius Caesar developed a code using simple letter substitution. In English, his variation would look like this:

A B C D E F G ..... X Y Z

D E F G H I J ..... A B C

Demonstrate Caesar's code and ask the students how the code alphabet differs from the regular English alphabet. *(The code alphabet shifts three letters to begin the code; the three letters that were shifted from the beginning are placed at the end.)*

Instruct the students to include one word of at least six letters in code and in English to help their partners decipher the messages.

T H A N K S

G S Z N Q H

SUBJECT-VERB AGREEMENT

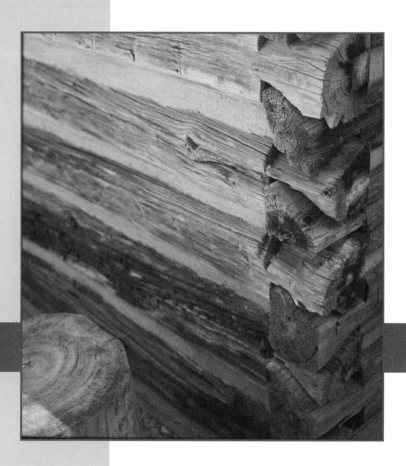

Objectives

Students will

1. deduce the differences between singular/plural verbs and subjects.

2. conclude that plural nouns and plural first-, second-, and third-person pronouns take the same forms of the verb *be* in the present and past tenses.

3. identify the verb form that agrees with the subject.

4. identify and differentiate between singular and plural indefinite pronouns.

5. choose the correct verb to agree with an indefinite pronoun as subject.

6. discover rules about subject-verb agreement with compound subjects.

7. choose the correct singular or plural verb to agree with a compound subject.

8. write sentences using correct subject-verb agreement with compound subjects.

9. label subjects and verbs in sentences.

10. identify and correct subject-verb agreement problems.

In times and places where nails have been scarce or expensive, people have devised ways to build houses without them. Notice how the logs in the picture have interlocking notches to make them fit together. Some master builders were able to set logs so well that no chinking or filling was needed between them.

Good writers know a different kind of notching. One kind of "notching" in writing has to do with making the subject of the sentence fit the verb. If the subject and verb don't fit together, no amount of chinking will help.

Subject-Verb Agreement

ETYMOLOGY

Agreement has its roots in Latin. The Latin prefix *ad-*, meaning *to*, was combined with a form of the Latin word *gratus*, meaning "pleasing." When two people agree, they are pleasing to one another. In subject-verb agreement, the subject and the verb are pleasing together.

Every verb must agree in **number** with its subject. In other words, a singular subject must have a singular verb, and a plural subject must have a plural verb. When the subject and the verb match in number, we say that they agree.

Singular: The boy *practices* basketball every day.
He *practices* basketball every day.
Plural: The boys *practice* basketball every day.
They *practice* basketball every day.

Notice that verbs form their plurals differently from nouns. A noun usually forms a plural by adding *s* or *es* (one boy, two boy*s*). A verb, however, usually forms a plural by dropping *s* or *es* (boy practice*s*, boys practice).

	Singular	Plural
Present	The boy *practices* every day.	The boys *practice* every day.
Past	The boy *practiced* every day.	The boys *practiced* every day.
Future	He will *practice* every day.	They will *practice* every day.

Notice also that this change occurs only in the present tense. Past and future tense verbs do not show number.

page 27
Plural forms of nouns

page 62
Present tense

Subject-Verb Agreement   **183**

Teaching Strategy: Introduction

Discuss the etymology of *agreement* on page 183. Better understanding of the term will lead to better understanding of the concept.

Scriptural Application

Discuss the use of the word *agreed* in Amos 3:3. Ask students what this verse teaches about the friends we have.

Teaching Strategy: Induction

Write these sentences on the board or overhead transparency:

- Log cabins remained important to early settlers.
- Five U.S. presidents lived in log cabins.
- Abraham Lincoln resided in one of them.
- A log cabin used many trees.

Ask student volunteers to rewrite the sentences, changing the verb tenses to the present tense. Instruct students to identify the verbs first and then the subjects in each rewritten sentence. Ask them whether they notice a pattern developing in the sentences. Elicit from the students that the singular verbs end with an *s* but the plural verbs do not and that the opposite is true of the subjects. Discuss the material about non-*be* verbs on page 183.

ESL Strategy

Use ESL Helps page 49 (Support Materials CD) for practice in adding *s* to third-person singular verbs.

page 51

Recognizing verbs

An exception to this rule for verbs is the verb *be*. The verb *be* is different from other verbs. To make *be* agree in number with the subject, you must know its forms.

Special Forms of the Verb *Be*				
	Present		Past	
	Singular	Plural	Singular	Plural
First-person pronouns	am	are	was	were
Second-person pronouns	are	are	were	were
Third-person pronouns and all nouns	is	are	was	were

All singular nouns and third-person singular pronouns *(it, he, she)* take *is* for the present tense and *was* for the past tense.

Present: That girl *is* a new student.
She *is* my cousin.
Past: She *was* a student at Highland Christian in Asheville.
Her father *was* a teacher there before they moved here.

All plural nouns, first-person and third-person plural pronouns *(we and they)*, and the second-person pronoun *(you)* take *are* for present tense and *were* for past tense.

Present: The neighbors *are* here.
They *are* the Kings.
You *are* welcome to come too.
Past: Last week our teachers *were* at a conference.
We *were* out of school for three days.
They *were* learning more about teaching.
You *were* out of school too, weren't you?

The first-person singular pronoun *(I)* takes *am* for present tense and *was* for past tense.

Present: I *am* glad to meet you.
Past: I *was* happy to hear you sing.

IN SUMMARY

In a sentence the subject and the verb must agree in **number**.

A singular subject must have a singular verb; a plural subject must have a plural verb.

The verb *be* has special singular and plural forms.

Teaching Strategy

Combination with Chapter 3: Verbs
Review the forms of *be* presented in Chapter 3.

Teaching Strategy: Induction
Write these sentences on the board or overhead transparency:

- Our friends <u>are</u> here for dinner.
- We <u>are</u> eager for their visit.
- They <u>are</u> always on time.
- You <u>are</u> usually on time as well.
- Yesterday the Nelsons <u>were</u> in their yard.
- They <u>were</u> diligent at their work.
- You <u>were</u> able to help them, weren't you?
- Unfortunately, we <u>were</u> out of town.

Ask the students to draw conclusions about the verb forms used in the sentences. Guide them to notice that plural nouns and plural first-, second-, and third-person pronouns take *are* for present tense and *were* for past tense.

Discuss the information about forms of *be* on page 184.

ESL Strategy
Use ESL Helps page 50 (Support Materials CD) for practice in using the forms of *be*.

Evaluation
Encourage students to find examples of proper subject-verb agreement. Ask the students to report their findings to the class.

Label the subject _S_. Underline the verb form that agrees with the subject.

1. Ruth's story *(is, are)* a Bible story that ends happily.

2. Ruth *(decides, decide)* that she will remain with her mother-in-law, Naomi.

3. Ruth *(gathers, gather)* stalks of grain that have been dropped by reapers in a field.

4. One day Boaz *(sees, see)* Ruth in his field.

5. The reapers *(begins, begin)* to allow Ruth to gather whatever grain she needs.

6. The ladies *(rejoices, rejoice)* at their good fortune.

7. Boaz *(realizes, realize)* that he is in love with Ruth.

8. Desiring to marry Ruth, Boaz *(goes, go)* to make an agreement with Ruth's nearest kinsman.

9. The kinsman *(allows, allow)* the marriage.

10. In the end, Boaz *(marries, marry)* Ruth.

 Learning Christianly

Consistently choosing subjects and verbs that agree is the mark of a skilled writer. Many people, however, never achieve this skill because they are not convinced it is worth the effort. Why should no Christian think this way?

 Learning Christianly

Many good answers may be offered. Consider giving the students an answer that will point them to the nature of God. Excellence in writing and grammar should be important to the Christian because it is important to the Christian's God. God brought the world into being through language (Gen. 1:3), He sustains it through language (Heb. 1:3), and He communicates how His creatures may be saved through language (John 1:1-18; 3:16). Throughout history, when humans have encountered God, they have responded by using language in a refined and skilled way. Many of the psalms are simply attempts to tell God in a skillful way how wonderful He is. The first two chapters in the Gospel of Luke record how several different people (some of them poor and uneducated) responded to God's announcement of salvation with poetry. Tell your students that they ought to learn to use language skillfully because they need to be able to tell others about what they believe. But then tell them that even if they were the only humans alive, they should still learn to use language skillfully because such learning pleases God. He writes and speaks well, and, since we are made in His image, we glorify Him and please Him when we write and speak well.

9-2 REVIEW THE SKILL

Label each subject S. Underline the verb form in parentheses that agrees with the subject.

1. The Lord *(requires, require)* obedience from Christians.
   - The Lord — S; *requires*

2. Righteous people *(is, are)* willing to be obedient.
   - people — S; *are*

3. Ron's sisters *(is, are)* eager to learn verses about obedience.
   - sisters — S; *are*

4. They *(teaches, teach)* Ron verses about obedience.
   - They — S; *teach*

5. Their father *(talks, talk)* about obedience in family devotions.
   - father — S; *talks*

6. They *(was, were)* sure that God would help them to be obedient.
   - They — S; *were*

7. God *(is, are)* pleased to help them learn obedience.
   - God — S; *is*

8. When we *(is, are)* obedient, we show our love for God.
   - we — S; *are*

9. Ron's mom *(quizzes, quiz)* him on his verses once a week.
   - mom — S; *quizzes*

10. Last week she *(was, were)* pleased when Ron recited every verse correctly.
    - she — S; *was*

Agreement with Indefinite Pronouns

Unlike many pronouns, indefinite pronouns do not have separate forms for subjective and objective case. They do, however, show number. Most indefinite pronouns are singular; some are plural; and some can be either singular or plural. An indefinite pronoun used as a subject must agree with the verb in the sentence.

> **Singular:** Everyone *likes* my mom's brownies.
> **Plural:** Many *like* her lemon pie even more.

page 93

Indefinite pronouns

page 200

Indefinite pronouns

Always Singular				
another	each	everything	neither	one
anybody	either	less	nobody	somebody
anyone	everybody	little	no one	someone
anything	everyone	much	nothing	something

Always Plural				
both	few	fewer	many	several

Singular or Plural					
all	any	more	most	none	some

Sometimes just knowing the meaning of an indefinite pronoun does not tell you whether the pronoun is singular or plural. In such cases you can tell whether the indefinite pronoun is singular or plural only by noticing the way it is used in the sentence.

Teaching Strategy: Introduction

Before beginning this lesson determine whether students need to review indefinite pronouns. For information on indefinite pronouns, see Chapter 4.

Teaching Strategy: Demonstration

Materials
- Peanuts (or candies or nonfood items such as beads)

Pass out at least three peanuts to each student. (If a student is allergic to peanuts, substitute another item.) Ask questions and make statements about the peanuts to elicit responses regarding whether the pronoun used is singular or plural. *(May I have one? Please give me several. I would like both.)* After using the obvious choices from the singular and plural indefinite pronoun chart on page 186, proceed to the less obvious pronouns. *(Each tastes better than the last. Another is a good idea.)* You can continue through the list of pronouns by telling students to pretend that each

peanut is a person. *(Someone needs me to take him for a walk.)* Encourage students to make connections between pronouns with similar endings *(one, someone, no one, everyone, anyone).*

Singular: All of the pie *is* gone.
Plural: All of the pieces *are* gone.

In the first example, *all* is singular (and takes the singular verb *is*) because it refers to just one thing—the pie. In the second example, however, *all* is plural (and takes the plural verb *are*) because it refers to several things—the pieces.

In spoken English, the preposition is often dropped: *all the pie.*

A prepositional phrase after an indefinite pronoun as a subject does not *change* the agreement of the subject and the verb; it *reveals* the number of the subject.

Some indefinite pronouns are plural; some are singular; some can be either singular or plural.

An indefinite pronoun used as a subject must agree in number with its verb.

9-3 PRACTICE THE SKILL

Label the subject S. Underline the verb form that agrees with the subject.

1. *S*
   Everyone in our astronomy class *(is, are)* eager to see the comet in March.

2. *S*
   Many of the students *(is, are)* going to bring either binoculars or telescopes.

3. *S*
   All of the students *(knows, know)* that seeing a comet is a unique experience. Natasha and Venika are especially excited about the comet.

4. *S*
   Neither *(plans, plan)* to miss the comet.

5. *S*
   Several students *(is, are)* interested in studying astronomy when they go to college.

6. *S*
   No one *(complains, complain)* about the idea of coming to school at nighttime.

7. *S*
   If someone *(brings, bring)* a pizza along, the trip will be even more enjoyable.

8. *S*
   Many *(thinks, think)* that this trip will be fun and educational.

9. *S*
   All of the comet *(is, are)* going to be clearly visible that night.

10. *S*
    Most of the students *(has, have)* seen Halley's comet, but this is the first comet that I have ever seen.

Teaching Strategy: Induction

Point out the chart of indefinite pronouns on page 186. After discussing the indefinite pronouns that are either always singular or always plural, tell students that there is also a group of indefinite pronouns that can be either singular or plural. Write the following sentences on the board or overhead transparency:

- Most of the horses are inside the fence.
- Most of the herd is ready to be moved.
- Some of the choir is present.
- Some of the boys are sick.

Ask students to draw conclusions about what makes the same indefinite pronoun singular in one sentence and plural in the other sentence.

Label each subject *S.* Underline the verb form in parentheses that agrees with the subject.

1. Everybody *(wants, want)* to look for seashells along the beach.

2. No one *(minds, mind)* getting up early in the morning to go looking for shells.

3. Few *(is, are)* interested in the clamshells that wash up on the shore in masses.

4. Fewer *(desires, desire)* getting stung by a jellyfish.

5. Somebody *(yells, yell)* in delight when he finds a big starfish.

6. At this beach, one *(does, do)* not need to go too far into the water to find shells.

7. Many *(finds, find)* beautiful shells at this beach.

8. Nobody *(likes, like)* to go away empty-handed.

9. All of the people *(was, were)* happy to find some seashells on the morning expedition.

10. Most *(likes, like)* the sand dollars and conch shells best.

page 5

Finding subjects and predicates

page 151

Conjunctions

page 10

Subjects and predicates in inverted order

Agreement with Compound Subjects

Making the verb agree with its subject can appear to be tricky if the subject is compound. However, the rules are actually very simple. If the two parts of the compound subject are joined by the conjunction *and,* the verb must be plural.

> **Plural:** Ruth *and* Esther *are* the two biblical books with a woman's name for a title.
> **Plural:** Montana *and* Wyoming *contain* parts of Yellowstone Park.

If the two parts of the compound subject are joined by the conjunction *or* or *nor,* the verb must agree with the subject closer to it.

> **Singular:** Hamburgers or *pizza is* on the menu tonight.
> **Plural:** Pizza or *hamburgers are* on the menu tonight.

If the compound subject joined by *or* or *nor* appears in a sentence with inverted order, the verb will still agree with the subject closer to it.

> **Singular:** *Is pizza* or hamburgers on the menu tonight?
> **Plural:** *Are hamburgers* or pizza on the menu tonight?

Teaching Strategy: Induction

Read the following sentences aloud to the students and ask them to identify what is similar about them: Justin and Quincy are friends. Cole and William recognize each other. Jeanette and Sue sing duets. *(All use the conjunction* and *in the subject and have plural verbs.)*

Now read the following sentences and ask what is similar and what is different about them: Sandwiches or a salad is for lunch. A salad or sandwiches are for lunch. The Caribbean or South American countries are popular for vacations. South American countries or the Caribbean is popular for vacations. *(All use the conjunction* or, *but the order of the two subjects is different, making the verb a different number.)* Elicit from the students some rules about compound subjects and their verbs. Use page 188 to discuss answers.

Evaluation

Instruct students to write sentences using compound subjects and indefinite pronouns. Encourage the students to use a variety of conjunctions. Assign a topic to help them get started. After they complete their sentences, ask students to trade papers with a classmate. Each student should check his classmate's sentences for correct subject-verb agreement. If he finds an error, the students should discuss the error and possible solutions.

IN SUMMARY

Compound subjects joined by *and* take a plural verb.

Compound subjects joined by *or* or *nor* take a verb that agrees in number with the subject closest to the verb.

9-5 PRACTICE THE SKILL

Label the subject *S*. Underline the verb form that agrees with the subject.

1. Young Orville and Wilbur Wright often *(plays, play)* with toy helicopters.

2. The boys or their father *(visits, visit)* the library regularly to obtain books about flying.

3. A book by Otto Lilienthal or books by Octave Chanute *(is, are)* among their favorites.

4. Neither Wilbur nor Orville *(graduates, graduate)* formally from high school.

5. Their bicycle business or their small newspaper company *(takes, take)* most of their time.

6. However, both Wilbur and Orville *(wants, want)* to build gliders someday.

7. A front rudder or different angles for the glider's wings *(presents, present)* new possibilities for flight.

8. The sand dunes and the high wind *(makes, make)* Kitty Hawk, North Carolina, a perfect place for gliding.

9. Finally, in December of 1903, Orville and Wilbur separately *(flies, fly)* a machine-powered airplane for the first time.

10. The Wright Brothers' development of accurate air pressure tables or their unrelenting experimentation *(is, are)* their most important contribution to man's ability to fly.

Subject-Verb Agreement   **189**

Enrichment

Materials

• Family photographs

Ask students to bring in a family photograph with several persons in it. Instruct them to write three sentences with compound subjects describing the picture. Direct students to trade photographs and papers and to evaluate them for correct subject-verb agreement.

REVIEW THE SKILL

Combine the two sentences, using a compound subject. Use the verb form that agrees with the subject of your sentence.

1. The crocodile is called a crocodilian.
   The alligator is called a crocodilian.

   The crocodile and the alligator are called crocodilians.

   _____

2. The students are confused about the differences between alligators and crocodiles.
   The teacher is confused about the differences between alligators and crocodiles.

   The students and the teacher are confused about the differences

   between alligators and crocodiles.

3. A crocodile lives at our local zoo.
   Two alligators live at our local zoo.

   A crocodile and two alligators live at our local zoo.

   _____

4. Are the alligators' snouts pointy?
   Or is the crocodile's snout pointy?

   Are the alligators' snouts or the crocodile's snout pointy?

   _____

5. Perhaps the alligators are more aggressive.
   Perhaps the crocodile is more aggressive.

   The alligators or the crocodile is more aggressive.

   _____

6. The alligators have long bodies and short legs.
   The crocodile has a long body and short legs.

   The alligators and the crocodile have long bodies and short legs.

   _____

7. The crocodile has one tooth longer than the other teeth.
   The alligators have one tooth longer than the other teeth.

   The crocodile and the alligators have one tooth longer than the other

   teeth.

8. Is the crocodile's long tooth visible?
   Are the alligators' long teeth visible?

   Is the crocodile's long tooth or the alligators' long teeth visible?

   _____

9. The alligator is similar to the crocodile.
   The crocodile is similar to the alligator.

   The alligator and the crocodile are similar.

   _____

10. Crocodiles lay eggs.
    Alligators lay eggs too.

    Crocodiles and alligators lay eggs.

    _____

Intervening Phrases, Predicate Nouns, and Inverted Order

Intervening Phrases

Sometimes we may lose track of which word in a sentence is the subject. For example, words that come between the subject and the verb may confuse us. Always find the true subject of the sentence in order to make the verb agree with it.

One common interrupter is a negative phrase. A negative phrase is a statement of contrast that often appears between the subject and the verb. The verb must agree in number with the subject, not the words in the negative phrase.

> The *racket,* not the tennis balls, *is* new.

The subject of this sentence is the singular noun *racket;* therefore, the verb must also be singular. The plural noun *balls* is part of the negative phrase; it is not the subject of the sentence.

Another common interrupter is a prepositional phrase. If a prepositional phrase comes between the subject and the verb, it does not affect the agreement of the subject and the verb. (Remember, though, that for some indefinite pronouns the prepositional phrase clarifies the agreement.)

> The two *books* on the shelf *show* pictures of Hawaii.
> The *pictures* in the first book *are* colorful.

The object of the preposition can never be the subject of the sentence. The verb must agree in number with the subject, not the object of the preposition.

page 144

Prepositional phrases

Teaching Strategy: Introduction

Remind the students that they already know about inverted order from Chapter 1. If necessary, review this concept with students.

Teaching Strategy: Discussion

Explain briefly the problems in the identification and agreement of subjects and verbs caused by intervening phrases, predicate nouns, and inverted order. Then tell the students to pretend to be doctors who will diagnose potential problems with three sentences. Write the three potential problems and the following sentences on the board or an overhead transparency:

- The dogs, not the pony, perform in the center ring.
- There are several items to be discussed.
- Miriam's gift to the class was cookies and hot chocolate.

Ask the students to match the problems to the sentences.

Predicate Noun of a Different Number

Sometimes the predicate noun and the subject do not have the same number; one is singular, and the other is plural. The verb must agree with the subject, not with the predicate noun.

> His *donation* to the party *was* apples from the family orchard.

The verb *was* agrees with the singular subject *donation*. The number of the predicate noun *apples* does not change the agreement of the subject and the verb.

Inverted Order

Sometimes the verb comes before the subject in a sentence. When this happens we say that the subject is delayed. For example, the word *there* is almost never a subject, but it sometimes appears at the beginning of the sentence in the usual place of a subject. In these sentences the subject follows the verb, and the verb must agree with the subject, not with the word *there*.

Singular: There *is* one *earth.*
Plural: There *are* many other *planets.*

Remember that most interrogative sentences and some declarative sentences are written so that the verb comes before the subject. Be sure to find the subject of the sentence so that you can make the subject and verb agree.

Plural: Where *are* the *ingredients* for tonight's dinner?
Plural: On the counter *sit* the *groceries.*

page 55
Linking verbs and predicate nouns

page 10
Subjects and predicates in inverted order

IN SUMMARY

Negative phrases do not affect subject-verb agreement.
Prepositional phrases do not affect subject-verb agreement.
Predicate nouns do not affect subject-verb agreement.
Inverted sentence order does not affect subject-verb agreement.

9-7 PRACTICE THE SKILL

Label the subject *S*. Underline the verb form that agrees with the subject.

1. *(Is, Are)* the Ruiz family planning to go camping this summer?

2. There *(was, were)* the possibility that they were not going to go.

3. Marco and his brother, not the entire family, *(is, are)* going camping for a week.

4. Their idea of a good camping trip *(is, are)* a week in the mountains with few modern conveniences.

5. The maps on the table clearly *(shows, show)* the way the brothers will go to the campsite and various hiking trails throughout the park.

Evaluation

Encourage students to examine the newspaper for examples of correct and incorrect subject-verb agreement, especially when the sentences include intervening phrases, predicate nouns, and inverted order. Announce that each student who brings to class a certain number of examples specified by you will receive extra credit.

Enrichment: Speech Link

Questions and Answers

Invite a guest speaker to class. Tell students in advance the speaker's identity and topic. Prior to the speaker's arrival, students should write three to five questions that they wish to ask the speaker about his topic. Instruct each student to check his questions for correct subject-verb agreement. Allow the guest speaker five to ten minutes of class time for his presentation. Allow time for students to ask some of their questions.

One on One: Take your student to interview an expert in some field that interests him (a pilot at the local airport, a librarian, a merchant). Instruct your student to prepare a list of questions using correct subject-verb agreement. After he interviews the expert, he should write a report about what he learned. Instruct your student to check his paper for correct subject-verb agreement. Allow him to present his report orally to an audience of family members or neighbors.

6. "Pietro, where *(is, are)* the sleeping bags?" Marco asked his brother.

7. "There *(is, are)* sleeping bags in the attic," Pietro replied.

8. The sleeping bags in the far corner of the attic *(belongs, belong)* to Marco and Pietro.

9. Their mother's contribution to the preparations *(was, were)* two coolers of the boys' favorite foods and beverages.

10. Their younger brother Felipe, not their sisters, *(wishes, wish)* that he could go camping too.

 9-8 REVIEW THE SKILL

Label each subject S. Underline the verb form in parentheses that agrees with the subject.

1. There *(is, are)* many different utensils for food.

2. *(Is, Are)* you aware of some of them?

3. Of course, the fork, not the hands, *(is, are)* most popular in North American culture.

4. In some cultures, however, a person often *(eats, eat)* with his hands.

5. The utensil of choice for many Asian people *(is, are)* the chopstick.

6. A pair of chopsticks *(serves, serve)* well—if you know how to use chopsticks!

7. For the inexperienced diner, the chopsticks, not the food, *(is, are)* the problem.

8. Sometimes servers in an Oriental restaurant *(gives, give)* diners practice chopsticks.

9. Into the air *(flies, fly)* bits of food.

10. Remember, practice with the utensils *(makes, make)* perfect.

A. Label the subject *S*.

B. Underline each verb.

C. If the subject and verb do not agree, write the correct verb form in the blank.

D. Write *C* if the sentence is correct. Be prepared to explain your answer.

___C___ 1. Angels have an important role in God's plan for humanity.

___C___ 2. Michael and Gabriel are the names of two specific angels.

___has___ 3. Michael, of all the angels, have the power of God against Satan and the fallen angels.

___shows___ 4. Everyone show interest in Michael's final victory over Satan and his fallen angels.

___praise___ 5. In the Book of Revelation, the angels often praises the Lord around His throne.

___are___ 6. There is several different terms for angels in the Bible.

___have___ 7. A few of Gabriel's jobs has been recorded in God's Word.

___does___ 8. As with all the angels, Gabriel do his jobs in obedience.

___is___ 9. Gabriel's announcement are good tidings to Zachariah and his wife, Elisabeth.

___is___ 10. The function of the angels are obedience to God.

TAKING NOTES

My son, keep my words, and lay up my commandments with thee. . . . Bind them upon thy fingers, write them upon the table of thine heart.
Proverbs 7:1, 3

Do these verses mean that someone took notes on a sermon like we do today? Not necessarily. However, we have a written record of the wisdom that Solomon gave. Solomon says that his sayings are for the good of the hearer and will profit the hearer spiritually and physically. Note taking helps the hearer focus on the sermon and enables the hearer to remember the ideas for later reflection and incorporation into his life. Solomon commands that the listener pay attention to the Holy Spirit–inspired words of Scripture.

Your Turn

Take notes on a Sunday morning or evening sermon.

Overview of Writing Process

Planning—(Not appropriate to assignment)

Drafting—Taking notes on a sermon

Revising—Evaluating how to make notes more effective

Publishing—Recapping the sermon for a fellow student (optional)

Objectives

Students will

1. take notes on a sermon.

2. evaluate the effectiveness of their notes in helping them remember the sermon.

Taking Notes

Lesson Support

Support Materials CD
Rubrics—p. 113

Scriptural Application

Ask a volunteer to read Proverbs 7:1 and 3 aloud. Remind the students that taking notes in church can help them to remember the biblical lessons they learn from their pastors' sermons.

Introduction

Ask students whether they can remember their pastors' sermon topic from last Sunday. If anyone responds, commend him and ask what helped him to remember that sermon. Instruct the students to read the opening paragraph on page 104 and to identify the two reasons that note taking is important. *(helps the hearer focus and enables him to remember)* Challenge the students to become good note takers. Explain that note taking helps focus their attention and helps them process information from the pastor.

Planning Strategies

Encourage students to arrive early at the service and to sit near the front where they can see and hear the pastor. Distractions can hamper the students' ability to listen well.

Briefly discuss the principles of organization in note taking. Point out that not every sermon is highly structured but that note taking should always organize the material being presented as efficiently as possible.

Planning

Gather the necessary materials. Choose paper that is large enough to allow you to structure your notes effectively. A notebook provides a place to store your notes as well as a continuing record of what you are learning.

Prepare your heart. Don't fidget or daydream but focus on the sermon. Ponder what God will say to you through His Word and the preacher.

Listen attentively to the speaker. Be aware of content and organizational clues. Speakers often use cues to help their listeners follow the sermon.

- Transitions such as *next* or *finally*
- Enumerated points such as *first, second,* or *last*
- Alliterated main points
  God's Providence
  God's Presence
  God's Purpose
- Similar structures
  To bring men and women to Christ
  To conform us to the image of Christ
  To deliver us from our flesh
  To empower us to fulfill the ministry of Christ

Drafting

Record information about the sermon. On a new sheet of paper or in your notebook, write the speaker's name, date, text, title, or topic.

Write quickly. Try to record the ideas that the speaker gives rather than the actual words he uses. Taking notes is not the same as taking dictation.

Write down the skeleton of the sermon as a simple outline. Distinguish main points and subpoints. Use key words or phrases, not full sentences.

  I. Main point
   A. Subpoint
   B. Subpoint
  II. Main point

Write down ideas that are new to you or that apply to you in a specific way. Use key words that will help you to remember the important ideas.

Revising

Review your notes. While the message is still fresh in your mind, read your notes. Fill in any additional information that will clarify the sermon.

Make a clean copy of your notes to save. If your notes are messy from your effort to write quickly, copy them neatly onto a fresh sheet of paper.

Publishing

Exchange your notes with another student. Encourage him to comment on the content of your outline and on the notes you have taken.

Include your sermon notes in your writing folder. Use your notes to encourage you or to challenge you to search the Scriptures diligently.

Subject-Verb Agreement 195

Drafting Strategy

Encourage the students to write each note on a separate line and to use key words and phrases rather than entire sentences. Remind them to include enough information to clarify the context later.

Revising Strategy

Encourage the students to make a clean copy of their notes, incorporating any changes or additions they have made as they reviewed their notes.

Publishing Strategies

Allow each student to choose a partner and to recap the sermon he heard for his partner, using only the notes he took.

Instruct the students to evaluate their notes. Ask them to write a sentence answer to each of these questions and to record their answers at the end of the notes.

- Which point in the sermon impressed me the most?

- Which point seemed least clear to me as I read back over my notes?

- How can I take notes more effectively next time?

Scriptural Application

Remind students of the consequences of not remembering God's words. Read the warning God gave to the children of Israel about forgetting to keep His commandments (Deut. 8:11, 19-20).

Evaluation

For help in grading this assignment, see "Grading Writing Assignments" (p. x) and Rubric 9 (Support Materials CD, p.113).

PRONOUN-ANTECEDENT AGREEMENT

Lesson Support

Student Text

Chapter Review 10—pp. 415-16

Support Materials CD

Warm-Ups—pp. 21-22
Teaching Helps—p. 37
Concept Reinforcements—p. 73
Bulletin Boards—p. 209

Teaching Strategy: Introduction

Review the definitions of *pronoun* and *antecedent* from Chapter 4. Remind the students of the mirror analogy in Chapter 4. Pronouns are the reflections, and nouns are the real image. Direct the students' attention to the photograph and discussion on pages 196-97.

Do you feel as if you are seeing double when you look at this photo? A reflection is produced when light waves are thrown back from a surface. Before mirrors were invented, people looked at their reflections in places like pools and polished metal.

Sometimes there are reflections in sentences as well. When a noun is replaced later in the sentence by a pronoun, that pronoun throws back meaning the way the surface of the water throws back the image of the trees. Writers are responsible to make pronoun "reflections" mirror the noun exactly.

Agreement with Personal Pronouns

Just as subjects and verbs agree in number, pronouns and their antecedents also agree in **number.** If the antecedent is a singular noun, the pronoun referring to it must also be singular. Pronouns, unlike verbs, often show gender. In other words, some pronouns are masculine, some are feminine, and some are neuter. Pronouns and their antecedents must agree in **gender** as well as number. If the antecedent is a masculine noun, the pronoun referring to it must also be masculine.

 The Latin prefix *ante* means "before," and the Latin verb *cedere* means "to go." The antecedent of a pronoun "goes before" it.

Where is *Javon? He* is late for class.

The pronoun *he* is replacing the noun *Javon.* The antecedent is a singular, masculine noun; therefore, the pronoun is also singular and masculine.

What should you do if the antecedent does not show gender? If the antecedent clearly refers to a person, use a singular, masculine pronoun.

A *student* should always bring *his* textbook to class.

Some nouns, especially those referring to animals, can be neuter, masculine, or feminine, depending on the context of the sentence. For example, is the noun *bear* masculine or feminine or both or neither? Notice how the gender of the pronoun changes in the following examples.

The *bear* slept in *its* den.
The *bear* protects *her* cubs.

page 84

Pronouns and antecedents

page 86

Personal pronouns

Pronoun-Antecedent Agreement **197**

Teaching Strategy: Discussion

Write these sentences on the board or overhead: *Where is Javon? He is late for class.* Direct the students' attention to the first example sentences on page 197. Ask these questions: What is the pronoun? *(He)* What is the antecedent that the pronoun is replacing? *(Javon)* Point out that the pronoun *he* is the reflection of the noun *Javon.* Explain that a pronoun must agree with its antecedent. Ask how they know to use *he* to replace *Javon. (Both words are singular and masculine.)*

Teaching Strategy: Discussion

Ask the students which pronoun should replace an antecedent that does not show gender. Refer to the next example sentence on page 197: *A student should always bring his textbook to class.* Explain that if the antecedent clearly refers to a person, a singular, masculine pronoun replaces the noun. Discuss the last example sentences on page 197: *The bear slept in its den. The bear protects her cubs.* Ask the students why two different pronouns were used to replace the antecedent *bear. (The first sen-*

tence does not show gender. The second sentence indicates that the bear is female.) Continue discussing the examples on page 198 of antecedents that are joined by conjunctions. Remind the students that pronouns must agree in number with their antecedents.

The first sentence does not show gender. The author does not indicate whether the sleeping bear is female or male. The pronoun *her* in the second sentence, however, tells us that the bear is the cubs' mother. Always consider the meaning you are trying to convey with your sentence when choosing a pronoun to replace an antecedent. If the antecedent is compound, look at the conjunction joining the parts of the antecedent. If the nouns are joined by *and,* the pronoun must be plural. If the nouns are joined by *or* or *nor,* the pronoun must agree with whichever noun is closer to it.

Plural: Brittany *and* Joseph welcomed *their* baby sister Erica.

Singular: The monkeys *or* the *elephant* will appear in the center ring for *its* finale.

Plural: The elephant *or* the *monkeys* will appear in the center ring for *their* finale.

Notice that the pronouns agree in both number and gender with their antecedents.

In Summary

Pronouns must always agree in **number** and in **gender** with their antecedents.

10-1 PRACTICE THE SKILL

Fill in each blank with the pronoun that agrees with its antecedent.

its 1. For over a thousand years, people have admired the cat for _?_ beauty and grace.

his 2. If a person killed a cat in ancient Egypt, that person had to pay with _?_ life.

their 3. The Greeks and Romans admired cats for _?_ ability to kill rodents.

his 4. In China or Japan, a writer often made the cat one of _?_ favorite subjects.

its 5. During the Middle Ages, people killed thousands of cats. They distrusted the cat because of _?_ association with evil.

their 6. The death of so many cats may have been an indirect cause of the Black Death, to which many people lost _?_ lives.

its   7. The disease caused _?_ victim's family and friends much sorrow.

its   8. The Black Death left _?_ impression on nearly everyone, rich or poor.

their   9. Cats caught the rodents that carried the Black Death. Slowly cats regained _?_ popularity.

their   10. Today, one cat or several cats can live happily and comfortably with _?_ owner.

10·2   REVIEW THE SKILL

Fill in each blank with a pronoun that agrees with its antecedent.

her   1. In 1775 Maria Theresa of Austria gave birth to _?_ fifteenth child, Maria Antonia.

his   2. Louis XV of France agreed to the marriage between Maria Antonia and _?_ son Louis.

their   3. Marie Antoinette and Louis became queen and king of France four years after _?_ wedding.

her   4. Marie Antoinette rarely allowed the serious affairs of court to enter _?_ mind.

its   5. New clothes or an expensive piece of jewelry often made _?_ appearance in Marie Antoinette's chambers.

his   6. Louis XVI soon proved inept in handling the serious financial problems of _?_ country.

their   7. On July 14, 1789, the French people led a revolt against _?_ government.

their   8. They made Louis XVI and Marie Antoinette _?_ prisoners.

his   9. Members of the aristocracy or any subject loyal to the monarchy could be sent to _?_ death instantly.

her   10. On October 16, 1793, Marie Antoinette died as _?_ husband had, on the guillotine.

page 93

Indefinite pronouns

page 186

Indefinite pronouns

Agreement with Indefinite Pronouns

Sometimes an indefinite pronoun is the antecedent of a personal pronoun. The personal pronoun must be singular if the indefinite pronoun it refers to is singular, or plural if the indefinite is plural. The personal pronoun always has the same number (singular or plural) as its antecedent.

Singular: *Each* has *his* bicycle.
Plural: *Both* have *their* bicycles.

If the indefinite pronoun is one that can be either singular or plural, look at the context of the sentence to determine its number. If the indefinite pronoun refers to only one thing, the personal pronoun should be singular. If the indefinite pronoun refers to more than one thing, the personal pronoun should be plural.

Singular: *Some* of the painting has lost *its* color.
Plural: *Some* of the paintings remain in *their* original frames.

Indefinite pronouns themselves do not show gender, but the context of the sentence may indicate a gender. Choose a personal pronoun that will agree with its indefinite pronoun antecedent in both number and gender.

Feminine: *One* of the girls has brought *her* textbook.
Neuter: *One* of the kittens has bent *its* whiskers.

What should you do if the context of the sentence does not indicate a specific gender but does clearly refer to people rather than animals or objects? If the indefinite pronoun is singular, use a singular, masculine pronoun. Do not use a plural personal pronoun to refer to a singular indefinite pronoun.

Wrong: *Everyone* clapped *their* hands at the end of the performance.
Right: *Everyone* clapped *his* hands at the end of the performance.

Refer to the chart of indefinite pronouns on page 186 in the subject-verb agreement chapter if you are unsure whether a certain indefinite pronoun is singular or plural.

IN SUMMARY

A personal pronoun that refers to an indefinite pronoun must agree in number with the indefinite pronoun.

A personal pronoun that refers to an indefinite pronoun must agree in gender with the context of the sentence.

Use the singular masculine pronoun to refer to an indefinite singular pronoun if the sentence does not indicate a specific gender.

Teaching Strategy: Discussion

Refer to the example sentences on page 200. Explain that indefinite pronouns do not have antecedents, but an indefinite pronoun can be an antecedent for a personal pronoun. Review the information about "Agreement with Indefinite Pronouns" on page 186 in Chapter 9. Point out the charts that show indefinite pronouns that are always singular, indefinite pronouns that are always plural, and indefinite pronouns that can be singular or plural. Return to page 200 to continue discussing

the example sentences. Remind the students that indefinite pronouns themselves do not show gender, but the context of the sentence sometimes indicates a gender. Explain that we sometimes must rely on the context of the sentence in order to determine how the pronoun should agree with the indefinite pronoun that is functioning as the antecedent.

Scriptural Application

Ask a student to read aloud I Corinthians 14:33. Direct the students' attention to the statement "God is not the author of confu-

sion." Explain that avoiding confusion by learning to speak and to write correctly is a God-honoring way to be a testimony to others.

Reinforcement

Use Teaching Helps page 37 (Support Materials CD) to review both subject-verb agreement and pronoun-antecedent agreement.

Underline the indefinite pronoun. Underline the personal pronoun in parentheses that agrees with it.

1. <u>All</u> of the students like to play *(her, <u>their</u>)* favorite outdoor games on warm, sunny days.

2. <u>One</u> of the boys persuaded the others to help *(<u>him</u>, them)* start a softball game.

3. <u>Each</u> brought *(<u>his</u>, their)* own glove.

4. <u>Several</u> of the girls decided to begin *(her, <u>their</u>)* own softball game.

5. <u>Either</u> the boys or the girls could have the field for *(his, <u>their</u>)* game.

6. <u>Some</u> of the boys suggested that the girls join *(him, <u>them</u>)*.

7. <u>Most</u> of the girls decided that *(she, <u>they</u>)* would challenge the boys.

8. <u>Someone</u> on the boys' team thought that *(<u>his</u>, their)* team had won.

9. <u>All</u> of the girls agreed that the victory was *(hers, <u>theirs</u>)*.

10. At the end of the game, <u>everyone</u> agreed that *(<u>he</u>, they)* had enjoyed playing the game.

Enrichment: Speech Link

Nominations for Agreement

Tell the students that they will hold a mock election. You will be taking nominations for office. Announce that each student will interview another student and then write and deliver a three- to five-sentence nomination speech for that candidate. Nomination speeches should exhibit proper pronoun-antecedent agreement. You may wish to divide the class into small groups; instruct each group to write a nomination for one of its group members.

One on One: Instruct the student to write a nomination for the guest speaker from the previous chapter.

Underline the indefinite pronoun. Underline the personal pronoun in parentheses that agrees with it.

1. In the Middle Ages <u>many</u> of the boys followed (*his, <u>their</u>*) fathers' examples and became knights.

2. Aspiring to be a knight, <u>each</u> began (*<u>his</u>, their*) training at age seven.

3. <u>All</u> started (*its, <u>their</u>*) training by serving noblemen as pages.

4. <u>No one</u> serious about becoming a knight took (*its, <u>his</u>*) training lightly.

5. <u>Each</u> of the dubbing ceremonies was recognized for (*<u>its</u>, their*) importance.

6. <u>Many</u> of the young men spent the night before (*his, <u>their</u>*) dubbing ceremonies in prayer at the church.

7. To become a knight, <u>someone</u> swore allegiance to (*its, <u>his</u>*) king, country, and the church.

8. <u>Some</u> of the knights lost (*his, <u>their</u>*) lives in battle.

9. As a knight, <u>one</u> had (*<u>his</u>, their*) own coat of arms, which helped identify him on the battleground.

10. <u>Most</u> of the knights believed (*his, <u>their</u>*) participation in the Crusades, also called the Holy Wars, pleased God.

Fill in the blank with the appropriate pronoun.

_it_ 1. Coffee is one of the world's most popular beverages, and the United States consumes more of _?_ than does any other country.

their 2. Brazil and Colombia are known for _?_ high production of coffee beans.

himself 3. A legend says that anyone who eats coffee berries or leaves can keep _?_ awake.

them 4. In Arabia some used coffee as a medicine, probably because the drink made _?_ feel more alert.

them 5. Coffee berries grow best in a tropical climate, where most are handpicked by the people who grow _?_ .

their 6. First, workers pick berries from coffee plants; then machines separate the berries' pulp from _?_ seeds.

them 7. Once machines discard the outer layers and keep the seeds, the workers are ready to roast _?_ .

they 8. The beans are roasted for sixteen to seventeen minutes, during which time _?_ will reach approximately nine hundred degrees.

them 9. A vacuum tin or paper bags of coffee beans will be sent to stores where grocers will put _?_ on the shelf.

_it_ 10. Shoppers buy coffee beans or preground coffee and brew _?_ at home.

Pronoun-Antecedent Agreement   **203**

Most of the sentences in the short story below contain errors in subject-verb agreement or pronoun-antecedent agreement. Correct the eleven errors.

No one fully understand the truth about the Trojan War. Much has been written about the conflict, but some of the facts is obscured. Sometimes the legends are true; sometimes it is false. The facts and legends seem to say this: for ten years the Greek army attacks the city of Troy but cannot conquer them. Neither the Greek army nor the Trojans is willing to give in. Each side claims various victories for themselves. In one battle the Trojans receive aid from the Ethiopians and the Amazons. Finally the Greeks devise a plan to defeat its enemies. They build a giant wooden horse and place it outside the walls of the city of Troy. Inside the horse sit part of the Greek army. Believing that the horse will bring protection, the Trojans pull them inside the city. During the night Odysseus and the Greek army emerges from the horse and conquers the sleeping city. Troy is burned, and the Greeks are victorious. To this day the term *Trojan horse* means something or someone used to deceive or sabotage an enemy.

No one fully understands the truth about the Trojan War. Much has been written about the conflict, but some of the facts are obscured. Sometimes the legends are true; sometimes they are false. The facts and legends seem to say this: for ten years the Greek army attacks the city of Troy but cannot conquer it. Neither the Greek army nor the Trojans are willing to give in. Each side claims various victories for itself. In one battle the Trojans receive aid from the Ethiopians and the Amazons. Finally the Greeks devise a plan to defeat their enemies. They build a giant wooden horse and place it outside the walls of the city of Troy. Inside the horse sits part of the Greek army. Believing that the horse will bring protection, the Trojans pull it inside the city. During the night Odysseus and the

Greek army emerge from the horse and conquer the sleeping city. Troy is

burned, and the Greeks are victorious. To this day the term Trojan horse *means*

something or someone used to deceive or sabotage an enemy.

_____

_____

_____

_____

DEFINING TERMS

Now faith is the substance of things hoped for, the evidence of things not seen.
Hebrews 11:1

"How do you spell —— ?" "Look it up in the dictionary!" This scenario is familiar to most of us. An entry in a dictionary offers much more than just the spelling of a word and the appropriate definitions, however. Among other things you can also find

- etymologies or the backgrounds of words.
  (The term southpaw *comes from the practice in baseball of arranging the diamond with the batter facing east to avoid the afternoon sun. A left-handed pitcher facing west would therefore have his pitching arm toward the south of the diamond.)*

- pronunciation guides.
  (Lou Gehrig's name is pronounced gér´ ig, with the e *like* pet *and the* i *like* pit.*)

- biographical information.
  (Billy Sunday was originally a professional baseball player [1883-91] who began preaching in 1896 and became a Presbyterian minister in 1903.)

- geographic location.
  (Cooperstown is a residential village of east central New York west-south-west of Schenectady. The National Baseball Hall of Fame is located there.)

- illustrations of selected entries.
  (The dictionary has a photo of Babe Ruth taken in the 1930s as well as a photo of an aerial view of a baseball diamond.)

Your Turn

Write a creative definition that goes beyond the dictionary; expand your thinking to other associations of the word you chose to define.

Planning

Determine which word to define. Choose one of the following terms: loyalty, writer, baseball, or family.

Begin with the dictionary. Look up the meaning of the word. Then write the definition of your word on a piece of paper.

Defining Terms

Lesson Support

Support Materials CD
Rubrics—p. 114

Scriptural Application

Ask the students what the word *hope* means. *(Answers will vary.)* Allow a brief discussion and then invite a volunteer to read Hebrews 11:1 aloud. Discuss the meaning of *hope* as it is used in Scripture. Knowing the full definition of *hope* helps us to understand passages that carry the concept of confident expectation, such as Titus 2:11-13. Encourage students with the knowledge that the hope of salvation in Christ is sure.

Introduction

Ask the students whether they have ever heard someone use a word incorrectly to mean something it doesn't. *(Answers will vary.)* Share this quotation attributed to the philosopher and writer Voltaire: "If you would converse with me, you must first define your terms." Discuss the importance of well-defined terms. If people chose to use their own meanings for terms, then conversations would never truly take place—each person would understand the words differently. In any situation where words are important, whether spoken or written, it is important for the speaker to define his terms. Emphasize the usefulness of the dictionary and direct the students' attention to the first paragraph on page 205.

Consider the reality of hope as mentioned in Proverbs 13:12.

The first definition was originally a children's joke, and one can certainly see the humor in the play on the word *outstanding.* A farmer spends most of his life working in his fields, and because the food he grows is crucial to life, he should be honored for his work.

In the second definition much can be done with the concept of *spice.* Spices add flavor and interest to cooking and make us enjoy our food. So variety adds interest to life and helps us enjoy it.

Consider both the denotative and connotative meanings of the word. The denotative meaning is the exact meaning found in the dictionary. The connotative meaning is the dictionary meaning along with emotional meanings associated with it.

Expand your thinking to other associations of the word. At this point, write down the connotative meanings of the word. For example, consider the word *hope.* If you look up *hope* in the dictionary, you will probably find a definition that includes the idea of fulfilled expectations. But hope is not always as certain as the dictionary implies. We are all familiar with this idea: we hope that it won't rain out the ball game; we hope there will be ice cream for dessert; we hope that we will get what we want for our birthdays. These connotations imply a type of wishful thinking. A really good definition of *hope* would include both the denotative meaning of the word and its associated, or connotative, meanings.

Include the *who, what,* and *why* of the word. The answers to these questions will be part of a complete definition. For example "Who uses this term?" and "Why is it an important word?"

Drafting

Develop your definition of the word. Incorporate ideas from the dictionary definition as well as the connotative ideas that you have found.

Put your definition into standard definition format. Remember that the correct pattern is subject, linking verb, and then predicate noun or predicate adjective. Be careful to use good grammar. A good definition of *hope* might be this:

> A hope is a wish that may or may not carry expectations. It all depends on the source of hope. If someone hopes for something that God has promised, he fully expects it to happen. If someone bases his wish on luck or chance, his hope carries little comfort. Therefore, it is important for the Christian to hope for things that God approves or promises. Then his course will be nearer to trusting than to gambling.

Revising

Reread your definition. Determine whether there are ways to improve or clarify your ideas. Did you include both denotative and connotative ideas? Did you answer all the *who, what,* and *why* questions? If not, revise now.

Check your definition for precision. Is your choice of words exact? Is your definition clear? Does your definition convey the meaning that you intended for it to convey?

Proofread for correctness. Be sure that your sentence structure is accurate and clear. Check your definition for correct spelling and punctuation too.

Publishing

Display your definition. Post your definition as part of a class bulletin board. Be prepared to respond to any comments from your peers regarding your definition.

Make a mini-dictionary. Arrange the definitions that your class has written alphabetically. Then publish the definitions as a booklet.

Teaching Strategy

Ask students to give a **denotative** definition of *hope. (to wish for something with expectation of its fulfillment)* Ask the students what **connotations** (associations) the denotative definition leaves out. *(the variations in probability of receiving the thing hoped for)* Refer to "Between the Innings" on page 207 and use the word pairs from the top margin note on page 206 to help students see how connotations can shade meanings of words.

Planning Strategy

Instruct each student to choose one of the words listed on page 205 to define. Remind the students to find a dictionary definition first and then to brainstorm for other connotations and associations.

Drafting Strategy

Lead the students through the steps for drafting a definition. Caution them to avoid "is when" and "is where" constructions in their definitions. Discuss the format and content of the sample definition of *hope.*

Revising Strategy

Peer Response

Direct each student to trade his definition with a partner and to evaluate his partner's work. Encourage each student to consider his peer's comments and to revise his definition accordingly before submitting it.

Publishing Strategy

Encourage the students to include their definitions in their writing folders.

Shades of Gray

Between Innings

"When *I* use a word, . . . it means just what I choose it to mean—neither more nor less." Do you agree with this opinion? Or do we all have to agree on what words mean?

Notice the difference between these two statements: *The Eagles won their game last night. The Eagles triumphed in their game last night.* In the dictionary, *win* and *triumph* mean the same thing: to gain a victory. But these two words have different *connotations.* Which one sounds bigger? Which one sounds better? A triumph seems more dramatic and important than a win.

A connotation is a meaning in addition to the dictionary meaning. What would you think if someone described you as dressing *simply?* You would probably consider that remark a compliment. But what if he said you dressed *plainly?* Not as good, right? Both words mean that the style of dress is uncomplicated and uncluttered, but the first has a much more positive connotation.

To write clearly, you must be aware not only of the dictionary meanings of your words but also of the connotations of your words. Otherwise, you might seem as self-centered as the speaker quoted in the first paragraph. The speaker was Humpty Dumpty in *Alice's Adventures in Wonderland*—and we all know what happened to him.

- The snow fell on the city. *(neutral)*
- The snow buried the city. *(negative)*
- The snow gently blanketed the city. *(positive)*

News broadcasters are trained to write unbiased statements. Read the following three sentences to your students and point out the differences.

- The new candidate spoke to 500 people in the Civic Auditorium, which holds 2000 people. *(neutral)*
- The refreshing candidate spoke to citizens of our community in a prominent, large auditorium. *(positive)*
- The candidate, a novice, spoke to a sparse audience in a near-empty auditorium. *(negative)*

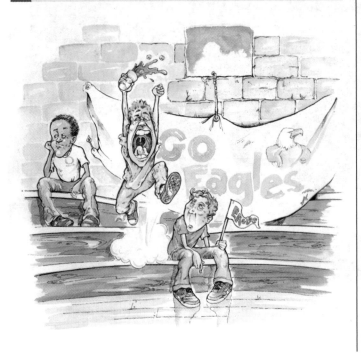

Pronoun-Antecedent Agreement   **207**

Evaluation

For help in grading this assignment, see "Grading Writing Assignments" (p. x) and Rubric 10 (Support Materials CD, p. 114).

Enrichment

Discuss definitions that go beyond the dictionary. Write the following definitions for display: *A farmer is a man outstanding in his field. Variety is the spice of life.* Use the margin notes on page 206 to discuss each definition with the students, pointing out the irony, humor, and imagery.

Enrichment

Direct the students to substitute a synonym for one of the main words in familiar sayings such as "Honesty is the best policy." Discuss how the switch changes the meaning.

Enrichment

Encourage students to find definitions of *faith* in the Bible.

PRONOUN USAGE

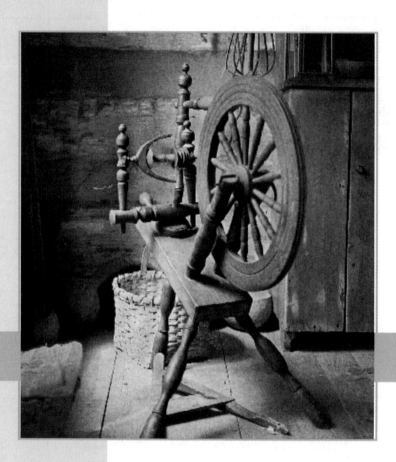

Objectives

Students will

1. use the subjective case for pronouns functioning as subjects and predicate nouns.

2. apply the same rules for compound subjects and predicate nouns as for single subjects and predicate nouns.

3. use the objective case for pronouns functioning as direct objects, indirect objects, and objects of prepositions.

4. apply the same rules for compound objects as for single objects.

5. distinguish between the uses of certain troublesome pronouns, such as *we/us* and *who/whom.*

6. use possessive pronoun/contraction pairs correctly.

7. use correct personal pronoun courtesy order.

8. use reflexive and intensive pronouns correctly.

9. revise sentences to eliminate the non-standard forms *hisself* and *theirselves.*

10. revise sentences to eliminate unclear pronoun reference.

Lesson Support

Student Text

Chapter Review 11—pp. 417-18

Support Materials CD

Warm-Ups—pp. 23-24
Concept Reinforcements—pp. 74-77
Bulletin Boards—p. 210

Yarn made by beginning spinners is often lumpy and so thin in places it is likely to break. Experienced spinners make yarn that is even and smooth. The reason for the difference is that experienced spinners know how to keep the right degree of tension between the wool they hold and the yarn being wound by the wheel.

Writers spin words into sentences, controlling the thread of thought. Careless writers can make lumps in their sentences. For example, "David told John that he thought his bike was stolen." The lump in that sentence is that we don't know whose bike was stolen. The antecedent of *his* could be either David or John. The thread of thought breaks.

Using Subjective and Objective Case Pronouns Correctly

Singular

	Subjective Case	Objective Case	Possessive Case
First Person	I	me	my, mine
Second Person	you	you	your, yours
Third Person			
neuter	it	it	its
masculine	he	him	his
feminine	she	her	her, hers

Plural

	Subjective Case	Objective Case	Possessive Case
First Person	we	us	our, ours
Second Person	you	you	your, yours
Third Person	they	them	their, theirs

page 86

Personal pronouns

Pronouns that are used as predicate nouns are in the subjective case because they refer to the subject of the sentence.

The chart shows the four characteristics of all personal pronouns: person, number, gender, and case. This unit will teach you how to use the different forms of these pronouns correctly.

Using Subjective Case Correctly

Pronouns that are subjects and predicate nouns must be in the **subjective case.**

Subject: *Wendell Willkie* fought against the New Deal.

S   InV
He fought against the New Deal.

Teaching Strategy: Introduction

Ask the students to turn to the personal pronoun chart on page 86 (Chapter 4), or display it on the overhead projector. Review with the students the four characteristics of personal pronouns: person, number, gender, and case.

Teaching Strategy: Discussion

Discuss "Using Subjective Case Correctly" on pages 209-10. Emphasize that only subjective case pronouns can fill the subject and predicate noun positions in sentences. Discuss the example sentences. Ask students to volunteer their own example sentences for class discussion.

Predicate Noun: In 1940 the candidates for president were *Willkie* and Roosevelt.

         S   **LV PN**
In 1940 the candidates for president were *he* and
  PN
Roosevelt.

In informal speech this rule is not always followed. The most common change is saying "It's me" for "It is I." Because "It's me" has become so common, usage experts tell us that "It's me" is acceptable to most people in informal speech. "It is I" would be the best usage for, say, a secretary who speaks with strangers. You should use it in writing and in formal speech. Notice a similar problem that can be easily avoided: when a telephone caller asks to speak with Rachel, should Rachel answer "This is she" or "This is her"? She could avoid the problem entirely by answering, "This is Rachel."

Compound Subjects and Predicate Nouns

Use the same rules for compound subjects and predicate nouns as you use for single subjects and predicate nouns.

        Single: *I* invited her to the recital.
Compound: *He and I* invited her to the recital.

If you are unsure which pronoun case to use in a compound, try dropping the other half of the compound. The correct choice will usually be clear.

        Original: Sean and *(I, me)* invited her to the recital.
    Subjective: *I* invited her to the recital.
     Objective: *Me* invited her to the recital.
Correct Choice: *Sean and I* invited her to the recital.

Using Objective Case Correctly

Pronouns that are direct objects, indirect objects, and objects of prepositions must be in the objective case.

Direct Object: Franklin Delano Roosevelt defeated *Willkie*.

           S   **TrV DO**
Franklin Delano Roosevelt defeated *him*.

Indirect Object: The voters gave *Roosevelt* the presidency.

      S TrV IO   **DO**
The voters gave *him* the presidency.

Object of Preposition: The loss was a disappointment to *Willkie*.

    S LV   **PN**   **OP**
The loss was a disappointment to *him*.

Compound Objects

Use the same rules for compound objects as you use for single objects.

        Single: I invited *her* to the recital.
Compound: I invited *Juan and her* to the recital.

Learning Christianly

When a student reads, he is reading another person's grammar. Part of the reason that some writing is difficult to read is that a student may not yet be prepared to understand the grammar. Learning to excel in grammar will open new doors for your students. They will be able to read many wonderful books and stories that are written with a higher level of grammar, such as the grammar they are learning now.

Learning Christianly

In the middle of a course like this, you may start to wonder how practical grammar really is. Sure, excellent grammar will allow you to be a better writer, and that is important. But have you ever thought about how grammar is useful in other ways? How would pursuing excellent grammar help you to be a better reader?

Teaching Strategy: Discussion

Discuss the appropriate use of the informal "It is me" and the formal "It is I." Discuss the example sentences on page 210 in the section "Compound Subjects and Predicate Nouns."

Teaching Strategy: Demonstration

Demonstrate how to "pull apart" sentences with compound elements in order to determine the correct pronoun:

• Marie and *(I, me)* are playing a piano duet.

    I am playing a piano duet.
    Me am playing a piano duet.

• Marie and *I* are playing a piano duet.

Teaching Strategy: Discussion

Review the information and the example sentences in the section "Using Objective Case Correctly."

If you are unsure which pronoun case to use in a compound, try dropping the other half of the compound. The correct choice will usually be clear.

Original:	I invited Juan and *(she, her)* to the recital.
Subjective:	I invited *she* to the recital.
Objective:	I invited *her* to the recital.
Correct Choice:	I invited *Juan and her* to the recital.

IN SUMMARY

Subjective case pronouns work as subjects and predicate nouns in sentences.

Objective case pronouns work as direct objects, indirect objects, and objects of prepositions in sentences.

11-1 PRACTICE THE SKILL

In the first blank label the function of each underlined noun *S* (subject), *DO* (direct object), *IO* (indirect object), *PN* (predicate noun), or *OP* (object of the preposition). Fill in the second blank with the correct pronoun to replace the underlined noun.

OP	her	1. We read about <u>Babe</u>.
S	She	2. <u>Her</u> name was Mildred Didrikson Zaharias. <u>Babe</u> is best known as Babe Didrikson.
PN	she	3. One of the most versatile women athletes ever was <u>Babe</u>.
S	she	4. When Babe was young, <u>Babe</u> ran errands in the neighborhood.
IO	her	5. This gave <u>Babe</u> good training.
DO	her	6. Her mother could call <u>Babe</u>, and she would come in a flash.
S	she	7. During high school <u>Babe</u> wanted to play basketball, but the coach thought that Babe was too short.

Teaching Strategy: Demonstration

Review the "pulling apart" method for finding the correct pronoun.

- Susan placed her lunch tray beside Dale and *(I, me)*.
  - Susan placed her lunch tray beside *I*.
  - Susan placed her lunch tray beside *me*.
- Susan placed her lunch tray beside Dale and *me*.

_IO_	_her_	8. Babe's hard work eventually brought <u>Babe</u> success as one of the best players in the state.
_OP_	_her_	9. In 1932, the National Women's Track and Field Championship was awarded to her team. The team was made up of <u>Babe</u> alone.
_DO_	_her_	10. Later that year the spectators watched <u>Babe</u> as she won two gold medals and broke four world records at the 1932 Los Angeles Olympics.

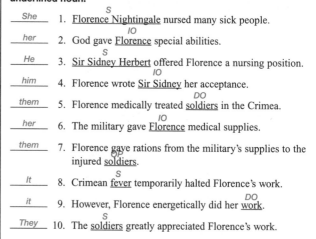

11·2 REVIEW THE SKILL

Above each underlined noun, label its function S (subject), DO (direct object), IO (indirect object), PN (predicate noun), or OP (object of the preposition). Fill in each blank with the correct pronoun to replace the underlined noun.

She 1. <u>Florence Nightingale</u> nursed many sick people.
           ^S

her 2. God gave <u>Florence</u> special abilities.
              ^{IO}

_He_ 3. <u>Sir Sidney Herbert</u> offered Florence a nursing position.
     ^S

him 4. Florence wrote <u>Sir Sidney</u> her acceptance.
                  ^{IO}

them 5. Florence medically treated <u>soldiers</u> in the Crimea.
                      ^{DO}

her 6. The military gave <u>Florence</u> medical supplies.
                ^{IO}

them 7. Florence gave rations from the military's supplies to the injured <u>soldiers</u>.
                          ^{OP}

_It_ 8. Crimean <u>fever</u> temporarily halted Florence's work.
        ^S

_it_ 9. However, Florence energetically did her <u>work</u>.
                            ^{DO}

They 10. The <u>soldiers</u> greatly appreciated Florence's work.
      ^S

Underline the correct pronoun. Fill in the blank with the function of the pronoun: *S* (subject), *DO* (direct object), *IO* (indirect object), *PN* (predicate noun), or *OP* (object of the preposition).

__DO__ 1. Oren's parents have invited Oren, Donald, Jennifer, and *(me, I)* to their home in Colorado this summer.

__S__ 2. Jennifer and *(me, I)* will go to Pikes Peak while we are in Colorado.

__IO__ 3. Oren and Donald have been to the top of Pikes Peak twice. Oren told us that his father had given Donald and *(he, him)* two of his horses for their trip to the top.

__IO__ 4. When we arrived at Oren's parents' house, Oren's father lent Oren, Jennifer, Donald, and *(me, I)* four horses.

__OP__ 5. Oren's father gave the calmest horses to Jennifer and *(me, I)* because neither of us had ever ridden a horse before.

__S__ 6. Oren and Donald led the way up the mountain. Oren and *(he, him)* told us a little of the history of Pikes Peak.

__PN__ 7. Oren gave some interesting details about the history of Pikes Peak. Since everything he said was new to us, the most enthralled ones were Jennifer and *(I, me)*.

__DO__ 8. Pike had led an expedition to explore Pikes Peak in 1806. Lack of supplies forced *(he, him)* and his men to end the expedition.

__PN__ 9. In 1820 Stephen Long led an expedition to the top of the 14,110-foot-high mountain. The first people ever to go to the top were *(him, he)* and his exploring party.

__DO__ 10. Everyone enjoyed the ride to the top of Pikes Peak. Information about the history interested Jennifer and *(me, I)* greatly.

11-4   **REVIEW THE SKILL**

Underline the correct pronoun. Fill in the blank with the function of the pronoun: *S* **(subject),** *DO* **(direct object),** *IO* **(indirect object),** *PN* **(predicate noun), or** *OP* **(object of the preposition).**

_OP_ 1. Nichole's mother remarked to Shandra and *(her, she),* "Mrs. Harris is ill."

_S_ 2. Shandra told Mrs. Harris, "Nichole and *(I, me)* want to help you with your household chores."

_OP_ 3. Mrs. Harris gratefully accepted the offer from Nichole and *(she, her).*

_S_ 4. Shandra's brother Jason said that he would help too. *(Him, He)* and his friend Dean would do the yard work.

_IO_ 5. Shandra said to Nichole, "Jason and Dean will do the yard work. Mrs. Harris has given you and *(me, I)* housework."

_S_ 6. While Jason and Dean did the yard work, Shandra and Nichole stayed busy. *(She, Her)* and Nichole cleaned the kitchen, living room, dining room, and bathroom that afternoon.

_OP_ 7. Dean brought a bouquet inside. "Give these to Mrs. Harris," he said. "They are from Jason and *(me, I).*"

_S_ 8. Shandra put the flowers into a vase, and *(she, her)* and Nichole took them into Mrs. Harris's room.

_S_ 9. After she had thanked Mrs. Harris for the invitation, Nichole said to her, "Shandra, Jason, Dean, and *(me, I)* were happy to help you with your work."

_DO_ 10. Nichole told her mother, "Mrs. Harris said she will invite Jason, Dean, Shandra, and *(me, I)* over to dinner some night in appreciation for our work."

Using *We* and *Us* Correctly

Problems with pronoun case sometimes occur when the pronouns *we* and *us* are used with a noun. Be careful to use the subjective case pronoun *we* for subjects and the objective case pronoun *us* for objects.

> *We* classmates gave our teacher a surprise birthday party.

> She sent a thank-you note to each of *us* students.

Notice that the noun does not affect the case of the pronoun. In the first sentence, the pronoun is the subject; therefore, the subjective case *we* is the correct choice. The pronoun in the second sentence is the object of the preposition *of;* the objective case pronoun *us* is the correct choice.

In each example, the noun following *we* or *us* is an appositive. Students will learn about appositives in grade 9. Emphasize that the pronoun itself is the subject or object in the sentence.

Teaching Strategy: Discussion

Discuss the sections "Using *We* and *Us* Correctly" on page 214 and "Using *Who* and *Whom* Correctly" on page 215. Emphasize the functions: *we* and *who* fill subject and predicate noun positions in sentences; *us* and *whom* fill object positions in sentences.

Scriptural Application

Ask a student to read Ephesians 4:29 aloud. Remind the students that learning correct English honors God and helps us to avoid offending others with incorrect speech. Mention that employers also expect workers to use appropriate speech in order to avoid offending anyone intentionally or unintentionally.

Using *Who* and *Whom* Correctly

The interrogative pronouns *who* and *whom* are often confused. Use the subjective case pronoun *who* for subjects and use the objective case pronoun *whom* for objects.

page 89

Interrogative pronouns

Subject:	*Who* wrote the editorial in this week's school newspaper?
Direct Object:	*Whom* did you interview?
Object of Preposition:	About *whom* did you write?

If you are not sure whether the pronoun in an interrogative sentence should be subjective or objective, try rearranging the order of the sentence. You will usually be able to see the sentence pattern clearly.

> You did interview *whom.*
> You did write about *whom.*

IN SUMMARY

Use the subjective case pronouns *we* and *who* for subjects and
the objective case pronouns *us* and *whom* for objects.

11-5 PRACTICE THE SKILL

Underline the correct pronoun.

1. *(We, Us)* have just finished reading Sir Arthur Conan Doyle's short story "The Speckled Band."

2. *(Whom, Who)* is the detective in the story?

3. Sherlock Holmes's powers of deduction amazed *(us, we)* readers.

4. Holmes knew the solution before *(us, we)* could figure it out.

5. *(Who, Whom)* would have thought of using a snake to commit murder?

6. It really did not surprise *(us, we)* too much when we learned the guilty person's name.

7. *(We, Us)* thought it was exciting when Holmes drove the snake back up the bell rope.

8. *(Who, Whom)* did the angry snake bite instead of the intended victim?

9. According to *(us, we)*, the guilty person deserved his punishment.

10. *(We, Us)* students enjoyed the story so much that our teacher has told us that we will read "The Blue Carbuncle," another Sherlock Holmes story.

11-6 REVIEW THE SKILL

Underline the correct pronouns.

1. *(We, Us)* memorized the entire book of I John.

2. *(Whom, Who)* gave you the assignment?

3. Mr. Rathburn assigned the project to *(us, we)* quiz team members.

4. Mark said to Peter and me, "*(We, Us)* already know some of the verses."

5. *(Us, We)* all spent one hour every day on our project.

6. Mark and I read the verses and put them into a logbook. *(We, Us)* recorded our progress in it daily.

7. *(Whom, Who)* does not think I John is worth the effort?

8. To *(whom, who)* did you recite your verses?

9. Mr. Rathburn said that he was pleased with *(us, we)* for our efforts.

10. *(We, Us)* quizzers learned much from doing this project.

page 310

Apostrophe

Problem Pronouns

Possessive Pronouns and Contractions

Some possessive pronouns and contractions are homonym pairs. Homonyms are words that sound the same (and may or may not have the same spelling) but mean different things. Be careful to spell the possessive personal pronouns correctly—without apostrophes.

Your/you're

> *Your* is a possessive pronoun.
> Don't forget *your* camera.

> *You're* is a contraction of *you are.*
> *You're* going to see Old Faithful.

Its/it's

> *Its* is a possessive pronoun.
> *Its* stream shoots nearly two hundred feet into the air.

> *It's* is a contraction of *it is.*
> *It's* a geyser that erupts about once every hour.

216   Chapter 11

Teaching Strategy: Introduction

Discuss the definition of *homonym*. Ask students for examples of homonyms.

Teaching Strategy: Discussion

Explain that some problem pronouns are similar to homonyms. Review the list of the same-sounding pronoun pairs on pages 216-17. Emphasize that a possessive personal pronoun does not have an apostrophe.

Teaching Strategy: Demonstration

Use this example to demonstrate the technique for testing what message a word is intended to convey:

- The dog needs *(its, it's)* leash.
  - The dog needs *its* leash. (Does the leash belong to the dog?)
  - The dog needs *it's* leash. (The dog needs it is leash.)
- The dog needs *its* leash.

Their/they're

Their is a possessive pronoun.
My aunt and uncle saw it, but *their* pictures are not as colorful as the one on the post card.

They're is a contraction of *they are.*
They're on the desk with the post cards from my grandparents.

Theirs/there's

Theirs is a possessive pronoun.
My snapshots are with *theirs.*

There's is a contraction of *there is.*
There's Aunt Lora by Old Faithful.

Whose/who's

Whose is a possessive pronoun.
Whose snapshot is the best?

Who's is a contraction of *who is.*
Who's standing behind Aunt Lora in this picture?

Courtesy Order

When you use personal pronouns in pairs, put the one referring to yourself last.

Helen wrote to him and me.

Always mention the person you are speaking to first in any personal pronoun pair.

You and I will answer.

I will give the stamps to you and him.

page 89

Interrogative pronouns

page 86

Personal pronouns

IN SUMMARY

Do not confuse possessive pronouns with similar-sounding contractions; possessive pronouns do not contain apostrophes.

When using personal pronoun pairs, always mention the person spoken to first and yourself last.

Teaching Strategy:
Discussion

Discuss the information about courtesy order on page 217.

PRACTICE THE SKILL

Correct any pronoun or contraction error by underlining the incorrect pronoun and writing the correct word above it. Write *C* in the margin beside any sentence that is correct.

You   I
1. I and you are going to play chess.

C 2. It's not hard to learn to play chess.

whose
3. I am one who's experience in chess has taught me to plan out a strategy before moving one piece.

Who's
4. Whose moving a piece first in this game?

your
5. Since you're pieces are light-colored, you will go first.

They're
6. Guard the king and queen carefully! Their the most valuable pieces.

its
7. The queen is valuable because of it's ability to move as far as it can in any direction.

You're
8. Your not allowed to put your king in danger.

C 9. If your king is captured, you lose the game.

There's
10. Theirs a draw when a game ends with neither player winning.

11-8 **REVIEW THE SKILL**

Correct any pronoun error by underlining the incorrect pronoun and writing the correct one in the blank. Write *C* if the sentence is correct.

you and me	1. The teacher gave the assignment to write a report on Vikings to me and you.
their	2. The Viking men were large, and they're facial expressions were fierce.
C	3. When the Vikings raided villages, they sometimes made the citizens their prisoners.
It's	4. Its important to know, however, that some Vikings did other things besides raid villages.

_____their_____	5. Many Vikings spent part of <u>they're</u> time farming or doing other skills, such as woodworking and metalworking.
_____C_____	6. Some Vikings became famous for their explorations.
_____Who's_____	7. <u>Whose</u> the Viking who discovered Greenland?
_____C_____	8. Eric the Red gave the island the name Greenland in the hope that its name would attract settlers.
_____whose_____	9. Eric the Red is also the Viking <u>who's</u> son Leif sailed to North America to explore new territories.
_____there's_____	10. Archaeologists have learned much about the Vikings, but undoubtedly <u>theirs</u> more waiting to be discovered.

Reflexive and Intensive Pronouns

Be careful to use reflexive and intensive pronouns correctly. Never use a reflexive or intensive pronoun in place of a personal pronoun. Remember that reflexive pronouns always refer to the same person or thing as the subject. Therefore, you cannot use a reflexive pronoun as a direct object, an indirect object, or an object of the preposition unless it refers to the subject. Never use an intensive pronoun unless there is another noun or pronoun for it to intensify. Use a personal pronoun instead.

page 91

Reflexive and Intensive pronouns

ETYMOLOGY

Reflexive is from a Latin word meaning "to reflect." A reflexive pronoun "reflects" another noun in the sentence.

Intensive comes from a Latin root meaning "to stretch out," that is, "to extend." An intensive pronoun "extends," or gives emphasis to, another word in the sentence.

> **Wrong:** They presented the award to Trudi and *myself.*
> **Right:** They presented the award to Trudi and *me.*

The pronoun *myself* is incorrect because it does not refer to the subject *they.* The personal pronoun *me* is correct.

> **Wrong:** Trudi and *myself* thought Mikail deserved it more.
> **Right:** Trudi and *I* thought Mikail deserved it more.

The pronoun *myself* is incorrect because it does not refer to any other word in the sentence. The personal pronoun *I* is correctly used as the subject.

Teaching Strategy:
Discussion

Review the information about reflexive and intensive pronouns from page 91 in Chapter 4 of the student text. Discuss the information about reflexive and intensive pronoun usage on pages 219-20, including the nonstandard forms *hisself* and *theirselves.*

Never use the nonstandard forms *hisself* or *theirselves*. Instead use *himself* or *themselves*.

Wrong: Alex only drew attention to *hisself* by shouting.
Right: Alex only drew attention to *himself* by shouting.

Wrong: They built the house *theirselves*.
Right: They built the house *themselves*.

IN SUMMARY

Never use a reflexive or intensive pronoun in place of a personal pronoun.

Avoid the nonstandard forms *hisself* and *theirselves*.

11-9 PRACTICE THE SKILL

Underline the correct pronoun.

1. Janelle and *(I, myself)* wanted to visit Zoo Atlanta.

2. Joel *(himself, hisself)* had been to the zoo five times already.

3. Dad asked Joel, "Why don't you go with your sisters rather than letting them go by *(theirselves, themselves)*?"

4. Joel decided to go with Janelle and *(myself, me)*.

5. Janelle *(herself, herselves)* enjoyed taking pictures of the animals.

6. Joel bought ice cream for *(himself, hisself)*.

7. He also bought ice cream for Janelle and *(myself, me)*.

8. Joel did not want to see the reptiles, so Janelle and I went by *(ourself, ourselves)*.

9. *(I, Myself)* appreciated the good day I was able to spend with my brother and sister.

10. Later, Joel *(himself, hisself)* admitted that he had really enjoyed his sixth visit to the zoo because he was with his sisters.

Fill in the blank with an appropriate reflexive or intensive pronoun.

_____ourselves_____	1. Kris and I worked on the project _?_ .
_____himself_____	2. Weston wanted to do the project by _?_ .
_____themselves_____	3. Alicia and Kerri finished their project by _?_ .
_____himself_____	4. Weston _?_ was the last one to finish.
_____myself_____	5. I _?_ thought that teamwork made the job easier.
_____ourselves_____	6. We _?_ did a very good job on our project.
____herself, himself____	7. Kris _?_ was surprised that we worked so well together.
_____ourselves_____	8. We were pleased with _?_ for all our hard work.
_____himself_____	9. Weston decided to help _?_ next time by working with a friend.
_____ourselves_____	10. Kris and I told him that we would help him _?_ .

Clear Pronoun Reference

Every pronoun must have an antecedent. We say that a pronoun refers to its antecedent. The antecedent of a pronoun is the noun that the pronoun replaces; the antecedent usually precedes the pronoun.

> Judy likes dogs, but she is allergic to cats.

In some poorly written sentences the antecedent of a pronoun is unclear.

> Leroy saw Sung Soo when he was mowing the lawn.

In this sentence it is unclear who mowed the lawn. We cannot tell for sure what the antecedent of the pronoun *he* is. Does *he* refer to Leroy or to Sung Soo? Sentences with unclear pronoun references need to be revised to clarify the antecedents of the pronouns. If we assume that Leroy was mowing the lawn, there are at least three revisions that make the antecedent clear. Sometimes we replace the pronoun with a noun.

> Leroy saw Sung Soo when Leroy was mowing the lawn.

page 84

Pronouns and
Antecedents

Teaching Strategy: Introduction

Ask the following questions: What is a pronoun? *(a replacing word)* What is an antecedent? *(usually a noun that the pronoun is replacing)* Is it easier to find the antecedent first or to find the pronoun first in the sentence? *(usually easier to find the pronoun first)* Remind the students that sometimes a pronoun may have two or three nouns before it; students need to look carefully to find the correct antecedent.

Teaching Strategy: Discussion

Discuss the example on page 221: *Leroy saw Sung Soo when he was mowing the lawn.* Ask the students for other examples with too many possible antecedents. Ask other students to suggest ways to restate the sentences clearly. Discuss the example on page 222: *Rosanna visited the Alamo. They have a historical museum there.* Ask the students for other examples of sentences without antecedents. Ask other students to suggest ways to restate the sentences clearly.

Enrichment

"Pronounced Feuding": Divide the class into two teams. One student from each team will step to the front of the room for each pronoun usage challenge. (If you prepared the index cards to use with the Chapter 4 personal pronoun drill, use them again now. Pronoun usage drills should be a combination of case, person, and number questions.) Choose a card or announce a pronoun description. (first person, singular, subjective case) The first student to compose a sentence that uses the correct pronoun will gain ten points for his team.

Because this kind of revision often sounds awkward, we usually rearrange the parts of the sentence; sometimes we rewrite the sentence completely.

> When Leroy was mowing the lawn, he saw Sung Soo.
> Leroy, who was mowing the lawn, saw Sung Soo.

Some pronoun reference problems are caused not by too many possible antecedents but by no possible antecedent.

> Rosanna visited the Alamo. They have a historical museum there.

The word *they* has no clear antecedent in this sentence. You can correct this problem by rewriting the sentence to get rid of the unnecessary pronoun.

> Rosanna visited the historical museum at the Alamo.
> The Alamo, which Rosanna visited, has a historical museum.

IN SUMMARY

Every pronoun must have a single, clear **antecedent**.

11-11   PRACTICE THE SKILL

Revise each of the following sentences to make the pronoun reference clear. *(Answers will vary.)*

1. Bonnie and Diane studied for her Bible test.

   Bonnie had a Bible test, and Diane helped her study for it.

   _____

2. Bonnie told Diane that she needed to do well on this test.

   Bonnie admitted that she needed to do well on this test.

   _____

3. Diane and Bonnie agreed that she needed the most help with the Old Testament material.

   The girls agreed that Bonnie needed the most help with the Old

   Testament material.

Award three points to the other team if they catch the student using the correct pronoun but with faulty reference. Award one additional point if a student on the same team catches the error. Award five points for questions answered correctly on the rebound. The spokesperson for the opposing team may answer after collaborating with his teammates or consulting the text.

4. Diane told Bonnie that she was having trouble understanding the Minor Prophets. They studied for many hours.

   According to Diane, Bonnie was having trouble understanding the

   Minor Prophets. The girls studied for many hours.

5. On the morning of the test, Diane and Bonnie prayed that she would do well.

   On the morning of the test, the girls prayed that Bonnie would do

   well.

6. Diane and Bonnie were happy about the results of her test.

   The girls were happy about the results of Bonnie's test.

7. Bonnie and Diane agreed that reviewing the test material together helped her remember things.

   Bonnie knew that reviewing with Diane had helped a lot.

8. Diane reminded Bonnie that praying before the test had undoubtedly helped her too.

   According to Diane, prayer had helped Bonnie also.

9. Bonnie told Diane that she wanted to go out to eat to celebrate.

   Bonnie suggested going out to eat to celebrate.

10. Diane took Bonnie to Pavlov's Pizza Palace. They have pizza with jalapeño peppers there.

    Diane took Bonnie to Pavlov's Pizza Palace, which serves pizza with

    jalapeño peppers.

Learning Christianly

Has anyone ever knocked on your door and tried to sell something to your parents? You may even remember someone who came to your door and spoke with very poor grammar. You probably felt sorry for him, that he hadn't had more opportunity to learn good grammar. But his difficulties with the English language might also make you more hesitant to take him and what he is selling seriously. Christians are called to go into all the world and share the gospel of Christ with others (Matt. 28:19-20). How would the skills of good writing and grammar help you in this calling?

Learning Christianly

A witness with good writing and grammar skills would be a more effective witness for Christ than one without these skills. He would certainly have more opportunities to speak to others, because he would feel comfortable speaking in various settings. In addition, though, a Christian with well-developed writing and grammar skills would be able to present the gospel in a natural, compelling way. Those who have mastered the English language are able to communicate the gospel in a manner that is fitting for something so valuable.

Rewrite each sentence to make the pronoun reference clear. *(Answers will vary.)*

1. Malissa told Meghan that she was going to Charleston in a few weeks.

   Malissa was planning a vacation to Charleston, and she told Meghan

   she would be leaving in a few weeks.

2. Malissa wanted to go to Charleston Place. They have a hotel on the upper level of the building and some exclusive shops on the lower level.

   Malissa wanted to go to Charleston Place, which has a hotel on the

   upper level and some exclusive shops on the lower level.

3. Meghan heard Malissa's vacation plans while she was waiting for the program to begin.

   While she was waiting for the program to begin, Meghan heard

   Malissa's vacation plans.

4. Meghan and Malissa agreed that she should take some time to see some of the beautiful houses near the Battery.

   Meghan suggested that Malissa take some time to see some of the

   beautiful houses near the Battery.

5. Malissa said that she might take a stroll along one of the beaches. They have some beautiful seashells there.

   Malissa said that she might take a stroll along one of the beaches

   where she can find some beautiful seashells.

6. Malissa told Meghan that she was also going to visit Fort Sumter.

   Malissa planned to visit Fort Sumter also.

7. While she was in Charleston, Malissa visited The Oceania Restaurant. They serve excellent seafood there.

   While she was in Charleston, Malissa visited The Oceania

   Restaurant, which serves excellent seafood.

8. Later Malissa and Meghan looked at her pictures from Charleston.

   Later the girls looked at Malissa's pictures from Charleston.

   _____

9. Both of them laughed when they saw the picture of her falling into the ocean.

   Both of them laughed when they saw the picture of Malissa falling

   into the ocean.

10. Meghan and Malissa both knew that she had had a wonderful vacation.

    Both girls knew that Malissa had had a wonderful vacation.

    _____

11-13 USE THE SKILL

Correct any pronoun error by underlining the incorrect pronoun and by writing the correct one above it. Write _C_ beside any sentence that is correct.

1. Louis Joliet and Jacques Marquette were explorers <u>who's</u> discoveries *(whose)* were important to the settlement of the American frontier.

2. Louis Joliet <u>hisself</u> *(himself)* was a fur trader living in New France (now Canada) when his government chose them to lead an important expedition.

3. <u>Him</u> *(He)* and Marquette were to explore the upper Mississippi River.

C 4. He attempted to find a Mississippi River route to the Pacific Ocean for the New French government.

5. <u>They're</u> *(Their)* voyage began in 1673 at Lake Michigan and continued through the area that is now Wisconsin.

6. Soon the two explorers realized that the river flowed south, not west; <u>he</u> *(they)* guessed that it flowed to the Gulf of Mexico instead.

7. Although <u>their</u> *(they're)* known for the Mississippi River exploration, Joliet and Marquette were not able to complete the expedition by <u>himself</u>. *(themselves)*

8. The Indians and Spaniards among <u>who</u> *(whom)* the men traveled were hostile.

9. Alone on the return trip to New France, Joliet lost all the maps and other records when <u>their</u> *(his)* canoe tipped over.

10. Amazingly, his knowledge allowed the explorer <u>themselves</u> *(himself)* to reconstruct some maps from memory.

Locate and correct the thirteen errors in the paragraph: subject-verb agreement errors, pronoun-antecedent agreement problems, and pronoun usage problems.

Seoul are one of the largest cities in the world. Seoul has many modern buildings yet contain some ancient palaces. Yi Songgye founded it in memory of his ancestors. He built hisself the Chongmyo Royal Shrine. One of the ancient buildings in Seoul are the Changdok Palace. They keeps it well preserved. Most of the people in Seoul lives near the Palace. Their is also sports facilities in Seoul. The Koreans used Olympic Park for the 1988 Seoul Olympics. They also provide theirselves with entertainment from theaters and musical performances. Their love of them result in many theatrical companies within the city limits of Seoul. Through much development, Seoul itselves has changed dramatically within the past few decades.

Seoul is one of the largest cities in the world. Seoul has many modern

buildings yet contains some ancient palaces. Yi Songgye founded it in

memory of his ancestors. He built himself the Chongmyo Royal Shrine.

One of the ancient buildings in Seoul is the Changdok Palace. The

caretakers keep it well preserved. Most of the people in Seoul live near the

Palace. There are also sports facilities in Seoul. The Koreans used Olympic

Park for the 1988 Seoul Olympics. They also provide themselves with

entertainment from theaters and musical performances. Their love of

drama results in many theatrical companies within the city limits of Seoul.

Through much development, Seoul itself has changed dramatically within

the past few decades.

GIVING DIRECTIONS

And Moses sent them to spy out the land of Canaan, and said unto them, Get you up this way southward, and go up into the mountain: And see the land, what it is; and the people that dwelleth therein, whether they be strong or weak.

Numbers 13:17-18

"The shortest distance between two points is a straight line." How often have you heard that statement? Or how about this common expression: "It's about fifteen miles as the crow flies." "As the crow flies"—if only it were that easy to get from Point A to Point Z without going over, through, and around Points B-Y! Unfortunately, when it comes to destinations, they often lie over bridges, through intersections, and around corners. Look at this set of directions. How effective is it?

> I declare to my nephew, Guido Spada, my sole heir, that I have buried in a place which he has visited with me, namely, in the caves of the little island of Monte Cristo, everything I possess in ingots, gold, money and jewels, that I alone know of the existence of this treasure, and that he will find it by lifting the twentieth rock in a straight line from the small creek to the east. Two openings have been made in these caves; the treasure is in the furthest corner of the second one.

The Count of Monte Cristo by Alexandre Dumas

Giving directions is an important skill. While sometimes the consequences of poor directions are no more serious than a missed turn, at other times major damage can result from inaccurate or incomplete directions. Giving precise directions will bring about the desired result: the arrival at the correct destination with a minimum of fuss.

Your Turn

Write out directions from your house to another specified location.

Planning

Select a location. Think about places that you frequent often such as your church, your school, your grandparents' home, or the local grocery store where your family shops. Be sure that your choice is a location that is familiar to you.

Make a list of streets and landmarks. Do not pay attention at this point to the exact order or importance of streets or landmarks that you can think of between your house and the location that you have chosen. Rather, randomly write any of these that come to your mind.

Look over your entries and determine those that are most important. You will need to delete unnecessary information. Including too much information or too many landmarks can distract the person following the directions. Choose only those that clarify your route.

Arrange these ideas in proper order. When telling a friend how to get from here to there, it is best to begin *here* and work your way to *there*. After you have presented a step in the directions, going back to fill in something that you forgot only confuses the reader and results in inaccurate directions.

Overview of Writing Process

Planning—Listing streets and landmarks

Drafting—Formulating directions from list

Revising—Assessing accuracy of directions; rewriting for clarity

Publishing—Trading directions with a classmate; handing in revised assignment to teacher

---

Objectives
Students will

1. prepare directions.

2. rate directions by standards.

3. write directions to a store.

4. write directions to some other place in the school.

Giving Directions

Lesson Support

Support Materials CD
Writing Worksheets—p. 99
Rubrics—p. 115

Introduction

Ask students to write a set of directions for how to get from where they are sitting to some other place in the school or on the school grounds. Tell them not to disclose the destination. When the students have completed their directions, ask them to trade with some else. The reader should write down on the paper what he thinks the destination is. Then lead the students in a discussion of the qualities that make those directions clear and helpful.

Scriptural Application

Ask a volunteer to read Numbers 13:17-18 aloud. When Moses gave directions to the twelve spies who were sent to Canaan, he was careful to be clear and specific. Read Luke 22:8-12 aloud. Show students that the directions in that passage are orderly, simple, complete, and accurate. Ask the students how we know the directions were good. Then read Luke 22:13 aloud.

Planning Strategies

Introduce the assignment on page 227. Allow time in class for each student to begin listing the streets and other landmarks between his house and the location he has chosen.

Remind the students to arrange their directions in proper order. Explain that the organization of their directions should be both spatial and chronological, listing the streets and landmarks in the order that someone would find them as he moves from the first location to the destination.

Write a draft of your directions. Pretend that you are going from your home to your destination. As you write your draft, make sure that your directions follow a pattern similar to "First you turn onto Street A and go two blocks before you turn left. Then you proceed to the statue in the middle of the square."

Avoid including unnecessary details. Describing too many landmarks on the way to the destination can cause the person following your directions to be distracted and to miss a turn. Choose a few distinctive landmarks that are large or obvious; they are easy to notice and they allow the follower to concentrate on the directions themselves, not the scenery.

Give accurate, complete directions. Your directions will not get the desired result if you count on your follower to read your mind. Remember that the reason for the directions is to help the other person on an unfamiliar trail. Caesar Spada's directions to his nephew, Guido, certainly seem precise. Notice the detail of the "twentieth rock" and the "straight line from the small creek to the east." Remember though that no two people understand things exactly the same. Using the detail of "the second [cave]" could present problems. Does one count from right to left or from left to right? Would the numbering of the caves be affected by the way one approached them? In the story the Count has no trouble retrieving the treasure, but in real life, directions like "It's the third exit from the end" are hard to follow. The goal is to arrive at the destination with as little lost time and effort as possible, not to drive to the end and then to backtrack three exits!

Read through your directions. In each step of the directions, consider whether or not you have been clear in your landmarks, street signs, and left or right turns. Do the steps of the directions follow in a logical order?

Exchange directions with a peer. Encourage your peer to identify parts of the directions that are not clear or accurate.

Revise and proofread for correctness. Incorporate any suggestions or corrections that your reader has given you. Then proofread your directions for correct grammar, spelling, and mechanics. Make a clean copy of your assignment.

Publish a directions guide. As a class project, publish a guide to local places. Include each class member's assignment in the directions guide.

Read your directions for your family. Ask your parents to listen to your directions. Encourage them to comment on the exactness of your route.

Drafting Strategies

Instruct the students to use sentences that are clear and direct in their directions. Warn them against including excessive details and numerous steps in a single sentence.

Use the points of the compass to emphasize the necessary elements of good directions. Display these reminders and challenge the students to keep these ideas in mind as they draft their directions:

- North—Numbered
- South—Simple
- East—Entire
- West—Well-defined

Revising Strategy

Peer Response

Distribute a copy of Writing Worksheet 11 to each student. Instruct each student to trade papers with a partner and to use the worksheet to evaluate his partner's directions. After students have returned the directions and evaluations to the original writers, allow the students to revise their directions as necessary.

Publishing Strategies

Ask volunteers to read their directions without revealing the destination. Allow students to guess the destinations.

Post the students' directions on a class bulletin board. Encourage the students to answer questions from visitors who read their directions.

Evaluation

For help in grading this assignment, see "Grading Writing Assignments" (p. x) and Rubric 11 (Support Materials CD, p. 115).

"The facts are the same in every case, Inspector. No locks were picked, no windows were broken or left open, no doors were forced open, no possible way to gain unlawful entry without detection, and yet it was done." Officer Bell ran his fingers through his hair. His widened eyes and disheveled hair were difficult to ignore.

Inspector Jameson stroked his chin.

"Five burglaries this month and no clues, no fingerprints, no suspects, not one shred of evidence," said Bell. "These have to be inside jobs! The only possible way to enter these homes is with keys. It has to be!"

"These burglaries are connected, Bell," said Inspector Jameson. "The facts we have tell us that. Look at this chart I've been constructing." Inspector Jameson stood up. "I still say someone outside is doing this. Let's go back to those houses, Bell. Perhaps the obvious has been overlooked. I'll meet you downstairs. You'll—ah—need to comb your hair before we go anywhere."

Reinspection of the homes brought no new leads. The doors and windows of all the houses were as they should be. The only marks anywhere were a few scratches on the inside handles of the doors and a smudge on the wall alongside two of the doors. Jameson pointed out the scratches to Officer Bell.

"The scratches are only on the inside," Bell said. "You said someone on the outside came in, not vice versa. Besides, they are small. Nothing out of the ordinary about a scuffed door handle or a smudge."

The Inspector said, "Let's see how long these marks have been here. Mr. Cohn, could you step over here?"

Mr. Cohn, the owner of the home, approached the Inspector and Officer Bell. The Inspector asked, "Mr. Cohn, would your dog have barked at an intruder or scratched the door?"

"Oh, he wasn't our dog. He was a lost dog we took in. He just appeared in our yard one day and was such a nice dog we decided to keep him till we could find his owner. My wife liked the dog because he was so quiet and knew so many commands and tricks. As for the scratches, I had never noticed the scratches before. I couldn't tell you whether they are recent or not."

"I remember liking that dog," said Officer Bell. "I saw him when we came after the burglary. He's a big golden retriever, isn't he? Really well behaved and gentle. I can't imagine him going after anyone. Where is he now?" Bell was a soft touch for dogs and cats.

"Oh, he's back where he came from. His owner placed an ad in the newspaper. We called him yesterday. He was a nice guy and glad to have the

Critical Thinking

Ask the students about their experiences with dogs. What are some tricks dogs can do? What kinds of things can professionally trained dogs be taught to do? How would these special skills benefit someone who is handicapped?

If possible, invite a dog trainer to bring a dog to the classroom to demonstrate its skills.

Suggest reading *Sound Friendships* by Elizabeth Yates (available from BJU Press) about a deaf girl and her Hearing Dog.

After discussing the questions on page 230, lead the students to this conclusion: *The robber is a dog trainer. He has trained a retriever to turn door knobs. He carefully "loses" the dog in yards he has checked out earlier. When no one is home, he orders the dog to let him in. He later collects the dog after advertising for it in the newspaper.*

dog back. The dog was glad too. He whined and jumped like a puppy when the guy came to get him."

Later that day, the Inspector and Officer Bell continued discussing the difficulties of the burglaries. The Inspector looked over his chart again. "No evidence of entry, no fingerprints, no witnesses. All we do have are five burglaries and maybe some scratches on the inside of the houses. How was it done? I wonder if anyone else had a dog. Did we find that out? Did anyone hear any barking? Someone might have looked to see a dog barking and seen something we could use."

"I'll call the other homeowners," said Bell. Later he reported to the Inspector. "This is odd, Inspector. I was able to reach three other homeowners. Mr. Spanner and Mr. Gibson had each found a lost retriever a few days before the burglaries and were trying to find the owners just like Mr. Cohn. Mr. Reame also had a dog that disappeared during the burglary, but didn't want to mention it before because his kids had found the dog in their yard and wanted to keep it. The family thought the dog would come back later, but it hasn't. How about that, Inspector. Curious, isn't it?"

Inspector Jameson didn't hear Officer Bell's question. He was busy looking through the newspaper.

1. *Why did Inspector Jameson think, by looking at his chart, that all the burglaries were connected?*

2. *If the Inspector had added a column to his chart headed "Dogs," which houses would get a check mark?*

3. *If you were Inspector Jameson, where would you be looking in the* Chicester Times? *What would you be looking for? Whom could you call for a possible lead on solving this case?*

- Jameson noticed that the details are almost identical in each case.

- The houses belonging to Reame, Spanner, Gibson, and Cohn would get a check mark for dogs; only the house belonging to Williams—the one with no scratches near the door—would not.

- Jameson is probably looking at the lost and found classified ads. He is looking for an ad asking for the return of a lost golden retriever. He could call Jane Dyes, the *Chicester Times*'s sales contact for classified ads.

INSIDE:
Robberies Increase
Details on B1

Golf Tournament begins today.

Thursday, June 15   Chicester County

Local School Named Best in County

by Bruce Ulmer
Times Staff Writer

Yesterday afternoon Mayor Price announced that Central High School has been named the best school in Ada County. At a news conference Price said, "This unique high school is superior in all aspects of education and administration."

The mayor cited Central's dedicated faculty as a primary factor in the school's success.

Price also mentioned the degree of student involvement at Central. Each school surveyed has strong extracurricular programs in sports, music, and debate. Central High School also features a school newspaper, a student writer's guild, and a popular drama club.

Price presented Jeanne Travois, principal of Central High School, a certificate with this inscription: "The Annual School Excellence Award of Ada County is hereby presented to Central High School for its superior standards in both academics and administration."

Chicester Times
104 Watson St.
Chicester
Publisher - Al Ross
City Editor - Frank Cook
Classified Ads - Jane Dyes
Call 555-0318

Today's weather forecast: Warm and windy. High near 80°F with 20 percent chance of rain.

Jack Mason described his grief at seeing the Logan Station burn. "The station has always been a sort of tourist attraction for visitors passing through this community."

Logan Corner Railroad Station was established in 1855 by Mr. Michael Williams. Mr. Williams, a man of much influence in the state house, persuaded his colleagues of the benefits of a station in Logan. Many famous persons passed through Logan Station throughout the years, including Abraham Lincoln.

"When my great-great grandfather passed on," explained Williams, "the state house decided that it would be better for the railroad to run through Millrock, which was a larger town nearby. The town has lost a priceless treasure."

Inside Chicester Times

Arts	B2
Business	A3
Classified Ads	
Auctions	D1
Lost/Found	D2
Rentals	D1
News	B1
Sports	C1
Weather	D4
World News	A1

Fire Destroys Historical Site

Early Tuesday morning the Logan Corner Railroad Station burned to the ground. Alerted by a smoke alarm, Hazel Williams crawled to the nearest exit and used a pay phone to call 911. Williams has been a live-in resident of the historical site for nearly fifty years.

Firefighters battled the blaze for nearly four hours but were unable to save the railroad station building. Firefighter

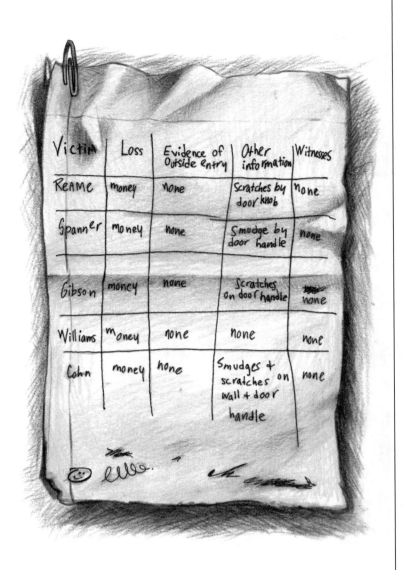

CHAPTER 12

Chapter Goals

Students will

1. learn the correct use of adjectives and adverbs.

2. understand the correct use of *not* and of *good* and *well.*

3. learn the correct use of positive, comparative, and superlative forms of adjectives and adverbs.

USING ADJECTIVES AND ADVERBS CORRECTLY

Objectives

Students will

1. recognize function and position of adjectives and adverbs.

2. correctly identify adjectives and adverbs.

3. identify and avoid using double negatives.

4. identify the positive, comparative, and superlative forms of adjectives and adverbs.

5. use the comparative form of a modifier to describe two persons, things, or actions.

6. use the superlative form of a modifier to describe three or more persons, things, or actions.

Lesson Support

Student Text
Chapter Review 12—pp. 421-22

Support Materials CD
Warm-Ups—pp. 25-26
Concept Reinforcements—pp. 78-79
Bulletin Boards—p. 210

Do you know someone who talks very little? Is he thought of as having good sense? Alexander Pope wrote, "Words are like leaves; and where they most abound, much fruit of sense beneath is rarely found."

Sprinkling many adjectives and adverbs into your sentences will not make them more effective or even more pleasing. The extra words only clutter the text, making it less meaningful and definitely less memorable. Good writers know how to use adjectives and adverbs correctly—and sparingly—to allow more light to fall on meaning.

Adjective or Adverb?

Adjectives and adverbs sometimes confuse people. Because both are modifiers, some writers incorrectly use an adjective when they should use an adverb, or they use an adverb where an adjective should be used. In order to choose the correct modifier, you must know what type of word you are modifying. Carefully analyze your sentences to determine whether an adjective or adverb is needed. Remember to use adjectives, not adverbs, to modify nouns and pronouns. Use adverbs, not adjectives, to modify verbs, adjectives, and other adverbs.

Adjective: Today's temperature is (normal, normally).
Today's temperature is normal.

Adverb: The temperature is (normal, normally) warm.
The temperature is normally warm.

Notice that both sentences follow the sentence pattern S-LV-PA. In the first sentence the adjective *normal* is necessary to complete the sentence pattern. Also, the adjective modifies the subject *temperature,* a noun. In the second sentence the adverb *normally* is the correct choice because it answers the question "to what extent?" about the adjective *warm.*

The words *good* and *well* are especially confusing to some people. Remember that *good* is an adjective and that *well* is an adverb.

Wrong: Her performance was well.
Right: Her performance was good.

The adjective *good* is correct in this example. Because it follows the linking verb *was,* we know it is a predicate adjective that modifies the subject (a noun). The adverb *well* is incorrect because an adverb cannot modify a noun.

Wrong: Lila played good at the music contest.
Right: Lila played well at the music contest.

page 55 — Linking verbs

page 102 — Adjectives

page 128 — Adverbs

Using Adjectives and Adverbs Correctly 233

Teaching Strategy: Introduction

Review the information about adjectives and adverbs from Chapters 5 and 6 by asking students questions about the modifiers' functions and their usual positions in sentences.

Teaching Strategy: Discussion

Discuss the paragraph "Adjective or Adverb?" on page 233 of the student text, noting the use of *good* and *well.* Ask a student to explain the difference between the two words. (Good *is an adjective that modifies a noun or a pronoun;* well *is an adverb that tells* how *or* to what extent.)

If students question the use of *well* as an adverb only, explain that there are two exceptions. *Well* can act as an adjective when it means "in good health." It is also a noun (The water in the *well* was deep) that can act as an adjective when modifying another noun (The cleaning bucket was made of plastic, but the *well* bucket was made of wood).

Scriptural Application

Discuss the examples of *good* and *well* from Scripture. Genesis 1:31—"And God saw every thing that he had made, and, behold, it was very *good.* And the evening and the morning were the sixth day." Matthew 3:17—"And lo a voice from heaven, saying, This is my beloved Son, in whom I am *well*-pleased." II Kings 4:26—"Run now, I pray thee, to meet her, and say unto her, Is it *well* with thee? is it *well* with thy husband? is it *well* with the child? And she answered, It is *well.*" (Emphasis added.)

In this example, the adverb *well* is correct because the verb *played* is the word being modified. *Well* answers the question "how?" about the verb. The adjective *good* is incorrect because an adjective cannot modify a verb.

The words *real* and *really* can also be confusing. The two words are not interchangeable in formal speech or writing. *Real* is an adjective that means "true or genuine." *Really* is an adverb that means "truly."

IN SUMMARY

Use adjectives to modify nouns or pronouns.
Use adverbs to modify verbs, adjectives, or other adverbs.

12-1 PRACTICE THE SKILL

In the first blank, label the underlined word *Adj* (adjective) or *Adv* (adverb). In the second blank, write the words modified.

Adv	*do begin*	1. In a marathon the runners do not begin too <u>fast</u>.
Adj	*finish*	2. The key is a <u>fast</u> finish.
Adv	*hung*	3. My shoe hung <u>loose</u>.
Adj	*rock*	4. I tripped on a <u>loose</u> rock.
Adj	*tree*	5. I leaned against the <u>nearest</u> tree and fixed my shoe.
Adv	*came*	6. The other runners came <u>nearer</u>.
Adv	*fell*	7. As I turned the corner, the others again fell <u>back</u>.
Adj	*entry*	8. I came into the <u>back</u> entry of the stands and crossed the finish line first.
Adv	*finished*	9. The runner from France finished <u>later</u> than I.
Adj	*response*	10. The <u>later</u> response of the newspaper reporters gave our trainers the credit for our excellent running times.

Evaluation

As you conduct oral drills with the students, notice which questions students have trouble answering correctly. Review those principles before presenting future lessons.

Scriptural Application

Point out examples from Scripture of adjectives and adverbs and ask whether students can think of more. See who can come up with chapter and verse with their examples.

Enrichment

Divide the class into groups of three students. Assign one student from each group to be "Adverb," another to be "Adjective," and the third student to be "Recorder." Write this sentence on the board or overhead transparency: *The doctor operated.* Ask students to list as many appropriate adjectives and adverbs as possible. Although all members of the group should suggest words, Adjective should concentrate on adjectives, and Adverb should concentrate on adverbs. The group that

lists the most modifiers for the sentence wins the game.

Fill in each blank with an appropriate adjective or adverb. Avoid the use of *very*. *(Answers will vary.)*

unusually
1. The students were ? excited.

fantastically
2. The school gym was decorated ? with streamers and banners.

Bright
3. ? balloons formed an arch over the doorway.

huge
4. A ? table in the center of the room held colas, sloppy joes, and chips.

well
5. Everyone thought that the decorations for the pep rally had been designed ? .

eager
6. The students were ? for the pep rally to begin.

enthusiastically
7. The coach and the team led cheers ? .

stray
8. No one saw the ? dog enter the gym.

immediately
9. The dog ran ? to the food table.

disastrous
10. What happened next was ? ! "Oh, well," said the student body president, "at least the brownies were saved!"

 12-3 PRACTICE THE SKILL

Underline the correct modifier.

1. Edgar Allan Poe's mystery and suspense stories are written *(good, well)*.

2. Even today, Poe's works remain *(enjoyable, enjoyably)* for old and young readers.

3. Poe was born on January 19, 1809, to actress Elizabeth Poe. Elizabeth's performances on the stage were done *(brilliant, brilliantly)*.

Using Adjectives and Adverbs Correctly   **235**

4. When Poe was two years old, his mother became ill and *(eventual, eventually)* died. A rich merchant named John Allan took Poe into his home.

5. Poe's behavior toward Allan was not *(good, well)*, however.

6. In 1827 Poe had a small volume of poetry published *(private, privately)*. His writing career had begun.

7. Poe later married Virginia Clemm; he spoke *(fond, fondly)* of her.

8. Many of the circumstances surrounding Poe's life were not *(good, well)*.

9. Rufus Griswold, Poe's biographer, did not like Poe, and the biography he wrote was *(terrible, terribly)* distorted.

10. On October 8, 1849, Poe died in Washington Hospital. The cause of his death remains *(mysterious, mysteriously)* to this day.

Learning Christianly

Answers will vary. Encourage the students to consider two main reasons. First, it is difficult for us to learn language because we are creatures whom God has limited. This limiting allows for a number of blessings. It allows us to show our fellow man that we love him because we must labor to learn to communicate with him well. We also gain a heightened appreciation for the privilege of communication and for any communication that is skilled and effective. Because skill in language must be learned, we are encouraged to depend on and admire the older generation, who are the ones that must teach us skill in language. Second, it is difficult for us to learn language because we are fallen beings. Because we are sinners, we naturally desire to live independently of God. By making communication difficult, God reminds us that we need something greater than ourselves to help us and to give meaning to our lives.

Learning Christianly

Learning how to use adjectives and adverbs correctly can be challenging, and this challenge reminds us that becoming skilled at writing and grammar does not come naturally. Why do you think that learning to communicate well in this world does not come naturally to us?

12-4 REVIEW THE SKILL

Underline the correct modifier. Be able to give a reason for your answer.

1. Tom, your first sermon was *(good, well)*.

2. You spoke *(good, well)* all the way through it.

3. David was feeling *(bad, badly)*, so he couldn't come.

4. I understood your main points. They were *(clear, clearly)*.

5. Pastor Grant *(real, really)* appreciated your help.

6. The sound system crackled *(bad, badly)* at one point.

7. Despite that problem, even the smallest children listened *(good, well)*.

8. Your little brother whispered *(loud, loudly)* that you are a real preacher now.

9. Your sincerity was very *(evident, evidently)*.

10. It was obvious that you studied *(hard, hardly)* for the sermon.

Teaching Strategy: Introduction

Write this sentence on the board or overhead transparency: *There's not no pizza left.* What does a person who says something such as this mean? *(There isn't any pizza left.)* Ask the students to examine the sentence more carefully. What does it truly express, if one looks at it completely logically? *(If there is "not no pizza left," the logical meaning of the sentence would be that there must be some pizza left!)* Tell them this is why, in grammar as well as mathematics, people often say two negatives make a positive.

Teaching Strategy: Discussion

Discuss the section "Double Negatives" on page 237 of the student text. Ask students for other examples of double negatives they have heard in conversation.

Reinforcement

Students may be interested to know that in Spanish, double negatives are permitted in certain situations. For example, the Spanish word for *never* is *nunca,* which may follow the verb even when *no* precedes it. Thus it is grammatically correct to say *Pedro no canta nunca* (Pedro does not sing never). While we may be used to people saying statements in English such as "He doesn't never sing" (or "He don't never sing") and while we may understand what the speaker actually means by such a statement, these types of sentences are considered substandard. In order to maintain a good testimony, Christians need to avoid letting their good be evil spoken of; avoiding double negatives is one small way of doing this. Encourage students to avoid double negatives in their speech and writing.

Double Negatives

In some languages, adding more negative words to a sentence just makes the negative stronger. But in the standard English of today only one negative is used. Using another negative word along with the adverb *not* is an error in usage called a **double negative**. One of the negative words should be eliminated.

Negative comes from a Latin root that means "to say no."

> **Wrong:** I do*n't* have *nothing.*
> **Right:** I do*n't* have anything.
>   I do *not* have anything.
>   I have *nothing.*

> When a sentence with the word *some* is made negative, *some* is replaced with *any*.
>
> Examples:
> 1. Norman bought *some* ice cream.
>   Norman didn't buy *any* ice cream.
> 2. We have *some* new books.
>   We don't have *any* new books.

Adjectives and Adverbs in Comparisons

Many adjectives and adverbs have comparative and superlative forms. Be careful to use these forms correctly. Use the **positive form** when you are describing only one thing or action. Use the **comparative form** *(er* or *more)* when you are comparing two things or actions. Use the **superlative form** *(est* or *most)* when you are comparing three or more things.

> **Comparative:** Paco is older than his friend Kai.
> **Superlative:** He is not the oldest boy in his class, however.
> **Comparative**: We often eat lasagna, but we eat spaghetti more often.
> **Superlative:** We eat pizza most often.

Be sure to avoid **double comparisons.** A double comparison is a usage error similar to a double negative. You can correct the error by eliminating one of the comparative or superlative words.

> **Wrong:** Is the cheetah the *most fastest* animal on earth?
> **Right:** Is the cheetah the *fastest* animal on earth?

page 128

Adverbs

page 105

Comparing with adjectives

page 134

Comparing with adverbs

ESL: Be aware that some languages allow double or triple negatives in one sentence for emphasis. Emphasize to ESL students that standard English does not allow double negatives.

Teaching Strategy: Introduction

On the board or overhead transparency, create three columns labeled *positive, comparative,* and *superlative.* Ask a student to use the positive form of either an adjective or an adverb in a sentence as you record it. Then ask other students to supply sentences using the comparative and superlative forms of the same word. Continue the activity until you have a list of several sentences with adjectives and adverbs in comparison.

Teaching Strategy: Discussion

Discuss with the students "Adjectives and Adverbs in Comparisons" on page 237 of the student text.

Evaluation

Refer again to your list of students' examples of adjectives and adverbs in comparison. Ask the students to find examples of the rules they have just studied in the student text. If any of the examples do not use the modifier correctly, ask a volunteer to suggest revisions.

One on One: Prepare a short list of adjectives that can be used in comparisons. Take turns forming the positive, comparative, and superlative forms in sentences. Begin by using the positive form in a sentence. *(Someone in our family is* tall.*)* Your student should reply by using the comparative form in a sentence. *(Joel is* taller *than I am.)* You should then finish by using the superlative form. *(Dad is the* tallest *person in the family.)* For the next round, ask your student to begin with the positive form.

Do not use another negative word with the adverb *not*.

Use the **comparative form** of a modifier to describe two things or actions.

Use the **superlative form** of a modifier to describe three or more things or actions.

Do not use *more* or *most* with a modifier that ends in *er* or *est*.

12-5 PRACTICE THE SKILL

Underline the correct modifier.

1. Jerry doesn't know *(nothing, anything)* about computers.

2. Jayne, however, thinks that using a computer is *(more better, better)* than using a typewriter.

3. Computers are often *(quieter, more quieter)* than typewriters.

4. A regular typewriter cannot do *(no, any)* graphics.

5. Because a computer usually has a spell checker, it is *(more helpful, helpful)* to poor spellers than a standard typewriter.

6. Jayne says that one cannot store *(no, any)* information in a standard typewriter.

7. Jerry and Jayne took a computer class together. Jerry said that Jayne did better because she is *(more smarter, smarter)* than he is.

8. Of all the students in the computer class, Jayne was in the computer lab *(more frequently, most frequently)*.

9. The time she spent in the lab was worthwhile. Jayne did not have *(any, no)* mistakes on her homework assignments.

10. Jayne thought that the computer class was the *(more beneficial, most beneficial)* of all her classes for that semester.

238   Chapter 12

Enrichment

Divide the class into groups of three or four students. Assign each group one or two adjectives or adverbs that can be used in comparison form. Each group should use each adjective or adverb in each form to describe a situation. *(The hungry student was satisfied with an apple at the picnic. The hungrier student was satisfied with a double cheeseburger at the picnic. The hungriest student was not satisfied at the picnic.)*

Underline the correct modifier. Be able to give a reason for your answer.

1. I think that I did _(well, good)_ on my literature test.

2. I studied for this test _(most diligently, more diligently)_ than I did for the first test.

3. I did not waste _(no, any)_ time in beginning to study for the test.

4. I _(most often, more often)_ study in the library.

5. It is a good idea to begin studying for a test _(most immediately, immediately)_.

6. _(Often, Oftener)_ my mom wants me to study right when I get home from school.

7. I eat a snack in the kitchen since I am not allowed _(no, any)_ food in my bedroom.

8. Mom rarely says that she doesn't have _(anything, nothing)_ for my afternoon snack.

9. My _(favorite, most favorite)_ snack is hot cookies.

10. Mom makes the _(best, bestest)_ milk-chocolate cookies ever!

12·7 **USE THE SKILL**

Cross out any incorrect adjective or adverb. Write the correct word above it.

1. Of all the structures in the world, the Eiffel Tower may be the most
   famous
   ~~famousest~~.

2. It is situated ~~beautiful~~ _beautifully_ against the Paris skyline.

3. The tower's builder, Alexandre Gustave Eiffel, did a ~~well~~ _good_ job.

4. At 984 feet, the Eiffel Tower stood ~~more taller~~ _taller_ than any other structure in Paris at the time.

Using Adjectives and Adverbs Correctly   **239**

5. The tower contained 12,000 metal parts, and each part was numbered
   separately
   ~~separate~~ for easy assembly.

6. The tower was planned *really* ~~real~~ well; most of the 2.5 million rivets were

   installed ahead of time.

7. Because of good prior planning, the project proceeded *smoothly* ~~smooth,~~ and ~~not~~

   no one was killed in the building process.

8. The tower was completed relatively *quickly* ~~quick~~—in just twenty-six and a

   half months.

9. The tower's builder also designed many other structures *well* ~~good;~~ the

   framework for the Statue of Liberty is another of his *greatest* ~~most great~~ creations.

10. Because it is so well built, the Eiffel Tower moves only *minimally* ~~minimal,~~ even

    in hurricane-force winds.

Locate and correct the twenty-four errors in the paragraph: subject-verb agreement errors, pronoun-antecedent agreement problems, pronoun usage problems, and adjective/adverb usage problems.

Dolphins are close associated with whales and porpoises. Dolphins has lungs, so it must surface regular to breathe air. A dolphin grasps it's prey with a beaklike snout with as many as two hundred cone-shaped teeth. Dolphins swallows they're prey of fish and squid whole. Dolphins often travels in groups, and it plays and hunts food together. Its sense of hearing is sophisticated. They also communicates among itself. Dolphins uses different sounds to mean different things. The entire surface of its bodies have a keen sense of touch. Their vision are good, but he has no sense of smell. All of their senses functions above and below the water. The chief enemy of dolphins are sharks. The killer whale, a kind of dolphin, and the bottle-nosed dolphin is the dolphins most frequently trained for aquariums and zoos. They shows the most apparent friendliness toward people.

Dolphins are closely associated with whales and porpoises. Dolphins have

lungs, so they must surface regularly to breathe air. A dolphin grasps its

prey with a beaklike snout with as many as two hundred cone-shaped

teeth. Dolphins swallow their prey of fish and squid whole. Dolphins often

travel in groups, and they play and hunt food together. Their sense of

hearing is sophisticated. They also communicate among themselves.

Dolphins use different sounds to mean different things. The entire surface

of their bodies has a keen sense of touch. Their vision is good, but they

have no sense of smell. All of their senses function above and below the

water. The chief enemy of dolphins is sharks. The killer whale, a kind of

dolphin, and the bottle-nosed dolphin are the dolphins most frequently

trained for aquariums and zoos. They show the most apparent

friendliness toward people.

Using Adjectives and Adverbs Correctly   **241**

Planning—Choosing a game; outlining the steps in explaining the game

Drafting—Writing instructions for the game

Revising—Testing instructions on a family member; revising for clarity

Publishing—Showing to family member; handing in to teacher

Objectives

Students will

1. use directions to play a new game.
2. write their own directions for a familiar game.

EXPLAINING THE RULES OF A GAME OR SPORT

Therefore all things whatsoever ye would that men should do to you, do ye even so to them.

Matthew 7:12

What happens when your friends talk you into playing a game that you don't really understand? It is frustrating at first, isn't it? You wish someone had taken the time to explain *beforehand* that those blank tiles could stand for any letter or that you should have saved your *z* tile for the triple letter score space on the board. Becoming skilled at explaining the rules of a game will enhance both your enjoyment of games and your friends' enjoyment of those games.

Your Turn

Write an overview and directions for a simple game such as Hangman or Ticktacktoe.

Planning

Choose a game that you know how to play. Be sure that you understand the game and directions well. How can you hope to explain what you do not know? Let's consider the game of Draw Two.

Determine what information is necessary and what can be picked up as the game is actually played. Stick to the necessary information. Do not overload the reader with more information than he needs. Some things about a game are learned best by doing them.

In the game of Draw Two, experience will teach the player the best strategy for building words that contain a large number of points. (Each letter tile includes a number representing its point value.) Using words that contain many vowels will often restrict his ability to make other words later on.

Define any unfamiliar terms. Most games have their own language. These terms may be familiar to you but will be unclear to someone who does not know the game.

The terms used in Draw Two are common ones: *tile* is the only new term, and it refers to the individual letter pieces from the Scrabble game.

Use comparisons to familiar games if possible. These details give the reader a reference point.

Discussing Draw Two in the context of the familiar game of Scrabble makes the new game easier to understand. The goal, rules, and scoring of Draw Two are all similar to Scrabble.

Explaining the Rules of a Game or Sport

Lesson Support

Support Materials CD
Writing Worksheets—p. 100
Rubrics—p. 116

Scriptural Application

Ask a volunteer to read Matthew 7:12 aloud. Discuss the verse, using the following information. Did you ever realize that something as mundane as the rules of a game reflect elements of biblical truth?

People create rules so that games will be just and fair. Rules ensure that each person participating is treated equally. The Bible defines justice and fairness in the Golden Rule of Matthew 7:12. Playing by the rules of a game is one way to demonstrate the Golden Rule to others.

Teaching Strategy

Materials
• Tiles from a Scrabble game

Ask the students to read the directions for playing Draw Two on page 242. Divide the class into groups of no more than five students and direct each group to play Draw Two. Reconvene as a class and discuss how the game went. Ask the following questions: Were the directions in your text clear? Was the order in which things were explained helpful? *(Answers will vary.)*

Planning Strategies

Encourage students to read the steps of the planning stage on page 242. Briefly discuss the logic and order of writing instructions. Review the outlining skill the students used in Chapter 7 and tell them that they will find it helpful to outline the

Drafting

Organize your instructions logically. Do not assume that the other person knows what you know or can figure out what you mean. In fact, you will often be better off to assume that the reader knows little if anything about the game.

Be clear and precise. As with any explanation, the goal is to be understood by the other party. Often one aspect of the game depends on another, so understanding the game as a whole is impossible if one part remains unclear.

Give an overview of the game. An overview is often helpful since it allows the reader to have a context for the details that you will give him. Include the goal of the game and any materials needed.

> Draw Two is a word game similar to Scrabble. Using the Scrabble tiles, each player will construct his own crossword-shaped puzzle similar to the one large puzzle made in a regular Scrabble game. Scoring for the games uses the same principles as the Scrabble game.

Write your directions. Cover the entire game in a logical fashion. The best approach is to explain the game chronologically, from start to finish. Look at the directions for the Draw Two game.

> Lay all the tiles from any Scrabble game face down in the middle of the playing surface. Have each player draw seven tiles and turn them over in front of him. When everyone has his tiles, play begins. Each player creates his own crossword-puzzle shape as in a regular Scrabble game, trying to use all his tiles. As in Scrabble, using a letter both horizontally and vertically will result in a higher score since the letter then counts twice.

> As soon as one player uses all seven of his tiles in proper form, he shouts, "Draw Two," and all the players must then draw two tiles from the pile regardless of the number of tiles they still have to use from the first draw. Play continues until all the tiles have been drawn from the pile and a player has used all his tiles.

> If necessary, a player may rearrange any or all of his puzzle at any time in the game. If at any time no player is able to use all his tiles, the players may agree to draw two tiles each from the pile.

> When the game ends, count the number of points earned by each player. The easiest way to tally each player's score is to count all horizontal words and then all vertical words. Subtract any unused tiles from each player's score. The game continues until a player reaches a predetermined number of points, such as five hundred.

---

steps of their games before they write out the instructions.

Brainstorm with students to generate ideas for simple games whose rules they could explain. Warn them that they should not attempt to give directions for a game that they have never played. Allow them to begin the planning stage during class.

Drafting Strategies

Encourage the students to set aside a block of time to complete the first drafts of their overview and directions. Remind them that they must understand the procedures of the game before they can write about it.

Instruct each student to put himself in his reader's position as someone who is not familiar with the game. Is the vocabulary accurate? Are the directions clear? Do the ideas follow in a logical order?

Revising Strategies

Distribute a copy of Writing Worksheet 12 to each student. Direct the students to test their completed instructions on a family member. The family member should evaluate the instructions by completing the questions on the worksheet. Tell the students to incorporate any useful suggestions.

Challenge each student to evaluate his writing by answering the following questions on a separate piece of paper and attaching the answers to the writing assignment when he submits it:

- Did I plan adequately before I began writing?
- Did the order in which I presented the directions succeed?
- Did my reader have problems understanding the directions to the game?
- Did the reader successfully play the game or sport?

Demonstrate any part of the game that you can. Examples help us to learn more easily. Lay out a sample of your puzzle before play actually begins to help the reader visualize his goal. Notice the example of the Draw Two puzzle.

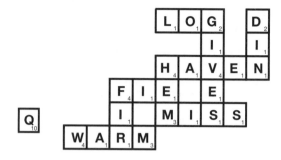

Scoring the sample puzzle will help as well.

Horizontal score:	42
Vertical score:	27
Total:	69
Unused Q:	-10
Total	59

Playing a practice round of the game, if possible, will also help the players understand the game without the pressure of competition. A visual demonstration can be worth a thousand words of explanation.

Revising

Look carefully at your directions. Did you identify your game in the opening sentence of the directions? Do your instructions follow a logical pattern? Have you defined any terms that are unfamiliar to the reader? If you find any problems, rework those steps in your explanation of the game.

Proofread your directions. After you have incorporated revisions and changes in your directions, check your work for errors in grammar, spelling, and mechanics.

Make a clean copy of your assignment. Incorporate any corrections that you identified in the proofreading stage. Make your final copy.

Publishing

Exchange directions with a classmate and play that person's game. Play the game exactly according to the directions written by the other person. Evaluate the directions for the game as you play.

Publish a book of games. Compile the directions for each student's game into a booklet. This booklet can be a source for many hours of enjoyable activity.

Scriptural Application

Point out that God's instructions in Exodus for building the tabernacle were very thorough and detailed. So too His plan for our lives is thorough and detailed. He is concerned about even the smallest details of our obedience to His plan.

Publishing Strategy

Allow students to post their instructions on a school bulletin board for other students to see. Provide copies of the game instructions for anyone who would like to have them.

Evaluation

For help in grading this assignment, see "Grading Writing Assignments" (p. x) and Rubric 12 (Support Materials CD, p. 116).

Scriptural Application

Ask a volunteer to read Psalm 32:8 aloud. Point out that God promises to instruct His children and to teach them through His Word. His instructions and directives regarding salvation and daily living are clear and easily understood. The Christian's words and actions should provide clear direction to Christ.

Enrichment

Allow students to work in groups of two to make up a new game of their own and to write instructions for it.

Enrichment

Assign a more complicated game such as Red Rover or Capture the Flag or soccer as an out-of-class writing exercise. Collect and read the directions aloud to the class for feedback on the comprehensiveness of the directions.

Restating Again

Would that title mean saying something two times or three? The real answer is three. When you restate something, you are saying the same thing twice. When you add the word *again,* then, that would make three times. If you were meaning only two times, then *restating again* is a *redundancy.*

How are the following phrases redundancies?
- nine A.M. in the morning
- unfilled vacancy
- a good improvement
- the honest truth
- a terrible disaster
- a free gift
- the exact same thing

You create a redundancy when you use unnecessary words.

Redundancies make your writing difficult to follow and hard to understand. Try to eliminate them totally and completely from whatever you write or author.

Grand Slam: Writing Across the Curriculum

Below are the words from a famous hymn that we often sing. Because the words are so familiar to us, we may not think about their meaning. Read through a few of the lines from the song.

> Long may our land be bright
> With freedom's holy light;
> Protect us by Thy might,
> Great God, our king!

What do these lines mean to you? Think about two words from these lines: "freedom" and "protect." Write about what freedom means to you or what you may see is happening to freedom in America at this time.

Ask students to make a list of as many redundancies as they can in exactly two minutes. Determine which student listed the most redundancies or which student listed the most redundancies that no other student listed. Ask volunteers to read aloud their lists.

Writing Across the Curriculum

Obtain a copy of Samuel F. Smith's "America" in order to read the entire poem to the students. ("America" by Samuel F. Smith is on page 330 of *EXPLORATIONS IN LITERATURE for Christian Schools,* Second Edition, BJU Press.)

Discuss the meaning of the word *freedom.* What happens to the freedom of a person imprisoned for a crime? Do people really have the freedom to do whatever they please? Is doing only what pleases an individual really freedom? Why or why not?

Read John 8:36 with the students. How does an understanding of biblical *freedom* change one's view of freedom in society?

USING TROUBLESOME WORDS CORRECTLY

Objectives

Students will

1. distinguish the correct uses of these troublesome verbs: *lie/lay; rise/raise; sit/set.*

2. eliminate *ain't* from both their speech and writing.

3. investigate the correct uses of some words that cause confusion because of pronunciation, spelling, or meaning.

4. use certain homonyms correctly.

Lesson Support

Student Text

Chapter Review 13—pp. 423-24

Support Materials CD

Warm-Ups—p. 27
Concept Reinforcements—pp. 80-81
Bulletin Boards—p. 211

Teaching Strategy: Introduction

Direct the students' attention to the photograph at the beginning of Chapter 13. Discuss the introduction on page 247. Choose two sentences from Warm-Ups page 27 (Support Materials CD) to demonstrate the importance of choosing the correct word. Ask students to explain the differences between a pair of words such as *pain* and *pane.*

> "The difference between the *almost*-right word and the *right* word is really a large matter—it's the difference between the lightning bug and the lightning." Mark Twain made this statement in a letter to a friend.
>
> What words would you say are lightning bugs? Which are lightning? Many times the answers depend on the effect you want your writing to produce. Writers who produce "lightning" know how to choose the most striking words and how to keep the troublesome words in a jar.

Using Troublesome Words Correctly

Pairs of words that have similar spellings or pronunciations are often confused and used incorrectly. Often these words have similar meanings as well, making their correct use even more difficult. The following list gives definitions and examples for some commonly confused words.

Troublesome Verbs

There are three pairs of verbs that are to many people especially confusing. The confusion most often comes from mistaking a transitive verb for an intransitive verb. Knowing the principal parts of these verbs will help you to use them correctly.

page 53

Transitive and
Intransitive verbs

Lie/lay

When the verb *lie* means "to recline," it never has a direct object. It is an intransitive verb, used only in the S-InV sentence pattern.

                S InV
lie: Every day now, I **lie** on the sofa.

             S InV
lay: Yesterday I **lay** on the sofa.

         S   InV
lain: I **had lain** on the sofa for half an hour when you called.

Teaching Strategy: Discussion

Review transitive and intransitive verbs. (Transitive verbs need direct objects to help complete the meaning of the verb; intransitive verbs do not need direct objects to complete the meaning of the verb.) Mention that one of the difficulties with *lie* and *lay* is that *lay* is a principal part for both verbs. (*Lay* is the third principal part for the verb *lie* and is also the first principal part for the verb *lay*.) Discuss "Troublesome Verbs" on pages 247-48.

Enrichment

Ask students whether they are familiar with the child's prayer "Now I lay me down to sleep." Does this prayer use the word *lay* correctly? Or should it read, "Now I *lie* me down to sleep"? (Lay *is correct; it is a transitive verb with the direct object* me.) Ask the students to rewrite the first line to use *lie* correctly. (*Delete the word* me: *Now I* lie *down to sleep.*)

The verb *lay* means "to put or place." It is a transitive verb; therefore, it takes a direct object.

            S TrV   DO
lay: Every day now, I **lay** the book on the table.

             S TrV   DO
laid: Yesterday I **laid** the book on the table.

           S TrV   DO
laid: I **had laid** the book on the table before you came.

Rise/raise

The verb *rise* means "to go up." It is an intransitive verb.

          S   InV
rise: The balloon **rises** gracefully.

      S InV
rose: It **rose** yesterday.

      S   InV
risen: It **has risen** before.

The verb *raise* means "to make something go up." It is a transitive verb.

     (Aux) S TrV   DO
raise: Does she **raise** violets?

        S TrV   DO
raised: She **raised** roses for many years.

        S   TrV   DO
raised: She **has raised** other plants also.

Sit/set

The verb *sit* means "to be in a seated position." It is an intransitive verb.

          S InV
sit: Every day now, I **sit** at the piano.

          S InV
sat: Yesterday I **sat** at the piano.

        S   InV
sat: I **had sat** at the piano for more than an hour without playing the same song twice.

The verb *set* means "to put or place." It is a transitive verb.

          S TrV   DO   DO
set: Every day now, I **set** the cup and saucer on the shelf.

          S TrV   DO   DO
set: Yesterday I **set** the cup and saucer on the shelf.

         S TrV   DO   DO
set: I **had set** the cup and saucer on the shelf, but they fell off.

13·1 PRACTICE THE SKILL

Underline the correct verb.

1. This morning I *(rose, raised)* at six o'clock.

2. I usually *(lay, lie)* in bed for a few minutes, but this morning I got out of bed right away.

3. I *(rose, raised)* the window and was glad to see that it was not raining. The first day of our vacation was starting out well.

4. I took my suitcase outside and *(sat, set)* it beside the car.

5. My cat *(lay, laid)* on the sofa and watched us getting ready to leave. She looked worried.

6. I *(lay, laid)* my jacket beside her, and she curled up inside it.

7. My dad *(set, sat)* the last of the suitcases inside the trunk of the car.

8. My sister Leissa and I were going to *(set, sit)* on the back seat of the car.

9. Earlier, I *(had lain, had laid)* a book on the back seat. I can usually read in a car.

10. The sun *(had raised, had risen)* by the time we left for our trip to Quebec.

11. By the time we arrived in Quebec, Leissa and I were tired. We *(had sat, had set)* in the car for ten hours.

12. In the hotel room, we *(set, sat)* the suitcases down on the floor by the closet door.

13. I *(laid, lay)* down on one of the beds and took an hour-long nap.

14. While I was sleeping, the rest of the family visited Aunt Meg. She is a horticulturist who likes to *(raise, rise)* unusual plants in her garden.

15. When Leissa and my parents returned to the hotel, the sun had already *(set, sat)*. Everyone was happy, and I knew that I was going to enjoy my first trip to Quebec.

Learning Christianly

While struggling to learn the difference between *lie* and *lay* or *sit* and *set*, some students complain that they are working to learn something that doesn't matter very much. "Everyone I know talks this way. Why learn something that nobody else finds important?" If a friend of yours asked you that question, how would you respond? Remember to "think Christianly."

Learning Christianly

The distinctions your students are learning in this chapter about troublesome words are not something that you (their teacher) or we (the writers of this textbook) have made up. They are observations that many well-educated people have said characterize people who know how to use this language effectively. Make sure your students don't look at the topic of this chapter (and in every chapter of this book) as "rules of English." Ask your students to view them instead as "traits of success." People who master these traits are opening the door to broader success and influence through their use of English. Your students' friends may not notice the correct usage of *lie* and *lay*, but many influential people whom they will meet throughout life will. If a student says that learning this material is a waste of time, then he is revealing that he does not properly value one of two very valuable things. He either undervalues the message that he as a Christian has been entrusted with by God, or he undervalues the people whom he will meet who need this message. The first shows a lack of love for God; the second shows a lack of love for other people. If a student thinks about writing and grammar in the right way, he realizes that the two most important commands in the Bible imply that this class is very important (cf. Mark 12:29-31).

Circle each incorrect verb and write the correct verb on the blank.
Write **C** if the sentence is correct.

_____sit_____ 1. On warm summer evenings, my grandfather and I liked to (set) for hours on the back porch.

_____raised_____ 2. The roses my grandfather had carefully (risen) looked beautiful in the moon's silver light.

_____set_____ 3. On many evenings my grandmother would come out and (sit) down two tall glasses of cool, freshly squeezed lemonade.

_____C_____ 4. Sometimes I would walk out onto the lawn. There I would lie flat on my back and look up at the stars.

_____rise_____ 5. Often my grandfather would (raise) from his chair and walk out to where I was lying. He told me the names of some of the constellations.

_____raised_____ 6. In the distance I could see the chicken coop. My grandmother had (risen) chickens for many years.

_____rise_____ 7. On evenings that my grandmother joined us, my grandfather would (raise) from his chair, go out into the yard, and cut off a rose from one of the bushes. He would place it in Grandmother's lap.

_____lain_____ 8. Now I am older, and I watch my own children lying on the lawn where I had (laid.)

_____C_____ 9. Now I sit and show my children some of the same constellations my grandfather showed me.

_____lay_____ 10. Other times, though, I remain on the porch and allow myself to (lie) aside the cares of the day and to think back to the quiet, peaceful summer evenings with my grandfather and grandmother.

Other Troublesome Words

Some words have a pronunciation, spelling, or meaning that is similar enough to another word to cause confusion. Other troublesome words are nonstandard forms or misspellings of other words. Be sure that you can use these words correctly.

page 111

Articles

a/an: *A* is used only before words that begin with a consonant sound.
An is used before words beginning with a vowel sound.

She lit **a** candle.
She searched with **an** anxious heart.

accept/except: *Accept* is a verb that means "to receive"; it is never a preposition.
Except is a preposition that means "not including."

All of the winners **except** one will **accept** their prizes at the awards ceremony.

ain't: *Ain't* is a nonstandard contraction for *am not*. Replace *ain't* with *am not, is not, are not, have not, has not,* or an accepted contraction, such as *isn't, aren't, haven't,* or *hasn't.*

Wrong: I **ain't** going to the parade tomorrow.
Right: I **am not** going to the parade tomorrow.

alot/a lot: *Alot* is not a word; it is a misspelling of *a lot.*

Wrong: She has **alot** of snacks left over from last night's party.
Right: She has **a lot** of snacks left over from last night's party.

alright/all right: *Alright* is not a word; it is a misspelling of *all right.*

Wrong: Yes, he fell; but he is **alright.**
Right: Yes, he fell; but he is **all right.**

between/among: *Between* is a preposition generally used when comparing just two items or people.
Among is a preposition used when comparing three or more items or people.

He divided the money **between** the two boys.
The students in the class divided the work **among** themselves.

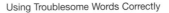

Underline the correct word.

1. Lady Ellesdayle decided to hold *(a, an)* party.

2. The daughters of her poor neighbors eagerly *(accepted, excepted)* the invitation that Lady Ellesdayle had kindly extended to them.

3. All of the daughters were going *(accept, except)* Margaret, who was too young to attend a party.

4. Margaret pouted and said, "It *(ain't, is not)* fair that I cannot go to the party."

5. Camisha and Elizabeth hoped that their Sunday dresses would be *(alright, all right)* to wear.

6. Camisha, Elizabeth, and Mary each wished that she could have a new dress, but they knew that their parents did not have *(alot, a lot)* of money.

7. To decorate their dresses, the three girls divided some late roses *(among, between)* themselves.

8. Lady Ellesdayle was *(an, a)* elegant lady. She looked beautiful in her blue satin gown.

9. Lady Ellesdayle smiled when she saw the girls. "Thank you for *(excepting, accepting)* my invitation," she said. "I have been wanting to meet my new neighbors."

10. After the party, Lady Ellesdayle allowed the girls to take some leftover cake home with them. As the girls divided the cake *(among, between)* themselves, Camisha said, "I don't think Lady Ellesdayle is snooty at all. She is the nicest person I've ever met."

**Circle any incorrect word and write the correct word in the blank.
Write *C* if the sentence is correct.**

an _____ 1. In 1957 the Soviet Union launched ⓐunmanned satellite into space.

C _____ 2. One month later the space dog Laika received a lot of attention for being the first living creature in orbit.

between _____ 3. Soon the United States sent *Explorer I* into space, and the race ⟨among⟩ the two nations to send a man into space was on.

aren't _____ 4. Unfortunately, the Americans ⟨ain't⟩ the ones who won the race.

all right _____ 5. A cosmonaut named Yuri Gagarin returned to earth ⟨alright⟩ after orbiting the earth once.

accepted _____ 6. Alan Shepard Jr. ⟨excepted⟩ the role of being the first American in space.

among _____ 7. Shepard was chosen from ⟨between⟩ his many peers as an aircraft readiness officer for the Atlantic naval fleet.

A lot _____ 8. ⟨Alot⟩ of people don't realize that Shepard didn't orbit the earth on his first mission.

a _____ 9. *Friendship 7* was manned by astronaut John Glenn, who later became ⟨an⟩ senator.

C _____ 10. From 1969 to 1972, every Apollo mission except *Apollo 13* (which made an emergency return to earth) landed on the moon.

Homonyms

Homonyms are words that sound the same and may or may not have the same spelling. Many homonyms make confusing pairs of words.

capital/capitol/
Capitol: A *capital* is a town or city that is a center of government. A *capitol* is the building in which a state legislature meets. The *Capitol* is the building in Washington, D.C., in which the U.S. Congress meets.

Did you know that St. Paul is the **capital** of Minnesota?
Cass Gilbert designed the **capitol** with its large marble dome.
He also designed the Supreme Court Building near the **Capitol** in Washington, D.C.

desert/dessert: *Desert* can be used as a noun to mean "a wasteland" or as a verb to mean "abandon." *Dessert* is a noun indicating a dish, usually sweet, served as the last course of a meal.

Have you ever visited the Mojave **Desert?**
Only a coward would **desert** his comrades in battle.
Chocolate ice cream is my favorite **dessert.**

pain/pane: A *pain* is an unpleasant physical sensation. A *pane* is a piece of glass used in a door or window.

The **pain** in his side could be a symptom of appendicitis.
The softball broke the upper **pane** of the neighbor's front window.

pray/prey: *Pray* is a verb that means "to make an earnest request." *Prey* can be used as a verb to mean "to hunt" or "to victimize" or as a noun to mean "an animal that is hunted" or "a victim."

Hannah **prayed** for a son from the Lord.
Con artists often **prey** on elderly people living alone.
The lion devoured its **prey.**

principal/
principle: *Principal* can be used as a noun to mean "a person who holds the highest rank" or as an adjective to mean "main or most important." *Principle* is always a noun that means "a basic truth or guiding policy."

Does the **principal** hire the new teachers?
Who has the **principal** role in this year's school play?
Do you understand the **principles** of geometry?

Teaching Strategy: Introduction

Review the definition of *homonym*. Ask students for examples of homonyms they know.

Teaching Strategy: Discussion

Discuss the homonym information and example sentences on pages 254-55 in the student text. After the students complete Practice the Skill 13-5 and Use the Skill 13-6, ask volunteers to state the definition of the word they chose for each question.

Discuss "More Homonyms and Troublesome Words" and the example sentences on page 257 in the student text.

Enrichment: Speech Link

Divide the class into small groups. Provide each group with the title of a well-known children's story, such as "Three Little Pigs." Assign each group three or four pairs of troublesome words from Chapter 13. Instruct each group to write a short version (ten to twelve sentences) of their assigned story, using both of the words from each assigned pair. For performance, one student may be the narrator while the others act out the story, or each actor may say his own lines. Encourage students to bring props and costumes for a genuine performance. Allow students to use lighting and sound effects if possible.

One on One: Direct your student to write a short play (as described above). Encourage him to cast family members and neighbors in his play. Remind him that one person can play more than one role by changing his costume when he is off-stage.

profit/prophet: *Profit* can be used as a verb to mean "to benefit or earn" or as a noun to mean "a gain or income." *Prophet* is a noun that means "a predictor" or "the interpreter through whom God speaks."

Mark will **profit** from this computer instruction.
She deposited the **profits** from the bake sale in the school's account.
Elijah thought that he was the only **prophet** of the true God.

13-5 PRACTICE THE SKILL

Underline the correct word.

1. Our seventh-grade class has been studying about Pennsylvania. This spring we went to Harrisburg, the *(capitol, capital, Capitol)* of Pennsylvania.

2. The *(capital, capitol, Capitol)* was modeled after the Paris Opera House.

3. The *(principal, principle)* thing people remember about Pennsylvania is that it was in Philadelphia that the United States Constitution was adopted.

4. It was also in Philadelphia that the Continental Congress met to lay down the *(principles, principals)* of government.

5. Benjamin Franklin, who suggested that Congress *(prey, pray)* before each session, lived in Pennsylvania.

6. In Philadelphia, Robert Green invented a popular *(desert, dessert)*, the ice-cream soda.

7. The *(panes, pains)* in the windows of your house may have come from Pittsburgh, Pennsylvania. One of the world's largest glass manufacturers is based there.

8. The third day of our trip, our *(principal, principle)* took us to Gettysburg, where Abraham Lincoln delivered his famous Gettysburg Address.

9. I must admit that I did *(profit, prophet)* from our trip to Pennsylvania.

10. Next year when we study United States government, we will visit the *(capital, capitol, Capitol)* in Washington, D.C.

Circle any incorrect word and write the correct word in the blank. Write C if the sentence is correct.

capital   1. In October, Martine and her family visited Denver. Denver is the (Capitol) of Colorado.

capitol   2. Elijah Myers and Frank Edbrook were the two architects who designed the (capital) with its gold-plated dome.

_C_   3. Martine learned that there are two senators and six representatives from Colorado serving at the Capitol in Washington, D.C.

profit   4. After the tour, the family went to see a Denver Broncos game. Martine did not know much about football, but she did (prophet) from her parents' explanations during the game.

pain   5. One of the players broke his leg during the game. He looked as if he was in a lot of (pane.)

_C_   6. After the game, Martine and her family went to Brown's Palace to get something to eat. Over dessert, they talked about other places to see in Denver.

principal   7. Martine's mother, an artist, thought that the Museum of Western Art would be the (principle) place to see.

_C_   8. Martine and her brother, however, did not think that they would profit from such a trip.

principles   9. The family decided to go to the Museum of Western Art and to the United States Mint. They thought that it would be interesting to learn the (principals) of moneymaking at the mint.

prayed   10. The family enjoyed their trip to Denver. Before leaving to go home, they (preyed) for safety in traveling.

More Homonyms and Troublesome Words

role/roll: *Role* is a noun that means "a part or position that an individual plays." *Roll* can be used as a noun to mean "a register or list" or "a portion of bread" or as a verb to mean "to turn over."

He is playing the title **role** in the production of *Hamlet*.
Is your name on my class **roll?**
Roll the bowling ball toward the pins.

**stationary/
stationery:**   *Stationary* is an adjective that means "unmoving."
Stationery is a noun that means "writing paper."

The large saw at the mill is fastened to a **stationary** stand.
My aunt sent me a letter on beautiful blue **stationery.**

than/then: *Than* is a conjunction used to introduce the second part of a comparison. *Then* is an adverb usually indicating time.

Is Anna older **than** Alison?
Hit the ball and **then** run around the bases.

to/two/too: *To* is a preposition often indicating direction. *Two* is a number word often used as an adjective. *Too* is an adverb that means "also" or "very."

Are you going **to** the store?
Yes, I need **two** onions for this recipe.
Please buy me a banana **too.**
You can't have **too** much fruit in your diet.

wear/where: *Wear* is a verb that means "to have on" or "to damage."
Where is an adverb indicating place or position.

Did your **wear** your coat?
Long use will **wear** out these shoes.
Where is the library?

were/we're: *Were* is the third-person plural form of the past tense of the verb *be*. *We're* is a contraction of *we are*.

We **were** late for school yesterday.
We're not going to be late today, however.

13-7 PRACTICE THE SKILL

Underline the correct word.

1. *(Were, We're)* going to put on a production of William Shakespeare's *Macbeth*.

2. Hovsep, who does well in all his speech classes, is playing the leading *(role, roll)*.

3. Candyce printed announcements on good quality *(stationary, stationery)* and posted them in public buildings in the neighborhood.

4. On the evening before opening night, we will have a dress rehearsal and *(than, then)* go to the director's house for fellowship and light refreshments.

5. *(To, Two, Too)* other students and I are working on the stage crew.

6. The Playhouse is the place *(wear, where)* we will be performing the play.

7. Roberto said that he was coming to see the play. Jenni said she was coming *(to, two, too)*.

8. The actors and actresses will *(where, wear)* Shakespearian costumes.

9. We *(were, we're)* pleased with the performance of the cast in past years.

10. I think this play will be better *(than, then)* last year's.

William Shakespeare, Macbeth, *Bob Jones University Classic Players*

**Circle any incorrect word and write the correct word on the blank.
Write C if the sentence is correct.**

stationery   1. The editor-in-chief of the Stone Valley Christian
School yearbook sent banquet invitations on pale
blue ⟨stationary.⟩

too   2. Debbie decided to go, and Kuri said that she
would go ⟨two.⟩

_C_   3. Kuri asked Debbie, "Should I wear my blue
dress or my green dress?"

than   4. Debbie said, "I think your green dress is prettier
⟨then⟩ your blue one."

where   5. The Greene Room was ⟨wear⟩ the banquet was to
be held.

_We're_   6. There were assigned tables at the banquet.
Debbie whispered to Kuri, "⟨Were⟩ sitting at
Jack's table!"

_C_   7. Kuri was so nervous about sitting next to the
editor-in-chief that she dropped a roll into her
soup.

_to_   8. After almost everyone had finished eating, Jack
went up ⟨too⟩ the platform and began giving out
awards for the exceptional jobs done by members of the yearbook staff.

then   9. Toward the end of the awards ceremony, Jack
paused; ⟨than⟩ he smiled at Kuri. "And in recognition of her hours of hard work, the 'Best Staff
Member of the Year' award is presented to Kuri
Carrington."

two   10. The ⟨to⟩ girls were excited about Kuri's award and
could not wait to tell everyone they knew.

Fill in each blank with the correct word from the chapter. Use the clues given in parentheses.

_____sat_____ 1. Detective Piers Templeton _?_ quietly at his desk and listened as his client Majel Flemming told her story. *(to be in a seated position)*

_____laid or set_____ 2. Majel said that she had _?_ the emerald ring on the dresser. When she awoke from her nap, the ring was gone. *(to put or place)*

_____a lot_____ 3. The emerald ring was worth _?_ of money. *(much)*

_____among_____ 4. Majel wanted Piers to discover who _?_ the twelve guests had stolen the ring. *(comparing three or more people or objects)*

_____desert_____ 5. Although Majel did not have the money to pay his fee, Piers decided that he would not _?_ his client. *(abandon)*

_____to_____ 6. Piers went _?_ the house where the theft had taken place and began to investigate. *(indicates direction)*

_____Where_____ 7. Piers asked each of the guests, "_?_ were you yesterday about four o'clock in the afternoon?" *(indicates place or position)*

_____raised_____ 8. Majel's room was dark when Piers entered. He _?_ a blind to let in some light. *(make something go up)*

_____stationery_____ 9. Piers looked carefully at the crumpled pieces of paper in the trash can. There was a letter written on _?_ that had an insurance company's letterhead. *(writing paper)*

_____profit_____ 10. Piers discovered that Majel would actually _?_ from the theft. The insurance company would pay $500,000 in case of theft. *(to benefit)*

<u>_were_</u> 11. Piers also knew that all of the other guests' alibis <u>?</u> backed up by irrefutable evidence. *(plural form of the past tense of* be*)*

<u>_principal_</u> 12. Piers now knew who had stolen the ring and why. The <u>?</u> thing was to prove that he was right. *(main or most important)*

<u>_between_</u> 13. As he walked in the garden, Piers noticed that some of the soil had been disturbed. There was a small indentation in the soil <u>?</u> two rosebushes. *(comparing two items or people)*

<u>_laid or set_</u> 14. Piers came into the room where Majel was waiting for him and <u>?</u> a small object on the table. It was a soil-encrusted emerald ring. *(to put or place)*

<u>_principle_</u> 15. As the police arrested her, Majel learned an important <u>?</u>. It never pays to tell a lie. *(basic truth or guiding policy)*

Using Troublesome Words Correctly   **261**

Locate and correct the fifteen errors in the paragraph: subject-verb agreement errors, pronoun-antecedent agreement problems, pronoun usage problems, adjective/adverb usage problems, and errors involving troublesome words.

Cheetahs live mainly in the grassy areas of Africa and are the faster of all animals in short distances. Cheetahs hunt during the day rather then at night. They prefer small pray, such as an young antelope. Cheetahs lay in tall grass and pounce upon they're prey. Alot of times an hyena, leopard, or lion steal the cheetahs' food. The cheetahs' slender bodies and extreme long legs helps them move rapid. They have brownish yellow coats with black spots accept on the throat and underparts. These parts are white. Today, the number of cheetahs are declining; it is hunted for their pelts, and farmland has taken over their habitat.

Cheetahs live mainly in the grassy areas of Africa and are the fastest of all
animals in short distances. Cheetahs hunt during the day rather than at
night. They prefer small prey, such as a young antelope. Cheetahs lie in tall
grass and pounce upon their prey. A lot of times a hyena, leopard, or lion
steals the cheetahs' food. The cheetahs' slender bodies and extremely
long legs help them move rapidly. They have brownish yellow
coats with black spots except on the throat and underparts. These parts
are white. Today, the number of cheetahs is declining; they are hunted for
their pelts, and farmland has taken over their habitat.

ANSWERING ESSAY QUESTIONS

Seest thou a man that is hasty in his words? there is more hope of a fool than of him.

Proverbs 29:20

Writing an in-class essay by itself or as part of a test need not be difficult. Think of the steps that a cook would follow in making a fruit pie. Simply make the crusts and then add the filling. Rather than being intimidated by an essay question, you can concentrate on what you know if you use this strategy. Consider the recipe for an in-class essay "pie."

2 crusts, bottom and top:	Topic sentence and summary sentence
Sliced apples or other fruit:	Specific facts
Sugar and flour (for the goo):	Transitions and stylistic aids

Your Turn

Write a one-paragraph in-class essay on one of the following topics:

- Describe your favorite vacation.
- Compare football and soccer.
- Contrast summer and winter or spring and fall.
- Explain why the chapel time at your school is important.

Planning

Analyze the assignment. When you are given a question to answer, read it carefully and make sure that you know what it is asking. Focus on the key terms in the questions, such as describe or explain, compare or contrast. These terms will determine the type of filling your pie needs.

Craft a preliminary topic sentence. The foundation, or "bottom crust," of your essay will be your topic sentence. Use the key words from the assigned topic or the essay question itself and create a statement (rather than a question) to guide you as you plan your answer. During the drafting stage you will refine this statement as a proper topic sentence.

Compile the content of your essay. The content of your essay is the filling of your in-class essay pie. Jot down ideas that you may want to include in your answer. Avoid generalities and be specific. For example, if you are asked to describe your favorite African animal, do not merely say that the cheetah has spots. A leopard also has spots. Tell your reader that although a cheetah has spots as a leopard does, someone can tell the two apart by the dark lines under the cheetah's eyes that make him look at though he has been crying. Details help to fulfill the requirements of the term *describe.* Then consider the ideas that you have written down. If any points do not directly answer the question, delete them.

Drafting

Begin with your topic sentence. The first sentence of your answer should state your main idea clearly. Refine your preliminary topic sentence from the planning stage. If you are given just a topic in class, create a specific topic sentence that indicates what your focus will be. For example, if you are asked to write an in-class essay about dogs, your topic sentence might be "Dogs make great helpers." If the test question asks you to "Describe the

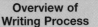

Overview of Writing Process

Planning—Prepare thesis and outline

Drafting—Write the essay from the plan

Revising—Evaluate the essay using PIES

Publishing—Proofread and hand in the essay

Objectives

Students will

1. write an in-class essay.
2. evaluate the draft with the PIES system.

Learning Christianly

Why are writing and grammar taught in the same textbook? Is it just an attempt to combine two topics into one course, like combining physical education and math into one class? Or is there a better reason? Given your familiarity with both writing and grammar, consider the following statement and respond to it: "Learning about grammar doesn't make a student a more effective writer."

Learning Christianly

Writing and grammar are vitally interconnected. In fact, we could almost say that one exists because the other exists. Because we have writing, we should learn how to write well; and much of learning how to write well leads us to grammar. On the other hand, when we learn grammar, we want to put it to use, and we do so with writing. God has made His creation to be a unified place, a "universe." Nothing is irrelevant in His world, not grammar or any other pursuit. Discovering the significance and usefulness of God's world is part of the Christian's calling (Gen. 1:28).

Answering Essay Questions

Lesson Support

Support Materials CD

Writing Worksheets—p. 101
Rubrics—p. 117

Scriptural Application

Ask a volunteer to read Proverbs 29:20 aloud. Point out that the key to writing a good essay is to take time to reflect on the answer. This reflection will give the writer the opportunity to make connections between ideas or to see the big picture. Remind the students that if they don't take time to think through their answers first, they may end up saying something foolish.

Introduction

Materials

- A piece of a double-crust pie (optional)

Show the piece of pie, if you have it. Otherwise talk about how a double-crust pie looks and how it is made. After the students have read pages 263-64, discuss the information. Explain that an essay can be compared to a pie. Ask what part of the pie hold up all the rest of the pie. *(bottom crust)* Point out to students that the topic sentence holds up the whole essay. Ask them to name some tactics for writing a good topic sentence. *(changing the question to a statement; focusing on key terms)* Then ask them what "filling" the essay should contain. *(specific details; at least three sentences)* Then ask the students to identify the qualities of a good restatement, or "top crust." *(does not repeat thesis exactly; recaps idea; gives a sense of completion)* process of making a peanut butter and jelly sandwich," your topic sentence might be "Making a peanut butter and jelly sandwich is a simple process." Notice how much of the question appears in the topic sentence.

Develop your supporting sentences. Craft supporting sentences from the details that you recorded earlier. A thorough essay will have at least three complete sentences as filling between the bottom and top crusts. For the topic sentence "Dogs make great helpers," you could give several examples of ways dogs help people. Some dogs help the disabled, some help with work like herding sheep, some help police officers track criminals, and some help the government to stop drug smuggling.

Organize your supporting details. Just as a recipe has a logical order for mixing the ingredients, so your essay should move logically from one idea to another. After you determine the best order for your support, create that "sugary goo" that holds your facts together by using transitions between sentences. Transitions do not need to be complex; use words like *first, next,* and *last* to give a sense of progression to your essay.

End with a restatement of the topic sentence. Like a double-crust pie, a well-written essay also has a "top crust" that concludes the essay by restating the main point. This last sentence of the essay should not repeat the topic sentence exactly. Its purpose is to recap the main idea of the paragraph and to give the reader a sense of completion. Notice the topic sentence, supporting sentences, and restatement in this example paragraph for the following assignment: Explain why baby-sitting is a good job.

> Baby-sitting is a great job. First, it is a good way to earn money. Second, baby-sitting has more variety than most other jobs. You can play outside, eat an ice-cream cone, make fun crafts, or learn a new game all in a few hours. Finally, baby-sitting is an excellent way to learn responsibility. Baby-sitting is one of the best ways to earn money for interesting work and to learn important lessons at the same time.

Revising

Evaluate your paragraph. Did you respond to the essay question? Does your topic sentence guide the paragraph? Did you cover all the points that you intended to cover? Check your facts. Have you been accurate? Do you need more details? Does your concluding sentence restate the main point? If you follow the recipe—understand the question, create a topic sentence, organize your support, write an orderly paragraph, and reinforce your idea—you will have a blue-ribbon essay.

Save some time to proofread. Even if you spend most of your time on planning and drafting instead of revising, be sure to allow enough time to proofread for correct grammar, spelling, and punctuation.

Publishing

Post your essay on a bulletin board. After your paragraph has been evaluated, you may wish to incorporate your teacher's suggestions and then to make a clean copy for display on the classroom bulletin board.

Include your essay in your writing folder. Keep a copy of your answer and your teacher's comments. Review them periodically to understand how to write a more effective essay answer in the future.

Planning Strategy

Discuss key terms in the essay question that will help guide them. *Describe* means that that student should tell about the topic using specific details to draw a word picture for the reader. *Explain* calls for the student to tell why something is the way it is or how a person should do something. *Compare* and *contrast* ask the student to discuss either how two things in the question are the same or how they are different.

Drafting Strategy

Before directing the students to begin drafting their essay answers, analyze a model essay with the class. Display a question and distribute copies of an anonymous essay answer. Discuss the strengths and weaknesses of the answer. Ask the students to comment on what the writer has done well and what the writer has failed to address. Then encourage them to keep these strengths and weaknesses in mind as they write their own essay answers.

Revising Strategy

Distribute a copy of Writing Worksheet 13 to each student. Instruct the students to evaluate their essays using the PIES system and then to make any necessary changes to their essays before submitting them to you.

Scriptural Application

Remind students that God will evaluate His whole creation on what He has outlined in His Word. Read Psalm 96:10-13.

Resurrecting Dead Words

When we call an object by the name of something different from itself as a means of comparison, we use a metaphor. For example, you call the device attached to your computer a *mouse*. It's not really a rodent. In fact, it's quite different. But it is similar enough for almost anyone to see the connection.

Sometimes metaphors have been used for so long that we no longer recognize the original connection of unlike things. We hardly stop to think that *table leg* is a metaphor. People in the late 1800s did, however. They even sometimes went so far as to cover the legs with skirts for modesty's sake.

It can be fun to bring an overused metaphor to life again, to make the comparison stand out. What metaphor is at work in the phrase *book jacket?* A publisher putting out a book on formalwear might revive the metaphor with a clever cover.

Grand Slam: Writing Across the Curriculum

To prepare a travel brochure to a real or an imaginary place, fold a white piece of paper ($8\frac{1}{2}$" x 11") in half. Write a real or imaginary place name on the front of the paper. You may wish to use special lettering and to decorate the page with images that would possibly be seen in the place.

Next, open the page to its full size. Look for various pictures to represent the best features of the place and attach them to the inside of the folder. Write a brief description under the pictures to "sell" the idea of taking a trip to your real or imaginary place.

On the back of the folded paper, give information about the climate in the area. State information about what kind of clothing is needed and what kinds of accommodations are available. Give any other information that you believe a person would need in order to have an enjoyable visit. Write a memorable slogan to summarize the reasons someone would choose this place as the ideal vacation spot.

Ask students which of the following phrases gives a more descriptive picture or clearer comparison:

- a noisy school bell
- a school bell as noisy as the fire truck's siren

Ask students to write down several appropriate clichés. Have them create fresh metaphors to replace the clichés. Ask volunteers to read their creations aloud. Remind students that it takes practice to create effective metaphors.

- Cliché: His throw was as straight as an arrow.
- Fresh metaphor: His throw was as straight as the back of a church pew.

Publishing Strategy

Encourage students to submit their essay assignment to the school newspaper for publication.

Evaluation

For help in grading this assignment, see "Grading Writing Assignments" (p. x) and Rubric 13 (Support Materials CD, p. 117).

Writing Across the Curriculum

Instruct the students to list several advertising jingles or slogans that they hear often. Take a survey to determine which slogans were repeated the most often. Ask the students to examine their lists of slogans. What do most advertising slogans have in common? *(They are usually short; they often rhyme; they sometimes include a play on words.)*

Remind the students to analyze their audience before they create their brochures. Instruct the students to ask themselves, "Who would enjoy visiting this place?"

This question will help the students identify their target audience and choose pictures that will appeal to that audience.

Challenge the students to match each picture they choose with a descriptive word or phrase. These words and phrases can form the bases for their slogans.

Chapter Goals

Students will

1. learn to capitalize proper nouns, words in a title, and proper adjectives.

2. learn the parts of a letter that should be capitalized.

3. learn to apply correctly the rules of capitalization to other writing.

CAPITALIZATION

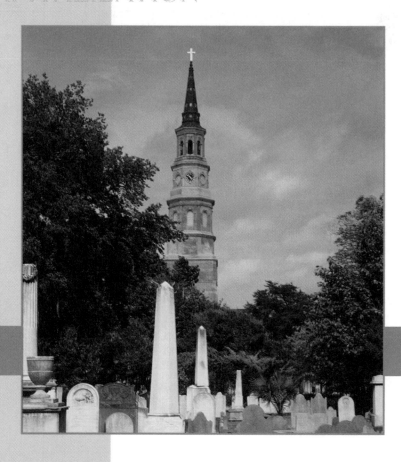

Objectives

Students will

1. correctly capitalize proper nouns.

2. correctly capitalize words in a title.

3. correctly capitalize proper adjectives.

4. correctly capitalize certain parts of a letter.

5. correctly apply the rules of capitalization to other forms of writing.

Lesson Support

Student Text

Chapter Review 14—pp. 425-26

Support Materials CD

Warm-Ups—pp. 29-30
Concept Reinforcements—pp. 82-83
Bulletin Boards—p. 211

Teaching Strategy:
Introduction

Direct the students to write this sentence on a piece of paper: *My name is __.* (Each student will write his own name in the blank). Then ask the students what words they capitalized in the sentence. Direct the students' attention to the photograph on page 266. Ask the students to study the light contrast on the church steeple. Explain that just as this lighting draws attention to certain areas of the photograph, so do capital letters draw attention to certain words.

The photographer took advantage of the setting sun when this photograph was taken. What does the light draw your attention to? It draws your eyes through the cemetery to the church steeple and then up to the brilliantly lit cross. The highest point in the picture is highlighted for visual emphasis.

Language has means of emphasis as well. In English, certain words are capitalized to emphasize their importance. Capitalizing a word is like shining a light on it.

Capitalization

In general, the rule is that we capitalize proper nouns and their abbreviations but that we do not capitalize common nouns. The problem comes when we must decide which nouns are common and which are proper. The rules of capitalization below can help you decide.

Proper Nouns: People and Places

Names and initials

Dee **A**nne **D**aly, **J**ohn **A**. **H**olmes **J**r.

Capitalize words for family relationships when they are used as proper nouns.

I asked **D**ad for a bicycle for my birthday.

If a word for a family relationship is modified by an adjective, it is not being used as a proper noun and should not be capitalized.

Do you think your **m**other can fix the sewing machine?
My favorite **a**unt is **A**unt **M**argie.

Personal titles used with a name

President **L**incoln, **Q**ueen **E**lizabeth I, **D**r. **R**icardo **S**anchez, **C**aren **S**mith, **P**h.**D**.

(*But:* Do not capitalize titles used in place of a person's name. *The council president wrote a letter to the mayor of the city.*)

Specific geographic names

Countries and continents

Zimbabwe, **A**frica

page 35

Identifying common and proper nouns

Capitalization   **267**

Teaching Strategy: Discussion

Discuss the material in "Proper Nouns: People and Places." Ask the students for more examples of proper nouns that name people or places.

Scriptural Application

Again direct the students' attention to the photograph on page 266. Remind the students that just as a capital letter in a word is like shining a light on that word, so someone's Christian testimony should be like shining a light on his life. (Matthew 5:16—"Let your light so shine before men, that they may see your good works, and glorify your Father which is in heaven.")

Cities and states

Tempe, **A**rizona

Streets and roads

Continental **D**rive, **W**est **M**aple **A**venue (*But:* the road)

Recreational areas

Superior **N**ational **F**orest, Sea **W**orld, Rice **P**ark (*But:* the park)

Bodies of water

Hudson **B**ay, Nile **R**iver, **P**acific **O**cean (*But:* the river)

Geographic Features

Old **F**aithful, Rocky **M**ountains, Gobi **D**esert (*But:* the desert)

Sections of the country or world

the **P**anhandle, the **F**ar **E**ast

(*But:* Do not capitalize direction words when they refer only to the compass directions. *Fred went east on Route 52. Fred lives in the **E**ast.*)

Heavenly bodies

Saturn, the **W**hirlpool **G**alaxy, **O**rion

(*But:* Capitalize the words *earth, sun,* and *moon* only when they appear with a list of other heavenly bodies. Never capitalize *earth* when it is preceded by *the.*
*Venus, **E**arth, and **M**ars are closer to the **S**un than Jupiter, Saturn, and Pluto.*
*The **m**oon is shining brightly tonight.*
*"The **e**arth is the Lord's, and the fulness thereof; the world, and they that dwell therein"* [Ps. 24:1]).

14·1   PRACTICE THE SKILL

Cross out each capitalization error. Write the correction above it.

1. This past summer, Derek's only cousin, ~~j~~Jean-~~p~~Paul Fourier, came to visit him.

2. Jean-Paul had come all the way from ~~b~~Belgium to visit Anthony.

3. Derek's favorite uncle, Richard ~~f~~Fourier, is a neurosurgeon in ~~e~~Europe.

Evaluation

Assign Practice the Skill 14-1 and Review the Skill 14-2 as an oral activity. Instruct the students to state both the correct answer and the reason for the answer. This technique will help you evaluate students' understanding.

4. Derek asked his ~~D~~*d*ad whether he and Jean-Paul could visit ~~a~~*A*tlanta on a weekend.

5. Derek's father replied, "Yes, and your mother wants to take a family trip to ~~c~~*C*allaway ~~g~~*G*ardens while Jean-Paul is here."

6. While they were in Atlanta, Derek and Jean-Paul went to a planetarium showing. The show focused on ~~m~~*M*ars.

7. Later the boys went to some of the shops on ~~p~~*P*eachtree ~~s~~*S*treet.

8. On the way back to the hotel, the boys got lost. They had gone ~~N~~*n*orth instead of ~~S~~*s*outh on the ~~S~~*s*treet.

9. During the last week of Jean-Paul's vacation, he went with Derek's family to a popular vacation spot near Pine Mountain. While they were there, the family had a picnic by the ~~L~~*l*ake.

10. After his vacation was over, Jean-Paul told Derek that he had really enjoyed his first trip to the ~~S~~*s*outh.

14-2 REVIEW THE SKILL

Cross out any capitalization error. Write the correction above it.

1. ~~M~~Mother's sister, ~~a~~*A*unt ~~m~~*M*ackenzie ~~l~~*L*eigh, has seen many natural wonders.

2. The ~~g~~*G*rand ~~c~~*C*anyon is a massive rock canyon in Colorado.

3. This ~~C~~*c*anyon contains huge mesas and valleys.

4. Paricutin, one of the world's youngest volcanoes, is located in ~~m~~*M*exico ~~c~~*C*ity, ~~m~~*M*exico.

5. The Great ~~b~~*B*arrier ~~r~~*R*eef in ~~q~~*Q*ueensland, ~~a~~*A*ustralia, protects the ~~c~~*C*oral ~~s~~*S*ea from invaders.

6. Mt. ~~e~~*E*verest is located in the ~~h~~*H*imalayan ~~m~~*M*ountain ~~r~~*R*ange.

7. My ~~A~~*a*unt also visited ~~v~~*V*ictoria ~~f~~*F*alls in Zimbabwe.

8. In $\overset{S}{\text{S}}$candinavia, she viewed the Aurora $\overset{B}{\text{b}}$orealis, also known as the $\overset{N}{\text{n}}$orthern $\overset{L}{\text{l}}$ights.

9. She has seen many spectacular wonders in the $\overset{E}{\text{e}}$ast.

10. Her favorite vacation spot is $\overset{A}{\text{a}}$sia $\overset{M}{\text{m}}$inor, where $\overset{A}{\text{a}}$lexander the $\overset{G}{\text{g}}$reat ruled.

Other Proper Nouns

Certain religious terms

Names of religions whether true or false

Christianity, Buddhism

All nouns and pronouns referring to the one true God

If you pray to God, He will hear you.

(*But:* Do not capitalize words referring to mythological gods other than their proper names: *The month of June is named for the Roman goddess Juno*.)

The words *Holy Bible* or *Bible* and the parts of the Bible and the names of sacred writings of other religions

Gospels, New Testament, Deuteronomy, Koran

Names of large constructions

Buildings and structures

Empire State Building, the Great Wall

Monuments

Vietnam Veterans Memorial

Aircraft and spacecraft

Spirit of St. Louis, Discovery (*But:* airplane, space shuttle)

Ships

Constitution, Titanic

Trains

the *New Orleans*

Names of organizations and businesses as well as their abbreviations

Businesses

Sears, GE, Peter's Grill

Learning Christianly

We capitalize God's names because He is worthy of respect and of our humility before Him. He is the most significant being in the universe, and any way that we can show Him respect is worthy of our consideration.

Learning Christianly

Have you ever wondered why we capitalize God's name and any other nouns or pronouns referring to Him? Christians are in a perfect position to explain why we capitalize any name referring to God. Given what you know about God from your study of the Bible, why is it appropriate to capitalize His names?

Brand names of business products

Ford Mustang, Kleenex (*But:* a Ford car, facial tissue)

Political parties

Republican Party, GOP

Governmental departments

Department of Education, EPA

Schools

Hampton Christian Academy, Winthrop College, UCLA

Clubs

4-H Club, Science Club, the Girl Scouts

Members of most organizations

a Girl Scout, a Democrat

Programs

Operation Safety

Nationalities, races, languages, and flags

Nationalities

Koreans, Australians

Races and Ethnic Groups

Caucasian, Hispanic

Languages

Latin, American Sign Language

Flags

the Union Jack, Old Glory

Calendar items

Months

December

Days

Sunday

Holidays

Labor Day

ESL: Point out that an **s** is added when the word is used as a noun, but the **s** is removed when it is used as an adjective.

A.D. and B.C.

Notice that **B.C.** (before Christ) properly follows the year and that
A.D. (*anno domini,* "in the year of the Lord") properly comes before
the year.

Socrates died in 399 **B.C.**
Leif Ericson sailed to Newfoundland about **A.D.** 1002.

(*But:* Do not capitalize the seasons. *My favorite season is **a**utumn.*)

Historical and special events, documents, and periods

Historical events

Battle of **G**ettysburg, **W**ar of 1812

Special events

Olympics, **W**inter **C**arnival, **A**wards **B**anquet

Documents

Declaration of **I**ndependence, **T**reaty of **P**aris

Periods

Industrial **R**evolution, **M**iddle **A**ges

14-3   PRACTICE THE SKILL

Cross out each capitalization error. Write the correction above it.

1. Leia and ~~l~~Laura decided to visit ~~w~~Washington, ~~d.c.~~D.C., on their vacation.

2. They flew from ~~h~~Honolulu, ~~h~~Hawaii, on an ~~A~~airplane. They knew that going
   by plane would be faster than going by ship, although riding on the
   ocean liner ~~u.s.s.~~U.S.S. ~~e~~Emerald did look like a lot of fun.

3. One of the first places the girls visited was the ~~c~~Capitol. While they were
   there, they visited ~~l~~Leia's ~~C~~cousin, Kumiko Noguchi, who works as an
   aide to one of the ~~S~~senators.

4. The girls later went to see the ~~l~~Lincoln ~~m~~Memorial. A picture of this
   memorial is stamped on the back of the ~~u~~United ~~s~~States penny, and if one
   looks carefully enough, one can see the statue of ~~a~~Abraham ~~l~~Lincoln
   etched on the coin.

5. Laura and Leia took a stroll down ~~p~~**P**ennsylvania ~~a~~**A**venue. They wanted to take a tour of the ~~w~~**W**hite ~~h~~**H**ouse.

6. The girls did not see the president or his family while they toured the ~~w~~**W**hite ~~h~~**H**ouse.

7. One of the last places that ~~l~~**L**aura and ~~l~~**L**eia visited was the ~~s~~**S**mithsonian ~~i~~**I**nstitution's National Museum of ~~n~~**N**atural ~~h~~**H**istory. There they saw many fascinating things, such as the beautiful Hope Diamond.

8. Before going home, the girls visited the ~~n~~**N**ational ~~z~~**Z**oo. They saw many unusual animals there, including a white tiger.

9. The girls enjoyed their trip, but they were sad when they realized that few of the people involved in the government are ~~c~~**C**hristians.

10. They decided to pray each day that ~~g~~**G**od would send more ~~c~~**C**hristians into the government and that other government officials would accept ~~c~~**C**hrist as their ~~s~~**S**avior.

14-4 REVIEW THE SKILL

Cross out any capitalization error. Write the correction above it.

1. This summer a group of us from ~~s~~**S**onshine ~~c~~**C**hristian ~~a~~**A**cademy went to ~~f~~**F**rance on a mission trip.

2. Most of us were members of the ~~f~~**F**rench ~~c~~**C**lub, but some were non-members who had studied ~~f~~**F**rench in school.

3. Part of our ministry involved handing out French ~~b~~**B**ibles and tracts to the people we met on the ~~s~~**S**treet.

4. Another part of our ministry was ~~o~~**O**pération ~~e~~**E**nfant, a program in which we invited children to ~~b~~**B**ible ~~c~~**C**lub.

5. Although many of the ~~f~~**F**rench people are ~~c~~**C**atholics, we met people of other religions while we were there.

6. We saw ~~g~~God working in the hearts of many unsaved people, and we led several to ~~c~~Christ.

7. We spent one ~~s~~Saturday sightseeing in ~~p~~Paris. I asked someone to take a picture of us standing in front of the ~~e~~Eiffel ~~t~~Tower.

8. We also rode the ~~t~~Train à ~~g~~grande ~~v~~vitesse, or ~~TGV~~TGV, a fast-moving train. It was an exhilarating experience.

9. I am interested in the ~~f~~French ~~r~~Revolution and was able to find out many interesting things about the revolution while we were in ~~f~~France.

10. Early in ~~o~~October, ~~d~~Dr. ~~b~~Bernson, our school's administrator, asked several of us to give testimonies of how ~~g~~God had blessed in our ministry in ~~f~~France.

14·5 **REVIEW THE SKILL**

Cross out any capitalization error. Write the correction above it.

1. ~~c~~Christopher ~~c~~Columbus was born in the early ~~a~~Autumn of ~~a.d.~~A.D. 1451.

2. Columbus believed that he could reach ~~a~~Asia by sailing ~~W~~west across the ~~a~~Atlantic ~~o~~Ocean.

3. He appealed to Spain's ~~k~~King ~~f~~Ferdinand and ~~q~~Queen Isabella to give him financial support for the journey.

4. When ~~c~~Columbus announced that he planned to use whatever money he gained to recapture Jerusalem from the ~~m~~Muslims, he gained the support of many ~~j~~Jews, including those who had converted to ~~c~~Christianity.

5. Finally, on August 3, 1492, ~~c~~Columbus and his crew sailed westward on three ships, the *~~n~~Niña*, the *Pinta*, and the *~~s~~Santa ~~m~~Maria*.

6. Columbus had few navigational instruments. He knew how to measure the latitude by the ~~n~~North ~~s~~Star, however.

7. On October 12, one of the crew members spotted land. Columbus
   believed they had reached the islands of the *E̶ast I̶ndies*.

8. Columbus called the inhabitants of the islands *I̶ndians*. He did not
   know he had landed on islands in the *C̶aribbean S̶ea*.

9. The new world he had discovered was named after another man,
   A̶merigo V̶espucci.

10. Today, however, Americans remember *C̶olumbus* and his discovery
    every October with a holiday called *C̶olumbus D̶ay*.

More Proper Nouns: Titles

Capitalize the first and last words in a title as well as all other important
words. Do not capitalize an article, a coordinating conjunction, or a preposition of fewer than five letters unless it is the first or last word in the title.

Newspapers

> *Los Angeles Times*

Literary works

> **"Old China,"** *The Scarlet Letter*

Works of art

> *The Thinker*

Musical compositions

> **"Nothing Between My Soul and the Savior,"** Handel's *Messiah*

Magazines

> *Reader's Digest*

Television and radio programs

> *Wall Street Week in Review*
> *Morning News Notebook*

Plays

> *Hamlet, The Importance of Being Earnest*

Specific courses of study

> **Algebra II, History 101**
> (*But:* His best subject is algebra. Do you have your history book?)

Introduction

Briefly review the rules for capitalizing proper nouns that name people or places.

Teaching Strategy: Discussion

Discuss the information and examples for "More Proper Nouns: Titles." Before you discuss capitalizing proper adjectives, review briefly the adjective's function in the sentences from Chapters 6 and 12. Discuss the information and examples on page 279 for "Common Nouns Not Capitalized."

Scriptural Application

Point out to students that the material they have learned up to this point is all interrelated. For example, if they learned well the grammar and usage information about adjectives, they will easily identify proper adjectives and capitalize them correctly. Similarly, lessons people have already learned in their walk with God affect their lives today, and lessons they learn today will affect their lives in the future.

Evaluation

Examine the capitalization in your students' writing assignments. If the student understands the principles, he will use correct capitalization in his writing.

Enrichment

Divide the class into two teams. One member from each team will stand at the front of the room next to an empty chair. Tell the students that you will call out a general category. The team member at the front will write on the board a proper name for the topic. The contestant who

Cross out each capitalization error. Write the correction above it.

1. Several students from our school class hiked to ~~b~~asin ~~l~~ake. *(B L)*

2. They climbed to the top of ~~t~~win ~~m~~ountain, the one featured on the front cover of ~~m~~ountaineer ~~m~~onthly. *(T M / M M)*

3. A few of the students tried to find some leaves for their ~~s~~cience 101 project. *(S)*

4. Others chose to sit on the edge the of lake and sing hymns such as "~~t~~his ~~i~~s ~~m~~y ~~f~~ather's ~~w~~orld." *(T / I M F W)*

5. An article appeared in the school newspaper, the ~~b~~anner, about their hike in the mountains and their enjoyment of creation. *(B)*

6. Instead of going to the mountains, some other students purchased tickets to the play ~~a~~ ~~c~~hristmas ~~c~~arol. *(A C C)*

7. The students were excited because they had studied ~~c~~harles ~~d~~ickens's novel in ~~e~~nglish class. *(C D / E)*

8. After the play they went to ~~g~~annini's ~~p~~izzeria for dinner. *(G P)*

9. Someone picked up a copy of the ~~e~~vening ~~i~~ndependent to read the comics for the day. *(E I)*

10. The newspaper also had a review of the previous night's performance of ~~a~~ ~~c~~hristmas ~~c~~arol as well as the symphony orchestra's performance of ~~b~~eethoven's ~~n~~inth ~~s~~ymphony. *(A C C / B N S)*

Cross out any capitalization error. Write the correction above it.

1. The ~~l~~iterary ~~s~~cholar, a monthly publication produced by ~~d~~anfield ~~u~~niversity, has articles of interest for all ~~e~~nglish students. *(L S / D U / E)*

2. In its ~~m~~ay issue, the ~~l~~iterary ~~s~~cholar stated that the television show ~~m~~asterpiece ~~t~~heater was showing a series based on some of ~~n~~athaniel ~~h~~awthorne's short stories. *(M / L S / M T / N H)*

276   Chapter 14

---

first writes a correct word and then sits in the chair gains one point for his team. Then another member from each team goes to the front to begin the next round. The team with the highest score wins. Some suggested categories include rivers, businesses, baseball teams, newspapers, books, cities, teachers, artists.

Enrichment: Speech Link

Instruct each student to write a paragraph describing a specific person, place, or thing with which he is familiar. Encourage the students to be as specific as possible by using proper nouns. Allow each student to read his report to the class. Suggest to the students that they may want to illustrate their speeches with photographs or other illustrations.

3. The stories include "Ethan Brand," "The Minister's Black Veil," and "Rappaccini's Daughter."

4. The Literary Scholar had a special article on a composer who wrote a song based on "Rappaccini's Daughter." The name of the piece is "Beatrice, or The Ill-Fated Lady."

5. At the end of the television series, there will be a two-part dramatization of The House of the Seven Gables.

6. The instructor in our Literature class encouraged us to watch the series.

7. Since Nathaniel Hawthorne is one of my favorite writers, I plan to record the entire series on videotape.

8. Our instructor, Dr. James Westcott, wrote his doctoral dissertation about Nathaniel Hawthorne.

9. In the Spring semester, Dr. Westcott will be teaching an entire class on Hawthorne.

10. I am sure that the Course will be very interesting and informative.

Proper Adjectives and Other Words

Proper adjectives

(*But:* Do not capitalize a word modified by a proper adjective unless the two together form a proper name. *The **B**ritish **I**sles are home to many people who are not **B**ritish citizens.*)

The word *I*

Breanna and **I** will make the decorations.

First words

In a sentence

The man said that his favorite poet is Lewis Carroll.

In a line of dialogue

Then he said, "**H**is best poems are very entertaining."

In a line of poetry

'**T**was brillig, and the slithy toves
Did gyre and gimble in the wabe:
All mimsy were the borogoves,
And the mome raths outgrabe.

page 116

Proper adjectives

Certain parts of a letter

The first word and all nouns in the greeting

Dear **A**leta and **F**amily,

The first word in the complimentary closing

Yours truly,

Cross out each capitalization error. Write the correction above it.

~~d~~[D]ear ~~e~~[E]mily and ~~f~~[F]amily,

~~i~~[I] arrived in ~~l~~[L]ondon on ~~s~~[S]aturday. ~~a~~[A]ll went well except that I had a little trouble with my luggage, which got rerouted to a different plane. The people at the airport were very helpful, though. I guess that ~~b~~[B]ritish citizens are not so arrogant as we might think. ~~t~~[T]omorrow I am going to Cumbria, where the ~~e~~[E]nglish poet ~~w~~[W]illiam ~~w~~[W]ordsworth grew up. ~~s~~[S]everal scenes from Wordsworth's famous poem *The ~~p~~[P]relude* are set in the area. ~~t~~[T]he first few lines of the poem are

> Oh there is blessing in this gentle breeze,
> A visitant that while it fans my cheek
> Doth seem half-conscious of the joy it brings.

Our cousin ~~m~~[M]atthew said, "~~s~~[S]ome of William Wordsworth's poetry is beautiful." I am planning to travel to ~~s~~[S]tratford-upon-~~a~~[A]von also. ~~s~~[S]ince I took a special interest in ~~s~~[S]hakespeare while I was a student at ~~y~~[Y]ates ~~c~~[C]ollege, ~~i~~[I] want to spend some extra time there. At the end of the summer ~~i~~[I] will return to ~~l~~[L]ondon to do some leisurely shopping. ~~i~~[I] hope all is well. I look forward to visiting you this ~~c~~[C]hristmas up in frigid ~~n~~[N]ew ~~e~~[E]ngland!

~~l~~[L]ove,

~~j~~[J]anet

Cross out any capitalization error. Write the correction above it.

Dear Aletheia,

I could hardly believe it when I saw on the calendar that it is November 7 and I had forgotten your birthday! I hope that it was wonderful. This time of the semester is really busy here at college, so it is no wonder that time is seeming to go by so quickly! In a few weeks I will be taking final exams. The only one that I am really concerned about is my History of World Civilizations exam.

I just finished writing a paper about Edgar Allan Poe's poem "The Raven." It is a fascinating poem. You may have heard it. The first lines are

Once upon a midnight dreary,

While I pondered, weak and weary,

Poe's poetry and stories are interesting. I remember that you read "The Tell-tale Heart" at your recital.

I would write more, but some friends and I are going to the Westmoreland Mall tonight. Tell Mom and Dad that I said hello. See you in Spokane in a few weeks!

Love,

Zoe

Common Nouns Not Capitalized

Some common nouns are often mistakenly capitalized as proper nouns. Do not capitalize common nouns.

Common names of flowers, trees, animals, and birds

daisies, oaks, collies, parakeets
(*But*: American Beauty rose, Norway spruce, Irish setter)

Games, foods, and musical instruments that are not brand names

football, pizza, flute
(*But*: Monopoly, Totino's pizza, Steinway piano)

Capitalization 279

Members of a class or a group that is not a proper name or title

We have fifty seniors this year.
A **gaggle** of geese flew above us.

14·10 PRACTICE THE SKILL

Cross out each capitalization error. Write the correction above it.

A new ~~G~~group of ~~S~~students enters senior high school each year. Although some ~~F~~freshmen struggle with this transition, many enjoy the new opportunities offered. As the school year progresses, ~~S~~students adjust to tougher academic requirements and find time for ~~E~~extracurricular activities. The more active students may play on the ~~B~~basketball team or join a musical ~~E~~ensemble, while other students may choose to take private ~~P~~piano lessons, help the ~~S~~senior class, or work on the ~~N~~newspaper. Other students may decide to work in the science lab and grow ~~I~~idaho potatoes, beans, or carrot tops. Most students will find some enjoyable activity when they get to ~~S~~senior ~~H~~high.

14·11 REVIEW THE SKILL

Cross out any capitalization error. Write the correction above it.

1. The state of Pennsylvania is located in the ~~M~~middle ~~A~~atlantic region of the country and has various ~~S~~seasonal attractions.

2. In ~~W~~winter, a person may wish to visit the ~~P~~pennsylvania ~~F~~farm ~~S~~show, which is held annually in the capital city of Harrisburg; but in summer, a person may wish to visit Harrisburg's surrounding towns and cities.

3. One such town is Hershey, where the aroma from the chocolate factory invites vacationers to enter such restaurants as ~~F~~friendly's and ~~H~~hershey ~~P~~pantry.

4. Some companies that make chocolate get their cocoa beans from various countries on the ~~s~~outh ~~a~~merican continent.
   (corrections: S, A)

5. Visitors to the city of ~~p~~hiladelphia learn much about American ~~H~~istory.
   (corrections: P, h)

6. Germantown, which is part of Philadelphia, was founded in the late 1600s after people of ~~g~~erman heritage arrived in 1683 on the ship ~~c~~oncord.
   (corrections: G, C)

7. Benjamin Franklin, who was from Philadelphia, is well known for his books *The Autobiography of ~~b~~enjamin ~~f~~ranklin* and *The ~~W~~ay to ~~W~~ealth.*
   (corrections: B, F, W, W)

8. Near Philadelphia is ~~l~~ongwood ~~g~~ardens, which has one of the most magnificent horticultural displays in the world. There one may see beautiful flowers and shrubs such as the ~~r~~ose of ~~s~~haron.
   (corrections: L, G, R, S)

9. The capital city, Harrisburg, sits on the banks of the Susquehanna ~~r~~iver, which flows into the ~~c~~hesapeake ~~b~~ay.
   (corrections: R, C, B)

10. Harrisburg contains places of historical interest, such as the ~~j~~ohn ~~h~~arris ~~m~~ansion and the ~~w~~illiam ~~p~~enn ~~m~~emorial ~~m~~useum.
    (corrections: J, H, M, W, P, M, M)

14·12 USE THE SKILL

Cross out each capitalization error. Write the correction above it.

1. In 1852, a group of ~~P~~ioneers from ~~i~~llinois founded a town that they named Seattle. The town was named after ~~c~~hief ~~s~~eattle, leader of the ~~s~~uquamish and ~~d~~uwamish tribes.
   (corrections: p, I, C, S, S, D)

2. ~~T~~oday, ~~s~~eattle is the largest city in Washington. It is also the transportation center of the ~~p~~acific ~~n~~orthwest.
   (corrections: T, S, P, N)

3. The ~~C~~ity is bordered on the ~~W~~est by Puget ~~s~~ound and on the east by ~~l~~ake Washington.
   (corrections: c, w, S, L)

4. Since World ~~w~~ar II, manufacturing has been a major source of ~~s~~eattle's economy. The ~~b~~oeing ~~c~~ompany is one of the largest aircraft manufacturers in the ~~u~~nited ~~s~~tates.
   (corrections: W, S, B, C, U, S)

Capitalization **281**

5. The well-known producer of video games, ~~n~~**N**intendo, also bases itself near Seattle. Betty MacDonald, the author of *The egg and i*, lived there too.

6. One of the largest buildings on the ~~w~~**W**est ~~c~~**C**oast is located in this city. It is the seventy-six-story ~~c~~**C**olumbia ~~s~~**S**eafirst ~~c~~**C**enter.

7. Another famous landmark is the 605-foot-high Space ~~n~~**N**eedle.

8. The ~~k~~**K**ingdome, a dome-shaped stadium, was in downtown ~~s~~**S**eattle. The Seattle Seahawks, a professional football team, played there until 1999.

9. Also impressive is the Seattle ~~p~~**P**ublic ~~l~~**L**ibrary, which has about two million books and operates twenty branches.

10. For a quiet afternoon, one might visit one of the city's three hundred Parks. ~~w~~**W**oodland ~~p~~**P**ark has an amusement area, gardens, and a zoo.

14-13 ⚾ CUMULATIVE REVIEW

Locate and correct the twenty-five errors in the paragraph: subject-verb agreement errors, pronoun-antecedent agreement problems, pronoun usage problems, adjective/adverb usage problems, errors involving troublesome words, and capitalization errors.

    The Allies surround the ~~g~~**G**ermans until their troops lie ~~stationery~~ *stationary* and cut off from ~~its~~ *their* supplies. Even though Hitler ~~do~~ *does* not ~~rise~~ *raise* the flag of surrender, ~~alot~~ *a lot* of soldiers ~~dessert~~ *desert* rather than fall ~~pray~~ *prey* to the Allied guns. May 7, 1945, ~~signify~~ *signifies* the end of ~~w~~**W**orld ~~w~~**W**ar II when the Germans sign a ~~unconditionally~~ *an unconditional* peace treaty with the ~~a~~**A**llied ~~f~~**F**orces. Because Hitler killed ~~hisself~~ on April 30, General Alfred Jodl signs the treaty for Germany. After six years of ~~pane~~ *pain* and suffering, Germany ~~final surrender~~ *finally surrenders* in Rheims, France. On May 8, Russia requires ~~an~~ *a* second surrender ceremony in Berlin, the ~~capitol~~ *capital* of Germany. Most countries, ~~accept~~ *except* those in the Axis powers, ~~calls~~ *call* this day Victory in ~~e~~**E**urope (VE) Day. Around the world, people honor the soldiers who fought ~~good~~ *well* for so many years.

WRITING A BIOGRAPHICAL SKETCH

> Josiah was eight years old when he began to reign, and he reigned thirty and one years in Jerusalem. . . . And he did that which was right in the sight of the Lord, and walked in all the way of David his father, and turned not aside to the right hand or to the left.
>
> *II Kings 22:1-2*

Biography: What does this word mean? According to its roots, *bio* has to do with life (as seen in words like *biology)* and *graph* has to do with writing (as in *calligraphy).* A biography then is the writing down of a person's life. If you look in a library, you will find biographies of all sizes, some as long as six volumes, such as Carl Sandburg's biography of Abraham Lincoln. Obviously, you do not want to write a six-volume biography, nor does your teacher wish to grade it!

So what is a biographical sketch? Just as an artist's small drawing has all the elements of the finished painting to give an idea of the finished work, so a biographical sketch has the elements of biography, but on a smaller scale. The Scriptures give us many biographical sketches. In II Kings 22, for example, just two verses reveal many important facts about King Josiah.

Your Turn

Interview a person whom you admire, such as a parent, a grandparent, a friend, a missionary, or a neighbor. Write a three-paragraph biographical sketch of the person. Include your interview notes with the finished sketch.

Planning

Read some sample biographical sketches. The encyclopedia contains many biographical sketches, and your literature book probably contains a brief biographical sketch about each author. The newspaper obituaries also often contain a type of biographical sketch.

Choose a person to interview. Think of someone that you wish others could know about. You may already know whom you want to interview. If you are not sure, take some time to think about someone whom you admire or respect, someone who has influenced your life, or someone that you particularly like. Primary sources of information are the person himself or people who knew him well. You can usually gather accurate information from these primary sources. Secondary sources—people who knew the people who knew the subject—are often unreliable. Your better choice, therefore, is to choose a subject with whom you can talk in person or by phone or can correspond with. If your subject is someone who has passed away, make sure his acquaintances are people you can contact directly.

Decide what information you want to find out about your subject. First, since you are writing only a short sketch, you must decide what is important; obviously, it would be impossible for you to include every detail of your subject's life. So if the subject is well known, you might focus on how he became well known. For example, Carl Sandburg's wife, Lillian, besides being the wife of that famous poet and biographer and the sister of Edward Steichen, a well-known photographer, was also remarkable in her own right for her business of raising goats. A biographical sketch would mention her important relationships and her personal accomplishments.

Formulate questions that you want to ask. Think of yourself as a journalist: many of the questions that a journalist asks are the questions that you should ask as well.

Overview of Writing Process

Planning—Choosing a subject; formulating interview questions; reviewing material gained through the interview

Drafting—Writing the biographical sketch

Revising—Evaluating with questions and revising as necessary

Publishing—Reading sketches to the class

Objectives
Students will

1. interview a primary or secondary source.

2. write a biographical sketch.

Writing a Biographical Sketch

Lesson Support

Support Materials CD
Writing Worksheets—p. 102
Rubrics—p. 118

Scriptural Application

Challenge students with the following question: What kind of biographical sketch could be written about you? In II Kings 22:2 one phrase describes Joash: "And he did that which was right in the sight of the Lord." Remind students that they are writing a record each day of their lives.

Introduction

Materials

• One newspaper obituary for every two students

Ask students to name places where they have seen biographical sketches. Assign each student a partner and give each set of partners an obituary. Instruct them to read the obituary and to write down the most noteworthy items mentioned about that person. Direct students to study the lists they have made of noteworthy items from the obituaries. Instruct them to formulate questions an interviewer might ask to get such information from his subject. Write their questions for display. As a class, identify each question as an open-ended question or a closed-ended question. Discuss the advantages of each type.

Planning Strategies

Ask the students to think of someone they admire because of an exemplary lifestyle or an accomplishment. Invite them to share the reasons they admire this person.

- **Who:** Find out the subject's full name (ask how to spell it even if you think you know; the spelling of names is notoriously unpredictable). Find out who his parents are and what they do for a living. Find out about his family. Does he have brothers and sisters? Is he married? Does he have children?

- **What:** Ask what the subject does for a living. Find out what he does that is not so well known as well as what he is better known for. What are his goals in life? Remember that the purpose of a biographical sketch is not only to present information in a logical manner but also to educate the reader, so share the little-known facts that you learn through your interview.

- **Where:** Find out the geographical facts associated with the subject. Where was he born? Where has he lived? Where has he traveled?

- **When:** Find out the chronological facts associated with the subject. When was he born? When was he married? When did he begin his career? When did he die?

- **Why:** Find out why the subject chose his career. Why does he think his job is important or worthwhile? Why is he important or interesting?

Include both open-ended and closed-ended questions in your interview. Open-ended questions generate more detailed answers, elicit opinions, allow explanations, provide quotable material, and use *what* and *why*. You might, for example, ask "What do you like about your job?" or "What was your childhood like?" Closed-ended questions elicit facts, provide specific answers (usually one-word answers) and use *when* and *where*. Examples of closed-ended questions are "Where do you work?" and "When were you born?"

Conduct your interview. As you conduct the interview, remember your manners.

1. Respect the time of the one you are interviewing: be on time and stay within the time limits.

2. Write out questions ahead of time, leaving room on your paper after each question to write the answer. Bring a pen to take notes. If possible, bring an audio recorder as well. Taking notes by hand as well as by recorder will eliminate the frustration of losing the entire interview if the recorder does not work.

3. Respect the subject's privacy. If your great-aunt does not want to tell you the year she was born, don't pester her about it!

4. Make sure that you understand the answers to your questions. Clarify any unusual terms that the subject uses and spell them correctly.

5. Make arrangements to contact the subject again in case you need to clarify your notes or have forgotten to ask a question. You might ask, "May I call you again if I have any questions as I write my sketch?" Most subjects will be happy to talk with you again if the need arises.

6. Thank the subject for his time and help. You will want to do so first at the time of the interview and then again a little later by means of a thank-you note.

Encourage them to choose that person or another admirable person to interview.

Tell the students to consult primary sources if at all possible. Remind them that they will obtain more valid and accurate information from primary sources.

Remind students that they can reveal certain feelings about a person either by telling the feeling or showing the feeling through details. Explain that a character sketch is much like a portrait: it preserves the memory of the person it portrays. Encourage the students to consider what details they want to learn about their sub-jects as they formulate their interview questions.

Scriptural Application

Read Philippians 2:3 aloud. Remind the students to respect both their subjects' time and their comments as they conduct their interviews.

Drafting Strategies

Instruct students to conduct their interviews and to write their sketches for homework. Remind them to organize the information clearly and to report the facts accurately.

Challenge the students to be selective in the words that they use. Encourage them to begin their sketches with an episode or dialogue that will gain the reader's attention. Remind them that a few well-chosen words that create a clear picture will be more effective that many words that paint a vague or ambiguous picture.

Revising Strategy

Distribute a copy of Writing Worksheet 14 to each student. Direct the students to an-

Drafting

Organize your notes. Chronological order is often effective. For example, you might begin with family background or the person's early life, then move to his preparation (schooling), and then discuss to his career. Topical organization is another way to prepare your sketch. You might write about the person's family background, then his career, and then interesting facts about him or significant quotations from the interview.

Be factual. Remember that a biographical sketch must be accurate. You are reporting the facts about the subject's life; you are not giving your opinions about that person.

Begin writing. Take a close look at the method of organization you have chosen. Set aside a block of time so that you can write without stopping. Follow the organization of your notes.

Revising

Read over what you have written. Have you answered the important *wh* questions about the person your interviewed? Is the organization of your paragraphs clear? Have you been factual in your writing?

Think about the beginning and ending of your sketch. Do the opening sentences catch the reader's attention? Have you used descriptive words that portray your subject clearly? Does the ending of your sketch sum up what you want to say about your subject? Is your reader left with any unanswered questions?

Make a clean copy. Incorporate any changes that you feel are necessary to improve your sketch. Proofread for correctness in grammar, spelling, and mechanics. Then write or print a clean copy to give to your teacher.

Publishing

Send a copy of your sketch to the person you interviewed. Your subject would probably like to know what you have said about him.

Share your sketch with people who know your subject. Friends, relatives, or classmates who know the person you wrote about might enjoy reading your sketch.

Read your sketch orally in class. Your teacher may set aside a class period in order to have an oral portrait gallery. Be prepared to read your sketch as part of the gallery presentation.

alyze their notes and rough drafts and then to revise their sketches as necessary.

Peer Response

After the students have analyzed their own sketches, match each student with a partner and direct them to exchange sketches. Instruct the peer readers to identify passages that are especially interesting or informative and then to identify confusing or unclear passages. After the students return the sketches to the original writers, direct each student to evaluate the peer's responses and to make changes that will clarify the biographical sketch.

Publishing Strategy

Encourage students to submit their sketches to the local newspaper. Tell the students to inquire from the local newspaper about times when the paper will feature family articles or tributes. Newspapers often feature special contributions near holidays such as Mother's Day and Father's Day.

Publishing Strategy

If students have written their biographical sketch about a relative, suggest that they read their biographical sketches as part of a family reunion.

Evaluation

For help in grading this assignment, see "Grading Writing Assignments" (p. x) and Rubric 14 (Support Materials CD, p. 118).

Enrichment

Instruct students to bring a newspaper obituary section to class. With the students examine the organization of a typical obituary. Referring to the models in the newspaper, lead the students in writing an obituary for Haman using information from the book of Esther.

CHAPTER 15

Chapter Goals

Students will

1. learn to use end marks, commas, semicolons, and colons correctly.

2. learn to use quotation marks correctly.

3. learn to use apostrophes, hyphens, underlining, and italics correctly.

PUNCTUATION

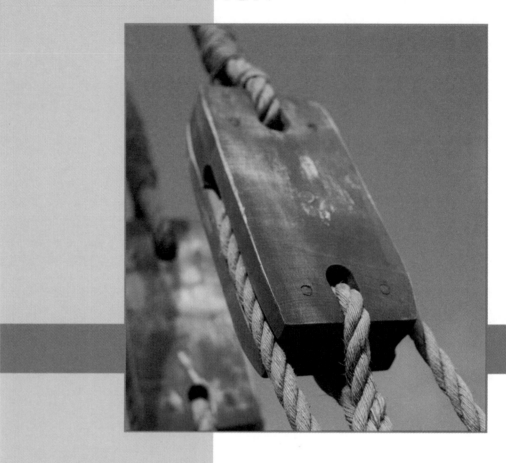

Objectives

Students will

1. correctly use periods, question marks, and exclamation points.

2. correctly use periods other than for end marks, including the decimal point.

3. correctly use the comma when it separates words or phrases in a series.

4. correctly use the comma when it separates words, clauses, or interjections.

5. correctly use the comma in quotations, dates, addresses, and letters.

6. correctly use the semicolon and colon.

7. correctly use quotation marks for enclosure, for direct and indirect quotations in dialogue, and with end marks.

8. correctly use quotation marks to enclose certain titles.

9. use underlining and italics correctly.

10. use apostrophes correctly to show omission, to form certain plurals, and to show possession.

11. use the hyphen correctly to divide or to show omission.

Lesson Support

Student Text

Chapter Review 15—pp. 429-30

Support Materials CD

Warm-Ups—pp. 31-32
Teaching Helps—p. 38
Concept Reinforcements—pp. 84-89

A pulley is a machine made of a rope and a wheel. It helps you lift things too heavy for you to lift by yourself. Pulling down on the rope on one side of the pulley will cause the rope on the other side to lift an object. The pulley changes the direction of the force of your pull.

Punctuation marks function something like pulleys. They can change the direction of your sentences. They also make sentences easier to read. Here's one example: "I have to hang up now. A friend just drove over Grandma." This is a terrible tragedy—but only of punctuation. Compare the correctly punctuated sentence: "I have to hang up now. A friend just drove over, Grandma." Good writers realize that proper punctuation, like a pulley, gives sentences a lift.

End Marks

Period

Use a period at the end of a declarative sentence.

> I spoke to Carlyle yesterday.

Use a period at the end of an indirect question.

> He asked me what I said.

Use a period at the end of an imperative sentence that does not express strong emotion.

> Please close the window.

Question Mark

Use a question mark at the end of an interrogative sentence.

> "Who is like unto thee, O Lord, among the gods?" (Exod. 15:11)

Exclamation Point

Use an exclamation point (sometimes called an exclamation mark) at the end of an exclamatory sentence.

> We won the championship game!

Use an exclamation point at the end of an imperative sentence that expresses strong emotion.

> Stop teasing your sister!

Use an exclamation point after an interjection that expresses strong emotion.

> Ouch! I stubbed my toe.

page 3

Sentence types

page 155

Interjections

Punctuation **287**

Teaching Strategy: Introduction

Prepare an overhead transparency of Teaching Helps page 38 (Support Materials CD). Using the transparency, demonstrate to the students the importance of using correct punctuation to avoid misunderstanding.

15-1 PRACTICE THE SKILL

Insert the correct end mark in each of the following sentences.

1. Has your class learned about the Plymouth Colony, Craig?

2. The Pilgrims landed at Cape Cod Bay.

3. This area was originally named Plimouth.

4. Boy, did they miss their destination of Virginia!

5. It took sixty-five days to sail from England to the New World.

6. What a trip!

7. Before they landed, the leaders composed the Mayflower Compact.

8. When did the Pilgrims meet Squanto?

9. Yuck! They prepared eel for their first Thanksgiving in 1621.

10. Read the next chapter by tomorrow.

15-2 REVIEW THE SKILL

Label each sentence as declarative, imperative, interrogative, or exclamatory. Add the correct end mark to each sentence.

interrogative 1. Have you ever heard the story of Paul Revere?

declarative 2. General Gage moved his British troops to Boston in 1774.

declarative 3. The British decided to destroy the American patriots' ammunition.

interrogative 4. How would the patriots know when the British were coming?

declarative 5. One patriot would signal by hanging lanterns in the church.

Teaching Strategy

Assign Practice the Skill 15-1 and Review the Skill 15-2.

Scriptural Application

Remind the students that to master a new topic in their English studies, they will need to apply what they have previously learned. If they learn well the first time through, the next section will be easier to understand. For example, if the students learn the types of sentences in Chapter 1, they will understand the correct use of end marks in Chapter 15 more easily. Isaiah 28:10 tells us that understanding is built precept upon precept, and line upon line.

<u>_imperative_</u>   6. Look at the two lanterns. or !

<u>_exclamatory_ or</u>   7. They will be here soon! or .
<u>_declarative_</u>

<u>_imperative_</u>   8. Tell Paul Revere to warn the people. or !

<u>_exclamatory_</u>   9. The British are coming!

<u>_declarative_</u>   10. Because of Paul Revere's warning, the patriots were ready for the British when they arrived in the morning.

Other Uses for the Period

A period usually follows an initial or each letter of an abbreviation.

> D. L. Moody (Dwight Lyman)
> Washington, D.C. (District of Columbia)
> M.Ed. (masters in education)

In recent years periods have been left out of some common abbreviations.

> USMC (United States Marine Corps)
> NASA (National Aeronautics and Space Administration)

A period follows the numbers and letters of an outline.

> I. First main idea
>> A. Supporting idea
>> B. Supporting idea
>>> 1. Supporting detail
>>> 2. Supporting detail
> II. Second main idea
> III. Third main idea

A period follows the numbers or letters in a list.

> 1. eggs
> 2. bread
> 3. milk
> 4. cheese

A period is used as a decimal point.

> $3.54
> 98.6°F
> 10.5%

Insert any missing periods, question marks, exclamation points, or decimal points in the following sentences.

1. Give me that book on astronauts.

2. Did you know that Sally K. Ride was the first female U. S. astronaut in space?

3. Sally Ride was born in Los Angeles, California, in 1951.

4. Amazing! She earned a PhD. from Stanford University in physics.

5. Did you know that she flew aboard the *Challenger* and the *Discovery* for NASA?

6. Wow! What an exciting job!

7. Have you read her book *To Space and Back*?

8. Dr. Ride gives an accurate, yet humorous, account of life aboard a space shuttle.

9. She dedicated her book to the memory of the astronauts aboard the *Challenger*.

10. Can you imagine? The *Challenger* had been in the air for only 73 seconds or 1.2167 minutes before it exploded. or !

Insert any missing periods, question marks, exclamation points, or decimal points.

1. George Washington Carver (or G. W.) was born a slave.

2. Mrs. Carver taught George how to work in the kitchen and the laundry room.

3. Boy! Did he ever have a secret touch with plants!

4. He received a B.S. in agriculture from Iowa State College.

5. George made many items from peanuts:

   a. axle grease

   b. coffee

   c. face powder

   d. milk.

6. Amazing! Who would imagine so many things from a peanut?

7. Didn't Carver teach at Booker T. Washington's Tuskegee Institute?

8. Yes, Thomas A. Edison even offered Carver a salary of $175,000.00!

9. Did you know that Carver was also a talented painter?

10. Carver preferred to work where he could help people.

Comma

Commas in a Series

Use a comma to separate three or more items in a series.

> Matthew, Mark, Luke, and John are the four Gospels.
> (*But:* Ruth and Esther are the only books of the Bible named for women.)
> The class read the novel, researched the author, and wrote a report.
> (*But:* The class studied the poem and memorized it.)

A comma sometimes separates two adjectives that modify the same noun. If you can reverse the order of the adjectives or replace the comma with the word *and* without changing the meaning, use a comma.

> A warm, gentle breeze blew off the gulf.
> A gentle, warm breeze blew off the gulf.
> A warm and gentle breeze blew off the gulf.
> (*But:* The new music teacher plays the clarinet.)

Use a comma to separate the first independent clause from the conjunction in a compound sentence. (*Do not use a comma before a conjunction that joins a compound predicate.*)

> The wind is blowing, and the air is cool.
> (*But:* The rain is falling heavily and flooding the streets.)

page 108

Adjectives

page 16

Comma splices and Fused sentences

page 151

Conjunctions

page 166

Compound sentences

If you and your students distinguish between true adjectives and determiners, explain that a comma never appears after a determiner. Only true adjectives will be separated by a comma.

Teaching Strategy: Introduction

Before teaching the lesson on commas, review the definitions and examples of modifiers, clauses, phrases, and conjunctions.

Teaching Strategy

If the students have trouble understanding comma use with clauses, review the definitions of a comma splice and a fused sentence from Chapter 1 and the definition of a compound sentence from Chapter 8. If the students have trouble understanding comma use with interjections, review the characteristics of interjections from Chapter 7.

Insert any missing commas and circle any unnecessary commas in the following sentences. Write _C_ to the left of the number if the sentence is correct.

1. Francis Scott Key worked as a prominent lawyer, served as Attorney General, and spoke as an opponent to slavery.

2. Key's strong, confident, and persuasive manner, made him an obvious choice to help Dr. William Beanes.

3. During the night the British soldiers awakened, arrested, and imprisoned Dr. Beanes.

4. Key, and John Skinner boarded the British ship and requested the release of Dr. Beanes.

C 5. President Madison's letter for release, Key's persuasive speech, and British soldiers' letters convinced the British to give Dr. Beanes freedom.

6. The British made Dr. Beanes, Francis Key, and John Skinner wait to leave until after the British attack upon Fort McHenry.

7. Key scribbled the words to "The Star-Spangled Banner" as he witnessed the forceful, British onslaught of cannons upon the fort.

C 8. The fort withstood the attack, and the flag waved in the air.

C 9. Francis Scott Key's strong national pride and relief at this comforting, stirring sight resulted in America's national anthem.

10. The flag flies twenty-four hours a day at Fort McHenry, Key's birthplace, and Key's gravesite.

Insert any missing commas and circle any unnecessary commas in the following sentences. Write C to the left of the number if the sentence is correct.

1. Many⊙loyal Englishmen opposed the ascension of a foreign Scottish ruler to their throne after Elizabeth's death.

2. James Stuart reigned on the English throne⊙and the Scottish throne until his death in 1625.

3. The weak, unattractive⌃and frail Charles became king after his father's death.

4. Historians depict James as greatly immoral⌃but they describe Charles as quite chaste and ethical.

C 5. Charles was not impressive to his parents, the Parliament, or the rest of England.

C 6. He did finally develop a strong bond with the Duke of Buckingham.

7. Charles's reign included wars within his country, with France⌃and with Spain.

C 8. Charles brought a moral, spiritual, and cultural influence to the court.

9. He purchased many paintings by Mytens⌃Van Dyck, and Rubens.

10. The English people never favored Charles⊙and eventually beheaded him.

Combine each pair of sentences into one sentence. Portions of most of the sentences have been underlined to help you. Be sure to use correct punctuation. *(Answers will vary.)*

1. Nicaragua lies <u>south of Honduras</u> and <u>north of Costa Rica</u>. Nicaragua lies <u>between the Pacific and Atlantic Oceans.</u>

   Nicaragua lies south of Honduras, north of Costa Rica, and between

   the Pacific and Atlantic Oceans.

2. <u>The Pacific Lowlands</u> is one of the three geographic regions in Nicaragua. <u>The Central Highlands</u> and <u>the Mosquito Coast</u> are also geographic regions in Nicaragua.

   The Pacific Lowlands, the Central Highlands, and the Mosquito Coast

   are the geographic regions in Nicaragua.

3. The <u>beautiful</u> city of Managua is the capital of Nicaragua. The <u>growing</u> city of Managua is the capital of Nicaragua.

   The beautiful, growing city of Managua is the capital of Nicaragua.

4. Nicaraguans grow <u>bananas</u> and <u>rice</u>. Nicaraguans grow <u>sugar cane</u> too.

   Nicaraguans grow bananas, rice, and sugar cane.

5. Nicaraguans <u>believe in a male dominant society</u>. The Nicaraguans <u>elected Violeta de Barrios Chamorro as president in 1990.</u>

   Nicaraguans believe in a male dominant society but elected Violeta

   de Barrios Chamorro as president in 1990.

6. The terrain of Nicaragua includes <u>mountains, valleys, and grasslands</u>. There are <u>rain forests</u> in Nicaragua also.

   The land of Nicaragua consists of mountains, valleys, grasslands,

   and rain forests.

7. Because of the tropical climate, each year Nicaragua has <u>about sixty inches of rain</u>. Nicaragua has an <u>average temperature of about 80°F.</u>

   Because of the tropical climate, each year Nicaragua has about

   sixty inches of rain and an average temperature of about 80° F.

8. Children are required to attend school in Nicaragua until the age of twelve. Many children do not have schools to attend.

Children are required to attend school in Nicaragua until the age

of twelve, but many children do not have schools to attend.

9. Granada and León are large cities in Nicaragua. Jinotepe is also a large city in Nicaragua.

Granada, León, and Jinotepe are large cities in Nicaragua.

10. Most of the people in Nicaragua speak Spanish and farm to earn a living. Most claim Roman Catholicism as their religion.

Most of the people in Nicaragua speak Spanish, farm to earn a

living, and claim Roman Catholicism as their religion.

Commas to Separate

A comma sometimes separates introductory words from the rest of the sentence.

> First, I want to tell you about mainland China.
> However, my slides are of only Taiwan and Hong Kong.

Use a comma to separate an introductory dependent clause from the independent clause in a complex sentence.

> Although the sun is shining, clouds are gathering on the horizon.

Use a comma or a pair of commas to separate a noun of direct address (a noun that names the person being spoken to) from the rest of the sentence.

> Luis, where is your coat?
> Where is your coat, Luis?
> Where, Luis, is your coat?

A comma or a pair of commas sometimes separates an interrupting phrase that could be left out of the sentence.

> Neil Armstrong was an American astronaut, as you know.
> He was, in fact, the first person to walk on the moon.

A comma sometimes separates an interjection from the rest of the sentence.

> Yes, I know the answer.
> Open your book to page 79, please.

page 169

Complex sentences

page 155

Interjections

Insert any missing commas and circle any unnecessary commas. Write C to the left of the number if the sentence is correct.

1. Though not as famous as their fathers White House children have made their own marks in history.

2. For example John Quincy Adams became the sixth president in 1825.

3. Esther Cleveland interestingly enough was the only child born in the White House.

4. Maria Monroe on the other hand receives special honor as the first to have her wedding in the White House.

C 5. Martin Van Buren's son married the niece of Washington Irving.

6. In some cases however, the grandchildren of the presidents lived in the White House.

7. Unfortunately the White House had not yet been built when George Washington's grandchildren and great-grandchildren lived with him during his presidency.

8. Mary Custis, who was George Washington's great-granddaughter married Robert E. Lee.

This photograph portrays President Eisenhower and his grandson David in 1955.

9. The marriage of Julie Nixon and David Eisenhower joined⊙two former White House children.

10. Furthermore‚President Eisenhower named Camp David, a presidential
retreat in Maryland‚after his grandson David.

15-9 REVIEW THE SKILL

Insert any missing commas and circle any unnecessary commas. Write C to the left of the number if the sentence is correct.

1. Have you ever gone ice skating‚Bob?

2. Well‚we should go to a skating rink sometime soon.

C 3. Even though most of the skilled skaters started young, people of all ages can learn.

4. Some kids‚however, start when they are two⊙or three years old.

5. Standing, walking‚and stopping are some of the basic skills in skating.

6. After mastering these skills, skating backwards‚some say, is not very difficult.

7. Ice skating‚with the invention of indoor skating rinks, can be enjoyed all year long.

C 8. To create a smooth surface Frank Zamboni invented the Zamboni. This machine resurfaces the ice.

9. Even though a Zamboni costs up to $50,000‚it can last ten, twenty‚and even thirty years.

C 10. I would love to drive a Zamboni sometime, but I will probably never get a chance.

Commas with Quotations, Dates, and Addresses
Commas in Letters

In a written dialogue a comma separates the direct quotation from the rest of the sentence.

> Magda asked, "What is the reference for the verse that says that all have sinned?"
> "It's Romans 3:23," Mr. Cooper replied.
> "Which verse," Jaime asked, "teaches us to obey our parents?"

In a date a comma separates the day from the year.

> May 11, 1858

A comma also follows a date within a sentence when the year is also given.

> She was born March 2, 1969, in Baltimore.
> (*But:* She was born March 2 in Baltimore.)

In an address a comma separates the city from the state or country.

> New Brighton, Minnesota
> Tokyo, Japan

A comma also follows a state or country when the city is also named within a sentence.

> Oslo, Norway, is his favorite European city.
> They went to Seattle, Washington, for their vacation this summer.
> (*But:* They went to Seattle for their vacation this summer.
> They went to Washington for their vacation this summer.)

A comma does not separate the state from the ZIP code in an address.

> Mr. Brad Abercrombie
> 2 Audley Lane
> Chapel Hill, North Carolina 27514

Use a comma after the greeting of a friendly letter and the closing of all letters.

> Dear Ronda,
> Sincerely yours,

Insert any missing commas and circle any unnecessary commas in the following letter.

628 West Main Avenue

Fredericksburg, OH, 44627

June 15, 2000

Dear Tim,

Thanks for writing me back. It sounds like you are learning a lot about living in, Africa. My teacher told us that on May 31, 1961, South Africa became a republic. I would like to learn more about this country.

People at church miss you. They ask me to tell them how you are doing. Mrs. West, asked, "Have you heard from Tim yet?" "Yes," I said, "I get a letter from him every month." I told her all about the elephants you saw on the reserve.

I cannot wait to see you in August. (Don't forget that August, 27 is my birthday!) Mom said we would be able to pick you up at the airport.

I hope you will write to me soon. I will be in Austin, Texas, during the month of July. You can send a letter to me at 4523 Sullivan Lane, Austin, TX 43211-4567.

Please write soon!

Your friend,

Kristen

Kristen

Insert any missing commas and circle any unnecessary commas.

B.P. 252

Koussui, Cameroon

West Africa

July(,)11, 2000

Dear Kristen,

Thank you for your friendly, informative letter. It is always good to hear from the USA.

I read the biographies of C. T. Studd, David Livingstone,and Mary Slessor(,) and learned much from their experiences. In 1841(,)David Livingstone became a missionary to Africa. When Mary Slessor heard that Livingstone had died,she told her mother, "I want to offer myself as a missionary." Within two years(,)Mary was in Africa.

I plan to arrive in Boston on August 12. First, I want to eat a hamburger! After that, I would like to visit our friends from church. I look forward to seeing you.

In Him,

Tim

Tim

Semicolon

A semicolon sometimes separates two independent clauses in a compound sentence.

> Ravi cooked the meal and set the table; his sister washed the dishes.

Colon

Use a colon to separate the chapter from the verse in a Bible reference.

> Isaiah 40:8

Use a colon to separate the hour from the minutes in a statement of time.

> 9:45 A.M.

Use a colon after the greeting of a business letter.

> Dear Mr. Noguchi:

Use a colon to introduce a list after an independent clause.

> You must assemble these ingredients for lemonade: lemons, sugar, and water.

page 166

Compound sentences

PRACTICE THE SKILL

Insert any missing semicolons or colons in the following sentences. Write *C* to the left of the number if the sentence is correct.

1. Joseph was a wise leader; he saved Egypt as well as other countries from starvation.

2. Joseph's story begins in Genesis 37:1.

3. Joseph's responsibilities included the following: assisting the pharaoh, collecting 20 percent of the surplus grain, and storing the grain for the time of famine.

4. Joseph was prepared to be a good administrator; he had learned necessary skills by being a faithful slave and prisoner in Egypt.

C 5. When the years of famine came, the country was adequately prepared.

6. All the people came to Joseph for food; he was prepared to help them.

C 7. Joseph sold the grain to the people and saved them from starvation.

Teaching Strategy: Introduction

Before teaching the lesson on semicolons, review with the students the information about compound sentences in Chapter 8.

Scriptural Application

First Corinthians 14:40 tells the people of God to do all things decently and in order. Punctuation should also be used decently and in order. If the punctuation is missing or incorrect, the meaning of a sentence may differ from what the writer intended.

8. Not only the Egyptians were saved by Joseph's foresight; other people suffering from the famine came to Egypt to see Joseph.

C 9. One group of visitors came to buy food, and Joseph realized that they were his brothers.

10. Joseph's wisdom helped many people; he saved his own family from starvation.

15-13 REVIEW THE SKILL

Combine the following sentences using either a comma and conjunction, a semicolon, or a colon. *(Answers will vary.)*

1. General Thomas "Stonewall" Jackson graduated from West Point. He was one of America's greatest military leaders.

   General Thomas "Stonewall" Jackson graduated from West Point;

   he was one of America's greatest military leaders.

2. Jackson demonstrated admirable character qualities. He demonstrated loyalty, dependability, and courage.

   Jackson demonstrated these admirable character qualities: loyalty,

   dependability, and courage.

3. Jackson wanted to keep the Union together. He fought for the Confederacy in the Civil War.

   Jackson wanted to keep the Union together, but he fought for

   the Confederacy in the Civil War.

4. Jackson was a religious man. He became a Christian when he was a young man.

   Jackson was a religious man; he became a Christian when he was

   a young man.

5. He loved the Scriptures. He read his Bible frequently.

   He loved the Scriptures; he read his Bible frequently.

   _____

6. He showed his concern for his troops in several ways. He read the Scriptures to them, preached to them, and prayed for them.

   He showed his concern for his troops by doing these things: reading

   the Scriptures to them, preaching to them, and praying for them.

7. He seemed to fear nothing in battle. He had great fear and respect for God.

   He seemed to fear nothing in battle, but he had great fear and

   respect for God.

8. Jackson was involved in numerous battles. He was involved in Bull Run, Richmond, and Antietam.

   Jackson was involved in numerous battles including the following:

   Bull Run, Richmond, and Antietam.

9. In the First Battle of Bull Run, Jackson and his troops stood firm. Another general cried, "There is Jackson standing like a stone wall."

   In the First Battle of Bull Run, Jackson and his troops stood firm;

   another general cried, "There is Jackson standing like a stone wall."

10. Stonewall Jackson died on May 10, 1863. Both the North and the South mourned his death.

    Stonewall Jackson died on May 10, 1863; both the North and the

    South mourned his death.

Insert any missing semicolons or colons in the following sentences. Circle any unnecessary semicolons, colons, commas, end marks, or decimal points.

November 9, 2000

Grace Flanders

5703 Washburn Road

Vassar, MI 48768

Dear Miss Flanders:

Thank you, Miss Flanders, for the article you submitted entitled "Holiday Helpers." We are happy to inform you that "Holiday Helpers" will be featured in the December issue of *Your Voice.*

For the use of your article, we would like to present you with a free issue of *Your Voice.* In addition, you may choose one of these three books for only $5.00: *Writing as a Craft, The English Manual for the Writer,* or the *Oxford English Dictionary.*

Your Voice would also like to invite you personally to be a guest at our next writers' banquet. The banquet will be held at Helena Hotel in Helena, Montana. Our theme verse for this year's banquet is I Corinthians 14:40. The banquet will begin at 7:00 P.M. on the night of January 15, 2001. At 8:00 P.M. we will gather in the conference room for a fascinating workshop on the topic "Organizing Your Written Work." You may attend a second workshop the following morning before you leave.

We encourage you to continue to submit articles for publication. These are the topics for the month of January: add-on bedrooms, children's sports, and health food.

Once again, thank you for writing. We hope to hear from you again.

Sincerely,

Betsy Kingston

Editor of *Your Voice*

Quotation Marks

Use quotation marks to show words taken from another source.

> John Donne wrote the words "No man is an island."

Use quotation marks to show the words of the speakers in a dialogue.

> "David, did you play miniature golf Saturday?" Tana asked.
> "Yes, but I didn't see you," David answered.
> "I was there with my friend Ann."
> "Oh, I remember her."

Quotation marks are not used with indirect quotations.

> David said that he remembered Ann.

Follow these rules for using other punctuation with quotation marks:

- Always place periods and commas before the quotation marks.

  > He said, "I remember her."
  > David thought for a moment. "I remember her," he said.

- Place question marks and exclamation points either before or after closing quotation marks, according to the meaning of the sentence. If the entire sentence is a question or an exclamation, place the question mark or exclamation point after the quotation marks.

  > Did you hear David say "I remember her"?
  > I can't believe you've never read "Birches"!

- If only the quotation is a question or an exclamation, place the question mark or exclamation point before the quotation marks.

  > Lane asked, "Do you smell smoke?"
  > "The house is on fire!" he exclaimed.

- Notice that no period or comma follows a question mark or an exclamation point.

Quotation marks are placed around the following kinds of titles.

short stories:	"Rikki-Tikki-Tavi"
chapters:	"Father Speaks"
short poems:	"Paul Revere's Ride"
essays:	"Our Blessed Land"
periodical articles:	"What It's Like When You Can't Read or Write"
songs:	"When I Survey the Wondrous Cross"
television or radio episodes:	"Charlie Coulson: Drummer Boy"

Teaching Strategy: Induction

Instruct the students to turn to the capitalization rules for titles on page 275 of the student text. Ask the students why some titles are in quotation marks and other titles are italicized. Lead them to realize that the titles in quotation marks are short works and the italicized titles are longer works.

Scriptural Application

A worker is known by his works. (Proverbs 20:11—"Even a child is known by his doings, whether his work be pure, and whether it be right.") Writers or students are also known by their works. Using correct punctuation can be an identifying mark. Carefulness and accuracy are important in all writing, whether formal or informal.

15·15 PRACTICE THE SKILL

A. Insert any missing quotation marks.

B. Circle any misplaced quotation marks.

C. Write C if the sentence is correct.

1. When asked if he could tell a sinner how to get to heaven, Dr. Walter Wilson would reply, "Yes, that is my principal business in life."

C 2. One time, Dr. Wilson was to board a train on June 28; however, because he had not received his ticket, he could not board the train until July 3.

3. A woman on the train saw Dr. Wilson reading his Bible and asked, "May I sit with you?"

4. When Dr. Wilson looked up to see a woman dressed in mourning clothes, what do you think he said but "Certainly?"

5. "Is there something I can help you with? Dr. Wilson asked.

C 6. The woman asked him, "Can you help me find Jesus?"

7. "Let's see what God has to say, replied Dr. Wilson.

8. After reading verses from God's Word and praying, the woman exclaimed, "I know now that my Savior has taken away my sins! "

9. The woman told Dr. Wilson, "I had planned to board this train on June 26, but my sister became ill, and my trip was delayed until July 3."

10. Dr. Wilson prayed, "Thank you, God, for showing me the reason for the delay."

A. Insert any missing quotation marks.
B. Circle any misplaced quotation marks.
C. Write C if the sentence is correct.

1. Rachel looked at her new baby sister through the nursery window and exclaimed, "She's beautiful!"

2. The doctor told Rachel's mother, "She has a collapsed lung; we will watch her for a few days."

3. Every day, Rachel visited her mother in the hospital and asked, "May I hold Hannah?"

4. Her mother replied, "She must grow stronger lungs first; then we may hold her."

C 5. The doctor told Rachel's mother that Hannah must stay in the hospital one more night.

6. What else could Rachel and her mother do but pray, "God, please help Hannah's lungs?"

7. The next morning, the doctor told Rachel's mother, "Hannah may go home today."

C 8. "Yea!" Rachel shouted.

9. Rachel asked her mother, "May I hold Hannah today?"

10. "Yes, today you may hold Hannah," replied Rachel's mother.

Underlining for Italics

In handwritten or typed papers, the following items are underlined. In printed books they are in italics.

Words and letters being discussed

How many i's are in the word <u>impossibility</u>?
How many *i*'s are in the word *impossibility*?

Names of large vehicles

ships:	*Mayflower*
planes:	*Spruce Goose*
trains:	*Orient Express*
spacecraft:	*Apollo 11*

Titles of long works

books:	*Caddie Woodlawn*
magazines:	*U.S. News & World Report*
newspapers:	*New York Times*
	(The word *the* is not part of a newspaper title.)
musical compositions:	Mendelssohn's *Elijah*
television or radio series:	*Miracles*
plays:	*Romeo and Juliet*

Names of works of art

paintings:	*American Gothic*
sculptures:	*Spoonbridge and Cherry*

15-17 ⚾ PRACTICE THE SKILL

A. Insert any missing quotation marks.

B. Underline any words that should be in italics.

C. Circle any unnecessary quotation marks or incorrectly italicized words.

D. Write C if the sentence is correct.

1. "Webster's New World Dictionary" defines an aircraft carrier as "a warship that carries airplanes."

2. In 1922 the first U.S. aircraft carrier was commissioned. It was named the Langley and could accommodate about thirty-five aircraft.

3. David Brown's book, "Aircraft Carriers," reports that the Saratoga, a carrier similar to the Langley, could carry up to ninety aircraft.

4. The article "Wheels over Water" appeared in a 1939 edition of the "Reader's Digest." This article tells the story of a fighter plane's attempting to land aboard the Lexington during a storm.

5. During the early 1940s, informative articles about aircraft carriers appeared in other leading magazines, such as "Popular Science," "Popular Mechanics," and "Life."

USS *Langley* in May 1928

A. Insert any missing quotation marks.
B. Underline any words that should be in italics.
C. Circle any unnecessary quotation marks or incorrectly italicized words.
D. Write *C* if the sentence is correct.

C 1. Many people associate Beverly Cleary's name with a character in her books, Ramona Quimby.

2. However, Ramona was only briefly mentioned in Cleary's first book, <u>Henry Huggins</u>.

3. In the final chapter of her autobiography, <u>My Own Two Feet</u>, Cleary tells of her efforts at writing a book. The chapter is called "A House, a Cat, a Letter."

4. "<u>Henry Huggins</u>" began as a short story entitled "Spareribs and Henry."

5. Someone encouraged her to add more short stories to "Spareribs and Henry" to make one book-length story.

6. One story Cleary added, entitled "(*The Green Christmas*)," was a new version of a short story she had written in high school.

7. Cleary finished her manuscript and sent "Spareribs and Henry," the book, to her publisher.

8. Before her manuscript could be published, Cleary had to change the title from <u>Spareribs and Henry</u> to "<u>Henry Huggins</u>."

9. Other books by Cleary include "<u>Ramona and Her Father</u>," "<u>Ramona Quimby, Age 8</u>," and "<u>Ramona the Brave</u>."

10. Cleary's mother encouraged her to write her stories by saying, "Make it funny."

Apostrophe

Use an apostrophe to show the omission of letters or numbers.

> Contractions: I + have = I've
>   could + not = couldn't
> Dates: 1929 = '29

Use an apostrophe to show the plurals of letters being discussed.

> the *d,* the *d*'s

Use an apostrophe to form the possessive of nouns.

- To form the singular possessive, add *'s* to the singular form of the noun.

man—man's	The man's hat blew into the water.
lady—lady's	Kevin turned to speak to the lady's daughter.
Gladys—Gladys's	Gladys's glasses lay on the windowsill.

- Traditionally, only an apostrophe is added to the proper names *Jesus* and *Moses*.

Moses—Moses'	God turned Moses' rod into a snake.
Jesus—Jesus'	Was Bartholomew one of Jesus' disciples?

- If a plural ends with an *s,* add only an apostrophe to make it possessive.

ladies—ladies'	The ladies' luncheon will be held at Turner's Restaurant.

- If a plural does not end with an *s,* add an *'s*

men—men's	Does your church sponsor a men's softball team?

 15-19   PRACTICE THE SKILL

Correct the following sentences by inserting apostrophes.

1. Havent you heard of the loyalty of Mordecai?

2. He overheard the terrible plan of the kings guards.

3. Mordecai warned King Ahasuerus of the mens intent to kill him.

4. How many *u*s are in Ahasuerus?

5. Mordecai worshipped only God; he wouldnt bow down to Haman.

6. Hamans pride was injured, and he made plans to kill Mordecai.

7. One night the king couldnt sleep, so he had his book of records read to him.

page 128

Adverbs

page 216

Possessive pronouns and contractions

page 30

Forms of nouns

8. The servants read the record of how Mordecai had saved Ahasuerus‸s life.

9. The king decided that some reward should be given for Mordecai‸s act of loyalty.

10. Haman had to lead Mordecai through all the city‸s streets and proclaim honor for Mordecai.

15-20 REVIEW THE SKILL

Underline each word that contains an apostrophe error and then rewrite the word correctly in the blank. If the sentence contains no errors, write *C* in the blank.

Congress's 1. Hiram Revels was <u>Congress'</u> first black member.

_C_ 2. He was born in 1822 and became a member of the Senate in '70.

didn't 3. Revels <u>did'nt</u> serve only as a senator.

_C_ 4. He pastored and taught in several churches in the North and Midwest.

slaves' 5. He cared for the former <u>slaves's</u> physical and spiritual needs.

Mississippi's 6. He later became the president of <u>Mississippis'</u> Alcorn College.

nation's 7. As secretary of state in Mississippi, he was still involved in the <u>nations</u> politics.

_'75_ 8. In <u>75'</u> he wrote a letter to President Grant expressing his disappointment with the corrupt government in Mississippi.

should've 9. He claimed that the government leaders <u>shouldv'e</u> been more honest and benevolent.

_C_ 10. Revels wouldn't quit preaching; he continued his ministry until his death in 1901.

Hyphen

Use a hyphen to divide words at the end of a line. (Divide words only between syllables; never divide a one-syllable word.)

Leave at least two letters and a hyphen on the first line.

Wrong: Three maidens tell Hercules not to be a-stonished at anything the old man says.

Right: Nathaniel Hawthorne tells the story of an ad-venturous quest for three golden apples.

Put at least three letters on the next line.

Wrong: The maidens tell Hercules to hold the craft-y man until he tells him the way to Atlas.

Right: The old man could change from one physi-cal form into another.

Leave the hyphen on the first line; do not carry it to the second line.

Wrong: The giant will not hold the sky on his shoul -ders again, but Hercules tricks him.

Right: Hercules holds up the sky while the enor-mous Atlas picks the apples.

Use a hyphen between the words of multiword numbers up to ninety-nine.

Twenty-four members of the youth group attended the meeting.

Use a hyphen between the two parts of a fraction that is written out.

They make up more than three-fourths of our class.

Use a hyphen to show the omission of a connecting word.

Your assignment is to read pages 21-25.
The revival services are May 17-23 this year.

15·21 PRACTICE THE SKILL

Insert any missing apostrophes and hyphens in the following sentences. Circle any wrong items. Write *C* if the sentence is correct.

1. Louisa May Alcott lived from 183288 and wrote mainly children's literature.

2. Her family's move from Philadelphia to Boston occurred during her childhood.

3. Her father's trip to Europe inspired plans for a large farm.

4. Mrs. Alcott's desire was for her four daughters' happiness.

Evaluation

Examine the punctuation in your students' writing assignments. If the student understands the principles, he will use correct punctuation in his writing. This examination, coupled with evaluation of practices, should be a good indication of students' progress.

Enrichment

Materials

- "Rikki-Tikki-Tavi" by Rudyard Kipling (*EXPLORATIONS IN LITERATURE for Christian Schools,* Second Edition, BJU Press)

Choose a children's story or narrative that contains a great deal of dialogue and various marks of punctuation, such as "Rikki-Tikki-Tavi." Alter several paragraphs to eliminate all punctuation. Divide the class into small groups. Give each group one altered paragraph. Instruct each group to insert the correct punctuation in its paragraph. Allow students to create appropriate sound effects for each punctuation mark (such as clicking their tongues, tapping pencils, or snapping their fingers). One student will read the paragraph for the class while the other group members supply the punctuation sound effects. Students will insert the correct sound every time that form of punctuation is needed.

5. Louisa and her sisters often heard stories of Jesus' life and of Moses' life.

C 6. The Alcotts' friends and neighbors included Ralph Waldo Emerson, Nathaniel Hawthorne, and Henry David Thoreau.

7. Louisa's first book, *Flower Fables,* was published when she was twenty-two years old and was written for Emerson's daughter Ellen.

C 8. Louisa was a Civil War nurse from 1862-63 in Washington, D.C.

9. Louisa's most famous book is *Little Women,* which she wrote when she was thirty-five years old.

10. *Little Women's* characters also appear in the book *Little Men.* These books represent two-thirds of the books about the March family.

15-22 REVIEW THE SKILL

Insert any missing apostrophes or hyphens. Write *C* if the sentence is correct.

1. Did you know that Queen Victoria's reign over Great Britain lasted sixty-three years?

2. The other British monarchs' reigns have not been as long as hers.

3. Victoria ruled during the years 1837-1901.

C 4. Many historians call this time the Victorian Age.

5. Her reign is famous for the expansion of Britain's properties in other parts of the world.

6. The British Empire included one-fourth of the world's land and population.

7. Charles Dickens was one of Britain's celebrities during the Victorian Age.

8. Have you ever read Dickens's novel *Nicholas Nickleby*?

9. Queen Victoria's family included five daughters and four sons.

10. The queen's eldest son became King Edward VII after his mother's death in '01.

 Learning Christianly

Have you ever read a fascinating story? Or have you ever heard someone read a poem that captured your imagination? One of the wonderful things about mastering a language is that it allows us to read and write beautiful things. Read Galatians 5:14. How can you love your neighbor better because of your access to some of the more beautiful things in our language?

 Learning Christianly

Part of loving our neighbors as ourselves is sharing beautiful things with them. When we share beautiful things, we show love to others in one of the ways that God has shown His love to us. In allowing us to live in a beautiful world, one that we do not deserve, God shows His love to us. God is also the source of beauty, and it is appropriate that we prize the beautiful things of this world because they come from Him. Even the talent to write and to create beautiful things comes from God. The Christian should seek to act like God in sharing beautiful things with others. Once your students have learned the skills of writing and grammar, they will be in an even better position to do so.

One on One: Instruct your student to restore the correct punctuation to the altered paragraph. Encourage him to create sound effects for each punctuation mark. Allow the student to read the paragraph aloud and to insert the sound effects at the appropriate times. Compare his version to the original and discuss your findings. Do the two versions differ? What are the differences? Why is one mark more or less effective than another (assuming both are correct)?

15-23 USE THE SKILL

A. Insert any missing punctuation marks: end marks, commas, semicolons, colons, quotation marks, apostrophes, and hyphens.
B. Underline any words that should be written in italics.
C. Circle any misplaced punctuation marks.

Louisa May Alcott wrote a series of books based on her own family's experiences. This series included the following titles: Little Women, Little Men, and Jo's Boys. Alcott used her own life as a model for Jo, the main character in all three of these books. "Little Women" was written when Louisa was thirty-five years old, and tells the antics of Jo and her three sisters: Meg, Beth, and Amy. The sisters' many mishaps draw them closer and teach them important lessons about life.

Jo's story continues in Little Men. The book chronicles the lives of Jo and her husband; the couple runs a boarding school. Imagine living with twelve boys! Further "adventures" at the boys' school continue in the final book, Jo's Boys.

15-24 CUMULATIVE REVIEW

Locate and correct the fifteen errors in the paragraph: troublesome words, capitalization, and punctuation.

Somehow the fledgling United States of America had to pay for the Revolutionary War. However, without the power of taxation, *there* ~~their~~ were few ways for the colonists to *raise* ~~rise~~ money. Congress had decided in 1775 to issue a new kind of ~~M~~*m*oney. Soon Congress had distributed so many new bills that they *were* ~~we're~~ almost worthless. Congress could not ~~prophet~~ *profit* from this valueless money. Individual state~~'~~s contributed money, but they could not give ~~to~~ *too* much. Some wealthy ~~a~~*A*merican colonists lent money to the government with the agreement that the loan would be paid back in full. Finally, it was gifts from other countries like Spain, France, and the ~~n~~*N*etherlands that rescued the young ~~N~~*n*ation.

CRAFTING A LETTER TO THE EDITOR

But sanctify the Lord God in your hearts: and be ready always to give an answer to every man that asketh you a reason of the hope that is in you with meekness and fear.

I Peter 3:15

Persuasion focuses on changing a person's thinking, choices, and behavior. A major indication that a person has been persuaded is his behavior. Successful persuasion results in someone's changing his actions. Wrong actions are often the result of negative or dishonest persuasion.

In a letter to the editor, the writer uses persuasion to sway others to take action on a certain issue. A letter to the editor is a response to an editor's opinion on the editorial page, an article published in the paper, or a topic of significance in the community. These letters are published on the editorial page of newspapers and magazines. If your school has a school newspaper, look to see whether it includes any letters.

Your Turn

Write a persuasive letter to the editor. Remember to suit the topic of the letter to the audience. (The readers of *USA Today,* for example, are not interested in the poor garbage pickup in your neighborhood.)

Planning

Choose an issue. Read a newspaper or a news magazine, listen to the news on the radio, or talk with a friend. Do you have strong emotional reactions to something that you read or heard? Perhaps you have strong feelings about several issues. As you consider a possible issue, you may find that your letter will be more successful if you choose a local issue.

Freewrite for several minutes. Write down everything you currently know about the issue. Then examine your notes. Are your ideas based on facts? Are there examples or expert opinions that support your ideas?

Identify your purpose. Based upon the ideas that you have written, what do you hope to accomplish with your letter? Do you want to argue your opinion in a way that will cause people to change their minds? Or do you want to persuade people to follow a course of action?

Many writers use emotion to persuade their readers. However, emotional appeal by itself is not often effective. Many persuasive writers use argumentation to present their viewpoint. Argumentation focuses solely on changing someone's mind about an issue, whereas persuasion tries to change not only someone's thinking but also his choices and behavior. When argumentation and persuasion are combined, the writer has a powerful tool at his disposal.

Drafting

Write an introduction. Use an introductory sentence or paragraph to identify who you are and why you are qualified to write your letter. Many letters to the editor come from doctors, preachers, professors, or other trained individuals. In their letters they state that they have had years of training in a particular field, and they may describe some of their experiences. This background information, called credentials, helps prove that the writer possesses enough knowledge to write about the subject. As a student, your credentials will probably not be your education or your job. Students' credentials could include a class project, a trip, or a special interest.

Support your opinions. Keep your letter simple. Use details to explain why you believe your position is the right one. Read the two example letters written by seventh-grade students about a topic that they believed was significant to the community.

> Dear Mr. Editor,
>
> I am Juan in the seventh grade at Oak Park School. I think the park's courts need another basketball hoop. I don't like shooting baskets with a bunch of other boys all the time. Some boys play rough, and kids get pushed around. I think the city needs to help kids play better ball by adding another hoop.
>
> Juan

> Dear Editor:
>
> My name is Santiago. I am a seventh grader at Oak Park School. One of my hobbies is playing basketball, and I hope to play for Oak Park this year. In fact, I practice shooting baskets every day after school at Rigley Park on Hastings Road.
>
> I like Rigley Park a lot except that it is always crowded in the afternoon. I counted thirty-five people on the courts the other day. Later that day a player was knocked to the ground while he was trying to rebound a ball. He went to the hospital because he broke his elbow.
>
> I think the city should add another court or another basketball hoop to the park. An additional hoop would relieve crowded conditions and would help prevent injuries caused by overcrowding.
>
> Sincerely,
>
> Santiago Carlton

Which letter do you believe would be published by the newspaper? Which letter do you believe would cause the city to add another basketball court? Santiago used details so that his readers would know which city park he was talking about. He also used specific examples about what happens because of insufficient space. In addition, Santiago tells why he is qualified to write about his topic, and his grammar skills are much better than Juan's.

Incorporate common arguments that are used as tools to persuade.
- **Simile:** a comparison that uses *like* or *as.* A letter to the editor urging people to vote in an upcoming election might include the following simile: "People who don't vote but then complain about the results of

---

if applicable. Warn the students against arguments based only on emotion or name calling; point out ineffective sample letters that rely on these weak strategies.

Planning Strategy

Remind students that success in changing someone's mind combines both rational (facts) and emotional (actions) appeal. Call the students' attention to the fact that they must believe strongly in something in order to be able to persuade someone else about that thing. Instruct the students to choose an issue and to begin planning

their letters. Remind the students to identify a clear purpose for their letters to the editor.

Drafting Strategies

Direct an in-class discussion on the topic of school uniforms. Briefly discuss advantages and disadvantages of school uniforms; then determine by vote whether the majority of the class is for or against them. Once the majority position has been settled, solicit reasons for the decision from various students, listing each reason for display. Allow the students to choose the

three strongest reasons to be the topic sentences of a letter. Designate one student as scribe and direct the class in composing a letter to the editor. Instruct the scribe to read the completed letter aloud to the class. Then encourage the students to use a similar composition process as they draft their own letters to the editor.

Direct the students' attention to the two sample letters on page 316. Discuss the differences between Juan's letter and Santiago's letter. Lead the students to notice Santiago's use of specific details by identifying himself, naming the park, and elections are like people who won't help make supper but then complain about the meal."

- **Metaphor:** a comparison that does not use *like* or *as.* "Our city taxes are a burden that is too heavy to carry any more" is a metaphorical comparison.

- **Testimonial:** information about the writer's credentials or personal experience. Testimonial is one way to prove that you are qualified to write about a topic. Santiago's statement "I practice shooting baskets every day after school at Rigley Park on Hastings Road" lets the reader see that Santiago has personally experienced the problem at the park.

- **Bandwagon:** device that urges people to become a part of a group. This device is often used in advertising and can be easily misused, so be careful if you include it. A statement such as "Everyone who thinks carefully about this problem will have to agree with me" is a bandwagon statement—but it may not actually be true! (Other people might think long and hard about a situation and come to a conclusion different from yours.) If you've ever said something such as "But Mom, everyone else is going!" you have used a bandwagon appeal. Did it work?

Write a conclusion. End your letter with your most important thought or recommendation. In the last paragraph of his letter, Santiago presents what he thinks the city should do. His concluding paragraph leaves the reader with the main reason for his letter.

Keep your letter simple. Write clear, grammatically correct sentences. Because the editor may need to shorten your letter for publication, make your letter brief and well organized.

Use correct form for your letter. Begin your letter with "Dear Editor." Be sure to close your letter with your full name and address. Newspapers and magazines automatically reject letters that are anonymous.

Revising

Evaluate your argument or ask a peer to evaluate it. Have you stated your opinion clearly? Have you used facts to support your argument? Did you include examples to prove your point? Is your letter convincing?

Proofread for correctness. Make sure that your letter is error free. Be alert for errors in grammar, spelling, and mechanics. You do not want to risk having your letter rejected because of careless mistakes.

Publishing

Send your letter for publication. If you have responded to a magazine article, send your letter to the magazine that published the article. If you addressed a local issue, submit your letter to the local newspaper.

Post your letter on a classroom bulletin board. If you are responding to an article from a magazine, your may wish to attach the article to your letter. Your readers will have a clearer point of reference to evaluate your letter. You might also include a comment sheet for readers' responses.

Include your letter in your writing folder. Include the article in your folder as well as your letter if you are responding to an article.

---

providing specific reasons for another court or hoop. Comment on his presentation of ideas and his use of correct form. Remind the students that their letters should be similarly strong and correct.

Revising Strategy

Peer Response

Instruct each student to exchange letters with a partner. Distribute a copy of Writing Worksheet 15 to each student. Direct each student to evaluate his partner's letter, answering the questions on the worksheet. When evaluations are finished,

instruct the students to read the comments and to revise their letters, correcting any weaknesses.

One on One: Evaluate your student's letter. After the evaluation, work together to draft a letter to the editor. Other possible topics include home school students' participation in local music or sports competitions.

Publishing Strategies

Provide time for students to read their letters orally to the class. Recommend that each student also present the article or

summarize the conversation or newscast that his letter to the editor references.

Create a bulletin board, poster, or collage of student letters. Display this in a hallway or other public place where students can read the letters. Consider providing space on the display for readers to respond to the letters.

Evaluation

For help in grading this assignment, see "Grading Writing Assignment" (p. x) and Rubric 15 (Support Materials CD, p. 119).

SPELLING

Lesson Support

Student Text

Chapter Review 16—pp. 431-33

Support Materials CD

Warm-Ups—p. 33
Concept Reinforcements—pp. 90-92
Bulletin Boards—p. 212

Does the pattern on these roofs remind you of anything? A reptile, perhaps? A diamondback rattler, to be specific? Writers notice patterns and use them to make unusual comparisons. But not all patterns are as easy to see. Sometimes it takes years for people to recognize a pattern of thought.

Patterns are at work, even in the words we use. These patterns help us make general rules for spelling English words. In a brief condemnation of a borough of New York City, Ogden Nash plays with a spelling pattern: "The Bronx? No, thonx!"

Spelling Hints

Spell by syllables.

Pronouncing distinctly each syllable of a long word will often help you spell correctly. Thinking about prefixes, suffixes, and other word parts can be helpful.

un + necessary	unnecessary
dis + appoint	disappoint
under + age	underage
mis + spell	misspell
personal + ly	personally
gentle + ness	gentleness

Suffix comes from two Latin words that mean "to fasten under." Today *suffix* is used only for something added at the end of a word.

Look up the spellings of doubtful words.

Use your dictionary to look up the spellings of words with confusing spellings. Even if you do not know how to spell the word, you should be able to make a reasonable guess about its spelling. Use the guide words to help you find it in the dictionary.

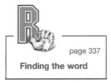

page 337

Finding the word

Keep a list of words that are problems for you.

A word should go on your list when you find that you have misspelled it.

Look for possible groupings among your problem words.

If you find a group of similar words, try to figure out or find a rule for that group. For instance, if you have problems with *ie* and *ei,* study that rule and write those words correctly.

Study your list of problem words systematically.

Begin by writing a word several times, concentrating on its appearance and its sound. Repeat this procedure on three or four different days within

---

Teaching Strategy: Induction

List these verbs with their first-person singular and progressive-tense forms on the board or overhead transparency: *cry, teach, rule, hit, permit.* Ask a student to pronounce the words for the class. Ask students to explain the spelling changes in the *s* and *ing* forms of each word. Ask the class to formulate rules for the spelling changes they have identified. Keep a record of the rules the class formulates.

Teaching Strategy: Introduction

Refer to the photograph and introduction on page 318 of the student text. Mention that patterns exist in the spellings of singular present-tense verbs and the plural forms of nouns.

Teaching Strategy: Discussion

Discuss "Spelling Hints" and the examples on page 319 of the student text. Lead a class discussion comparing the rules that the class formulated to the rules in the book. How are they similar? How do they differ? Mention that some of these words (such as *tax*) can function as verbs or as nouns. *(Johnny taxes my nerves with his gum chewing. The United States government requires its citizens to pay their taxes.)*

page 28

Spelling the plurals of nouns

page 51

Recognizing verbs

the next week. Then have someone quiz you on that word. If you can write the word correctly and without hesitation, transfer it to your "learned" list. If a problem or a doubt remains, keep working on the word.

Rules for Spelling Singular Present-Tense Verbs and the Plural Forms of Nouns

If the word ends in *ch, sh, s, x,* or *z,* add *es.*

march	marches
push	pushes
genius	geniuses
tax	taxes
buzz	buzzes

If the word ends in a consonant followed by *y,* change the final *y* to *i* and add *es.*

poppy	poppies
pony	ponies
rally	rallies
deny	denies

If the word ends in a vowel followed by *y,* add *s.*

key	keys
toy	toys

If the word ends in *f* or *fe,* consult your dictionary. For most, add *s;* for others, change the *f* to *v* and add *es.*

roof	roofs
safe	safes
leaf	leaves
shelf	shelves

If the word ends in *o,* consult your dictionary. For most, add *es;* for others add *s.*

tomato	tomatoes
echo	echoes
solo	solos
photo	photos

Add *s* to most other words.

look	looks
bug	bugs
menu	menus
bone	bones

Some nouns have irregular plural forms. Consult your dictionary for nouns with irregular plurals.

ox	oxen
goose	geese
deer	deer

320   Chapter 16

Teaching Strategy: Introduction

Ask the students what the general rule is for making English words plural. *(Add* s.*)* Show them the following paragraph on the board or overhead transparency: *In the summers my family takes a trip to my uncle's house near the citys of Minneapolis and St. Paul. My uncle has over one hundred sheeps on his farm. My six-year-old twin brothers say that their favorite part of visiting Uncle Jim is riding his two ponys. Uncle Jim told them, "I'm glad that you childs aren't triplets; if you were, I'd have to buy another pony!"* After reading the information together, ask the students which plural words in the paragraph are formed correctly. *(summers, brothers, triplets)* Which words are formed incorrectly? *(citys, sheeps, ponys, childs)* How should these plurals have been spelled? *(cities, sheep, ponies, children)* Ask the students what the activity shows us. *(Making words plural is often more complicated than simply adding an* s.*)* Explain to them that in part of today's lesson they will learn how to form irregular plurals—those that we do not merely add an *s* to—correctly.

A. Underline any misspelled word.
B. Write the word correctly in the blank.
C. Write *C* if the sentence is correct.

bodies, torpedoes   1. Seals are marine animals that have <u>bodys</u> shaped like <u>torpedos</u>.

fish/fishes, preys   2. A seal eats a variety of <u>fishs</u>. It also <u>preyes</u> on squid and shrimp.

teeth   3. Because they have sharp pointed <u>tooths</u> with no flat surfaces, seals cannot chew their food. They either grasp and tear it or swallow it whole.

rookeries   4. Every spring, seals go to breeding grounds called <u>rookerys</u>.

babies   5. The mother seals' <u>babys</u> are born at the rookery.

C   6. Seals have few enemies other than hunters.

beliefs   7. Some people hold strong <u>believes</u> that some seals should be protected because their species are becoming extinct. These people oppose hunting seals for any reason.

Sharks   8. <u>Sharkes,</u> killer whales, and polar bears are among the seal's natural enemies.

themselves   9. Seals defend <u>themselfs</u> in the water by diving deeper or by swimming between rocks. On land, they have little chance of escaping an enemy.

beaches   10. Sometimes people get an opportunity to watch certain types of seals swim near <u>beachs</u>.

A. Underline any misspelled word.
B. Write the word correctly in the blank.
C. Write *C* if the sentence is correct.

days	1. We spent five <u>dayes</u> at our grandparents' farm last summer.
bushes	2. Our grandparents live in a white farmhouse. Their front walk is lined with short, fat <u>bushs</u>.
tomatoes, boxes	3. One day my sister Sachi and I picked <u>tomatos</u> from the garden and put them into wooden <u>boxs</u>.
feet	4. Another time, we walked to the country store. My <u>foots</u> were sore because I was not used to walking so much.
carries, groceries	5. Every time our grandparents go to the store, Grandpa <u>carrys</u> most of the <u>grocerys</u>.
knits, gifts	6. Grandma <u>knites</u> well. She often makes hand-knit things and gives them as <u>giftes</u>.
calves	7. In the spring I like to visit the farm to see the adorable newborn <u>calfs</u>.
C	8. Sachi would rather see the sheep and lambs.
C	9. I remember the time that Grandma gave Sachi and me two of Lady's puppies.
grandchildren	10. Grandpa and Grandma told our parents that they are happy to have their <u>grandchilds</u> visit them at the farm.

Rules for Spelling with *ie* and *ei*

When the sound is "long *e*," put *i* before *e* except after *c*.

i before *e*	except after *c*
shriek	ceiling
shield	receipt
grieve	conceit

Teaching Strategy:
Discussion

Discuss "Rules for Spelling with *ie* or *ei*" and the examples on pages 322-23.

(*But: caffeine, leisure, protein, seize, sheik, weird. Either* and *neither,* in their more common American pronunciation, are also exceptions to this rule.)

When the sound is "long *a*," put *e* before *i*.

    freight   vein   weight

16-3   PRACTICE THE SKILL

A. Underline any misspelled word.
B. Write the word correctly in the blank.
C. Write *C* if the sentence is correct.

believe	1. I <u>beleive</u> that winter is a beautiful season, especially when there is a lot of snow.
sleigh	2. It is fun to take a ride in a horse-drawn <u>sliegh</u> on a wintry afternoon.
neighbors	3. Our <u>nieghbors</u>, the Sandersons, have a horse, and they often let us borrow it and their sleigh for a ride.
C	4. One day we received an invitation to go with them on a ride through the countryside.
niece	5. My <u>neice</u> and I were the only ones who could go.
C	6. Renee, who is eight years old, enjoyed the ride immensely.
leisurely	7. I also enjoyed the <u>liesurely</u> time with the Sandersons.
Neither	8. <u>Niether</u> Renee nor I complained about the cold weather.
conceive	9. I cannot <u>concieve</u> of a more relaxing way to enjoy the <u>beauty</u> of the winter scenery.
grieved	10. Some people are <u>greived</u> to see winter arrive, but Renee and I look forward to it.

Learning Christianly

Why is learning to spell in English difficult for some people? There are many answers to that often-asked question because many different factors have caused this difficulty. One factor is the presence of many loanwords. An English loanword is a word that English speakers take from another language and use as though it were English. Over the past three or four centuries, English has picked up many loanwords, each reflecting its own language's system of spelling. So if you ever get frustrated trying spell *chassis, clique, chutzpah,* or *fjord,* you can blame French, Yiddish, or Norwegian. But if you think about why English has so many loanwords, you begin to realize that our difficulty in learning to spell could actually be a blessing in disguise. Can you figure out what that blessing is?

Learning Christianly

English includes many loanwords because English culture, first through Great Britain and later through the United States of America, has interacted with many other cultures. The fact that English has adopted words from many other languages suggests that English-speakers have interacted with speakers of those other languages. More recently, English has become one of the primary languages of technology and politics. This influence has led speakers of other languages to learn English. When your students face the challenge of learning the English language, it can be encouraging to remember that learning English well enables Christians to share the gospel with those from other countries who have learned to speak English.

16·4 USE THE SKILL

A. Underline any misspelled word.
B. Write the word correctly in the blank.
C. Write *C* if the sentence is correct.

_____receive_____ 1. The Bible teaches that anyone can <u>recieve</u> Christ as his Savior.

_____C_____ 2. An atheist is someone who thinks that there is no God. He does not think there is such a thing as the gift of salvation.

_____deceived, believing_____ 3. Unfortunately, many people are <u>decieved</u> into <u>beleiving</u> that they do not need God.

_____C_____ 4. The old fiend, Satan, is the one who tells people these lies.

_____achievements_____ 5. Some people think that they can get to heaven through their own <u>acheivements</u>.

_____yield_____ 6. The only way to get to heaven is to <u>yeild</u> to the fact that you are a sinner and accept Christ as your Savior.

_____C_____ 7. Christians ought to tell others about the gift of salvation. They can begin by telling family members and neighbors.

_____C_____ 8. The need for people to become saved weighs so heavily on the hearts of some Christians that they devote their lives to full-time mission work.

_____seize_____ 9. It is encouraging when Christians eagerly <u>sieze</u> the opportunity to witness to an unsaved person.

_____chief_____ 10. The <u>cheif</u> thing that God wants Christians to accomplish on earth is to tell others about Him.

Rules for Adding Suffixes

Doubling a final consonant

If a one-syllable word ends with a single consonant preceded by a single vowel, double the final consonant before adding a suffix beginning with a vowel.

snob   snobbery

If a multisyllabic word with its main accent on the final syllable ends with a single consonant preceded by a single vowel, double the final consonant before adding a suffix beginning with a vowel.

occur   occurring

If a word ends with a single consonant preceded by a double vowel, do not double the final consonant before adding a suffix.

droop   drooped
greet   greeter

Changing final *y* to *i*

Change final *y* to *i* before adding a suffix if a consonant precedes the *y*.

baby   babied
plenty   plentiful
sixty   sixtieth

However, if the suffix itself begins with *i*, do not change final *y* to *i*.

cry   crying
carry   carrying

Dropping final silent *e*

Drop the final silent *e* preceded by a consonant before adding a suffix beginning with a vowel.

hope   hoping
like   likable
use   using

(But: *noticeable, courageous*)

Keep the final silent *e* before adding a suffix beginning with a consonant.

hope   hopeless
like   likely
use   useful

(But: *truly, argument, judgment*)

Learning Christianly

Have you ever seen a lawyer on television presenting a case on behalf of his client? Or have you ever heard a politician promising to represent others in getting a law changed or improving conditions in a certain area of town? If so, you have seen people pleading the cause of others in order to improve their lives. How will improving your writing and grammar skills allow you to show your love to your neighbor in this way?

Learning Christianly

One of the skills your students gain when they study writing and grammar is the skill of persuasion. When students are able to communicate well, people are more willing to listen to them and to take what they say seriously. Christians are called to love their neighbors as themselves because God loves people (Rom. 5:8). When your students have developed their abilities in writing and grammar, they will be in an ideal place to plead for others, whether they are in a courtroom or not. Developing refined skills in communication gives them the ability to persuade—through a letter to the editor in a local paper or through a call to a local politician. Because your students are taking the time to improve their skills with language, they will have more opportunities in the future to show their love to others as God has shown His love to them (Isa. 51:22; Heb. 7:25).

Evaluation

Evaluate your students' writing assignments for correct spelling. After the students complete a writing assignment, give each student his own list of spelling errors from his composition. Challenge each student to master the words he missed and to spell them correctly in future compositions.

Enrichment: Speech Link

Dictionary Spelldown

Assign five words to each student. Instruct each student to look up each word in the dictionary, write proper pronunciation for the word, paraphrase the definition, and use the word in a sentence. Announce that you will conduct a spelldown in class the next day. The students will try to spell any word you collect, not just those from their own lists. Collect the students' lists of words. Begin the spelldown by instructing all the students to stand. Select a student to start the game and choose a word from any list. Pronounce the word, read the definition of the word, and read the word in a sentence. Ask him to spell it. If he spells it correctly, he stays in the game; if he spells it incorrectly, he sits down and is out of the game. Move to the next student. Continue until only one student is left standing or until you run out of words.

page 62

Past tense

16-5 PRACTICE THE SKILL

Add the suffixes to the following words by writing the word correctly in the blank.

clueless	1. clue + less		_dragging_	9. drag + ing
traded	2. trade + ed		_barely_	10. bare + ly
beautiful	3. beauty + ful		_hooted_	11. hoot + ed
meeting	4. meet + ing		_hungrily_	12. hungry + ly
slipper	5. slip + er		_coming_	13. come + ing
fortieth	6. forty + eth		_hugged_	14. hug + ed
adorable	7. adore + able		_trying_	15. try + ing
happily	8. happy + ly			

16-6 USE THE SKILL

A. Underline any misspelled word.

B. Write the word correctly in the blank.

C. Write *C* if the sentence is correct.

ninetieth   1. Marcus and Olivia helped celebrate their grand-mother's <u>ninetyeth</u> birthday this year.

_C_   2. Marcus, who has an engaging personality, was the host of the party.

prettily   3. The room was decorated <u>prettyly</u> with green and maroon balloons and crepe paper.

preceding   4. Olivia and her sister Georgina used most of the <u>precedeing</u> week to bake their grandmother's favorite desserts.

setting   5. Marcus and some of the other relatives spent the day before the party <u>seting</u> up chairs and tables.

<u>spying</u>   6. All during the week, everyone made sure that
Grandmother was not <u>spiing</u> on them.

<u>likely</u>   7. Grandmother was curious, so it was <u>likly</u> she
would be tempted to spy.

<u>C</u>   8. On the day of the party, everyone clapped when
Grandmother came into the living room.

<u>eating</u>   9. While the guests were <u>eatting</u>, Marcus and
Olivia told stories about their childhood visits to
Grandmother's house.

<u>C</u>   10. Toward the end of the party, Grandmother
unwrapped a large present. Her eyes sparkled
when she saw a beautiful cuckoo clock.

16-7   REVIEW THE SKILL

Fill in each blank with the letter of the misspelled word. You may use your dictionary for help.

<u>a</u>   1. a. recieve
    b. naming
    c. churches
    d. feet

<u>c</u>   2. a. crying
    b. tomatoes
    c. monkies
    d. yield

<u>d</u>   3. a. artful
    b. deceive
    c. babies
    d. brushs

<u>b</u>   4. a. wives
    b. mooses
    c. foxes
    d. cats

<u>b</u>   5. a. sleigh
    b. potatos
    c. occurring
    d. buzzes

<u>a</u>   6. a. huged
    b. crosses
    c. chief
    d. donkeys

<u>d</u>   7. a. nameless
    b. pianos
    c. likelihood
    d. wiegh

<u>c</u>   8. a. moose
    b. dogs
    c. makeing
    d. halves

<u>a</u>   9. a. knifes
    b. dresses
    c. fishes
    d. pizzas

<u>a</u>   10. a. lookking
    b. vein
    c. fiftieth
    d. marries

Locate and correct the twenty errors in the paragraph: troublesome words, capitalization, punctuation, spelling, subject-verb agreement, and adjective and adverb usage.

Many folkes prefer hot cereal too cold cereal especially in the Winter. Either the low temperatures or the frozen precipitation make a bowl of hot cereal "inviting." Of course, babys eat alot of cooked cereal since its more soft for there tender gums and is alright for young Digestive Tracts. Some hot cerealses requires fifteen minutes of cooking time, others' need only three minutes. still others are made instantly with boiling water. Accept when one has much time, instant cereals are oftener the best option.

Many folks prefer hot cereal to cold cereal, especially in the winter. Either

the low temperatures or the frozen precipitation makes a bowl of hot

cereal "inviting." Of course, babies eat a lot of cooked cereal since it's

softer for their tender gums and is all right for young digestive tracts.

Some hot cereals require fifteen minutes of cooking time; others need

only three minutes. Still others are made instantly with boiling water.

Except when one has much time, instant cereals are often the best option.

EVALUATING A SCIENCE FAIR PROJECT REPORT

And this I pray, that your love may abound yet more and more in knowledge and in all judgment; That ye may approve things that are excellent.
Philippians 1:9-10

Have you ever heard someone say "It was as interesting as seeing the sap rise"? This expression indicates irony; the speaker sounds as though he is saying that something is interesting, but he is really saying that whatever activity he is describing is as boring as one could imagine. Yet, *is* this activity boring? Sap's rising is a scientific process. The sample science fair project and report below demonstrates how interesting this process really is.

Your Turn

Read the science fair project report at the end of this section and evaluate it as though you were a science fair judge. Use the following information about science fair projects and reports as your guide. Then write a paragraph that summarizes your evaluation.

Planning

Understand the correct contents and format of a science fair project report. The information below describes a typical science fair project and the elements that make up the science fair project report.

First, a scientist (or a student in a science class) asks himself a question. For example, you may wonder whether nourishment from a plant's roots reaches all the way to the top of the stem or just to the root system or leaves. More specifically, if you put a white carnation into a glass of water tinted with food coloring, will the tinted water color the white petals of the flower, or will it merely travel in the stem and leaves? This sort of question is what scientists call the hypothesis.

After forming a hypothesis, a scientist designs an experiment to prove or disprove his idea. To test the plant nourishment question, you could perform this experiment: Trim the end of the flower stem with a sharp knife and place the stem into the colored water. Observe the petals at regular intervals and keep a log of your observations—write down what you see and when you see it. Make drawings or photographs of the progress of the experiment. Describe in detail the amount of color in the petals, if any.

Finally, the scientist will report on his findings. The report should be able to stand alone as an explanation for the project and be complete enough to allow another person to repeat the experiment by following the same procedures. Although the requirements for science fair project reports vary from location to location, the following guidelines are generally accepted.

Title Page

The title should be a complete sentence or the statement of the science project's purpose. It should, however, suggest the topic of the experiment and cause the reader to turn the page and read about your experiment. Make the page attractive by using an appropriate font and color. For this experiment, a good title might be "Turning Blue in the Face: The Path of Sap in a Flower."

Overview of Writing Process
Planning—Reading the science report
Drafting—Filling out the chart
Revising—Writing a summary of the evaluation
Publishing—Handing in the assignment

Objectives
Students will
1. evaluate a science report.
2. summarize their evaluations.

Evaluating a Science Fair Project Report

Lesson Support

Support Materials CD

Writing Worksheets—p. 104
Rubrics—p. 120

Scriptural Application

Ask volunteers to read Philippians 1:9-10 and John 13:35 aloud. Then discuss these verses. The most basic Christian command is the command in John 13:35 to love. But this command is by no means the only one. As Philippians 1:9-10 teach, love must be combined with good judgment. The Christian needs to learn what is good (both what is morally upright and what is effective or beautiful) and then how to spot goodness when he sees it around him. Learning to identify what is good, what is almost good, and what is not even close is an important part of learning to "approve things that are excellent." Point out that learning to evaluate a science fair project report can be a step in developing the skill of discernment.

Introduction

Ask the students about their experiences at science fairs. Then ask them what they think it would be like to judge a science fair.

Teaching Strategy

To draw the students' interest to the project discussed in this lesson, display a white carnation in a glass of water tinted with food coloring. Leave the carnation on display as the students work on their assignments.

Table of Contents

The table of contents lists the items in the report and the pages on which they begin. Do not list the title page or the table of contents page itself.

Abstract

The abstract is the first item in the report. Think of it as a one-page summary of the entire project. All of the vital information about the project should appear on the abstract page. First, list the project title (from the title page); then state the purpose of your project. The statement of purpose is exactly what it sounds like: state what you hope to prove by your experiment. Next, state the hypothesis, which is the statement of the project question, followed by a brief description of the procedure and the results. Because it is an overview of the entire project, this page of the report is quite possibly the most important one of all.

Introduction

The introduction, next in the report, contains your statement of purpose and any background information about the project, such as how you became interested in the idea or what made you come up with your hypothesis. List any books you read or experiments done by others that prompted you to do your project.

Materials and Methods

Then comes the actual description of the experiment in the experiment and data section. Remember that someone should be able to follow this description and repeat your project. First write out the purpose of the experiment—what you hope to accomplish. Follow that statement with a list of the materials you used (and the amount needed of each) in the experiment. For the sake of those who may repeat your experiment, be complete. Finish the section with an explanation of the procedures. Be detailed with the steps you took to test your hypothesis. Your log will be vital here. Be sure to include all the measurements and data from your experiments. Arrange the information neatly and clearly, using graphs and charts. If you have a large amount of data, you may put the majority of it in an appendix at the end of the report and merely summarize the data in this section of the report.

Results and Discussion

The results and discussion section is a short (about one page) summary of what you learned. State the hypothesis again and then state whether you were able to prove or disprove it by your experiments. If this experiment has made you curious about other possible experiments, you may list these possibilities here.

Sources

On this page list all of the information about any written materials that you read or interviews that you did as part of the experiment or in preparation for it. Use proper bibliography page form.

Planning Strategies

Direct the students to read the information on pages 329-31. Then discuss the elements that a science fair project report should include and the criteria for those elements. Ask the students to read pages 332-35 as though they were judges at a science fair. Remind them to look for the elements required in a science fair project report.

Discuss the definition of the word *hypothesis:* a tentative explanation for an observation or phenomenon that can be used as the basis for an investigation.

Distribute a copy of Writing Worksheet 16 to each student. Ask the students to read the science report and to circle the appropriate responses. Explain that you will judge their evaluations for accuracy and completeness.

Drafting Strategies

Instruct each student to review his notes and to state his overall evaluation of the report in a single sentence. Then direct him to adapt that sentence as necessary to make it the topic sentence of his evaluation paragraph. Explain that the rest of the

paragraph should consist of sentences that support the topic sentence by giving details from the report.

Remind the students to acknowledge the report's strengths and to recommend possible improvements while keeping a positive, encouraging tone.

Revising Strategies

Ask each student to review his notes and then to review his evaluation. Are there any additional observations from his notes that he should include in his evaluation?

Acknowledgments

Acknowledgments are a list of those who helped you and how they did so. Although you should have done the majority of the science project yourself, you may have received some assistance. If your relatives helped, it is not necessary to give their names; you may say, "Thanks to my mother, who typed my report."

A good science fair project takes much work. But keep in mind that the qualities of a good scientist are precision, accuracy, and completeness. Attention to these details will give a project and report the credibility it needs to be a winner.

Preview the report. Before you read the report thoroughly, check to see that all the necessary elements are present. Has the writer presented both problems in his findings as well as successes? Has he included a log of results? Are there sources and acknowledgments for his work? Does the report follow the correct form?

Read the report. As you read, take notes. Has the writer developed a hypothesis? Does he include the necessary materials for the experiment? Does the experiment prove or disprove the hypothesis? Does he use clear scientific language to express his findings? Does the report present accurate, well-documented information? Does it follow a logical order?

Evaluate the writer's style. Did the writer get your attention with the beginning of his report? Does he present his material in a convincing way? You may want to use the categories of *purpose, organization, vocabulary,* and *details* to organize your notes.

Drafting

Begin with a topic sentence that will give direction to your paragraph. State your overall evaluation in a simple, direct topic sentence. The rest of the paragraph will explain the reasons for your overall evaluation.

Support your topic sentence. Let the organization of your notes be your guide as you write your paragraph. Each sentence in your paragraph should help to support the overall evaluation in your topic sentence by giving further details. Include the reasons for the evaluations that you give.

Use proper tone as you write. The tone of your writing reveals your attitude toward the subject and the writer. Keep in mind why you are writing the evaluation—you are a judge. The tone of your evaluation should be confident and courteous.

Revising

Take a fresh look at your paragraph. Reviewing your paragraph at a later time will help you to identify problems. Does the paragraph meet the expectations of the assignment? Is the evaluation clear and easy to follow?

Incorporate additions and revisions. Rewrite your paragraph, including any changes or additions that you decide are necessary.

Proofread your paragraph for correct grammar, spelling, and mechanics. Try reading the paragraph backwards, one word at a time.

Make a clean copy of your paragraph. Incorporate any additional corrections that you marked on your paragraph as you proofread.

Challenge student to analyze their evaluations. Is the evaluation only one paragraph with an appropriate topic sentence? Are the supporting sentences accurate factually and grammatically? Do the sentences say what the students intended? Are the ideas presented logically and clearly?

Publishing Strategies

Divide the class into groups of five students and direct each student to read his paragraph for his group. Instruct each group to discuss the differences in their evaluations. Remind the students that each evaluation should be the sole work of a single student but that some similarities are probably unavoidable.

Stage a mock interview. Allow students to take turns interviewing one another about their evaluation paragraphs. Encourage the audience to ask questions as well.

Scriptural Application

Read Psalm 139:23 aloud. Remind students that God will evaluate them according to the standards in His Word. Like the psalmist, Christians should want God to evaluate and to improve them. Then read James 1:2-4 aloud. Remind the students that Christians can rejoice when God tests them because His work in their lives is always meant for their good and His glory.

Reinforcement

If possible, allow your students to see the winning reports from a recent science fair. Explain that the judges chose the reports based on criteria that may not be exactly the same as the criteria your students used for this assignment.

Publishing

Share your evaluation with a peer. No two people have the same observations and evaluations. Make notes for yourself regarding the difference between your observations and your peer's.

Get an expert opinion. If possible, ask a science teacher to read your evaluation and to write comments about your paragraph. Include these comments with your evaluation in your writing folder.

Table of Contents

Abstract

The purpose of this project was to demonstrate that nutrients reach the petals of a flower, not merely the stem and leaves. The experiment measured the progress of colored water up the stem of a white carnation and into the petals. I noted the amount of color present in the petals at set intervals.

The resulting patterns of blue seen on the petals of the carnation confirmed my hypothesis that water travels throughout the entire flower, not just through the stem and leaves. These results cause me to wonder whether nutrients cause the opening of the flower head. It is common scientific fact that sap rises throughout a plant's stem and carries nutrients with it to the leaves and stem, but what is the effect of this transportation system on a flower blossom?

Enrichment

Encourage the students to volunteer to help read reports from elementary science fairs. Remind them to abide by the criteria set up for the particular fairs and to keep a positive, encouraging tone in their responses.

Evaluation

For help in grading this assignment, see "Grading Writing Assignments" (p. x) and Rubric 16 (Support Materials CD, p. 120).

Introduction

It is common knowledge that plants need water and other nutrients to grow. But exactly where in a plant are these nutrients found? It is logical to assume that they are found in the roots of the plant and probable to assume that they are found in the stems and leaves as well. Scientists have determined that sap (the liquid nutrients that travel upward from the roots of a plant) is found in the stems and leaves of a plant, but what about the petals? Since most flowers' blooms do not last a long time before dying, are nutrients found in the petals at all? Is the lack of nutrients responsible for the dying of the flower blossoms?

Before I could determine whether nutrients cause the opening of a flower head, I had first to determine whether a simple liquid such as water makes its way to the flower petals. To discover this, I placed a white carnation in colored water and charted the progress of the color in the petals.

My curiosity about this process resulted in this project to demonstrate that nutrients do indeed travel throughout a plant. My hypothesis is that water will travel from the bottom of a flower stem to the top, throughout the entire plant.

Materials and Methods

a white miniature carnation
a vase with water
dark food coloring (blue)

To determine whether nutrients will flow through a stem to the petals of a flower

1. Make a solution of the food coloring and water. I used 6 drops of blue food coloring in $\frac{1}{4}$ cup water since I used 1 white miniature carnation.

2. Trim the end of the carnation stem using a sharp knife. Cut at an angle to give the stem a maximum absorption surface.

3. Place the stem into the colored water.

4. Observe the carnation periodically and record any change in the petal color.

Results and Discussion

As it was stated in my hypothesis, I believe that sap flows through the entire plant: roots, stem, leaves, and flower petals. I believe that the nutrients contained in the sap and transported from the roots of a plant are responsible for the actual opening of a plant's blossoms. While this experiment did not confirm the second part of the hypothesis, it did answer the preliminary question of whether nutrients found in roots, stems, and leaves are present in the flower petals as well.

The experimental data showed that the colored water at the base of the carnation stem did travel up the stem and into the flower petals. This progress was fairly easy to chart by using colored water that contrasted with the flower petals. As the tinted water entered the white petals, they turned blue.

This experiment has prompted other questions about the progress of nutrients in a plant and various factors that affect that progress. Future experiments could explore the effect of freshness of the flower on the progress of the colored water. Is the progress of the colored water faster if the flower is cut and placed into the water immediately? Is the progress of the water affected by the degree to which the flower bud is closed? Are the results different with different flowers? Do the petals gradually lose their ability to transport water, and is that what causes them to die?

Sources

Hargis, Grace Collins. *Writing from Research for Christian Schools.* Greenville, S.C.: Bob Jones University Press, 1998.

"Sap." *1997 Grolier Multimedia Encyclopedia.* CD-ROM. Danbury, Conn.: Grolier, 1997.

Acknowledgments

I would like to thank my sister Eileen for her help in thinking of an idea for this project. I would also like to thank my science teacher, Mr. Howell, for his help, and my mom for buying the carnation for me.

Science Project Log

Saturday

8:10   Put 6 drops of blue food coloring into $\frac{1}{4}$ cup water. Cut the stem of a miniature white carnation and placed it into the colored water.

9:10   No change in petal color (I wonder whether roses work better?)

10:10   No change in petal color (Does the freshness of the flower change the speed of absorption?)

12:10   Bare traces of blue on outer edge of outer petals; center petals the same

1:10   More blue on outer petals; none on center yet

5:10   More blue on outer petals; center ones still white

Sunday

8:10   Outer petals still absorbing blue; center petals beginning to turn slightly

1:10   Center petals still hardly affected

4:10   Outer edges of outer petals quite blue; center still little affected

Monday

7:30   Little change from yesterday

Tuesday

7:15   No change from yesterday

Wednesday

7:10   No change from yesterday

Thursday

7:10   Carnation stem broken at level of the jar top; no noticeable difference from Friday's observation. Broken carnation allowed a glimpse of the underside of the flower bloom; significant veining with blue; I should have checked the progress of the water on the underside as well as on the top.

Modifications (to be made if experiment repeated)

1. Check progress of color on the underside of petals as well as on the top.
2. Try experiment with other flowers, such as roses.
3. Try experiment with buds that were cut more recently.

Observations

1. Notched edges of the petals had the most color.
2. Outer petals were affected more than inner petals.

CHAPTER 17

DICTIONARY SKILLS

Lesson Support

Support Materials CD
Bulletin Boards—p. 213

Teaching Strategy: Motivation

Bring a variety of dictionaries to class. Ask the students to look up the same word in several different dictionaries, e.g., *book.* How are the definitions different? How are they similar?

$\mathbf{A}$ **dictionary** is the most common tool used for learning about words and languages. The dictionary gives a word's spelling, syllabification, pronunciation, definitions, different forms, parts of speech, synonyms or antonyms, and capitalization. The information in a good dictionary is reliable because it comes from the speech and the writing that is most often accepted by educated people. Many dictionaries also list abbreviations, geographic names, and biographical names; they may even include a brief history of the English language or a handbook of style and usage. Notes and guides in your dictionary can help you understand the content of the dictionary. To use your dictionary in the right way, you will want to become familiar with all such helps.

page 353
How do I use specific reference works?

Finding the Word

At the top of each dictionary page you will find two words in large dark print. These **guide word**s tell you the first and last word defined on that page. Any word that alphabetically comes between those two words can also be found on that page. Using the guide words will save you much time when trying to find a particular word.

The **entry** is the word being defined (usually printed in bold type) and all the information about that particular word. Look here for the proper spelling of a word. Most dictionaries will also list other forms of the word. For example, an entry for a noun will list the noun's plural form; an entry for a verb will list the verb's principal parts. Remember that the entry word itself is always the base form of the word.

page 39
Compound nouns

17-1 PRACTICE THE SKILL

Underline the entry words that would appear on a dictionary page with the guide words *pledge / plesiosaur.*

1. <u>Pleiades</u>

2. Plexiglas

3. <u>plenary</u>

4. <u>plenty</u>

5. pleurisy

Teaching Strategy:
Introduction

Briefly tell the students the history of the dictionary: Ancient Romans and Greeks originated the first books containing lists of difficult words. In 1604, Robert Cawdrey compiled the first dictionary in English, *A Table Alphabeticall of Hard Wordes,* which contained about three thousand words. In 1721, Nathan Bailey produced the first English dictionary to contain more than just hard words, and it recorded about sixty thousand entries. Even the Brothers Grimm (of fairy-tale fame) wrote a German dictionary in the mid-1800s. Noah Webster published the first American dictionary in 1806; revisions of his 1828 version (70,000 words) are still used today. The most comprehensive dictionary in any language was the *Century Dictionary* (415,000 words), published from 1884-1928. It was published in 1933 as the *Oxford English Dictionary (O.E.D.).* A twenty-volume edition of the *O.E.D.* was published in 1989. The *O.E.D.* attempts to record every word in written English, giving the historical background for each.

Zag·ros Mountains (zăg′rəs). A range of W Iran forming the W and S borders of the central Iranian plateau and rising to 4,550.6 m (14,920 ft).

Za·har·i·as (zə-hār′ē-əs), **Mildred Ella Didrikson.** See **Mildred Ella Didrikson.**

zai·bat·su (zī′bät-soo′) *n., pl.* **zaibatsu. 1.** A powerful family-controlled commercial combine of Japan. **2.** A Japanese conglomerate or cartel. [J. : *zai*, wealth (< Chin. *cái*) + *batsu*, powerful person or family (< Chin. *fá*).]

zaire (zī′îr, zä-îr′) *n.* See table at **currency.** [Port., the Congo River < Kongo *n-zadi*, large river.]

Zaire (zī′îr, zä-îr′). Formerly (1885–1908) **Con·go Free State** (kŏng′gō) and (1908–60) **Bel·gian Congo** (bĕl′jən) and (1960–71) **Congo.** A country of central Africa astride the equator; achieved full independence from Belgium in 1960. Cap. Kinshasa. Pop. 29,671,407. — **Za·ir′e·an, Za·ir′i·an** *adj. & n.*

Zaire River. See **Congo River.**

za·kat (zə-kät′) *n.* The alms tax required of all Muslims by the shari'a.

Za·ma (zā′mə, zä′mä). An ancient town of N Africa SW of Carthage in present-day N Tunisia; site of the Roman defeat of Hannibal, which ended the Second Punic War (202 B.C.).

Zam·be·zi (zăm-bē′zē). A river of central and S Africa rising in NW Zambia and flowing c. 2,735 km (1,700 mi) to the Mozambique Channel.

Zam·bi·a (zăm′bē-ə). A country of S-central Africa; gained independence from Great Britain in 1964. Cap. Lusaka. Pop. 5,661,801. — **Zam′bi·an** *adj. & n.*

za·mi·a (zā′mē-ə) *n.* Any of various chiefly tropical American cycads of the genus *Zamia*, having a thick trunk, palmlike terminal leaves, and seeds borne in woody cones. [NLat. *Zamia*, genus name < misreading of *(nucēs) azāniae*, pine cone (nuts), prob. < Gk. *azamein*, to dry up < *azein*, to dry. See **as-**.]

zam·in·dar also **zem·in·dar** (zăm′ən-där, zĕm′-, zə-mēn-där′) *n.* **1.** An official in precolonial India assigned to collect the land taxes of his district. **2.** A landholder in British colonial India responsible for collecting and paying to the government the taxes on the land under his jurisdiction. [Hindi *zamīndār* < Pers. : *zamin*, earth; see **dhghem-** + *-dār*, -holder; see **dher-**.]

zan·der (zăn′dər) *n., pl.* **zander** or **-ders.** A common European pikeperch *(Stizostedion lucioperca)* valued as a food fish. [Ger. < LGer. *Sander*.]

Zanes·ville (zānz′vĭl′). A city of E-central Ohio E of Columbus; a former state cap. (1810–12). Pop. 26,778.

Zang·will (zăng′gwĭl′, -wĭl′), **Israel.** 1864–1926. British writer whose works include *Children of the Ghetto* (1892).

za·ny (zā′nē) *n., pl.* **-nies. 1.** A comic performer who assists or imitates a clown, acrobat, or mountebank. **2.** A comical person given to extravagant or outlandish behavior. — *adj.* **-ni·er, -ni·est.** Ludicrously comical; clownish. **2.** Comical because of incongruity or strangeness; bizarre. [Fr. *zani* < Ital. dial. *zanni* < *Zanni*, var. of Ital. *Gianni*, John, the name of servants who act as clowns in commedia dell'arte.] — **za′ni·ly** *adv.* — **za′ni·ness** *n.*

Zan·zi·bar (zăn′zə-bär′). **1.** A region of E Africa, comprising **Zanzibar Island** and several adjacent islands; became an independent sultanate in 1963 and in 1964 joined Tanganyika to form Tanzania. **2.** A city of Tanzania on the W coast of Zanzibar I.; founded in the 16th cent. Pop. 110,699.

zap (zăp) *Slang.* — *v.* **zapped, zap·ping, zaps.** — *tr.* **1.a.** To destroy or kill with a burst of gunfire, flame, or electric current. **b.** To kill or destroy as if by shooting. **c.** To strike suddenly and forcefully as if with a projectile or weapon. **d.** To expose to radiation; irradiate. **2.** To attack (an enemy) with heavy firepower; strafe or bombard. **3.** To use a remote control device to switch (channels on a television) or to turn off (a television set). — *intr.* To move swiftly; zoom. — *n.* Something that imparts excitement or great interest. — *interj.* **1.** Used to imitate a sound made by a gun when fired. **2.** Used to indicate a sudden occurrence. [Imit.]

Za·pa·ta (zə-pä′tə, sä-pä′tä), **Emiliano.** 1879?–1919. Mexican revolutionary who led an agrarian revolt (1910–19).

za·pa·te·a·do (zä′pə-tā-ä′dō, thä′pä-tā-ä′thō, sä′-) *n., pl.* **-dos.** A Spanish flamenco dance in which the performer stamps and taps rhythmically with the heels. [Sp. < *zapatear*, to tap with the shoe < *zapato*, shoe.]

Za·po·pan (zä′pō-pän′, sä′pō-). A city of SW Mexico W of Guadalajara. Pop. 345,390.

Za·po·ro·zhe (zä′pə-rô′zhə, zə-pə-rô′zhyĕ). Formerly **A·lek·san·drovsk** (ăl′ĭk-sän′drəfsk, ə-lĭk-sän′-). A city of S Ukraine W of Donetsk; founded 1770. Pop. 852,000.

Za·po·tec (zä′pə-tĕk′, sä′pō-) *n., pl.* **Zapotec** or **-tecs. 1.a.** A member of a Mesoamerican Indian people of southern Mexico, whose civilization reached its height around A.D. 300–900. **b.** A modern-day descendant of this people. **2.** Any of a group of related languages spoken in southern Mexico. [Sp. *Zapoteco* < Nahuatl *tzapotēcah*, pl. of *tzapotēcatl*, person from Tzapotlan < *Tzapotlan*, place name : *tzapotl*, sapodilla + *tlān*, place.] — **Za′po·tec′** *adj.*

zap·py (zăp′ē) *adj.* **-pi·er, -pi·est.** *Slang.* Lively.

Za·ra·go·za (zär′ə-gō′zə, thä′rä-gō′thä). See **Saragossa.**

Zar·a·thu·stra (zär′ə-thoo′strə). See **Zoroaster.**

za·re·ba also **za·ree·ba** (zə-rē′bə) *n.* **1.** An enclosure of bushes or stakes protecting a campsite or village in northeast Africa. **2.** A campsite or village protected by such an enclosure. [Ar. *zaribah*, pen for cattle.]

zarf (zärf) *n.* A chalicelike holder for a hot coffee cup, typically made of ornamental metal, used in the Middle East. [Ar. *zarf*, container.]

zas·tru·ga (zä-stroo′gə, zä-) *n.* Var. of **sastruga.**

z-ax·is (zē′ăk′sĭs) *n., pl.* **z-ax·es** (zē′ăk′sēz). *Math.* One of three axes in a three-dimensional Cartesian coordinate system.

za·yin (zā′yĭn) *n.* The seventh letter of the Hebrew alphabet. [Heb. < Aram.]

Zc *abbr. Bible.* Zechariah.

zeal (zēl) *n.* Enthusiastic devotion to a cause, an ideal, or a goal and tireless diligence in its furtherance. [ME *zele* < OFr. *zel* < LLat. *zēlus* < Gk. *zēlos.*]

Zea·land (zē′lənd). See **Sjaelland.**

zeal·ous (zĕl′əs) *adj.* **1.a.** One who is zealous, esp. excessively so. **b.** A fanatically committed person. **2. Zealot.** A member of a Jewish movement of the first century A.D. that fought against Roman rule in Palestine as incompatible with strict monotheism. [ME *zelote* < Lat. *zēlōtēs* < Gk. < *zēlos*, zeal.]

zeal·ot·ry (zĕl′ə-trē) *n.* Excessive zeal; fanaticism.

zeal·ous (zĕl′əs) *adj.* Filled with or motivated by zeal; fervent. — **zeal′ous·ly** *adv.* — **zeal′ous·ness** *n.*

ze·a·tin (zē′ə-tĭn) *n.* A cytokinin originally isolated from young corn kernels. [NLat. *Zea*, corn genus; see ZEIN + -IN.]

ze·bec or **ze·beck** (zē′bĕk′) *n. Naut.* Var. of **xebec.**

Zeb·e·dee (zĕb′ĭ-dē′). In the Bible, a fisherman whose sons James and John became disciples of Jesus.

ze·bra (zē′brə) *n.* Any of several swift, wild, horselike African mammals of the genus *Equus*, having distinctive overall markings of alternating white and black or brown stripes. [Ital. < OPort. *zevro, zevra*, wild ass.] — **ze′brine′** (zē′brīne′) *adj.*

zebra crossing *n. Chiefly British.* A pedestrian crosswalk.

zebra finch *n.* A small Australian bird *(Poephila guttata)* having black and white markings and popular as a cage bird.

zebra fish *n.* A small freshwater tropical fish *(Brachydanio rerio)* of India having horizontal dark blue and silvery stripes.

ze·bra·wood (zē′brə-wood′) *n.* **1.** Any of several African or tropical American trees having striped wood. **2.** The wood of any of these trees, used in cabinetmaking.

ze·bu (zē′boo, -byoo) *n.* A domesticated ox *(Bos indicus)* of Asia and eastern Africa having a prominent hump on the back and a large dewlap. [Fr. *zébu.*]

Zeb·u·lon also **Zeb·u·lun** (zĕb′yə-lən). In the Bible, a son of Jacob and Leah and the forebear of one of the tribes of Israel.

zec·chi·no (zĕ-kē′nō) also **zec·chin** or **zech·in** (zĕk′ĭn) *n., pl.* **-ni** (-nē) or **-nos** also **-chins** or **-ins.** See **sequin** 2. [Ital. < SEQUIN.]

Zech·a·ri·ah¹ (zĕk′ə-rī′ə) *n. Bible.* **1.** A Hebrew prophet of the 6th cent. B.C. **2.** See table at **Bible.** [Heb. *Zĕkaryāh* : *zekar*, remembrance + *Yāh*, God.]

Zech·a·ri·ah² (zĕk′ə-rī′ə). See **Zacharias.**

zed (zĕd) *n. Chiefly British.* The letter z. [ME < OFr. *zede* < LLat. *zēta*, zeta < Gk. See ZETA.]

Zed·e·ki·ah (zĕd′ĭ-kī′ə). 6th cent. B.C. The last king of Judah (597–586 B.C.), who led an unsuccessful uprising (588–586) against Nebuchadnezzar II and was sent to captivity in Babylon.

zed·o·ar·y (zĕd′ō-ĕr′ē) *n., pl.* **-ies. 1.** An Indian plant *(Curcuma zedoaria)* having yellow flowers and starchy tuberous rhizomes. **2.** The dried rhizomes of this plant, used as a condiment and in perfumes, medicines, and cosmetics. [ME *zeduarie* < Med.Lat. *zeduāria* < Ar. *zadwār* < Pers.]

zee (zē) *n.* The letter z.

Zee·land (zē′lənd, zā′länt). A historical region of SW Netherlands bordering on Belgium and the North Sea; part of Holland after the 10th cent.

Zee·man (zā′män′), **Pieter.** 1865–1943. Dutch physicist who shared a 1902 Nobel Prize.

Zeeman effect *n.* The splitting of single spectral lines of an emission spectrum into three or more polarized components when the radiation source is in a magnetic field.

ze·in (zē′ĭn) *n.* A prolamine protein derived from corn, used in the manufacture of various plastics, coatings, and lacquers. [NLat. *Zea*, corn genus (< Lat. *zéa*, emmer < Gk. *zeia*, one-seeded wheat, barley; see **yewo-**) + -IN.]

Zeist (zīst). A city of central Netherlands E of Utrecht. Pop. 60,478.

Zeit·geist (tsīt′gīst′, zīt′-) *n.* The spirit of the time; the taste and outlook characteristic of a period or generation. [Ger. : *Zeit*, time (< MHGer. *zīt* < OHGer.; see **dā-**) + *Geist*, spirit; see POLTERGEIST.]

zem·in·dar (zăm′ən-där, zĕm′-, zə-mēn-där′) *n.* Var. of **zamindar.**

zemst·vo (zĕmst′vō, zyĕm′stvə) *n., pl.* **-vos.** An elective council responsible for the local administration of a provincial dis-

Zambia

ă pat	oi boy
ā pay	ou out
âr care	oo took
ä father	oo boot
ĕ pet	ŭ cut
ē be	ûr urge
ĭ pit	th thin
ī pie	th this
îr pier	hw which
ŏ pot	zh vision
ō toe	ə about,
ô paw	item

Stress marks:
′ (primary);
′ (secondary), as in
dictionary (dĭk′shə-nĕr′ē)

17-2 ⚾ PRACTICE THE SKILL

Using the sample guide words, write the number of the page on which you would find each entry word.

lesson/level 780
lever/liberal 781
Liberia/licorice 782

_782_ 1. liberty   _782_ 6. license

_782_ 2. library   _780_ 7. levee

_780_ 3. letter   _780_ 8. Leuctra

_781_ 4. libel   _782_ 9. lichen

_781_ 5. levy   _781_ 10. liar

17-3 ⚾ PRACTICE THE SKILL

Using the sample dictionary page on page 338, answer each question.

z-axes 1. What is the plural form of _z-axis?_

zemindar 2. What is the alternate spelling of _zamindar?_

zedoaries 3. What is the plural form of _zedoary?_

zebrine 4. What is the correct spelling of the adjective form of _zebra?_

_b_ 5. What is the correct spelling of the word that means "a domesticated ox"?
  a. zeebu   c. zeboo
  b. zebu   d. zebyu

Pronouncing the Word

Most dictionaries show the entry word's **syllabification** by placing dots between each syllable. Recognizing syllable divisions will help you learn to pronounce words that appear difficult at first glance; a syllable of few letters is much easier to pronounce than a word of fifteen letters. Syllable divisions will also help your spelling. When you can hear the sound of the individual syllables, you will be less likely to leave out letters or even entire syllables when you spell the word.

Immediately after the entry word will be its **pronunciation;** this is a respelling that shows you how to pronounce the word correctly. Some of the symbols used in the respelling may be unfamiliar to you. Near the front of the dictionary and at the bottom of each page, a **pronunciation guide** lists the symbols used in that dictionary to represent sounds. Refer to the pronunciation guide when you are unsure how to read the entry word's respelling. The respelling usually shows syllable divisions by placing hyphens or other marks between each syllable. An accent mark indicates which syllables will be emphasized, or stressed, when pronounced. Some words may have more than one accent mark if more than one syllable is pronounced with stress. The largest accent mark indicates the strongest stress in a word.

page 62

Principal parts of verbs

17-4 **PRACTICE THE SKILL**

Using the sample dictionary page, fill in each blank with the number of syllables in the word. Underline the syllable that is stressed most strongly.

_3_ 1. Zam<u>be</u>zi

_2_ 2. <u>za</u>yin

_4_ 3. Zech<u>a</u>riah

_2_ 4. <u>ze</u>in

_1_ 5. Zeist

17-5 **PRACTICE THE SKILL**

Using the sample dictionary page, draw a vertical line between the syllables of each word. If the word has only one syllable, do not draw a vertical line.

1. zai|bat|su

2. zan|der

3. zeal

4. ze|a|tin

5. zed|dar|y

Teaching Strategy: Demonstration

Write the word *wash* on the board or overhead transparency. Ask several students to say the word and listen to the differences in their pronunciation. Point out that although there are differences, we can still understand each other. Discuss pronunciation differences with students. Explain that idiolectal and dialectal differences among students are to be expected. Ask students for other examples of pronunciation differences. What regions of the country are known for different pronunciations?

What makes one pronunciation the standard? Who decides? Look up pronunciation differences in a dictionary. How difficult do pronunciation variations make learning English for speakers of other languages?

PRACTICE THE SKILL

Using the sample dictionary page, answer the following questions.

___c___ 1. How do the two pronunciations of *zebu* differ?
  a. The *z* is pronounced differently.
  b. The *b* is pronounced differently.
  c. The *u* is pronounced differently.
  d. All of the above.

___c___ 2. How do the two pronunciations of *Zapotec* differ?
  a. The *z* is pronounced differently.
  b. The *o* is pronounced differently.
  c. Both of the above.
  d. None of the above.

___d___ 3. How do the two pronunciations of *Zeeland* differ?
  a. The *e* is pronounced differently.
  b. The *a* is pronounced differently.
  c. The *d* is pronounced differently.
  d. All of the above.

___a___ 4. How do the two pronunciations of *Zeitgeist* differ?
  a. The *z* is pronounced differently.
  b. The *z* and the *t* are pronounced differently.
  c. The *t* and the *g* are pronounced differently.
  d. None of the above.

___d___ 5. How do the two pronunciations of *zaire* differ?
  a. The *z* is pronounced differently.
  b. The *r* is pronounced differently.
  c. The *e* is pronounced differently.
  d. None of the above.

Using the Word

Most dictionaries will also include a **function label** to indicate the entry word's part of speech. Many words can function as more than one part of speech. For example, the word *walk* would have function labels for noun and verb.

Next you will find the **definition** or meaning of the word; some words may have several definitions. Be sure that you choose the one that best fits the meaning of what you are reading or writing. Always read all the definitions and then decide. Some dictionaries also list **synonyms** (words with the same or similar meaning) of the entry word.

After the definition in most dictionaries (but before the definition in some) is the **etymology**, or the word's history. Knowing the history of a word can sometimes help you to understand why that word is spelled a certain way or how the word came to have several different meanings.

Learning Christianly

Learning to use the dictionary is a basic skill in learning to do research of all kinds. Many people do not like to research subjects that they do not find to be interesting. However, many Christians have devoted their lives to research, and they believe that Psalm 24:1 gives them good reason for doing so. Read this verse and see whether you can determine how it applies to research.

Learning Christianly

Psalm 24:1 states, "The earth is the Lord's, and the fulness thereof; the world, and they that dwell therein." Research is the work of investigating various parts of this world. Because this world belongs to God, it is a place worth studying; therefore, all sorts of research are worthy of the Christian's attention.

page 386

Precise words

PRACTICE THE SKILL

Using the sample definitions, write the number of the definition that corresponds to the use of this entry word from the *American Heritage College Dictionary.*

> **chute** (shoot) *n.* 1. An inclined trough, passage, or channel through or down which things may pass. 2. A waterfall or rapid. 3. A parachute, such as one for pilots or skydivers.

_____1_____ 1. The machine includes a chute that delivers the parts to the assembler.

_____3_____ 2. Did his chute catch on the tree or the telephone pole?

_____2_____ 3. The chute flows into Lake Superior.

_____1_____ 4. The logs were sent to the mill by way of a wooden chute.

_____2_____ 5. We visited the chute on the Cascade River last summer.

Using the sample dictionary page, answer the following questions.

_____zanily_____ 1. What is the adverb form of the word *zany?*

_____Greek_____ 2. From what language does the word *zed* originally come?

_____earth_____ 3. What is the meaning of the Persian word from which we get the word *zamindar?*

verb, noun, interjection 4. What part(s) of speech is the word *zap?*

_____zelotes_____ 5. What is the Latin form of the word from which we get the word *zealot?*

LIBRARY SKILLS

Lesson Support

Support Materials CD
Bulletin Boards—p. 213

Teaching Strategy:
Introduction

Share with the students part of the history of the library: As long as people have written, people have kept their writings in libraries. Early writings were recorded on materials such as stone, bamboo, and papyrus. King Sennacherib of Assyria kept thousands of clay tablets in his palace in Ninevah as did his grandson

Ashurbanipal. (For more on Sennacherib see II Kings 18-19; II Chronicles 32; Isaiah 36-37.) Some of the oldest copies of the Scripture were housed in libraries. The earliest Greek translation of the Old Testament, the *Septuagint,* was kept in the Alexandrian Library in Egypt. The Dead Sea Scrolls, which were written on leather, probably once belonged to the library of a religious group called the Essenes. The first library in the United States was started with money and about four hundred books donated by John Harvard in 1638. Harvard University was named after

him. Melvil Dewey, who developed the library classification system named after him, was also one of the founders of the American Library Association and the *Library Journal*. He also started the nation's first school for librarians at Columbia University in 1887.

Enrichment

Consider taking the students on a field trip to your school library or a public library. Many libraries offer special tours or events for students.

What Can I Find in the Library?

Libraries today are not only places for quiet research and study but also exciting centers of activity. Modern libraries contain much more than books. You can often find magazines, newspapers, audio cassettes, videocassettes, and puppets. You can attend classes, listen to lectures, or view displays on interesting topics. Many large public libraries offer free computer access to the Internet. Going to the library is a helpful and enjoyable way to learn. Today's libraries provide a broad selection of information and tools for you to use. Before you can use these tools, however, you need to know where to find them.

Libraries usually are divided into several sections. Sometimes these sections are separate rooms in the library building. Sometimes the sections are an area of shelves set apart from the other shelves. Each section contains a different type of library material.

Books, of course, are still the main feature of most libraries. In fact, our word *library* comes from the Latin word *liber,* which means *book.* Librarians arrange books on shelves called stacks. These stacks usually take up the most space in any library.

Book grew out of an Old English word for "beech," a kind of wood. *Book* comes from the old practice of carving letters into wood.

The **periodical** section contains materials published at regular intervals, such as monthly magazines or daily newspapers. Because they are published regularly, periodicals are an excellent source for current information about a wide variety of topics.

The **reference** section contains materials that do not circulate. In other words, they cannot be checked out of the library. They remain in the library where they will always be available to everyone. Many libraries reserve an entire room for reference materials. A capital letter *R* or the abbreviation *REF* on a book's spine indicates that the book belongs in the reference section.

Many libraries now have a separate section for **audio-visual** materials. These materials may include audio cassettes, videocassettes, works of art such as paintings and sculptures, or even puppets and games for young children. Some libraries have equipment for using the audio-visual materials right there in the library; others allow you to check out the materials for home use. The letters *AV* usually refer to the audio-visual collection.

Most libraries place the books written for **children** and **young adults** in a separate area of the library. This area usually contains both circulating and reference books and may even have its own periodical section and audio-visual materials. The capital letters *J* (for juvenile) or *YA* (for young adult) on a book's spine indicate that the book belongs to this section of the library.

Learning Christianly

Mankind's study and research of the world is as old as mankind itself. In ancient times one of the most accomplished researchers was King Solomon. The wisdom and knowledge of this king of Israel was like no other, and his wisdom was not limited to strictly moral matters (I Kings 4:30-33). In Proverbs 2:1-5 Solomon talks about some of the basics of the right kind of wisdom and knowledge. What does he emphasize in these verses?

Learning Christianly

In just five verses in this passage, Solomon uses eight verbs to describe the pursuit of wisdom and knowledge. Several of these verbs suggest hard work and determination. Pursuing the right kind of wisdom and knowledge is difficult, like the pursuit of most any good thing. Additionally, though, Solomon mentions the fact that the "fear of the Lord" is connected with the pursuit of wisdom and knowledge. This Old Testament concept carries the idea of a right relationship with God and is also connected with knowledge in Proverbs 1:7. It is a reality of God's world that pursuing wisdom and knowledge is truly successful when the pursuer has a right relationship with God. God is the source of all wisdom and knowledge (Col. 2:2-3), so both having a right relationship with Him and seeking for these gifts of His are worthy pursuits.

Library Skills **345**

How Are the Books Arranged?

All books fall into one of two categories: fiction or nonfiction. **Fiction** books, although sometimes based on facts, tell about events from an author's imagination. Regardless of its topic, a fiction book is arranged on the shelf alphabetically by the author's last name. If two authors share the same last name, their books are arranged alphabetically by the authors' first names. If a library has more than one book by the same author, the author's books are arranged alphabetically according to the first words of the titles (not including *A, An,* or *The*). The list below shows the order in which these books would appear on a library shelf.

> *Jane Eyre* by Charlotte Brontë
> *Wuthering Heights* by Emily Brontë
> *The Deerslayer* by James Fenimore Cooper
> *The Mystery of Edwin Drood* by Charles Dickens
> *Oliver Twist* by Charles Dickens
> *A Tale of Two Cities* by Charles Dickens

The word *fiction* comes from the Middle English word *ficcion,* "invention," and the older Latin source *fictus,* "formed, molded." Fiction is writing that has been formed or invented by its writer.

Some libraries separate the **mystery fiction** and **science fiction** books from the other fiction books. These libraries will have shelves marked *mystery fiction* or *science fiction* where those books can be found. In addition, the book spines will usually be marked with the letters *MYS* for mystery fiction or *SCI* for science fiction.

Nonfiction books present facts on almost every subject. Books about airplanes, livestock, mythology, poetry, and government are examples of nonfiction books. Most libraries use the **Dewey Decimal System** to arrange nonfiction books. The arranging is called "decimal" because many of the numbers have decimal points. The numbers are found on the spine of each book, along with the author and the title.

Melvil Dewey developed this system to bring together all the different books on one subject rather than having them scattered throughout the library. He divided knowledge into ten subject categories. To these categories he assigned numbers.

000-099	Generalities (including encyclopedias and general reference works)
100-199	Philosophy and psychology
200-299	Religion (including mythology)
300-399	Social sciences (including government, education, and etiquette)
400-499	Language
500-599	Natural sciences and mathematics (including chemistry and biology)

600-699	Technology (including occupations and professions)
700-799	The arts (including sports)
800-899	Literature and rhetoric (including short stories and plays)
900-999	Geography and history (including travel and biography)

A **biography** is a book written by one person about another person's life; an **autobiography** is a book about the author's own life. Many libraries separate the biographies and autobiographies from the other nonfiction books and shelve them in a separate area of the stacks. A capital *B* or the Dewey Decimal number *920* or *921* on the spine of a book indicates that the book is a biography or an autobiography. Biographies and autobiographies are arranged alphabetically by the last name of the subject, not the author. For example, a biography about the missionary Adoniram Judson would be shelved with other biographies under *J* for Judson.

Some large libraries use the **Library of Congress System** instead of the Dewey Decimal System. The Library of Congress System uses letters and numbers instead of numbers only and has twenty-one subject categories instead of ten. For example, in one library the book *Birds' Eggs* may have the Dewey Decimal number 598.233 and the Library of Congress call number QL 675.W32. Be sure you understand the system that your library uses.

18-1 ⚾ PRACTICE THE SKILL

Number the titles and authors of the following fiction books in the order in which they would appear on the fiction shelves of a library.

_4_ Norton Juster, *The Phantom Tollbooth*

_9_ Rosemary Sutcliff, *Simon*

_7_ Stephen W. Meader, *Clear for Action*

_5_ Jim Kjelgaard, *Big Red*

_2_ Betsy Byars, *The Summer of the Swans*

_10_ Geoffrey Trease, *Web of Traitors*

_1_ Sheila Burnford, *The Incredible Journey*

_3_ Will James, *Smoky*

_6_ Stephen W. Meader, *Boy with a Pack*

_8_ Rosemary Sutcliff, *The Silver Branch*

18-2 **PRACTICE THE SKILL**

Using the Dewey Decimal chart on pages 346-47, write the numbers for the correct category of each of the following books.

_500-599_ 1. *Janice VanCleave's Geometry for Every Kid*

_000-099_ 2. *Encyclopaedia Britannica*

_700-799_ 3. *The Winter Olympics*

_200-299_ 4. *Myths and Legends of the Ancient Near East*

_300-399_ 5. *Perfect Pigs: An Introduction to Manners*

_800-899_ 6. *Aesop's Fables*

_900-999_ 7. *Clara Barton: Soldier of Mercy*

_000-099_ 8. *The Guinness Book of World Records*

_300-399_ 9. *How We Choose a President*

_700-799_ 10. *Favorite Operas*

_600-699_ 11. *Careers in Horticultural Science*

_100-199_ 12. *The Essence of Ancient Philosophy*

_900-999_ 13. *Everyday Life in Ancient Crete*

_400-499_ 14. *Indian Signals and Sign Language*

_600-699_ 15. *The Internal Combustion Engine*

How Are the Books Labeled?

Every book in the library will have a label on the spine of the book. For a nonfiction book, this label contains the book's **call number.** The call number is the Dewey Decimal number with the first letter of the author's last name under it. Sometimes the label will also contain a **section letter** (such as *R*) if the book belongs in a separate section of the library (such as reference). Fiction books usually do not have call numbers. A fiction book is labeled with the first few letters of the author's last name and the capital letter *F*. The label may also include a section letter if the book belongs in a special section, such as *MYS* (mystery) or *YA* (young adult).

The call number or letters that appear on a book's spine will also appear on the **catalog entry.** Traditionally, libraries used **card catalogs** as tools to help people find the books they wanted. Today, many libraries have converted their card catalogs to on-line **computer catalogs.** Both types of catalogs contain the same information in approximately the same format. Computer catalogs, however, offer the user more ways to search for information.

How Do I Use the Card Catalog?

A card catalog is a cabinet with small drawers, usually located near the library entrance. Here, cards contain information on each book in the library. The three types of cards in the card catalog are the author card, the title card, and the subject card. These cards are usually alphabetized all together (not separated into three groups) in the drawers. Each card has a different top line: the author card starts with the author; the title card starts with the book's title; and the subject card starts with the subject of the book. Each card will include the title, the author, the place of publication, the date of publication, the publisher, the number of pages, and the call number (for a nonfiction book).

To use the card catalog you need to know the author or the title or the subject of the book you want. Perhaps you want a book by a particular author, but you are not sure of the title. Find the author card, which is filed alphabetically according to the author's last name. If there is more than one author with that same last name, the cards under that last name will be arranged alphabetically by the first names. For example, under *Brontë,* the name *Brontë, Anne,* would come before *Brontë, Charlotte.* Both fiction and nonfiction books have author cards.

Title cards are placed alphabetically in the drawers according to the first word in the title (again, not including *A, An,* and *The*). There are title cards for both fiction and nonfiction books.

If you do not know the titles or authors of nonfiction books on a subject that interests you, look for subject cards in the card catalog. There may be more than one subject card for some books. Subjects include noteworthy people, geographic locations, languages, countries, and other topics of interest.

When you find the card for the book you want, first write down the call number from the upper left-hand corner of the card (for a nonfiction book); then copy the name of the author and the title of the book. With this information you can ask for the book or go to the shelf and get it yourself.

How Do I Use the Computer Catalog?

Instead of individual filing cards, a computer catalog contains electronic records for each book. Each record includes the same information you would find on an author, title, or subject card in the card catalog. In fact, a computer catalog may contain more information than a card catalog. For instance, some computer-catalog records include a summary of the book. The summary can help you decide whether the book will be helpful to you. In addition, most computer catalogs also contain information about each book's status. In other words, the computer catalog can tell you if a book is available or is already checked out. If the book is already checked out, the catalog may tell you when it is due to be returned.

Using the computer catalog is similar to using the card catalog. First, you need to know the author or the title or the subject of the book you want to find. Next, type the information you know into the computer, according to the instructions on the screen. The computer will begin to search for the book you need by comparing the words you typed to the information in its database. When it finds a match, the computer screen will display the record for that book. If the information you typed was not specific enough, the computer screen will display a list for you to choose from. For instance, if you type the subject rather than the title, the screen will list several books about that subject. To see the record for an individual book, simply type the number displayed next to that title on the list.

The computer catalog at one library may be somewhat different from the computer catalog at another library. Be sure to ask the librarian for help if you do not know how to use your library's computer catalog.

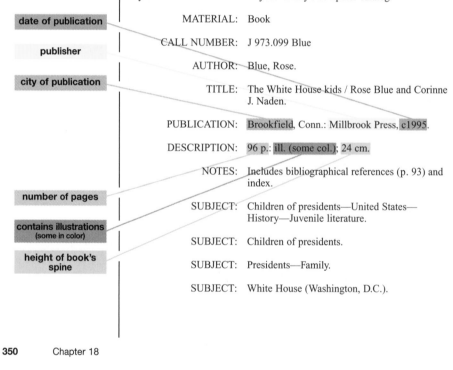

MATERIAL:	Book
CALL NUMBER:	J 973.099 Blue
AUTHOR:	Blue, Rose.
TITLE:	The White House kids / Rose Blue and Corinne J. Naden.
PUBLICATION:	Brookfield, Conn.: Millbrook Press, c1995.
DESCRIPTION:	96 p.: ill. (some col.); 24 cm.
NOTES:	Includes bibliographical references (p. 93) and index.
SUBJECT:	Children of presidents—United States—History—Juvenile literature.
SUBJECT:	Children of presidents.
SUBJECT:	Presidents—Family.
SUBJECT:	White House (Washington, D.C.).

Labels: date of publication, publisher, city of publication, number of pages, contains illustrations (some in color), height of book's spine

MATERIAL:	Book
CALL NUMBER:	598.233 Walters
AUTHOR:	Walters, Michael
TITLE:	Birds' eggs / Michael Walters; photography by Harry Taylor.
EDITION:	1st American ed.
PUBLICATION:	London; New York: Dorling Kindersley, 1994.
DESCRIPTION:	256 p.: col. ill.: 22 cm.
SERIES:	Eyewitness handbooks
NOTES:	Includes index.
SUBJECT:	Birds—Eggs.

Using the catalog entry above, answer the following questions.

Michael Walters 1. Who is the author of *Birds' Eggs*?

_256_ 2. How many pages are in *Birds' Eggs*?

Harry Taylor 3. Who is the photographer whose work appears in *Birds' Eggs*?

Eyewitness Handbooks 4. *Bird's Eggs* is part of what series?

Dorling Kindersley 5. What company published *Birds' Eggs*?

18-4 PRACTICE THE SKILL

A. Choose five topics from the list below.

B. Use your library's card catalog or computer catalog to find one book on each topic.

C. List the title, author, and call number for each book you choose.

1. Church history _____

_____

2. Holidays _____

_____

3. Ethics _____

_____

4. Zoology _____

_____

5. Old English _____

_____

6. Classical music _____

_____

7. Tokyo _____

_____

8. Dairy farming _____

_____

9. Journalism _____

_____

10. Greek drama _____

_____

How Do I Use Specific Reference Works?

Dictionaries

All dictionaries are pretty much alike, right? Actually, there are many different types, and you need to be acquainted with each one. An **unabridged dictionary** gives the most complete list of words and definitions. Although an abridged dictionary, or **desk dictionary**, is not as complete as the unabridged dictionary, it contains most of the words that you will need for your own reading and writing. Some desk dictionaries are designed for junior high students.

Abridge comes from the Latin word for "abbreviate," which means "to shorten."

A **foreign language dictionary** lists the words of another language and gives their meanings in English. Many foreign language dictionaries have two sections, one listing English words with their foreign language counterparts and the other listing words from a foreign language with their English translations.

Other dictionaries define special terms or provide information not found in a regular dictionary. A **dictionary of synonyms**, or **thesaurus**, gives words with similar meanings; some also give **antonyms**, words with opposite meanings. A **biographical dictionary** gives information on important people from the past and the present. A **geographic dictionary**, or **gazetteer**, lists places and their locations. It provides not only a correct pronunciation of the name of a place but also a description of its geographic features (such as rivers or mountains) and other helpful information (such as population).

Encyclopedias

Encyclopedias contain articles on almost every imaginable subject. These articles are arranged alphabetically. The volumes of an encyclopedia are usually labeled with one or more letters as well as with a numeral.

Find the article you need with the help of guide words at the top of each page. These words tell you the topic of the first article on each page, somewhat like the guide words that help you find words in a dictionary.

Check also in the index to find the pages where articles on your topic appear. Some sets of encyclopedias have an index in each volume, while others have a special volume (usually the last volume) that is the index for the entire set.

Investigate other references on the same topic when the encyclopedia gives them. They help you find articles with important additional information. These additional references, called cross-references, are often listed at the end of the article under a heading such as "See also."

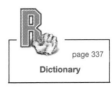

page 337
Dictionary

Almanacs

An **almanac** supplements the encyclopedia by giving more current information. An almanac includes tables of weights and measures, lists of sports statistics, names of award winners, information about government agencies and programs, summaries of recent events, and other miscellaneous facts. Most almanacs are published every year. You can find the information you need by looking in the almanac's index. An almanac's index may appear at the front, like a table of contents, instead of at the back, where most indexes appear.

Atlases

An **atlas** is a collection of maps. It can provide some of the same information as a geographic dictionary. Some atlases contain only political maps, which show political divisions such as countries, states, or cities. Other atlases include topographical maps, which show geographic features such as mountain ranges and bodies of water. The most commonly used atlases contain road maps, which show the roads connecting various cities. Some atlases also include information about populations, crops, weather, and similar facts. Every atlas has an index that lists the page number where you can find the map you need.

Books of Quotations

A **book of quotations**, such as Bartlett's *Familiar Quotations,* allows you to find a quotation by looking up its author, first line, or subject. Most books of quotations also list each quotation's original source and date.

Concordances

The Bible **concordance** gives key words from the Bible with lists of verses where the key words appear. When you can remember only part of a verse, look up an important word from the verse, a key word, in the concordance's alphabetical list.

For example, if you remember reading a verse that says something about temptation being common to man, you can look up *temptation* and find I Corinthians 10:13 as well as other verses listed under that topic. If the particular passage you want is not listed, try another key word. Not all key words or passages will be given in every concordance.

Some concordances are available in software form for use on computers. These products make searching the Scriptures even easier. For example, finding all the occurrences of the phrase "son of God" in a printed concordance would be time consuming, and you might miss references. But in a software version it can take less than a second.

Readers' Guide to Periodical Literature

The **Readers' Guide to Periodical Literature** is the most commonly used periodical index. In the same way that the card catalog or computer catalog can help you find a specific book, the *Readers' Guide* can help you find a specific periodical article. It lists articles from approximately two hundred fifty magazines by subject and by author. Each entry will tell you the article's subject, its title, its author, the magazine in which it appears, the issue number or date of the magazine, and the page numbers where you can find that particular article.

subject heading   FARGO (N.D.)   includes illustrations   beginning page number

Flooded Red River ruins crops. K. Johnston. il *Midwesterner* no15 p28-9+ My 1997

indicates article continues on other pages   date   article title   author   magazine title   issue number

18-5 PRACTICE THE SKILL

Identify the type of reference tool you would use to find the answer to each question: desk dictionary, foreign language dictionary, thesaurus, biographical dictionary, geographic dictionary, encyclopedia, almanac, atlas, book of quotations, concordance, or *Readers' Guide to Periodical Literature*.

___almanac___ 1. What baseball team won the 1956 World Series?

___desk dictionary___ 2. From what language does the English word *fantastic* originate?

___geographic dictionary___ 3. Which of the fifty states have cities named Maplewood?

___almanac___ 4. Which spacecraft was launched on November 3, 1973?

___concordance___ 5. How many verses in Proverbs include the word *believe?*

___thesaurus___ 6. What is an antonym for *resolution?*

___encyclopedia___ 7. Who discovered uranium?

___book of quotations___ 8. Who said "A good book is the best of friends"?

___foreign language dictionary___ 9. What is the Portuguese word for *cow?*

___encyclopedia___ 10. Where did soccer originate?

<u>Readers' Guide</u> 11. Which magazines published articles about Hale-Bopp in April 1997?

<u>atlas</u> 12. What is the average yearly rainfall in Sri Lanka?

<u>concordance</u> 13. In which verse does the apostle Paul mention "a thorn in the flesh"?

<u>biographical dictionary</u> 14. John Chapman is better known today by what nickname?

<u>encyclopedia</u> 15. What are some breeds of horses?

18-6 **PRACTICE THE SKILL**

CRUISING

Barging your way through Europe: river barge cruises. T. Innes. il *World Traveler* no79 p12+ O 1998

Use the entry from the *Readers' Guide to Periodical Literature* to answer each question.

1. Who is the author of the article? *T. Innes*

2. Is the article illustrated? How do you know?
   Yes. The abbreviation il means illustrated.

3. What is the title of the article?
   "Barging Your Way Through Europe: River Barge Cruises"

4. In which issue of the magazine did this article appear?
   number 79; October 1998

5. Is there more than one page for the article? How do you know?
   Yes. The plus symbol indicates that there are multiple pages.

Techno-Talk

A headline in an Internet trade publication declared that "Firewall Can Now Block Spam." To people not familiar with computer talk, this says that walls used to prevent fires from spreading between apartments can also keep out canned pork. But to people in the computer industry, it means there is a software program that can filter out unwanted e-mail.

We call words that are used only by people in certain fields *jargon*. To the outsider, jargon is almost impossible to understand. Christians use jargon too. How might this sound to someone who has never heard the gospel: "I covet your prayers as I go on visitation; pray that I will be a good testimony"?

The words *covet, visitation,* and *testimony* mean different things outside the Christian context. Jargon is language that excludes those not in the group. Christians should take care not to use words that confuse those who most need to understand.

Ask the students to name professions known for using jargon. (*scientists, computer technicians, medical personnel, news media, educators, and even students*)

Ask students to write a paragraph full of jargon. Instruct them to exchange paragraphs with other students. Challenge the students to rewrite the paragraphs using clear language.

CHAPTER 19

STUDY SKILLS

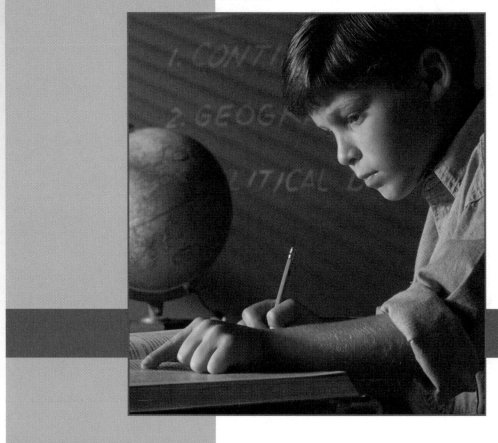

Lesson Support

Support Materials CD
Teaching Helps—p. 39
Bulletin Boards—p. 214

Developing an Interest

Do you ever have problems concentrating on what a teacher is saying because you are not interested in the subject? You are interested in certain subjects because God has given you these interests; therefore, you achieve good grades more easily in some classes than in others. However, you are not doomed to be bored or to achieve a lower grade if you are not interested in a certain subject (such as science or math). Interest can be developed.

Each class has something new or interesting. Look for one fact that can be useful or interesting to you. There are many ways to focus your attention and to discover interesting information.

1. Sit in your chair as if you are interested. Do not slouch.

2. Keep your eyes focused on your teacher to help you concentrate better.

3. Listen (or read) to learn. Try to learn while you are listening to the teacher or doing your class work. The more you learn in class, the less time you will have to spend studying outside class.

4. Write (or mark) important points. If the teacher or textbook emphasizes a point, write it down.

5. Practice guessing. Think ahead. What will the teacher or the book state next? Were you correct? If you were not, why not?

6. Connect the information that you are learning. How does what you are now learning relate to what you learned yesterday or in another class?

7. Ask questions, especially about information that you do not understand. If you are shy, write your questions down and then ask at least one question in each class until you become more confident.

Using the Parts of a Book

If you understand the parts of a book, you can find information in it quickly. Not all books have all of these parts, nor are they arranged in the same order in all books.

Every book begins with a **title page,** which gives the title of the book, the name of the author, the name of the publisher, and the place of publication. On the back of this page is the **copyright page,** which gives the year the book was copyrighted. *Copyright* is the legal right to that book; no one can reprint any part of it without permission.

A **table of contents** gives the chapter or unit divisions with page numbers in numerical order. A **list of illustrations** is similar to a table of contents; it tells where the pictures are in the text.

Some books also include **acknowledgments,** the names of people the author or editor wants to thank, and an **introduction** or **preface,** an explanation of the purpose of the book.

ESL: Not all countries have copyright laws, so this concept may be new to some of your foreign students.

Study Skills **359**

Teaching Strategy: Motivation

At the beginning of one class period, tell the class that you are requiring each of them to find at least one fact that somewhat interests him in today's lesson and that you will ask each one to write (at the end of the period) that fact on a piece of paper that will be turned in to the teacher. *Special note*: On the day you choose to do this activity, plan to include especially interesting material in your lesson. For instance, take the time to include a history fact, a science fact, something mathematical, and/or something regarding art or music. Remind your students periodically of what they should be doing. (Please be advised that even those students who simply write down any fact will still be listening better.) Continue this activity periodically, requiring the students to write an interesting fact (which you will collect at a required time) from other classes. Share what you are doing with the other teachers in your school so that other teachers may require the same type of behavior.

The major part of every book is the **text**. In both fiction and nonfiction books, the text is usually divided into units, sections, or chapters.

Other pages of information come after the text in many nonfiction books. The **bibliography** lists either the books that the author used in writing the text or the titles of some other books about the same subject.

An **appendix** includes extra helps, such as charts, diagrams, long lists, and notes of explanation. One kind of appendix is a **glossary,** which gives the definitions of special vocabulary used in the text. Many textbooks have glossaries and other appendixes.

An **index** is an alphabetical listing of key words and phrases with all the page numbers where they appear in the text. Sometimes the index will also list the page numbers for the illustrations.

You may notice that fiction books usually have only a title page, a table of contents, and a text. The main purpose of fiction is usually to entertain, not to inform; therefore, the other parts are not necessary.

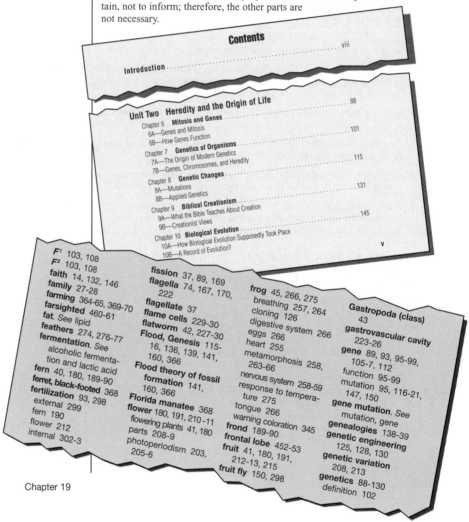

Teaching Strategy: Reinforcement

Direct the students to follow these instructions with the textbook from another class. Tell them to use the Index to determine which page contains information or an illustration for a topic you have selected; to use the Table of Contents and Index to determine which chapter contains specific information; to use the Glossary to discover the definition of certain terms; and to use the Title Page to discover publishing information.

Use the sample table of contents and index to find the answer to each question. Fill in each blank with the letter of the correct answer.

   _c_   1. In which chapter would you find the theory of fossil formation after the Flood?
            a. 7
            b. 8
            c. 9

   _c_   2. Which page would tell about the black-footed ferret?
            a. 189
            b. 229
            c. 368

   _c_   3. Which chapter contains information on genetic engineering?
            a. 6
            b. 7
            c. 8

   _b_   4. Which page would tell about parts of a flower?
            a. 203
            b. 208
            c. 210

   _a_   5. Fission is discussed in chapter
            a. 6.
            b. 7.
            c. 8.

   _b_   6. Genealogies can be found in the same chapter as
            a. farming.
            b. the Flood.
            c. genetic engineering.

   _b_   7. Which page would help you learn about flame cells?
            a. 227
            b. 229
            c. 231

   _c_   8. Which chapter includes Bible teaching about Creation?
            a. 7
            b. 8
            c. 9

   _c_   9. Genetics is discussed in all these chapter parts except
            a. 7A.
            b. 8B.
            c. 9B.

   _a_   10. The definition of genetics is discussed in the same chapter as
            a. F^2.
            b. fern fertilization.
            c. the function of genes.

19-2 · PRACTICE THE SKILL

Fill in each blank with the letter of the correct book section that would give you the information requested. Letters may be used more than once.

A. title page   E. bibliography
B. copyright page   F. appendix
C. table of contents   G. glossary
D. text   H. index

_A_ 1. the place of the book's publication

_G_ 2. the definition of a math term in the math text

_D_ 3. the main portion of the book

_C_ 4. a list of the chapter titles

_F_ 5. a special chart

_A_ 6. the name of the book

_C_ 7. the order of the textbook's main ideas

_E_ 8. the books that the author used when writing the text

_H_ 9. the pages on which a certain term is used

_B_ 10. the year the book was published

Reading Textbooks

In elementary school, your textbooks were filled with stories. Even your science and history textbooks were written to sound like stories. You have probably discovered that in junior high most of your textbooks are not written as stories. Therefore, you need to learn how to use different kinds of reading skills.

When you receive a new textbook, take a few minutes to see where you are headed. Survey your textbook by looking over the table of contents. The table of contents will tell you two important things: the major topics in the textbook and the logical organization the author uses to discuss those topics.

Textbook authors almost always organize their topics by units and chapters. For example, this textbook has three units: grammar, usage, and reference. Each unit is divided into chapters. In this book, the reference unit contains four chapters: Dictionary Skills, Library Skills, Study Skills (the chapter you are reading now), and Composition Skills.

Each chapter may be further divided into sections. This chapter has large bold headings and small bold headings. Each heading tells you which part of the topic will be discussed. The rest of the information is in regular paragraphs. Read each paragraph looking for the one topic in that paragraph. Once you have found that topic, look further to see what in-depth

---

Teaching Strategy: Demonstration

Have the students turn to the Table of Contents. Point out the textbook divisions noted there.

Teaching Strategy: Participation

Point out the headings on page 363. Have the students read the first paragraph under the heading "Improving Your Study Time." Ask them what the main topic of the paragraph is.

Evaluation

Using a textbook from another class, create questions for the students to answer from their reading.

information the paragraph includes about the topic. Also notice the pictures and illustrations. They are there to help you better understand what is being taught. Actually, reading a textbook can be easier than reading a novel because you have all these wonderful clues to help you along.

Improving Your Study Time

The purpose of studying is to learn the information. You might be surprised to discover that the students who make the best grades are not necessarily the most intelligent students in the class. They are usually the ones who have figured out the best methods of study.

Be prepared for every class period. Come to class with your textbook. Check before you get to class to be certain that you have everything (pen, paper, text, etc.) that you will need for that class. Take time every day

1. to write down each homework assignment in an assignment booklet.

2. to put each paper where it belongs.

3. to take home every book you need.

4. to have every book, paper, and other study tool before you begin your homework.

You may think that some homework or tests are beyond your ability. With the help of the Lord and with some organization, however, you can conquer many difficulties.

Scheduling Your Study Time

Life in junior high is very busy. Therefore, you need to use a schedule to make the best use of your study time.

First, you should develop a priority schedule. To create priorities means to "establish by order of importance or urgency" (from *The American Heritage College Dictionary*). Once a month you should take at least five minutes to think ahead. Think about the activities scheduled for that month: church activities, sports practice, jobs at home, due dates for school assignments. Write these events on a calendar. Then you will know what days you already have things planned if another activity comes up. If you know your schedule in advance, you can plan to work ahead on school projects.

Second, you should have a detailed homework schedule. An assignment notebook is a must. It is wise to write "to do" lists, because the average person's mind is crowded with too much information to remember everything that occurs. That is why even many adults have appointment books.

Write down every assignment as soon as the teacher gives it to you. If you have no homework in a certain class on one day, write the word *none* for this class in your assignment notebook. If you do not write anything, you might think that you have homework but forgot to write it down.

When your teacher assigns a long-term project, mark the due date on your calendar. Then plan a schedule for completing the assignment one part at a time. Give yourself a due date for each part of the project and mark these dates on your calendar. This strategy reminds you to continue working on the project until it is finished.

Learning Christianly

Studying is not easy but it is rewarding. Proverbs 25:2 is a great verse proving that a Christian can get excited about studying for Christian reasons. Read this verse for yourself and see what you think.

Learning Christianly

Back in Solomon's day not many people had the free time to give to studying. Most people had to work all day, so studying was in fact a privilege reserved for people such as kings. Proverbs 25:2 describes one of the marvelous realities of God's world. He has created it in such a way that there are many things we can study. Students today have a privilege that only ancient kings once had—to apply themselves in school to study the many facets of the world God has made.

Study Skills **363**

Scriptural Application

Share the story of Gideon's battle against the Midianites from Judges 7. When the Lord commanded Gideon to attack the host of the Midianites with only three hundred men, Gideon did not attack randomly. Defeating the Midianites was beyond his natural ability; Gideon needed good organization. A student may think that some homework assignments, quizzes, or tests are beyond his ability. With the help of the Lord and with some organization, however, the student can conquer these difficulties.

Teaching Strategy: Motivation

Distribute a copy of Teaching Helps page 39 (Support Materials CD) to every student and give students time in class to complete the quiz. Encourage the students to examine their answers and to change their study habits if necessary.

Enrichment

Create a calendar page for this month for every student. Instruct the students to write all their scheduled activities (church, school, family, and personal) and project due dates on the calendar. Allow the students to keep the calendar at their desks or in their notebooks. Refer to the calendar periodically at the beginning of class. Show them how to use the schedule to plan ahead.

Third, you should have a daily study schedule. You need to have a plan for your after-school study time. This plan must include the "when," "where," and "how" of study.

When: Your study time is limited. Your choices are right after school or between supper and bedtime. Do not wait until the next morning to do your homework. Between getting dressed and eating breakfast, you will not have enough time to study.

Where: Establish one place to study—your bedroom, the kitchen, the living room, or a special study room. Choose a place where you can be comfortable, but not so comfortable that you are tempted to fall asleep. If you have just one study place, your mind will become conditioned to study in that place.

How: Which subject do you study first and which last? Determine which subject is your most difficult. Then decide whether to study that subject first or last. Do you retain more information when you study your hardest subject first? Or do you remember best what you study last?

Once you have determined the order of your study, decide approximately how long the homework for each class usually takes. Of course, some evenings the timing will vary. You should always set aside some time to review. These review sessions save study time later by allowing the information to become more firmly rooted in your long-term memory.

Using Profitable Memory Techniques

Once you have completed your daily reading assignments and your written homework assignments, the only type of assignment left to do is studying for those quizzes and tests. What you study includes the information from class and the information in your textbook. Here are some techniques to improve your memory.

1. Determine to remember. In other words, pay attention as you study. Do not be mentally lazy.

2. Ask yourself questions about your notes and answer them aloud.

3. Make flash cards from note cards. Write the question on one side and the answer on the other side.

4. Create your own written quizzes. Put your quiz aside for a day or two. Then return to the quiz and try to answer the questions. The questions you cannot correctly answer are the ones to restudy.

5. Have a friend or family member quiz you orally.

6. Think of some picture which you can associate with the fact you are studying. For example, you have read that China throughout most of its history has had a policy of isolationism. (It discourages the influence of non-Chinese peoples and cultures.) You know about the Great Wall of China. You could think of China as enclosed by a huge wall keeping out everyone who does not already live in China. This strategy can help you remember China's isolationist policy.

7. Cluster the information you are learning. If your history teacher gives you a list of names to learn for the final exam, learn them by category groups: the names of Chinese rulers, the names of Japanese rulers, and so on.

Reinforcement

Every day for a week, take a moment at the end of class to check that each student has written down his homework assignments for that day. Repeat this process every few days for the next two weeks, without warning the students which days their assignment booklets will be checked. Encourage the students' parents to help them establish good study habits by checking progress at home.

Teaching Strategy

Instruct the students to keep a written record of the time it takes them to do each class's homework for an entire week. Then instruct them to list the classes in the order in which they do their homework. Ask the students why they chose that order. In other words, of what value is it to them to do their first subject first, their second subject second, and so on.

8. Use mnemonic [nĭ-mŏn´-ĭk] devices to help you remember.

    a. Create rhymes.

    > Predicate nouns, the subject rename.
    > To do their jobs, linking verbs they claim.

    b. Create acronyms and acrostics. An acronym is a word in which each letter stands for another word. An acrostic is a word in which each letter stands for a phrase or a sentence. Here is an example of an acronym:

    > To remember the names of the great lakes (Superior, Huron, Michigan, Erie, Ontario), take their first letters *(S, H, M, E, O)* and rearrange them into a single word: *HOMES.*

Improving Your Reading Comprehension

Your school career involves much reading. Although you do not always know the meaning of every word you read, you do not always have time to stop reading and to search for the meaning of each unfamiliar word. How can you discover the meanings of these words while you continue to read your assignments? You can "read around" the word itself, or you can analyze the parts of the word. You may not discover the word's exact dictionary definition, but you will know enough of the meaning to understand the concept being taught.

Definitions

Look for a definition. Sometimes the text gives a definition with the word. In this example, what does *joual* mean?

> The Canadian Indian spoke *joual* to the missionaries, a dialect of Canadian French using nonstandard grammar and English vocabulary.

Restatements

Look for a restatement. If the text does not give a definition of the word, look for extra information after the word that may explain the word's meaning.

> The *edentate* man, who found it impossible to eat anything requiring chewing, settled for some rice pudding and hot coffee.

What does *edentate* mean? The sentence explains that chewing is difficult for the man. You can probably guess that *edentate* means "lacking teeth."

Examples

Look for an example. The extra details in the rest of the sentence help you guess the meaning of the word you do not know.

> The *recalcitrant* young man resisted his teacher's authority and refused to apologize.

What does *recalcitrant* mean? The sentence gives two examples of the young man's attitude and behavior. From the context, you can determine that *recalcitrant* means "stubborn and defiant."

Enrichment

In this example of an acrostic, each letter in the word *snowflakes* stands for a line that gives factual information about snowflakes.

> **S**ix-sided doilies, too tiny for mice;
> **N**ot only well-crafted, but all made of ice.
> **O**ccurring as flat-plated crystals combine,
> **W**hite flakes fall in infinite styles of design.
> **F**ormed when the temp falls below thirty-two,
> **L**ighter than raindrops and drier than dew,
> **A**ll finally settle if the ground's frozen too—
> **K**ind of like blankets on winter nights do.
> **E**ach flake, like a wool fiber, traps in some air,
> **S**o whatever snow covers, it's *warm* under there!

Reference Link

Suggest to the students that they use the dictionary to look up the pronunciations of the example words. If necessary, review the principles in Chapter 17.

Write the definitions of the words in italics. Use contextual clues to determine the definitions.

1. The knight's *vambrace,* the piece of armor protecting his arm from the wrist to the elbow, was damaged during the battle.

   armor used to protect the forearm

2. The *deluge* last night caused the river and the sewers to overflow this morning.

   a heavy downpour or flood

3. The *jovial* man, who was never in a bad mood, laughed heartily at his guest's joke.

   marked by hearty conviviality and good cheer

4. Mother said I must have been starving since I left only a *scintilla* of mashed potatoes in the bowl.

   a minute amount; an iota or a trace

5. The teacher told the students to *cogitate,* think very carefully, before they answered the next question.

   to think very carefully

Word Parts

Look at the parts of the word. If you know the meaning of part of the word, you may be able to determine what the entire word means. Listed below are several prefixes, suffixes, and root words and their meanings.

- Prefixes

   A **prefix** is added to the beginning of a word.

Prefix	Meaning	Example
ante-	before	antecedent
e-/ex-	out, from	emit, exhale
in-	not	insane
inter-	between, among	interstate
intra-	within	intramural
per-	through	permit
super-	above normal	supervise

- Suffixes

  A **suffix** is added to the end of a word.

Suffix	Meaning	Example
-ion	action/condition	exception
-ous	having/possessing	spacious

- Roots

  A **root** is the main part of a word. Some roots can act alone as words without any prefixes or suffixes attached.

Root	Meaning	Example
ced/cede	to move, to yield	concede
cept	take	except
flu	flow	fluid
leg/lect	read, choose	illegible
mit/mis	send	permission
urb	city	suburban
vide/vise	see	supervise

 19-4 PRACTICE THE SKILL

Using the definitions of the prefixes, suffixes, and root words given above, guess the definitions for the words given below. Even if you do not know the entire definition, give the part that you do know.

1. vision _the condition of seeing; eyesight_

2. superscript _something written above (the other writing)_

3. perception _the act of perceiving (becoming aware of through the senses)_

4. flume _a passageway for water to flow through_

5. indestructible _not destructible, impossible to destroy_

6. interurban _between two city areas_

7. exclude _to keep or put out; to prevent from entering_

8. antechamber _a room before another room, an outer room that opens into another room_

9. neglect _to choose not to pay attention to something_

10. gracious _possessing kindness or courtesy_

Taking Tests

While part of your grade depends on how well you do on your homework and quizzes, another part of it depends on how well you do on your tests. Taking good notes, doing your homework, and studying your notes and homework weekly will help you to do better on your tests than you will do if you wait until the night before the test to begin studying. The more often you review, the more information your memory will retain.

How to Take Classroom Tests

1. Look over the test to discover what types of questions there are and to see how many questions you have to answer.

2. Read the directions to each section carefully.

3. Work through the entire test in one of two ways.

    a. Start at the beginning and keep going. Answer all those questions that you know and those that you are 50 percent to 75 percent certain of. Mark somehow those that you do not know or that you need to spend more time thinking about (circle the number, place a check beside the number, etc.). Come back to those later.

    b. Choose the most difficult section of the test and do it first. Be certain, however, not to spend too much time on that one section, or you will not have enough time to complete the easier sections. (Again, mark the questions with which you are having problems and come back to those later.) (Note: Be aware that sometimes information given in another question on the test may provide you with just the clue you need to answer one of the questions that you do not know the answer to.)

4. Try to answer all the questions, even if you have to guess at some.

5. Think before you write. It is always better to write a little about what you do know than to write a lot about what you do not know.

6. Write neatly. Correct answers will not count if the teacher cannot read what you have written.

How to Answer Objective Test Questions

Multiple Choice

1. Read the question carefully. Try to think of the answer before you look at the choices.

2. Read all the choices carefully. Ignore those that you know are wrong. (You might want to cross them out.)

3. Choose the best answer from the choices that are left.

Example: _d_   During World War II, what country controlled most of
the activity in the Pacific Ocean?
a. Germany
b. China
c. England
d. Japan

Matching

1. Read all the questions carefully. Try to think of the correct answer for
    each question before you look at the choices.

2. Match the questions and answers that you know are correct.

3. From the choices remaining, choose the best answer for each question.

Example: A. Aleksandr Solzhenitsyn
B. Elizabeth II
C. Pablo Picasso
D. Marie Curie
E. Franklin Pierce

____E____   1. American president

____C____   2. Spanish artist

____A____   3. Russian writer

____B____   4. English queen

____D____   5. French scientist

True/False

1. Read each item carefully. If any word in the item is false, the entire
    item is false.

2. Look for words such as *always, never,* or *only;* these words often signal
    a false item.

Example:

_____false_____Adverbs modify only verbs.

(Adverbs modify verbs, but they also modify adjectives and other
adverbs. The word *only* makes this statement false.)

Teaching Strategy: Discussion

Ask the students to explain their answers
for the matching activity. Point out that the
feminine names *Elizabeth II* and *Marie
Curie* are the only possible choices for
English queen. Furthermore, *Elizabeth II*
is the logical choice because monarchs are
often known by numbers as well as their
names. The students should use reasoning
to determine any answer they do not already know.

Short Answer

1. Answer accurately and completely those questions you know.

2. If you do not know the answer, guess as well as you can. You may get partial credit for your answer.

Example:

_____May_____ 1. Mother's Day in the United States is observed in what month?

_____November_____ 2. Thanksgiving in the United States is observed in what month?

_____June_____ 3. Flag Day in the United States is observed in what month?

How to Take Standardized Tests

According to your school's schedule, you will take standardized tests periodically. If you are familiar with the types of questions usually included on a standardized test, you will have a better chance of doing well on it.

Reading Comprehension

The reading comprehension section tests your ability to analyze a written passage. The questions may ask about the main ideas, details, or meaning of the passage. You may have to evaluate information or draw conclusions. Use these strategies for this part of the test.

1. Briefly look at the questions.

2. Read the paragraph and answer the questions you definitely know.

3. Then read the other questions carefully; eliminate the choices that you know are incorrect.

4. Choose the most logical answer from the choices remaining.

Example: One by one the French posts began falling to the British. Late in 1758 a British force ousted the French from Fort Duquesne. The British rebuilt the badly damaged fort and renamed it Fort Pitt.

_____C_____ In this paragraph the word *posts* means
A. wooden supports
B. mail deliveries
C. military bases
D. assigned positions

The paragraph has no information leading the reader to think that *wooden supports* or *mail deliveries* would be the correct choice. *Assigned positions* would come closer, but the contextual clues should signal that *military bases* is the best answer.

Vocabulary

The vocabulary section tests your knowledge of common English words. This section may include two types of questions. One type gives you part of a sentence or an entire sentence with a word in bold print. You choose from a list of choices the word that best matches the meaning of the word in bold print. Use your knowledge of contextual clues to help you choose an answer.

Example: _C_   The boat moved into the **harbor.**
    A. island
    B. outlet
    C. sheltered body of water
    D. water

Another type of question may list several sentences, all including the same underlined word. You choose from the list of choices the sentence in which the word has the same meaning as in the original sentence.

Example: _B_   The senator will take a <u>stand</u> for what he believes.
    A. Please <u>stand</u> for the doxology.
    B. Our pastor's <u>stand</u> is the same as our family's.
    C. I could <u>stand</u> having some breakfast.
    D. The bookcase will <u>stand</u> six feet high.

In the original sentence, *stand* means "a position one is prepared to uphold." *Stand* in the first choice means "to rise to an upright position." In the second choice, *stand* means "a position one is prepared to uphold." In the third choice, *stand* means "to benefit from." *Stand* in the fourth choice means "to measure to a specified height." The correct answer is the second choice.

Grammar, Usage, and Mechanics

Some standardized tests combine questions about grammar, usage, and mechanics in one section. Other standardized tests include several separate sections of questions. The questions may appear in several different formats. The test may show a sentence with several words underlined and labeled. Then you choose the word that contains an error. If the sentence is correct, choose the "no error" option.

Example: _A_   Sheila, our <u>Dog</u>, <u>climbs</u> the steps <u>carefully</u>. <u>No error</u>
                 A   B   C   D

The correct choice is *A* because the word *dog* should not be capitalized.

Another type of question may show you a sentence with part of the sentence underlined. You then choose one of several possible replacements for the underlined part. If the underlined part is correct, choose the answer that indicates no change is necessary.

Example: _B_   One of my dogs <u>is missing their</u> collar.
    A. are missing their
    B. is missing its
    C. are missing its
    D. (correct as is)

The correct choice is *B* because the pronoun *its* agrees with its singular antecedent *One* and the verb *is* agrees with the singular subject *One*.

Some standardized tests have separate sections for mechanics (capitalization and punctuation). The question may divide one sentence into several parts. Each part is listed separately. You choose the part that contains an error. If the sentence is correct, choose the answer that indicates no change is necessary.

Example: _D_   A. Candy went to the store
            B. and bought a collar
            C. for her dog.
            D. (no error)

Because each section of the sentence is correct, the correct answer is *D (no error)*.

19-5 PRACTICE THE SKILL

Reading Comprehension

When the United States entered the nineteenth century, it was a quiet land with family farms, small villages, and a few small cities on the Atlantic coastline. By the end of the century, however, crowded cities, busy factories, and mechanized farms stretched across the country. At the dawn of the twentieth century, the United States was on its way to becoming the greatest industrial nation in the world.

_D_   1. The topic of the above paragraph is
        A. American farming methods.
        B. villages and cities in the United States.
        C. the twentieth century.
        D. the industrialization of the United States.

Vocabulary

_B_   2. Settlers used wagons to carry their supplies over the narrow isthmus that separated the two large lakes.
        A. steel bridge
        B. strip of land
        C. mountain passage
        D. river

_C_   3. Kris received an autographed copy of his sister's novel.
        A. Amber tried to copy Ryan's actions.
        B. Pablo wrote the copy for the newspaper advertisement.
        C. The teacher wanted me to print another copy of my report.
        D. Biographical copy for people can be found in an encyclopedia.

Grammar, Usage, and Mechanics

_C_   4. Sarah, <u>who</u> wears <u>the</u> uniform, <u>ride</u> her bicycle.   <u>No error</u>
                           A   B   C   D

_B_   5. Everyone <u>clapped their hands</u> as Danika walked off stage.
      A. clapped their hand
      B. clapped his hands
      C. clapped its hand
      D. (correct as is)

_B_   6. A. David said to
      B. his Father,
      C. "Where is Aunt Beth?"
      D. (no error)

CHAPTER 20

COMPOSITION SKILLS: THE WRITER'S TOOLBOX

Lesson Support

Support Materials CD
Teaching Helps—pp. 40-41
Bulletin Boards—p. 214

What Is a Paragraph?

You are reading a paragraph right now. A **paragraph** consists of a group of sentences related closely to one main idea. The main idea of the paragraph is usually stated in the **topic sentence.** As you write, you indent each new paragraph to show that you are introducing another idea or point.

Besides the topic sentence, paragraphs contain **supporting sentences.** These sentences may use details, examples, illustrations, or other methods to support the topic sentence.

A **concluding sentence** joins all the ideas together so that the paragraph will be complete. Many concluding sentences restate the idea in the topic sentence.

Caring for Your Cat

Every cat owner is responsible to provide for three basic survival needs of his pet. The first need is food; any cat will die without food, of course. Another need is fresh water. A cat's water dish should be rinsed and refilled at least once a day. Finally, every cat (whether it lives indoors or out) needs a warm, dry place to sleep. Providing for these simple needs for his pet is the duty of a dependable cat owner.

> **Topic Sentence**
>
> **Supporting Sentences**
>
> **Concluding Sentence**

Planning

How Do I Choose a Topic?

Before you begin to write, you must choose a **topic.** Some people have trouble thinking of anything to write about; other people have so many ideas that they have trouble choosing just one. Choose a topic that interests you. If you are interested in your topic, your reader will be more interested in what you have to say. Here are some methods you can use to find topic ideas.

- **Individual techniques**

Make a list

Recall and list events, experiences, and memories from the past that you could write about. To jog your memory you may want to

- Read journal or diary entries.
- Look at personal photos or scrapbooks.
- Observe objects or scenes that you enjoy.
- Make a map of your neighborhood or home.

Various descriptions of the writing process name different numbers of steps. Some list as many as six steps; some list as few as three. You may have used a five-step writing process in which the revising stage is divided into two separate steps called revising and proofreading. The system you will use in this text names four steps in writing process: planning, drafting, revising, and publishing.

Ask yourself questions

Here are some questions to get you started. You may be able to think of more questions that will lead you to a topic.

- What are my favorite pastimes? Why?
- Whom could I pattern my life after? Why?
- What is a book I have enjoyed? Why?
- What is my best (or most difficult) subject? Why?
- What is the funniest thing that ever happened to me?

• Group techniques

Use brainstorming

Brainstorming is a useful tool for a group of students to use together. One student begins by stating a subject. Then the others list everything they can about that subject.

- Work in a small group of students.
- Bring up a subject in which you are interested.
- Start commenting on the subject.

Look at the example of a list from a brainstorming session. Notice that the students start with one word and end with many possibilities.

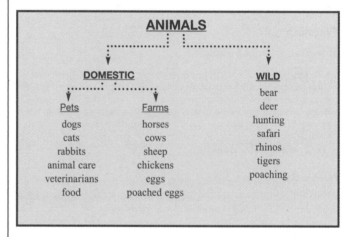

Work in pairs

Talk with another student about a topic you think you may use. Allow him to ask you questions about the topic in order to spark some creative ideas in your mind. Take notes as your partner asks you questions.

Teaching Strategy: Participation

Many different paragraphs could be developed from the ideas on the brainstorming diagram in the student text. Encourage students to come up with a variety of potential topics based on the diagram's information.

Teaching Strategy: Participation

Small groups of students can brainstorm together in class for short periods of time (perhaps five to seven minutes). Every student should contribute ideas; one student should record the group's ideas. The group could then choose one topic to develop into a paragraph, or each student could choose the topic that most appeals to him.

How Do I Narrow My Topic?

After you choose your topic, you may need to narrow it. For example, the topic "domestic" is too broad for a paragraph. One might think of household chores, tamed pets, or servants. The topic "cat" is also too broad because there are many different types of cats. Of course, some topics are too narrow. The topic "my cat's left ear" would be difficult to develop into an entire paragraph.

If you have chosen a broad topic, think of specific things about your topic that you could develop into a paragraph. One good topic idea from the brainstorming example is caring for a cat's basic needs. This topic combines the broad topic "cats" with the specific idea of "animal care."

How Do I Gather Information?

Now that you have decided on a topic, you need to gather information about your topic. List everything you already know about your topic. You can use the same methods for gathering information that you used to choose a topic: listing, asking questions, brainstorming, and working in pairs. Look at the example: this student gathers information on the topic "my favorite activity" by asking questions.

1. What is my favorite activity?
   playing soccer

2. When did I first try this activity?
   My friend Joe brought his new soccer ball to my house, and we started kicking it around the yard.

3. Did I enjoy the activity the first time I tried it?
   Yes, although my aim wasn't very good yet.

4. Why do I enjoy this activity?
   I like to run, and it's fun to see my skills improve. I also like working together as a team with the other players.

5. What is the most fun I have had with this activity?
   The time our team won the city championship was really exciting.

Does this student have enough information to write a good paragraph? If he is writing about his personal experience, he probably has enough information.

If you still need more information, you may want to research your topic. You could look for facts in books and periodicals from the library. Or you could interview someone you know who is an expert on your topic. If you use any information from a source, be sure to tell where you found the information.

Learning Christianly

Writing from research is an important skill that Christians need to acquire. Many Christians, however, think that acquiring this ability is a waste of time. The verse they tend to quote is Ecclesiastes 12:12. Read this verse in context. How would you respond to someone who thinks the verse is telling Christians to stop reading and writing?

Learning Christianly

The book of Ecclesiastes describes the pointlessness of a life lived without God. In the last chapter of his book, Solomon poetically describes the effects of old age on a person's body (12:3-7) and encourages young people at the same time: "Remember now thy Creator in the days of thy youth" (12:1). The chapter closes by explaining that "because the preacher [Solomon] was wise, he still taught the people knowledge" (12:9). In fact, Solomon "sought to find out acceptable words" (12:10), a skill that students learn in a course like this. According to Solomon, the words that wise people use are either like goads (something that stimulates a person to think) or like nails (something that gives people stability). Yes, it is true that there are too many books to read in a lifetime and that studying makes a person tired. But what God has called people to do is to have a right relationship with Him and to follow His commandments (12:13). One of those commandments appears to be seeking how to give people knowledge with the right words (12:9-11). Reading and writing are valuable skills that can be used in a service like this for God and others.

Composition Skills **377**

Considering Audience and Determining Purpose

After you decide on a topic and gather information, you must decide what information to include in your paragraph. How do you choose the information to include? Considering your audience and determining your purpose will help you decide your focus.

When you write, you are writing to a person and for a purpose. Perhaps you are writing a thank-you note to a friend, a science report for your teacher, or a book report to persuade another student to read the book.

The **audience** is the person or group to whom you are writing. Knowing your audience will help you choose effective words and structure as you write. For example, a letter to a friend would be worded differently from a science report for your teacher.

The **purpose** is the reason for your writing. Your purpose may be to describe, inform, persuade, or entertain. The reason to write your friend could be to inform him about what has been going on in your life, while the purpose for the science report would be to explain the procedure and outcome of an experiment or to persuade your audience that one detergent is better than another.

As you plan your paragraph, ask yourself these questions:

- Who is my audience? (fellow students? the editor of the local newspaper?)

- What is my purpose? (to persuade someone to do something? to describe an experience I had?)

- What information does my audience already know about my topic?

- What about my topic will interest my audience?

Be sure to include in your paragraph information that will interest your audience and help you to achieve your purpose.

Look again at the example in the previous section. What information should the writer include in his paragraph if his purpose is to entertain his teacher? Would he include different information if his purpose is to persuade another student to play soccer?

If the writer wants to persuade another student to play soccer, he would include the information from questions three, four, and five. He would emphasize the fun and excitement of playing soccer with other students.

Evaluation

Prepare an overhead transparency of Teaching Helps page 40 (Support Materials CD) or distribute a copy to each student. After students have completed the activity, ask volunteers to discuss the reasons for their answers. Lead the students to understand the logical connections between certain topic sentences and their intended audiences.

Read the following student paragraph and answer the questions at the end. *(Answers will vary.)*

Do we have to tear down the old department store building? It seems it could be put to another use. The students of Red Mill need a recreation center. It would give them a place to go that is safe and keep them off the streets after school. Parents would know where their children are. It would make money and be cheaper than building a new building. Please consider this proposal before it is too late.

to persuade   1. What is the purpose of this paragraph?

decision makers   2. Who is the intended audience for this paragraph?

students and parents   3. What other audience might be interested in this information?

Drafting

Writing a Topic Sentence

Now that you have chosen a topic, narrowed your subject, determined your purpose, and identified your audience, you are ready to write your paragraph. First, write your topic sentence. The topic sentence states the main idea of the paragraph. Look at this example.

Great Faith

Many Old Testament characters had great faith. Noah had enough faith in God to build an ark on dry ground. Abraham's strong faith enabled him to present his son Isaac as a sacrifice. Only because he believed in God's care could Moses give up his riches in Pharaoh's house to suffer with God's people. These people are given as examples to us so that we might become more faithful.

If someone asked you right now what the example paragraph is about, what would you say? You would probably say something like "Old Testament characters who had great faith." And you would be correct. If you said only "Old Testament men" or "faith," you would not be entirely accurate. The paragraph tells about Old Testament men, but it more specifically tells how they demonstrated their strong faith in God.

Composition Skills   **379**

Teaching Strategy: Discussion

Instruct the students to reread the example paragraph "Great Faith" on page 379, putting the topic sentence last. How does this change affect the paragraph? *(The ideas seem disconnected without a sentence to introduce them.)*

Teaching Strategy

Use these ideas to help your students locate and draft topic sentences:

- Read aloud good examples of topic sentences and supporting sentences from paragraphs written by former students. (Always keep a few paragraphs —good and bad—from each year to use as examples for future students.)

- Display several example paragraphs with clear topic sentences. Instruct the students to find the topic sentence in each paragraph.

- Display or read aloud a paragraph without a topic sentence. Instruct the students to write a topic sentence.

- Assign the students several ideas not yet developed into paragraphs. Instruct the students to write an appropriate topic sentence for each idea.

You could answer that question with the first sentence of the paragraph: "Many Old Testament characters had great faith." The first sentence is the topic sentence of the paragraph. It tells you both the subject and what will be said about the subject.

The topic sentence is usually, but not always, the first sentence in a paragraph. Because it introduces the topic, it is often helpful to the writer as well as to the reader if it does come first.

20-2 PRACTICE THE SKILL

Write a good topic sentence for the following paragraph. The sentence should both tell the subject of the paragraph and indicate what will be said about the topic. *(Answers will vary.)*

Miriam bravely went to Pharaoh's daughter in order to protect Moses. Esther, the beautiful queen of Ahasuerus, risked her life to save the Jewish people from Haman's scheme. Perhaps not as well known, but just as brave, was Jael, who killed an enemy of God's people. These women had the courage to do what had to be done.

Many Old Testament women were courageous.

_____

Esther before Ahasuerus by Claude Vignon,
From The Bob Jones University Collection

Developing the Supporting Sentences

Now that you have a topic sentence, you need sentences to support your topic. Your supporting sentences use the information that you gathered in the planning stage. Remember your audience and purpose: what kind of support will help you reach your goal?

Paragraph Development		
Kind	**Definition**	**Example**
Fact	A statement that can be proved	The moon travels around the earth as the earth revolves around the sun.
Example	An instance or event that occurred	Moonrise is that time of the appearance of the moon above the eastern horizon.
Statistic	A fact expressed in numbers	The average period of the moon's revolution around the earth is 29 days, 12 hours, 44 minutes.
Incident/ anecdote	Brief personal account that illustrates the point	Last night the moon looked beautiful through the trees behind our house.
Sensory details	The use of sense words—taste, touch, smell, etc.	When the moon is full, it looks more like a spongy ball than a piece of cheese.
Reasons	Explanation of a truth	We distinguish between a calendar month and lunar month because the two time intervals are not exactly the same.

Look again at the example paragraph about Old Testament characters who had great faith. Notice that all the sentences coming after the topic sentence support it by giving examples about the topic. Noah, Abraham, and Moses are specific examples of Old Testament characters who had great faith. An effective paragraph needs both a clear topic sentence and specific supporting sentences.

Organizing the Supporting Sentences

Now that you have your details, you need to think about the best way to organize the information. As you look at your information, think about the different ways in which you could put your paragraph together. Keep your audience and your purpose in mind. Choose the organizational method that best helps you reach your goals.

Paragraph Organization		
Method	**Definition**	**Good places to use**
Chronological order	A presentation of events in the order of their occurrence	Stories, history, biography, news reports, processes, or instructions
Spatial order	A description according to how something is arranged	Description of a place or an object
Order of importance	A move from least important to most important or vice versa	Persuasive writing, description

Notice how the different organizational methods are used to achieve different purposes in these examples.

Chronological Order

As Easy as Pie

Pie crust is easy to make. First measure flour, salt, and shortening into a bowl. Then use a pastry cutter to mix the ingredients until the dough resembles small peas. Next add one tablespoon of ice water at a time to the mixture until the dough can be gathered into a ball. Finally, pat the ball into a flattened disk and put it into the refrigerator to cool. Anyone can prepare this simple food in minutes.

The writer uses the words *first, then, next,* and *finally* to show the order of the steps to make pie crust. Using words like these helps your reader to understand clearly the process you are describing.

Spatial Order

What words indicate that this paragraph's development is spatial?

A Home Away from Home

The guest room at my aunt's house is a pleasant place to stay. A comfortable bed stands to the right of the door. In the corner is a small nightstand with a good reading lamp and a loud alarm clock. The next wall has a window with heavy curtains. On the wall across from the bed, a bureau with a mirror above it stands next to a desk and chair. The fourth wall contains a large closet with folding doors. A guest will enjoy his stay at my aunt's house.

Expressions such as *in the corner* and *across from the bed* help the reader picture the room being described. Notice that the writer begins to the right of the door and describes everything in order. Do not describe things randomly; your reader will have difficulty picturing the room.

Order of Importance

What words let the reader know what is of most importance and what is of least importance?

The Importance of a Good Vocabulary

Every student should try to increase his vocabulary. First, a good vocabulary helps the student understand what he reads. Second, a good vocabulary can help a student improve his grades. Most importantly, a good vocabulary allows the student to communicate more effectively with other people. Every student will benefit from improving his vocabulary.

The words *most importantly* signal the most important support for the thesis. Notice that the writer places the most important idea last. Last is the most effective position because people usually remember best what they read last.

Coming to a Conclusion

A good paragraph usually contains a good conclusion. As you end your paragraph, you want your audience to have a sense of closure—bringing your discussion to an end. There are several ways to conclude. One common method is to summarize your main idea. However, you could also give a solution to a problem or even ask your audience a question. The purpose of your paragraph will help determine how you end your paragraph.

Look at the example paragraphs in the previous section. Each of the paragraphs uses the summary method to conclude. Compare the first sentence (the thesis) in each paragraph to the last sentence (the conclusion). Notice that the writer uses the same idea stated in different words.

Now look at the following example. Which method does this writer use to conclude the paragraph?

A Useful Tree

The tree in the empty lot on Elm Street should not be cut down. It is not in anyone's way. It does not interfere with power lines. It gives extra shade to the houses on either side of the empty lot. And who knows how much the next person who buys the lot might wish he had a tree were the tree to be cut down?

The writer uses a question to conclude the paragraph. The question draws the reader into the discussion and leaves him thinking about the writer's thesis.

Choosing a Title

After you have finished writing your paragraph, you need to choose a title for your work. Choosing a title is important. The title tells the reader what you are about to discuss. A good title also captures the reader's attention. For example, "Dogs" is not a good title. It is too broad; it does not let the reader know anything about the paragraph's specific topic. A better title is "Dogs Are My Favorite Pets" or "Why Do Dogs Make the Best Pets?" Both of these titles let the audience know the paragraph's topic. The second title even indicates that the paragraph may give reasons that dogs make good pets. The second title also grabs the reader's attention by asking a question. Choose a title for your paragraph that interests your readers and indicates your topic.

Revising

No one writes a perfect paper on the first try. No experienced writer skips the process of revision, nor should you. Revision is the way you improve whatever you are writing at the time, and it will gradually help you produce better first drafts too.

Revising for Ideas

Revision of the first draft should always be *re-vision*—seeing the material again. That is, you look at the rough draft again to see whether you have said what you wanted to say and to see how you can improve the saying of it. You may want to take the following steps as you revise.

1. After you have written your first draft, put it aside for a while. Come back to it later. The lapse of time helps you see your draft more objectively, as other people will see it. You will be better able to notice problems in your paragraph.

2. Look for ways to improve your rough draft. Use your pencil to mark changes you want to make. You may circle words you want to change, cross out unrelated sentences, draw arrows to indicate you want to move a word to another position, insert a caret where you want to add a word, or make other changes.

3. Read your paper aloud. Just hearing the words will give you a better insight into how you used your words.

The chart summarizes specific areas you need to consider as you revise your paragraph: clarity of purpose, audience interest, unity of ideas, coherence, and emphasis.

Teaching Strategy:
Discussion and Modeling

Explain that all writers revise their work to make it the best possible writing. Help the students see that writing begins as a rough process. Encourage the students to use these techniques:

- Write on a legal pad. The informality of the paper shows that this draft is not the final one.

- Use only one side of the paper and write on every other line. The extra room allows the students to circle words; to draw arrows to move words or phrases; and to add new words, phrases, and sentences.

- Write an assignment with the students and revise yours as an example. Even if you write only one paragraph, your participation says, "I can do it; so can you."

Potential Problems	Solutions
Is my purpose clear in my topic sentence? (My topic sentence should clearly state my purpose for my audience.)	Be more specific; zero in on one idea.
Is my paragraph interesting to my audience? (Let one or more friends read it and give you their reactions.)	Try writing an alternate beginning. Use an interesting fact, question, or anecdote to get your audience interested.
Is my paragraph unified? (Every sentence in the paragraph should relate to the topic sentence.)	Leave out any sentence that does not belong or rewrite the sentence to make it pertinent to the topic.
Is my paragraph coherent? Do my sentences "stick together" well? (The relationships between ideas should be clear and logical.)	Use clear transitional words *(now, then, next, because, in addition, also)*. You may need to link some sentences with connecting words.
Does my audience know what I am emphasizing? (The best way to show emphasis is by position.)	Put the most important point of a paragraph at the beginning or at the end.

Look at this example of a student's revision for ideas.

How Rabbits Grow

~~Cats are very clever in the way they hunt mice, chipmunks, and rabbits. Some rabbits are domesticated, but most live in~~

Rabbits grow in distinct stages.

~~the wild.~~ (When they get older, they have thick fur.) Baby rabbits drink only their mothers' milk. Because of their constantly growing teeth, adult rabbits must gnaw on harder food like pellets or vegetables. If you want to learn more about how rabbits ~~or cats~~ develop, go to your local library.

Sentence one has nothing to do with the rest of the paragraph. Sentence two introduces the subject of domesticated and wild rabbits, but the rest of the paragraph discusses how rabbits grow. The writer deleted both sentences and wrote a new topic sentence to introduce the topic of a growing rabbit.

Sentences three, four, and five discuss the stages of rabbit growth. However, sentence three discusses an adult rabbit, sentence four discusses a baby rabbit, and sentence five bounces back to the characteristics of an adult rabbit. The writer fixed this problem by putting the stages in chronological order.

Sentence six mentions cats, which are not discussed in the paragraph. The writer deleted the phrase "or cats" from the concluding sentence.

Revising for Style

After you revise for ideas, look at your paragraph again to revise for style.

Precise Words

As you revise, correct the inaccurate or imprecise words. Precise words help you to get your message across to your reader clearly. Use precise nouns and verbs. Some words may be general (like *state* or *said*) and some words may be specific (like *North Carolina* or *shouted*). A thesaurus may help you find the specific word you need.

Showing, not Telling

Have you ever heard the expression "Don't tell me; show me"? Your paragraph will be more effective if you show, not just tell, your idea. Use words that refer to the senses—taste, hear, touch, smell, see—to show your audience what you are describing. Do not rely on adjectives and adverbs alone; try to use precise nouns and verbs too.

Notice the details in the following examples. Which example shows the reader its topic?

1. The meal was delicious.

2. Steam rose from the huge turkey. When the host began to carve, the tender meat fell away from his knife. Each juicy slice gleamed in the candlelight. The spicy aroma of the herb dressing teased each hungry guest.

The second example successfully shows the reader the delicious meal. The writer appeals to the reader's senses with precise words: *tender, juicy, gleamed, spicy,* and *aroma*.

Teaching Strategy: Introduction

Write these sentences on the board or over-head transparency and instruct the students to revise them:

- *The picture is pretty.*
- *Jonathan plays the oboe.*
- *The mother called her son.*

Encourage the students to use more precise and interesting words in order to show rather than tell the reader the ideas conveyed by the sentences.

Evaluation

Each day that you discuss proofreading, display a sentence or two for the students to proofread as class begins. Include errors with which the students are having trouble (for example, fragments or incorrect verb forms).

Rewrite the passage to make it more precise. Show the reader what is happening. *(Answers will vary.)*

The next morning we started for the lake. We arrived at the dock after traveling through fog. We rented a boat and waited until the fog lifted and then started out. We cast our lines. A fish struck mine and after a fierce battle, I landed him.

The next morning we started for Lake Lanier. After traveling through fog,

we arrived at the dock. We rented a rowboat and waited until the fog lifted;

then we started out. We cast our lines. Almost immediately a fish struck

mine. I resisted the urge to pull the fish in too fast. And it was a good thing!

It was a strong and determined bass, not eager to be taken. I reeled in

just a few inches, and the bass hauled back on the line so hard he came

half out of the water. I let the line out and then reeled it back in. After at

least ten minutes of this reeling in and out, I got him close enough to the

boat to net him. After this fierce battle, I finally landed him.

Composition Skills   **387**

Proofreading

Proofreading your paper is just as important as revising. Make sure that you made no errors as you wrote your final draft. Mistakes can occur accidentally as you rewrite or type your paper, but you need to find and correct them. Even if someone else types your paper, you are still responsible for any errors.

Good proofreading takes practice, but you can learn to do it well. The most important principle is this: do not expect to find every error (or every kind of error) in a single reading. Read in different ways to find different things.

Use these tactics to proofread your paragraph:

- Slow down by using a blank sheet of paper to cover the part you have not yet read.

- Read the paper aloud. You may hear an error that you did not see when you read the paper silently.

- Look at the words in reverse order; begin reading at the end of the paper and work toward the beginning. This tactic will force you to look at each word individually for spelling or capitalization errors.

Potential Problems	Solutions
Grammar	
Do I have any fragments or run-on sentences?	Figure out what is missing with a fragment and complete the sentence. Divide the run-on sentence and punctuate it correctly.
Usage	
Do my subjects and verbs agree and do my pronouns and antecedents agree?	Put a singular subject with a singular verb. Follow the correct rules for pronoun/antecedent agreement. Check the rules in Chapter 9 and Chapter 10.
Punctuation	
Have I omitted any punctuation marks or used any marks incorrectly? Have I used the correct end punctuation or omitted any end punctuation?	Read each sentence carefully. Check the rules in Chapter 15.
Capitalization	
Does every sentence begin with a capital letter? Are all proper nouns capitalized?	Look for specific places, people, events, and objects. Check each sentence.
Spelling	
Have I misspelled any words?	Look deliberately at every word.

Teaching Strategy: Participation

Distribute a copy of Teaching Helps page 41 to each student. Encourage the students to use this checklist as they proofread their work. You may want to distribute this checklist each time you assign a new writing project.

Finally, you may want to read the paper through more quickly a few times, looking each time for some particular problem area that has been difficult for you in the past. For instance, it is fairly easy to spot comma problems when you read looking only for commas.

Careful proofreading does take some time. It is only a little more time, however, compared to the time you have already invested in your paragraph. And it can make an important difference in people's impression of your work.

Publishing

Publishing your paper simply means that you are sharing it with someone else. You could publish your paper a number of ways:

- Send it to your local newspaper.

- Put together a class literary collection.

- Use your work for programs (Parent Teacher Fellowships, holiday programs).

- Read your work over the school's public address system.

- Share it with your English class.

- Read your work to someone at home.

- Mail it to a friend or relative.

Writing Folders

After you finish your final draft, you may want to put it in a folder or notebook. By the end of the year, you would have a collection of your work. You could include your rough drafts and final papers or just the final papers. You and your teacher may find these folders helpful because the folder allows you, your parents, and your teacher to see your progress over the weeks, semester, or year. The folder also can help you see mistakes you have made in the past so that you will not make them again.

Teaching Strategy

Do not require students to type their papers at this grade level unless a typing class has been offered in their curriculum.

Chapter 1: Sentences

Sentence Types and Punctuation

Identify each sentence as declarative, interrogative, imperative, or exclamatory. Write in the blank the letter that corresponds to the correct answer. Then supply the correct punctuation mark at the end of the sentence.

A. declarative
B. interrogative
C. imperative
D. exclamatory

_B_ 1. Have you heard of Sergeant Alvin York?

_A_ 2. He fought in World War I.

_D_ 3. His bravery was incredible!

_B_ 4. Did you know he won the Congressional Medal of Honor?

_C_ 5. Read on to learn about his heroic exploits.

Simple Subjects

Find the simple or compound subject in each sentence. Write in the blank the letter that corresponds to the correct answer.

_C_ 6. Sergeant York and many other men formed a special nationwide division of soldiers.
A. Sergeant
B. Sergeant York
C. Sergeant York, men

_B_ 7. At first York had requested his removal from the draft lists.
A. At
B. York
C. removal

_B_ 8. Can you imagine the loss to the American troops?
A. Can, imagine
B. you
C. loss

_B_ 9. Fortunately, someone in Washington denied his request.
A. Fortunately
B. someone
C. someone, Washington

_B_ 10. Superiors and comrades were surely glad for York's presence on the battlefield.
    A. Superiors
    B. Superiors, comrades
    C. York's

Simple Predicates

Find the simple or compound predicate in each sentence. Write in the blank the letter that corresponds to the correct answer.

_B_ 11. York's fame rests primarily on his actions in the Argonne Forest.
    A. fame
    B. rests
    C. primarily

_B_ 12. Early one morning York and his unit made and executed plans for a charge up a hill.
    A. York, unit
    B. made, executed
    C. charge, hill

_A_ 13. There was extremely stiff resistance from the enemy.
    A. was
    B. extremely
    C. resistance

_B_ 14. What would you have done?
    A. would
    B. would have done
    C. have done

_C_ 15. York's unit found an empty trench and sneaked behind enemy lines.
    A. found
    B. sneaked
    C. found, sneaked

Correct Sentence Structure

Identify each group of words as a correct sentence, fragment, comma splice, or fused sentence. Write in the blank the letter that corresponds to the correct answer.

    A. correct sentence
    B. fragment
    C. comma splice
    D. fused sentence

_C_ 16. The unit saw two German stretcher bearers, York and his men followed the Germans to their headquarters.

_B_ 17. Although the soldiers at the headquarters surrendered to York and his men.

_A_ 18. More Germans with machine guns joined the fight.

_____C_____ 19. York stood and fired against the Germans until his rifle became too hot, he next fought six men with bayonets single-handedly and killed all of them with a .45.

_____D_____ 20. The remaining German gunners surrendered York and his men returned to their camp with 132 prisoners.

Correcting Sentence Structure

Correct the sentences above for which you chose letters _B, C,_ or _D_. If the sentence is correct as it is, write _correct_ in the blank.

21. _The unit saw two German stretcher bearers. York and his men followed the Germans to their headquarters._

22. _Although the soldiers at the headquarters surrendered to York and his men, more Germans with machine guns joined the fight._

23. _correct_

24. _York stood and fired against the Germans until his rifle became too hot. He next fought six men with bayonets single-handedly and killed all of them with a .45._

25. _The remaining German gunners surrendered. York and his men returned to their camp with 132 prisoners._

Chapter 2: Nouns

Identifying Nouns

Questions 1-5: Underline each common noun once and each proper noun twice in the following paragraph.

Hair used to be a symbol of nationality. A Muslim wore a turban. In China the men shaved the front part of the head and tied the back. In Africa the women dyed their hair with red earth and grease. In America Aztecs showed many conquests by a ridge at the scalp.

5 common/2 Proper
6 common/1 Prop.
4 common/2 Prop

Forms of Nouns

Identify the form of each italicized noun. Write in the blank the letter that corresponds to the correct answer.

        A. singular
        B. singular possessive
        C. plural
        D. plural possessive

___D___ 6. *Women's* hair in the medieval era was very long.

___C___ 7. *Egyptians* wore wigs to protect their heads from the hot sun.

___A___ 8. An Inca chief wore a *headband* wrapped around his head five times.

___B___ 9. A *girl's* hairstyle indicated whether she was married.

___C___ 10. In the eighteenth century, women wore their hair over wire *cages*.

Forming Possessive Nouns

Identify the correct possessive form of each phrase. Write in the blank the letter that corresponds to the correct answer.

___C___ 11. the color of the hair
        A. hairs color
        B. hairs' color
        C. hair's color

___B___ 12. the arrangements of the hairdressers
        A. hairdressers arrangements
        B. hairdressers' arrangements
        C. hairdresser's arrangements

___B___ 13. the brightness of the ribbons
        A. the ribbons brightness
        B. the ribbons' brightness
        C. the ribbon's brightness

_C_ 14. the fullness of the wig
  A. the wigs fullness
  B. the wigs' fullness
  C. the wig's fullness

_C_ 15. the length of the mustache
  A. the mustaches length
  B. the mustaches' length
  C. the mustache's length

Count and Noncount Nouns

Questions 16-20: Look at the italicized common nouns in the following paragraph. Underline the count nouns. Double underline the noncount nouns.

Proper hair care is essential to any _hairstyle_. Shampoos help keep hair very healthy. Egg shampoos add extra sheen to hair. Lemon _shampoos_ cut out extra oils. Washing hair with just _water_ does not thoroughly clean the hair. Hair should be cleaned at least once every other _day_. Hairdressers help to clean and trim hair. Some people find _enjoyment_ in going to the hairdresser each week.

Compound Nouns

Write _Cpd_ (compound) in the blank if the italicized noun is a compound noun. Leave the blank empty if the italicized noun is not a compound noun.

cpd 21. Egyptian _noblemen_ shaved their hair close for coolness and cleanliness.

cpd 22. Even in ancient times, public _barbershops_ were common.

cpd 23. Jewels and ornamental _hairpins_ provided extra beauty.

cpd 24. Some cultures used _horsehair_ in making wigs.

_____ 25. Hair fashion changes from _generation_ to generation.

Chapter 3: Verbs

Simple Predicates

Find the simple predicate in each sentence. Write in the blank the letter that corresponds to the correct answer.

___A___ 1. Trees grow nearly everywhere on the earth's surface.
    A. grow
    B. nearly
    C. surface

___C___ 2. Literally thousands of varieties exist.
    A. thousands
    B. varieties
    C. exist

___C___ 3. Except in extreme cold or extreme dryness, trees can thrive anywhere.
    A. can
    B. thrive
    C. can thrive

___A___ 4. Size, longevity, and leaf type are distinctions of different tree types.
    A. are
    B. are distinctions
    C. types

___B___ 5. Despite their differences, all trees share many characteristics.
    A. Despite
    B. share
    C. characteristics

Action and Linking Verbs

Identify each italicized verb as action or linking. Write in the blank the letter that corresponds to the correct answer.

    A. action
    B. linking

___A___ 6. A tree surgeon *treats* wood and bark injuries in trees.

___A___ 7. Water and minerals *move* most quickly up and down in a tree.

___B___ 8. Side-to-side movement of water in the tree *is* somewhat slow.

___A___ 9. Therefore, the tree surgeon *must shape* any cuts into the tree to provide for the best healing.

___B___ 10. The repairs sometimes *appear* strange after the tree surgeon finishes.

Sentence Patterns: S-InV, S-TrV-DO, and S-TrV-IO-DO

Identify the sentence pattern for each sentence. Write in the blank the letter that corresponds to the correct answer.

> A. S-InV
> B. S-TrV-DO
> C. S-TrV-IO-DO

_B_ 11. The tree surgeon first cuts the dead bark away from the live tissue.

_B_ 12. He then paints the tree tissue with an orange shellac.

_C_ 13. Later the tree surgeon gives the tree a coat of another type of paint.

_A_ 14. The bark grows over the wound in about six months.

_A_ 15. Sometimes paint must be reapplied to the wound.

Sentence Patterns: S-LV-PN and S-LV-PA

Identify the sentence pattern for each sentence. Write in the blank the letter that corresponds to the correct answer.

> A. S-LV-PN
> B. S-LV-PA

_A_ 16. Bark injury is the least difficult type of injury.

_B_ 17. An injury to the tree cavity is more dangerous.

_B_ 18. A diseased tree may appear fine outwardly.

_B_ 19. The tree could be quite sick inside.

_A_ 20. The two types of treatment for diseased trees are closed-cavity and open-cavity surgery.

Verb Forms

Identify the correct verb form to complete each sentence. Write in the blank to the left of the sentence the letter that corresponds to the correct answer.

_B_ 21. Last week a tree surgeon _?_ on a tree in our back yard.
   A. operates
   B. operated
   C. had operated

_A_ 22. Every day for two weeks the tree _?_ many leaves.
   A. has lost
   B. will have lost
   C. loses

_C_ 23. On any job this tree surgeon always _?_ in the early morning.
   A. will work
   B. had worked
   C. works

_B_ 24. On our tree the surgeon used cement; before this job he _?_ an asphalt-dust mixture.
 A. uses
 B. had used
 C. will use

_B_ 25. He _?_ cement to all of his jobs from now on.
 A. applied
 B. will apply
 C. will have applied

Chapter 4: Pronouns

Pronoun Identification

Choose the correct pronoun to replace the italicized word or phrase. Write the correct answer in the blank.

his   1. Jonathan Swift published *Jonathan Swift's* well-known <u>Gulliver's Travels</u> in 1726.

_It_   2. *The book* tells the story of Lemuel Gulliver.

_He_   3. *Gulliver* is an English doctor who has amazing adventures.

her   4. Gulliver likes being at home with *Gulliver's wife* and their children.

them   5. But Gulliver's medical practice proves unprofitable, so Gulliver decides to sail as surgeon with *the crew of the <u>Antelope</u>*.

Pronoun Antecedent

Identify the antecedent of each italicized pronoun. Write in the blank the letter that corresponds to the correct answer.

_B_   6. During the voyage the ship runs into a storm, and *it* splits apart on a rock.
     A. voyage
     B. ship
     C. storm

_A_   7. Gulliver escapes into a boat with five other men, but *he* alone survives.
     A. Gulliver
     B. boat
     C. men

_B_   8. Having reached land and rested for several hours, Gulliver awakens to find his arms and legs tied to *their* positions on the ground and little people crawling on him.
     A. hours
     B. arms and legs
     C. people

_A_   9. He has unknowingly reached the island of Lilliput, and one of *its* important officials greets him from a specially-built platform a foot and a half off the ground.
     A. island
     B. officials
     C. platform

_C_ 10. The official and his people provide Gulliver with food—so tiny that he can eat three loaves of bread in one mouthful—but not at first with *his* freedom.
   A. official
   B. people
   C. Gulliver

Pronoun Identification

Identify each italicized pronoun as personal, demonstrative, interrogative, or indefinite. Write in the blank the letter that corresponds to the correct answer.

   A. personal
   B. interrogative
   C. demonstrative
   D. indefinite

_A_ 11. Eventually allowed to roam freely through the land, Gulliver receives permission to visit the capital city with its large wall and great palace.

_D_ 12. Later *someone* from the government explains an important national controversy to him.

_B_ 13. *Which* is the proper end of an egg to crack, the big or the little one?

_C_ 14. *That* is the question that had divided Lilliputians and helped stir up war with the neighboring island of Blefuscu.

_D_ 15. Feeling responsibility to *many* of the Lilliputians, Gulliver is persuaded to fight for them by walking off with a good part of the Blefuscans' fleet.

Pronoun Identification

Identify each italicized pronoun as reflexive, intensive, demonstrative, or indefinite. Write in the blank the letter that corresponds to the correct answer.

   A. reflexive
   B. intensive
   C. demonstrative
   D. indefinite

_B_ 16. Gulliver's adventures do not end in the land of the little Lilliputians, however; he *himself* is the midget at his next stop.

_C_ 17. *This* is Brobdingnag, the land of the giants.

_D_ 18. Almost *everyone* is as much bigger than Gulliver as he is than the Lilliputians.

_A_ 19. Here Gulliver discovers for *himself* what it is like to be held in someone's hand or to be shocked at someone's appetite.

_D_ 20. Through his adventures with bigger and smaller peoples, Gulliver sees the foolishness of pride for *anyone*.

Chapter 5: Adjectives

Identifying Adjectives

Questions 1-10: Underline each adjective in the following paragraph and draw an arrow to the word it modifies.

Antarctica is an icy continent. Most plants cannot survive in the dry climate.

The coldest temperature ever recorded (-128.6°F) was in Antarctica. Severe winds

also help explain why Antarctica is not an inviting place to live.

Comparing with Adjectives

Identify the correct form of the adjective in parentheses for each sentence. Write in the blank the letter that corresponds to the correct answer.

_____A_____ 11. In 1911, Roald Amundsen and Robert Scott began a *(famous, positive)* race to reach the South Pole first.
A. famous
B. more famous
C. most famous

_____C_____ 12. Scott's motor sleds travelled slowly in the snow, but Amundsen used much *(fast, comparative)* Eskimo dogs.
A. fast
B. more fast
C. faster

_____B_____ 13. Amundsen travelled the shortest but *(unfamiliar, superlative)* route.
A. more unfamiliar
B. most unfamiliar
C. most unfamiliarest

_____B_____ 14. Amundsen had a *(good, comparative)* plan and reached the South Pole several weeks before Scott's team arrived.
A. gooder
B. better
C. more good

_____A_____ 15. The *(dangerous, superlative)* part of trip was getting home. Amundsen's team arrived safely, but Scott and his five men died in Antarctica.
A. most dangerous
B. more dangerous
C. more dangerest

Common and Proper Adjectives
Underline the common adjectives once and the proper adjectives twice in the following sentences.

16. Before Antarctica had ever been seen, <u><u>Greek</u></u> scholars speculated that there could be <u>a</u> continent at <u>the</u> bottom of <u>the</u> earth.

17. Nathaniel Brown, <u>an</u> <u><u>American</u></u> sealer, was one of <u>the</u> <u>first</u> men to see <u>the</u> <u>southern</u> continent. _____

18. <u>The</u> <u>same</u> year, <u>a</u> member of <u>the</u> <u><u>British</u></u> navy, Captain Edward Bransfield, may have seen Antarctica.

19. <u>The</u> <u>stormy</u> <u><u>Antarctic</u></u> waters are very <u>dangerous</u> for sailors.

20. <u>Many</u> animals live in <u>the</u> waters, including whales and <u><u>Adélie</u></u> penguins.

Adjectives, Nouns, Independent Possessives
Identify each italicized word as an adjective, noun, or independent possessive. Write in the blank the letter that corresponds to the correct answer.

   A. adjective
   B. noun
   C. independent possessive

_A_ 21. Most of Antarctica is covered with ice. The *thickest* ice is 15,700 feet deep.

_A_ 22. Scientists from several different countries have *research* stations in Antarctica.

_B_ 23. Scientists have learned more about the history of the earth through their *research* in Antarctica.

_C_ 24. Many other scientists have interesting jobs, but *theirs* is certainly one of the most complex and difficult.

_A_ 25. Because of *their* studies, many facts have been discovered about the ozone layer.

Chapter 6: Adverbs

Identifying Adverbs

Questions 1-7: Underline each adverb in the following paragraph.

During sleep the eyes <u>usually</u> close and the body remains <u>fairly</u> still. In contrast, the brain is <u>not</u> still; it is <u>rather</u> active. Scientists have documented two types of sleep that take place in the brain: nonrapid eye movement (NREM) and rapid eye movement (REM). <u>Approximately</u> every ninety minutes the body changes from one type of sleep to the other. These two types are <u>entirely</u> different from each other, yet both are <u>quite</u> necessary for the body's proper function.

Modifiers

Identify the type of word that each italicized adverb modifies. Write in the blank the letter that corresponds to the correct answer.

        A. verb
        B. adverb
        C. adjective

___A___ 8. Several factors *definitely* influence sleep patterns.

___C___ 9. Scientists have learned several *remarkably* interesting facts.

___B___ 10. *Not* surprisingly, a lack of sleep makes someone more sleepy.

___A___ 11. Boredom *also* contributes to sleepiness.

___A___ 12. By contrast, new situations and worry *sometimes* prevent sleep.

___C___ 13. Other factors which influence the *exceedingly* delicate sleep process are noise and warmth.

___C___ 14. Even outside barometric pressure can be a *somewhat* important influence on sleep.

___B___ 15. Time of day is *very* definitely the most important factor in sleep.

___A___ 16. Travelers to other time zones *normally* feel sleepy during the same time they would in their home time zone.

___C___ 17. Full adjustment to a new time zone often takes *almost* ten days.

Positive, Comparative, and Superlative Adverbs

Identify the correct form of the adverb in parentheses for each sentence. Write in the blank the correct answer.

_____most often_____ 18. The average adult *(often, superlative)* needs between seven and eight hours of sleep per night.

_____best_____ 19. However, some adults perform *(well, superlative)* with as little as three hours of sleep.

_____most likely_____ 20. Babies and young children *(likely, superlative)* require more sleep than adults.

_____extremely_____ 21. Lack of sleep can be *(extremely, positive)* harmful.

_____most frequently_____ 22. People who lose just one night's sleep *(frequently, superlative)* suffer very little except tiredness.

_____more noticeably_____ 23. After two and a half days with no sleep, a person's behavior may become *(noticeably, comparative)* bizarre.

_____frighteningly_____ 24. Some people suffering from extreme lack of sleep may even experience *(frighteningly, positive)* real hallucinations.

_____worse_____ 25. Sleep deprivation also causes memory problems and generally makes a person perform *(badly, comparative)* on even a daily task.

Chapter 7: Prepositions, Conjunctions, and Interjections

Adjectival and Adverbial Prepositional Phrases

Underline each prepositional phrase and circle the object of the preposition. Identify each phrase as adjectival or adverbial. Write in the blank the letter that corresponds to the correct answer.

        A. adjectival prepositional phrase
        B. adverbial prepositional phrase

_A_ 1. Time is an indispensable part of our lives.

_B_ 2. Our daily schedules revolve around time.

_B_ 3. You eat lunch at noon.

_A_ 4. Then you have a three o'clock appointment with your dentist.

_B_ 5. You finish the day with an eight o'clock play performance.

_B_ 6. Each activity is regulated by time.

_A_ 7. Change is an important indicator of time's passage.

_B_ 8. Regular changes help divide time into units.

_A_ 9. The earth's rotation on its axis gives us days.

_A_ 10. Its revolution around the sun gives us years.

Prepositions and Adverbs

Identify each italicized word as a preposition or an adverb. Write in the blank the letter that corresponds to the correct answer.

        A. preposition
        B. adverb

_A_ 11. Hours, minutes, and seconds likely came *through* the Babylonians.

_B_ 12. Looking *up* at the sky, they divided a day into 24 parts, 12 for darkness and 12 for light.

_A_ 13. In addition, they split a circle into 360 parts, each of which was later further split *into* 60 smaller parts.

_B_ 14. Hours came *about* by the divisions of the day, and minutes and seconds by the divisions of the circle.

_A_ 15. Hours, minutes, and seconds came together *in* one timepiece with the refinement of the clock.

Conjunctions

Circle the conjunction in each sentence. Determine which parts of the sentence the conjunction joins. Write in the blank the letter that corresponds to the correct answer.

_____A_____ 16. A clock in Hong Kong (and) a clock in Bermuda are not set at exactly the same time.
      A. subjects
      B. predicates
      C. direct objects

_____B_____ 17. If they were, noon would be in the middle of the day in one place (but) in the middle of the night in the other.
      A. subjects
      B. prepositional phrases
      C. indirect objects

_____A_____ 18. Instead, clocks in each location register noon approximately in the middle of the day (and) midnight approximately in the middle of the night.
      A. direct objects
      B. objects of the preposition
      C. indirect objects

_____B_____ 19. Two methods of time measurement are local time zones (and) standard time zones.
      A. subjects
      B. predicate nouns
      C. direct objects

_____C_____ 20. Local time depends entirely on the position of the sun overhead (and) differs from location to location.
      A. direct objects
      B. subjects
      C. predicates

_____B_____ 21. Standard time zones establish identical times throughout given regions (and) create less confusion for travelers.
      A. subjects
      B. predicates
      C. objects of the preposition

_____B_____ 22. The world is divided into twenty-three full time zones (and) two half time zones.
      A. prepositional phrases
      B. objects of the preposition
      C. predicates

_____A_____ 23. Measurement of time (and) measurement of distance start with the prime meridian of Greenwich, England.
      A. subjects
      B. predicates
      C. direct objects

_____B_____ 24. Time moves forward one hour for each new time zone to the east (but) moves backward one hour for each zone to the west.
  A. subjects
  B. predicates
  C. indirect objects

_____A_____ 25. The International Date Line, an imaginary line, separates the time zones (and) signals a change in day.
  A. predicates
  B. direct objects
  C. prepositional phrases

Conjunctions and Interjections

Identify each italicized word as a conjunction or an interjection. Write in the blank the letter that corresponds to the correct answer.

  A. conjunction
  B. interjection

_____A_____ 26. Time is obviously important to man, *but* does God care about it?

_____B_____ 27. *Yes,* the Bible contains many references to the concept.

_____B_____ 28. *Really?* Where?

_____B_____ 29. *Well,* Hosea 10:12 warns the Israelites that it is time to seek the Lord.

_____A_____ 30. Romans 13:11 speaks of a time to wake to action, *and* Ephesians 5:16 commands all believers to make wise use of their time.

Chapter 8: Clause Structure

Clauses and Phrases

Identify each underlined group of words as a phrase, an independent clause, or a dependent clause. Write in the blank the letter that corresponds to the correct answer.

      A. phrase
      B. independent clause
      C. dependent clause

_B_   1. <u>There are fifty-three different countries in the continent of Africa</u>, where the people and their cultures differ widely.

_A_   2. Africa is <u>the third largest continent in the world</u>.

_B_   3. <u>A large part of the land is covered with tropical rain forests</u>, and animals such as gorillas and crocodiles live there.

_C_   4. Egypt is in the northeastern part of Africa, <u>where the Nile flows south to north</u>.

_B_   5. <u>It is the longest river in the world</u>; along its banks great civilizations have risen.

_B_   6. <u>The Nile is over four thousand miles long</u>.

_C_   7. Much of the land is covered by the Sahara, <u>which is the largest desert in the world</u>.

_A_   8. <u>Elephants and lions, two fascinating animals</u>, live in the grasslands of Africa.

_C_   9. <u>Although hunters have threatened the existence of several species</u>, fascinating wildlife is still abundant in Africa.

_A_   10. Mt. Kilimanjaro, <u>the highest mountain in Africa</u>, is 19,340 feet high.

Simple and Compound Sentences

Identify each sentence as simple or compound. Write in the blank the letter that corresponds to the correct answer.

      A. simple sentence
      B. compound sentence

_B_   11. An abundance of precious metals, including gold and diamonds, are found in Africa, but most of the people who live there are not wealthy.

_A_   12. Farmers without modern farming tools cannot make the best use of their land.

_A_   13. The poor people sometimes suffer from severe famines.

_B_   14. The medical conditions in rural Africa are very poor, and many people die of various African diseases.

_A_   15. The general life expectancy for Africans is only about fifty-four years.

Simple, Compound, and Complex Sentences

Identify each sentence as simple, compound, or complex. Write in the blank the letter that corresponds to the correct answer.

A. simple sentence
B. compound sentence
C. complex sentence

_C_ 16. Africa is a continent of many different ethnic groups, where religious and political unity is difficult.

_A_ 17. The various tribes of Africa speak innumerable languages and dialects.

_C_ 18. Since communication is vital to business, many Africans speak English as a second language.

_C_ 19. Although most Africans in the cities wear Western dress, many still prefer the traditional robes and head coverings.

_B_ 20. Numerous people in northern Africa share the Arabic language, but the languages in southern Africa are as diverse as the people.

_A_ 21. The governments of Africa have improved their educational systems.

_B_ 22. The literacy rate is quite low; fewer than half of the people can read and write.

_A_ 23. Since the 1940s, many more Africans have attended colleges in their own countries.

_A_ 24. Rice, bread, fruits, and vegetables are the main elements of the African diet.

_C_ 25. While conditions have improved in Africa, malnutrition, lack of education, and disease are still significant problems for the continent.

Chapter 9: Subject-Verb Agreement

Agreement

Questions 1-5: Find the errors in agreement in the following paragraph. Rewrite the paragraph correctly in the space provided.

How aware is you of the rules of etiquette? For many years Emily Post were the authority on etiquette, and copies of her book was on the shelves of all well-bred families. Some rules of etiquette has changed drastically since Post's book first came out in 1922; however, basic good manners is timeless. What are your thoughts on the following social customs of 1937?

How aware are you of the rules of etiquette? For many years Emily Post was the authority

on etiquette, and copies of her book were on the shelves of all well-bred families.

Some rules of etiquette have changed drastically since Post's book first came out in

1922; however, basic good manners are timeless. What are your thoughts on the

following social customs of 1937?

Agreement with Indefinite Pronouns
Underline the verb in parentheses that agrees with the subject of the sentence.

6. Few (*disagrees, disagree*) with Post's comments on conversation.

7. Anyone (*is, are*) capable of carrying on a conversation with a little effort.

8. All of the guidelines (*boils, boil*) down to thinking before you speak.

9. Nobody (*likes, like*) a bragger, so do not talk too much about yourself.

10. Most of the conversation problem (*is, are*) solved by the participants' resolve to be thoughtful speakers and interested listeners.

Agreement with Compound Subjects
Underline the verb in parentheses that agrees with the subject of the sentence.

11. Men and women (*has, have*) whole chapters devoted to their dress.

12. In 1937 hats and gloves (*was, were*) mandatory in many cases for a lady in public.

13. His nails or his haircut (*was, were*) evidence of a gentleman.

14. Carelessly tossed clothes or an unworn shoe without a shoetree (*was, were*) not appropriate.

15. A college student or other young men *(was, were)* warned not to coordinate outfits too

noticeably, though they might safely match golf stockings with sweaters and ties.

Intervening Phrases, Predicate Nouns, and Inverted Order

Circle the subject of each sentence. Underline the verb in parentheses that agrees with the subject.

16. Table (manners) *(is, are)* an especially important part of etiquette.

17. *(Is, Are)* each (utensil) used properly at your table?

18. The (fork) and the (spoon) never the knife, *(is, are)* the utensils that should enter your mouth.

19. The (tines) of a fork *(faces, face)* up for everything that does not involve cutting.

20. There *(is, are)* different (ways) of using a spoon, depending on the food.

21. (Soup), but not ice cream and cereal, *(requires, require)* a scooping movement away from

yourself and a sipping from the side of your spoon.

22. There *(is, are)* almost no (situation) in which fingers are appropriately used for messy foods.

23. Despite this precaution, a (finger bowl), in addition to a napkin, *(completes, complete)* each

guest's place at the home of a good hostess.

24. *(Has, Have)* (you) ever removed food from your mouth? Do not!

25. Finally, the (chewer) with his mouth open and the (talker) with his mouth full *(is, are)* never in

good taste.

Chapter 10: Pronoun-Antecedent Agreement

Agreement with Personal Pronouns

Fill in each blank with a pronoun that agrees with its antecedent.

his 1. Henry Ford is known throughout the world by _?_ association with the automobile.

its 2. Ford's hometown of Dearborn, Michigan, bears many marks of _?_ famous citizen.

their 3. Undoubtedly, many residents and _?_ guests have visited Greenfield Village and the Henry Ford Museum, showcases of history and technology established by Ford.

his 4. Both places are excellent spots for a teacher to take _?_ class on a field trip.

their 5. Does the teacher or the children learn the most from _?_ study of Ford's story?

its 6. Henry Ford devoted much energy to the development of the automobile, although he was not _?_ original creator.

his 7. Ford built _?_ first car in 1896 and established the Ford Motor Company in 1903.

their 8. These events were crucial in _?_ impact on Ford's future.

their 9. Ford and other company executives wanted _?_ product to be well built but affordable.

his 10. With the Model T, the common man had found _?_ car.

Agreement with Indefinite Pronouns

Identify the pronoun that agrees with the antecedent. Write in the blank the letter that corresponds to the correct answer.

_C_ 11. Few could part with enough of _?_ money to buy a Model T at the original price of $850.
   A. his
   B. her
   C. their

_A_ 12. No one can run a successful business if _?_ product is too expensive.
A. his
B. her
C. their

_A_ 13. Most of the extra expense of the product was due to _?_ high cost of production.
A. its
B. his
C. their

_A_ 14. Therefore, everyone in leadership contributed _?_ ideas for the best way to lower that cost.
A. his
B. her
C. their

_B_ 15. With the introduction of the assembly line, every department shortened _?_ production time.
A. his
B. its
C. their

_B_ 16. With everybody focusing on _?_ one task as parts moved along a conveyor belt, much less labor was required.
A. her
B. his
C. their

_B_ 17. Anything requiring less labor can have _?_ price lowered.
A. his
B. its
C. their

_C_ 18. In addition, many of the cars' parts became cheaper when _?_ suppliers were replaced with in-house producers.
A. her
B. its
C. their

_A_ 19. Finally, each of the major market regions received _?_ own plant where parts could be sent for assembly, cutting down on shipping costs.
A. its
B. his
C. their

_C_ 20. With all of these improvements, most of the nation's workers could afford cars for _?_ families by 1924, when the price had fallen to $290.
A. his
B. its
C. their

Chapter 11: Pronoun Usage

Subjective, Objective, and Possessive Cases

For each sentence, underline the correct pronoun in parentheses.

1. Robert E. Lee is remembered in the Hall of Fame for Great Americans because of *(him, his)* contribution to America.

2. Zach and *(I, me)* visited the Hall of Fame at New York University.

3. The hostess was pleased to give Zach and *(I, me)* a tour of the museum.

4. We saw the bust of Robert E. Lee, and Zach read its inscription to *(I, me)*.

5. I listened to *(he, him)* as he read, "Duty then is the sublimest word in our language."

6. Even when his responsibilities were small and insignificant, Robert E. Lee took care to fulfill *(they, them)* completely.

7. His superiors were always assured that *(he, him)* would complete his assignments.

8. Robert E. Lee's commitment to duty made him a successful general in the Civil War and an excellent example for *(we, us)*.

We, Us, Who, and *Whom*

Choose the correct pronoun to complete the sentence. Write in the blank the letter that corresponds to the correct answer.

        A. we
        B. us
        C. who
        D. whom

____A____ 9. _?_ students studied famous Americans in our history class.

____C____ 10. _?_ was the most famous general in the Confederate army?

____B____ 11. Our teacher told _?_ students to look for the answer in our history books.

____D____ 12. At Appomattox Court House, General Lee surrendered to _?_ ?

____C____ 13. Ulysses S. Grant, _?_ was very generous and kind to the general, accepted Lee's surrender.

Problem Pronouns

Choose the correct pronoun to complete the sentence. Write in the blank the letter that corresponds to the correct answer.

___B___ 14. Have you read _?_ assignment about the Civil War?
A. you're
B. your

___A___ 15. _?_ quite long, so I began reading it yesterday.
A. It's
B. Its

___A___ 16. Some other students finished _?_ last night.
A. theirs
B. there's

___B___ 17. They wanted to finish early; _?_ going to the basketball game tonight.
A. their
B. they're

___A___ 18. All of the students _?_ assignments are complete will probably be going to the game tonight.
A. whose
B. who's

Clear Pronoun Reference

Identify each sentence as having correct or incorrect pronoun reference. Write in the blank the letter that corresponds to the correct answer. If you choose *B*, rewrite the sentence correctly in the space provided.

A. correct sentence
B. incorrect pronoun reference

___B___ 19. Diannah and Hannah traveled to Gettysburg, Pennsylvania. They have a lot of Civil War memorabilia there.

Diannah and Hannah traveled to Gettysburg, Pennsylvania, where there is a lot

of Civil War memorabilia.

___B___ 20. Diannah told Hannah that she loved to visit Civil War sites.

Diannah said to Hannah, "I love to visit Civil War sites."

___A___ 21. The girls read about the famous battle at Gettysburg, and they learned that it was the turning point of the Civil War.

_____B_____ 22. The Confederate army met the Union army at Gettysburg in 1863. On July 3 they attempted to gain control of Cemetery Ridge.

The Confederate army met the Union army at Gettysburg in 1863. On July 3 the Confederates

attempted to gain control of Cemetery Ridge.

_____A_____ 23. The Confederates fought valiantly, but after a fierce battle, the Union army had prevented their advance.

_____

_____

_____B_____ 24. The day after the battle, General Lee decided that they would begin a retreat.

The day after the battle, General Lee decided that his army would begin a retreat.

_____B_____ 25. The Union army wanted to pursue the Confederates, but they safely returned to Virginia.

The Union army wanted to pursue the Confederates, but the remaining Confederates safely

returned to Virginia.

Chapter 12: Using Adjectives and Adverbs Correctly

Adjective or Adverb

Choose the correct word to complete the sentence. Write in the blank the letter that corresponds to the correct answer.

_B_ 1. Over nineteen million people live in the _?_ populated metropolitan area of Mexico City.
A. heavy
B. heavily

_B_ 2. Many people have moved to the city _?_ , and there has been an incredible growth in population.
A. quick
B. quickly

_A_ 3. Because of the increased population, finding _?_ housing for everyone is difficult.
A. sufficient
B. sufficiently

_A_ 4. Many middle-class residents have _?_ jobs and enjoy more modern homes.
A. good
B. well

_A_ 5. Crime is a _?_ problem in Mexico City, and alcohol and drug abuse only complicate the problem.
A. real
B. really

_B_ 6. Because the city is in a valley, pollution is not blown away _?_ .
A. easy
B. easily

_B_ 7. The government has enforced _?_ strict laws regarding pollution to help alleviate the problem.
A. real
B. really

_B_ 8. Because streets in Mexico City are very crowded, people travel _?_ by bus.
A. most
B. mostly

_A_ 9. The city contains a _?_ and sophisticated subway system.
A. fast
B. fastly

<u> A </u> 10. Mexico City is the home of El Palacio de Bellas Artes, a _?_ center for the performing arts.
A. cultural
B. culturally

Adjective and Adverb Modifiers

Label the italicized word *adj* (adjective) or *adv* (adverb) by writing the correct abbreviation in the blank.

<u> adv </u> 11. The Monument to Independence stands *high* in Mexico City at an intersection on the *Paseo de la Reforma.*

<u> adj </u> 12. The city contains very old Spanish buildings along with *high,* modern structures.

<u> adv </u> 13. Because of crowded traffic conditions, the cars often move *slowly.*

<u> adj </u> 14. The buses often are *slower* than the subways.

<u> adj </u> 15. During congested times, taking a car might be the *slowest* way to travel.

Double Negatives and Comparisons

Write in the blank the correct form of the word in parentheses.

<u> most developed </u> 16. Mexico City is one of the _?_ cities in the world. *(developed)*

<u> more luxurious </u> 17. Some residences are _?_ than others. *(luxurious)*

<u> any </u> 18. Poorer residents frequently do not have _?_ good jobs or homes. *(any)*

<u> more often </u> 19. For buildings, cement is used _?_ than wood. *(often)*

<u> finest </u> 20. Of all the museums in Mexico City, the National Museum of Anthropology is the _?_ . *(fine)*

Chapter 13: Using Troublesome Words Correctly

Troublesome Verbs

Choose the correct verb to complete the sentence. Write in the blank the letter that corresponds to the correct answer.

_____A_____ 1. Some items are used all the time while others mostly _?_ around.
   A. sit
   B. set

_____A_____ 2. Money _?_ to the top of the list of items used often, for few things are used more.
   A. rises
   B. raises

_____B_____ 3. Just think of how many times you _?_ money down for purchases.
   A. lie
   B. lay

_____B_____ 4. Or perhaps you prefer to _?_ your money aside in a bank account to earn interest.
   A. sit
   B. set

_____B_____ 5. In that case the bank _?_ money for itself by lending out what you have deposited.
   A. rises
   B. raises

_____A_____ 6. Either way, your money does not _?_ idle but is constantly moving from person to person.
   A. lie
   B. lay

_____A_____ 7. Money rarely _?_ in one place for any length of time.
   A. sits
   B. sets

_____A_____ 8. So what _?_ behind the desirability of money?
   A. lies
   B. lays

_____B_____ 9. We _?_ money to obtain things that we do not have but either need or want.
   A. rise
   B. raise

_____A_____ 10. With all of our needs and desires, it is no wonder that money rarely _?_ still.
   A. sits
   B. sets

Other Troublesome Words and Homonyms

Choose the correct word to complete the sentence. Write in the blank the letter that corresponds to the correct answer.

_____B_____ 11. There has always been a need _?_ the peoples of the world to find a way of getting what they want.
   A. between
   B. among

_____A_____ 12. The _?_ method in early days was barter, the trading of one item for another.
   A. principal
   B. principle

_____B_____ 13. Barter might still be used today in a country _?_ most people are farmers or the currency has become worthless.
   A. wear
   B. where

_____A_____ 14. The problem with barter, though, is that you must find someone who has what you want and is willing to _?_ what you have.
   A. accept
   B. except

_____B_____ 15. In addition, although barter is _?_ when it is the only option, it lacks certain qualities of money.
   A. alright
   B. all right

_____A_____ 16. For one thing, the value of items traded does not remain _?_ but varies.
   A. stationary
   B. stationery

_____B_____ 17. Also a cow, for instance, could cause _?_ of trouble for the trader who must travel far away to make his purchase.
   A. alot
   B. a lot

_____B_____ 18. Finally, it _?_ very easy to divide a cow if the item the trader wants is not worth the entire animal.
   A. ain't
   B. isn't

_____A_____ 19. To solve the problems posed by barter, metal coins and eventually pieces of paper _?_ introduced as units of money.
   A. were
   B. we're

_____A_____ 20. Originally paper notes were just signs that their holders had coins deposited at a bank, but later the paper took on the _?_ of money itself.
   A. role
   B. roll

Chapter 14: Capitalization

People and Places
Questions 1-5: Circle the capitalization errors in the following paragraph.

Empress Catherine II, also known as Catherine the great, was one of russia's most intense rulers. Ironically, Catherine was not even a Russian. She was a German. She involved Russia in many wars that led to possession of the Crimea and access to the Black sea. Catherine lived many years in St. Petersburg because she hated moscow. Catherine enjoyed the title Little mother.

Other Proper Nouns
Identify the word that is an example of a capitalization error. Write in the blank the letter that corresponds to the correct answer.

___C___ 6. Catherine the Great once said, "my heart cannot be happy, even for an hour without love."
   A. Great
   B. said
   C. my

___B___ 7. Nevsky Prospekt is the main Boulevard near the Winter Palace in St. Petersburg.
   A. Prospekt
   B. Boulevard
   C. Palace

___A___ 8. Russians are fascinated by western culture but also strangely resist most change in that direction.
   A. western
   B. direction
   C. no error

___A___ 9. Even though Catherine hated moscow, it was still the center of Russian Orthodoxy.
   A. moscow
   B. center
   C. Russian

___C___ 10. Catherine once said of herself, "I had in my heart a strange certainty that one day I should, by my own efforts, become empress of russia."
   A. herself
   B. empress
   C. russia

Titles, Proper Adjectives, and Common Nouns

Identify the word that is an example of a capitalization error. Write in the blank the letter that corresponds to the correct answer.

_____C_____ 11. Catherine supported the ideals of the European Enlightenment.
　　　　A. ideals
　　　　B. Enlightenment
　　　　C. no error

_____A_____ 12. Catherine married duke Karl Peter Ulrich of Holstein-Gottorp, later known as Tsar Peter III.
　　　　A. duke
　　　　B. Holstein-Gottorp
　　　　C. Tsar

_____B_____ 13. Catherine hated Peter so much that one of her cossack guards eventually murdered him after she overthrew him in a coup.
　　　　A. Peter
　　　　B. cossack
　　　　C. him

_____B_____ 14. Catherine realized the need for huge reform; she said, "people were careful not to talk of art or sciences, because they were ignorant about them."
　　　　A. she
　　　　B. people
　　　　C. sciences

_____A_____ 15. Catherine's Peasants were divided in their support of her political tactics.
　　　　A. Peasants
　　　　B. political
　　　　C. tactics

_____A_____ 16. The Sun was soon to set on one of Russia's most controversial leaders.
　　　　A. Sun
　　　　B. Russia's
　　　　C. leaders

_____B_____ 17. Catherine the Great died on november 6, 1796.
　　　　A. Great
　　　　B. november
　　　　C. no error

_____C_____ 18. Her body was buried in the Hall of pillars.
　　　　A. body
　　　　B. Hall
　　　　C. pillars

_B_ 19. The inscription on her tomb reads, "divided in Life, United in Death."
  A. tomb
  B. divided
  C. no error

_C_ 20. Catherine's elaborate funeral followed the traditions of the Russian orthodox Church.
  A. elaborate
  B. funeral
  C. orthodox

Chapter 15: Punctuation

End Marks, Periods, and Commas
Insert missing end marks, periods, or commas in each sentence.

1. Sweden is a beautiful country made up of many lakes, forests, and mountains.

2. Did you know that some parts of Sweden have dark, bitterly cold winters?

3. Those crystal-blue lakes are amazing!

4. Sweden is the fourth largest country in Europe, and it is located on the eastern part of the Scandinavian Peninsula.

5. Is Norway to the west of Sweden?

6. Stockholm, Sweden, the capital city, is an important sea port.

7. Many Swedes, of course, are known for their blond hair, fair complexion, and blue eyes.

8. Because Sweden is located by the water, the Swedes' diet consists mainly of seafood.

9. Because of their love for recreation, Swedes do a lot of camping, boating, and fishing.

10. Sweden's new constitution went into effect on January 1, 1975.

Semicolons, Colons, and Quotation Marks
Identify the punctuation mark missing from each sentence; identify also quotation marks that should be removed. Write in the blank the letter that corresponds to the correct answer.

        A. semicolon
        B. colon
        C. quotation marks
        D. remove quotation marks

__B__ 11. Sweden has five universities Uppsla, Lund, Göteborg, Stockholm, and Umeå.

__B__ 12. Midnight in Sweden is 6 00 p.m. in the eastern United States.

__A__ 13. Swedes eat a lot of wild game they also enjoy reindeer steaks.

__C__ 14. "I love wild rose hip juice, my sister told me.

__D__ 15. My uncle said that "his favorite thing to eat in Sweden was ligonberries."

Quotation Marks, Italics, Apostrophes, and Hyphens

Underline the word or phrase in parentheses that is punctuated correctly.

16. Sweden's national anthem is (*Du Gamla, du fria;* "Du Gamla, du fria").

17. The Swedish number *sjuttiofem* is equivalent to our English number (seventy five, <u>seventy-five</u>).

18. Dag Hammarskjöld, a Swedish author, wrote the book (<u>*Markings,*</u> "Markings").

19. Swedish <u>*(ä's, äs)*</u> are pronounced differently than English *a*'s.

20. Lakes make up about (<u>one-third</u>, one third) of Sweden.

21. (<u>Sweden's</u>, Swedens) eastern border separates Sweden from Finland.

22. Recently, Swedes (<u>haven't</u>, have'nt) used the land for farming as much as in the past.

23. The (Swedes, <u>Swedes'</u>) culture includes many celebrations and holidays.

24. Bernt Notke's sculpture (<u>*St. George and the Dragon,*</u> "St. George and the Dragon") is located in Stockholm's Great Church.

25. Hugo Alfvén's (<u>*Midsummer Vigil,*</u> "Midsummer Vigil") for orchestra follows the traditions of Swedish folk music.

Chapter 16: Spelling

Verbs and Nouns

Write the correct plural spelling of each underlined singular word.

_____nations_____ 1. A police officer enforces the laws of a <u>nation</u> and protects its people.

_____cops_____ 2. Informally, a police officer has sometimes been called a <u>cop</u>.

_____badges_____ 3. Some believe that this name was an abbreviation for *constable on patrol,* while others think that it came from an officer's copper <u>badge</u>.

_____territories_____ 4. Of the many types of police, the most common is probably the patrol officer, who prevents or responds to crime within an assigned <u>territory</u>.

_____autos_____ 5. A traffic officer works to ensure the safety of each <u>auto</u> and pedestrian.

_____thieves_____ 6. A detective investigates crime, perhaps looking for a murderer, a <u>thief</u>, or a drug runner.

_____keys_____ 7. Often his evidence proves the <u>key</u> to a conviction in court.

_____activities_____ 8. An undercover agent monitors the <u>activity</u> of a suspected criminal.

_____dispatches_____ 9. A worker in the central <u>dispatch</u> office links people who need help with officers who can help them.

_____heroes_____ 10. Special units contain many a <u>hero</u> who has rescued a lost person, freed a hostage, disarmed a bomb, or captured a criminal.

ie or *ei* and Suffixes

Identify the correctly spelled word to complete each sentence. Write in the blank the letter that corresponds to the correct answer.

___B___ 11. American police operate at several levels, each one __?__ its place under a different division of government.
   A. occupiing
   B. occupying

Chapter 16 Review   **431**

_____A_____ 12. City police enforce the laws within urban regions and range in size from the thousands of the _?_ force in New York City to just a handful in small towns.
   A. busiest
   B. busyest

_____A_____ 13. County police patrol wider regions under the direction of their _?_ officer, the sheriff.
   A. chief
   B. cheif

_____B_____ 14. State police, sometimes called _?_ , focus mainly on the highways.
   A. trooppers
   B. troopers

_____A_____ 15. Federal agencies pursue people who break federal laws or who cross state lines after committing crimes like _?_ or murder.
   A. robbery
   B. robery

_____B_____ 16. Private agencies _?_ licenses from the state to perform police work for individuals or organizations.
   A. recieve
   B. receive

_____A_____ 17. In other parts of the world, police systems perform _?_ services.
   A. comparable
   B. compareable

_____B_____ 18. Among those that may be familiar to you is our _?_ Royal Canadian Mounted Police.
   A. nieghbor's
   B. neighbor's

_____A_____ 19. Another would be the Metropolitan Police of London, with its _?_ offices at New Scotland Yard.
   A. controlling
   B. controling

_____B_____ 20. Most far-reaching of all is Interpol, an agency that fights international crime through its _?_ of cooperative effort.
   A. achievment
   B. achievement

Spelling

Questions 21-25: Circle the spelling errors in the following paragraph. In the blanks provided, correctly spell the words that you circled.

Soldiers typically performed police (dutyes) in ancient times. In 27 B.C. the emperor

Augustus set up a nonmilitary police force for the city of Rome. However, it was the (medeival)

(Englishmans) who placed law enforcement firmly in civilian hands by (divideing) their country

into small groups and holding families accountable for each other. Britain also produced Sir

Robert Peel, the father of modern police organizations and the source of the name *bobbies* for

London police officers. Early law in America ranged from watch groups keeping peace in New

England to vigilantes (seekking) justice in the Old West. Gradually, police work became more

professional, and officers were better trained.

duties, medieval, Englishmen, dividing, seeking

Glossary of Terms

Action verb   A verb that tells what someone or something does. (3)

Adjective   A word that modifies a noun. An adjective tells *what kind, which one, how many,* or *whose* about the noun it modifies. (5)

Adverb   A word that modifies a verb, adjective, or other adverb. An adverb tells *when, where,* or *how* about the verb it modifies. (6)

Antecedent   The word or phrase that a pronoun replaces. (4, 10)

Article   An adjective that shows whether a noun is being used in a definite or an indefinite sense. The definite article pointing to specific things is *the;* the indefinite articles pointing to nonspecific things are *a* (used before a consonant sound) and *an* (used before a vowel sound). (6)

Auxiliary   A verb that helps the main verb express a complete thought or special meaning. (3)

Being verb   A verb that tells what someone or something is. A being verb usually acts as a linking verb. (3)

Case   The characteristic of a noun or pronoun that reflects the way the word is used in the sentence. Pronouns have three case forms: subjective (sometimes called nominative), objective, and possessive. (4, 11)

Clause   A group of words that has both a subject and a predicate. Two types of clauses are independent and dependent clauses. (8)

Comma splice   The error that results when two sentences are joined by only a comma. (1)

Common noun   A general word for a person, place, thing, or idea; the opposite of a proper noun. (2)

Complete predicate   The complete verb and its modifiers and completers. It describes the subject or tells about the subject's action. (1)

Complete subject   The simple subject and its modifiers. It tells what the sentence is about. (1)

Complete verb   The main verb and any auxiliaries working together as the simple predicate in a clause. (1, 3)

Complex sentence   A sentence made of one independent clause and at least one dependent clause. (8)

Compound noun   A noun formed by joining two or more words to make a new word. (2)

Compound predicate   Two or more simple predicates joined by a conjunction. (1)

Compound sentence   A sentence made of two or more independent clauses. (3)

Compound subject   Two or more simple subjects joined by a conjunction. (1)

Conjunction   A connecting word that joins words or groups of words in a sentence. (7, 8)

Coordinating conjunction   A connecting word that joins sentence parts of the same type. Commonly used coordinating conjunctions are *and, but, or, nor,* and *yet.* (7)

Count noun   A common noun that can be made plural to show *how many.* (2)

Declarative sentence   A sentence that makes a statement and ends with a period. (1)

Demonstraßtive pronoun   A pronoun that points out the position of objects, persons, or places. *This, that, these,* and *those* are demonstrative pronouns. (4)

Dependent clause   A clause that cannot stand alone as a sentence. A dependent clause has a subject and a predicate but contains some other word that makes it express an incomplete thought. (8)

Direct object   A noun or pronoun in the predicate that receives the action of a transitive verb. (3)

Double comparison   An error created by using two comparative words together, such as *more better.* (5, 6, 12)

Double negative   An error created by using a negative word plus the adverb *not* to modify the same word. (12)

Exclamatory sentence   A sentence that expresses strong emotion and ends with an exclamation point. (1)

Fragment   A group of words wrongly punctuated as a sentence. (1)

Fused sentence   The error that results when two or more sentences are joined without punctuation or conjunction. (1)

Gender   The classification of third-person singular pronouns into masculine, feminine, and neuter. (4)

Imperative sentence   A sentence that gives a command or a request and ends with a period or an exclamation point. (1)

Indefinite pronoun   A pronoun that refers to persons and things in general terms. It refers to a large category, or part of a large category, without definitely specifying the particular individual or part. (4, 9, 10)

Independent clause   A clause that can stand alone as a sentence and that expresses a complete thought. (8)

Independent possessive   A possessive word that replaces a noun or a noun and its adjectives. (5)

Indirect object   The noun or pronoun in the predicate that (without a preposition) tells *to whom* or *for whom* the subject does something. It always appears after the verb and before the direct object. (3)

Intensive pronoun   A personal pronoun ending in *-self* or *-selves* emphasizing an already stated noun or pronoun in the sentence. (4, 11)

Interjection   A word that can stand alone and be punctuated as a sentence or can appear along with a regular sentence in which it takes no real part. It often expresses strong feeling and sometimes is called an *isolate.* (7)

Interrogative pronoun   A pronoun used to ask a question. These include *which, what, who, whom,* and *whose.* (4)

Interrogative sentence   A sentence that asks a question and ends with a question mark. (1)

Intervening phrase   A group of words that comes between the subject and the verb of a sentence. Common interrupters are negative phrases and prepositional phrases. (9)

Intransitive verb   A verb that does not need an object to express a complete thought. This verb does not send action toward anything or anyone. It occurs in the pattern S-InV. (3)

Inverted order   The wording that occurs when the verb comes before the subject in a sentence. Most interrogative sentences and some declarative sentences invert the normal subject and verb order. (9)

Linking verb   A verb that links the subject with a word that renames or describes the subject (a predicate noun or a predicate adjective). It functions something like an equal sign. It appears in either of these patterns: S-LV-PN or S-LV-PA. (3)

Modifier   A word that describes another word in a sentence. (5, 6)

Noncount noun   A common noun that cannot be made plural. (2)

Noun   The name of a person, place, thing, or idea. (2)

Number   The classification of noun forms and personal pronouns telling whether the noun or pronoun is singular or plural. (4, 9, 10)

Object of the preposition   The noun or pronoun (simple object) that follows the preposition and that the preposition relates to the rest of the sentence. The complete object of the preposition is the simple object and its modifiers. (7)

Person   The classification of personal pronouns into first person (the speaker), second person (the person spoken to), and third person (the person spoken about). (4)

Personal pronoun   One of the pronouns that are distinguished by person, number, gender, and case. (4)

Phrase   A word group that does not contain both a subject and a predicate. (8)

Possessive   A word that expresses ownership or belonging. It usually functions as a modifier. (5, 6)

Predicate   The part of the sentence that asserts something about the subject. It includes the main verb in the sentence. (3)

Predicate adjective   An adjective in the predicate that follows a linking verb and describes the subject. (3)

Predicate noun   A noun or pronoun in the predicate that follows a linking verb and renames or identifies the subject. (3)

Preposition   A word that relates its object (a noun or pronoun) to another word in the sentence. (7)

Prepositional phrase   A preposition and its complete object. An adjectival prepositional phrase functions as an adjective; an adverbial prepositional phrase functions as an adverb. (7)

Pronoun   A word that replaces a noun or a noun and its modifiers. (4, 10, 11)

Pronoun-antecedent agreement   Correct use of singular pronouns with singular antecedents and of plural pronouns with plural antecedents. (4, 10)

Pronoun reference   The relation of a pronoun to its antecedent. (4, 11)

Proper adjective   An adjective made from a proper noun. Proper adjectives must be capitalized. (5)

Proper noun   A specific name for a person, place, or thing. Proper nouns must be capitalized. (2, 14)

Reflexive pronouns   A pronoun ending in *-self* or *-selves* that is used as an object to refer to the same person or thing as the subject. (4, 11)

Run-on sentence   Two or more sentences joined with incorrect or no punctuation. It is usually called a *comma splice* or a *fused sentence.* (1)

Sentence   A group of words including a subject and a predicate that expresses a complete thought. (1)

Simple predicate   The main verb and any auxiliaries in the predicate. (1)

Simple sentence   A sentence made of one independent clause and no dependent clauses. (8)

Simple subject   The main noun or pronoun in the subject. (1)

Subject   The part of the sentence that expresses what the sentence is about. It includes the main noun or pronoun in the sentence. (1)

Subject-predicate pair   The two main parts, subject and verb, that go together in any given sentence. One subject may have two verbs, but they are still a pair. Compound and complex sentences have more than one subject-predicate pair. (8)

Subject-verb agreement   Correct use of singular subjects with singular verbs and of plural subjects with plural verbs. The first word of the complete verb agrees with the person and number of the subject. (1, 9)

Subordinating word   The word in a clause that makes that clause dependent upon another clause. (8)

Tense   Forms of a verb that indicate time, continuing action, or completed action or state of being. (3)

Transitive verb   A verb that needs a receiver for its action. It occurs in the sentence patterns S-TrV-DO and S-TrV-IO-DO. (3)

Understood *you*   The unstated subject of an imperative sentence. (1)

Verb   A word that expresses action or state of being. (3, 9)

A

adjective
    article 111
    comparing with 105-6
    correct usage of 233-34
    definition of 102
    diagramming of 108, 113-14
    possessive noun 27
    possessive phrase 113-14
    possessive pronoun 112-14
    predicate adjective 56, 58
    prepositional phrase as 146
    test frame for 102

adjective vs. adverb 233-34

adjectives not made plural (ESL) 116

adverb
    comparing with 134, 237-38
    correct usage of 233-34
    definition of 128, 130
    diagramming of 130
    irregular, regular 134
    prepositional phrase as 146-47

adverb vs. preposition 149-50

agreement
    pronoun-antecedent 197-98, 200
    subject-verb 183-84, 186-89

almanac 354

alot/a lot 251

antecedent
    agreement of pronoun with 197-98, 200
    clarity of pronoun reference 221-22
    compound 198
    definition of 84

apostrophe
    to form possessives 25-31, 310
    to show omission 310
    with plurals of letters 310

article
    definite (*the*) 111
    definition of 111
    indefinite (*a/an*) 111

articles (ESL) 111

atlas 354

auxiliary
    definition of 60-61
    examples of 60-61, 63, 65-66, 69

B

be, forms of 51, 184

book of quotations 354

books, library. *See* library books

books, parts of 359-60

C

capitalization
    common nouns not capitalized 279-80
    of proper adjectives 277
    of proper nouns 267-68, 270-72
    of titles 275

card catalog
    author card 349
    call number 349
    subject card 349
    title card 349

case. *See* pronoun case

clause
    definition of 163-65
    dependent, independent 164-65

colon
    in a Bible reference 301
    in a business letter 301
    in a statement of time 301
    to introduce a list 301

comma
    in a compound sentence 291
    in a series 291
    to separate 295
    with quotations/dates/addresses/letters 298

comma splice 16, 18

complete verb 60-61

complex
    components of 169
    definition of 169-70

compound nouns 39

compound nouns, stress in (ESL) 39

compound part of the sentence 151

compound pronoun. *See* reflexive pronoun
    and intensive pronoun

compound sentence
    components of 166-67
    definition of 166-67
    diagramming of 167

compound vs. complex sentence 169-70

computer catalog 350

concordance 354

confusing pairs of words 254-55

conjunction
    coordinating 151-53
    definition of 151, 153
    diagramming of 153
    functions of 152

contractions
    apostrophes with 310
    possessive pronouns and contractions 216-17

count and noncount nouns (ESL) 37

count noun 37-38

D

decimal point 289

definition 341

demonstrative pronoun 88-89

Dewey Decimal System 346-47

diagramming
    adjective 108, 113-14
    adverb 130
    compound sentence 167
    conjunction 153
    direct object 53
    indirect object 54
    interjection 155
    intransitive verb 53
    predicate adjective 56
    prepositional phrase 147
    transitive verb 53
    verb 53-54, 56

dictionary
    definition in 341
    entry in 337
    etymology in 341
    function label in 341
    guide words in 337
    pronunciation guide in 340
    pronunciation in 340
    stress of words in 340
    syllabification in 340

dictionary skills
    finding the word 337
    pronouncing the word 340

using the word 341

dictionary, type of
    biographical 353
    desk 353
    foreign language 353
    geographic (gazetteer) 353
    thesaurus (dictionary of
        synonyms/antonyms) 353
    unabridged 353

direct object
    definition of 53-54, 58
    diagramming 53
    distinguished from predicate noun 58
    sentence patterns with 53

double comparison 237

double negative 237

E

encyclopedia 353

end marks. *See* punctuation marks

entry word 337

ESL notes 4, 6, 28, 37, 39, 99, 111, 116, 180, 237

etymology 341

exclamation point 3, 287

F

function label 341

fused sentence 16, 18

future perfect tense 72-73

future tense 66

G

gender
    feminine 86-87, 197-98
    masculine 86-87, 197-98
    neuter 86-87, 197-98

good/well 233-34

guide words, dictionary 337

H

helping verbs. *See* auxiliary

homonym
    confusing pairs of 254
    definition of 254

hyphen
 to show omission 312
 with fractions 312
 with multiword numbers 312
 with word division 312

I

idiom, "to make a scene" (ESL) 180

indefinite pronoun 93-94
 agreement with 186-87, 200
 antecedent of 200
 number with 182-87, 200

independent possessive 114

indirect object
 definition of 53-54
 diagramming 54
 sentence patterns with 54

indirect quotation 305

intensive pronoun 91, 219-20

interjections
 definition of 155-56
 diagramming of 155
 functions of 155

interrogative pronoun 89

intonation (ESL) 4

intransitive verb 53-54

inverted order
 with questions 11-12
 with *there* 10, 192

irregular verb 62-63

italics. *See* underlining/italics

L

library
 audio-visual materials 345
 periodical section 345
 reference section 345

library books
 autobiography 347
 biography 347
 children's 345
 fiction 346
 mystery fiction 346
 nonfiction 346
 science fiction 346
 young adult/juvenile 345

library books, finding
 call number 349
 card catalog 349
 catalog entry 349
 computer catalog 349
 Dewey Decimal System 346
 section letter 349
 Library of Congress System 347

Library of Congress System 347

lie/lay 247-48

linking verb 55-57

M

modal auxiliary 60

modifier
 definition of 102
 examples of 128-30

N

noncount noun 37-38

noun
 as direct object 53, 58
 as indirect object 54, 58
 as object of the preposition 144
 as predicate noun 55, 58
 as subject 5-6
 capitalization of 25-36. *See also* proper
  noun
 common 35-36
 compound 39
 count 37-38
 definition of 25-26, 29
 distinguishing between PN and DO 58
 formation of compounds 39
 irregular plural 25-29
 noncount 37-38
 plural 25-28
 plural possessive 27, 25-31
 predicate noun 49-56, 58
 proper 35-36
 singular 27-28
 singular possessive 27, 25-31
 spelling plurals of 25-29, 320

number
 of indefinite pronouns 200
 of nouns 27-29
 of personal pronouns 86-87, 197-98

Suggested Teaching Schedule: Two Semesters

Week	Day One	Day Two	Day Three	Day Four	Day Five
1	1: Book Jacket* (22-23)	1: Sentences (xii-5)	1: Sentences (5-8)	1: Sentences (8-10)	1: Sentences (10-12)
2	1: Book Jacket (22-23)	1: Sentences (13-16)	1: Sentences (16-21)	Review	Test 1‡ (23)
3	2: Observation Journal (44-47)	2: Nouns (24-27)	2: Nouns (27-32)	2: Nouns (33-35)	2: Nouns (35-37)
4	2: Nouns (37-39)	2: Nouns (39-41)	2: Observation Journal (44-47)	Review (42-43)	Test 2 (47)
5	3: Verbs (48-52)	3: Verbs (53-55)	3: Verbs (55-57)	3: Verbs (57-60)	3: Verbs (60-62)
6	3: Verbs (62-64)	3: Verbs (65-68)	3: Verbs (68-75)	Review (76-77)	Test 3 (80-81)
7	3: Ads and Announcements (77-81)	3: Ads and Announcements (77-81)	4: Pronouns (82-85)	4: Pronouns (86-88)	4: Pronouns (88-93)
8	4: Letter to a Pen Pal (98-99)	4: Letter to a Pen Pal (98-99)	4: Pronouns (93-96)	Review (97-98)	Test 4
9	5: Adjectives (100-103)	5: Adjectives (104-7)	5: Adjectives (108-10)	5: Adjectives (111-12)	5: Adjectives (112-16)
10	5: Adjectives (116-18)	5: Adjectives (118-20)	5: Adjectives (124-25)	Review	Test 5
11	5: Found Poems (121-23)	5: Found Poems (121-23)	6: Adverbs (126-29)	6: Adverbs (129-31)	6: Adverbs (132-35)
12	6: Family Tradition Report (140-41)	6: Family Tradition Report (140-41)	6: Adverbs (136-38)	Review (139-40)	Test 6 (141)
13	7: Process Writing (161)	7: Prepositions, Conjunctions, Interjections (142-46)	7: Prepositions, Conjunctions, Interjections (146-49)	7: Prepositions, Conjunctions, Interjections (149-51)	7: Prepositions, Conjunctions, Interjections (151-154)
14	7: Process Writing (161)	7: Prepositions, Conjunctions, Interjections (155-58)	7: Prepositions, Conjunctions, Interjections (159-60)	Review	Test 7
15	8: Dramatizing a Scene (175-80)	8: Phrases and Clauses (162-66)	8: Phrases and Clauses (166-69)	8: Phrases and Clauses (169-71)	8: Phrases and Clauses (181)
16	8: Dramatizing a Scene (175-80)	8: Phrases and Clauses (171-73)	8: Phrases and Clauses (173-74)	Review	Test 8
17					
18	MIDTERM REVIEW AND MIDTERM EXAMINATION				

Suggested Teaching Schedule: Two Semesters

Week	Day One	Day Two	Day Three	Day Four	Day Five
19	9: *Taking Notes (194-95)*	9: Subject-Verb Agreement (182-86)	9: Subject-Verb Agreement (186-88)	9: Subject-Verb Agreement (188-89)	9: Subject-Verb Agreement (189-91)
20	9: *Taking Notes (194-95)*	9: Subject-Verb Agreement (191-92)	9: Subject-Verb Agreement (192-94)	Review	Test 9
21	10: *Defining Terms (205-6)*	10: Pronoun-Antecedent Agreement (196-98)	10: Pronoun-Antecedent Agreement (198-99)	10: Pronoun-Antecedent Agreement (200)	10: Pronoun-Antecedent Agreement (207)
22	10: *Defining Terms (205-6)*	10: Pronoun-Antecedent Agreement (201-2)	10: Pronoun-Antecedent Agreement (203-5)	Review	Test 10
23	11: *Giving Directions (227-28)*	11: Using Pronouns (208-12)	11: Using Pronouns (213-16)	11: Using Pronouns (216-19)	11: Using Pronouns (219-21)
24	11: *Giving Directions (227-28)*	11: Using Pronouns (221-23)	11: Using Pronouns (224-26)	Review	Test 11 (229-31)
25	12: *Explaining the Rules (242-44)*	12: Using Adjectives and Adverbs Correctly (232-34)	12: Using Adjectives and Adverbs Correctly (235-36)	12: Using Adjectives and Adverbs Correctly (237-39)	12: Using Adjectives and Adverbs Correctly (245)
26	12: *Explaining the Rules (242-44)*	12: Using Adjectives and Adverbs Correctly (239-40)	12: Using Adjectives and Adverbs Correctly (241)	Review	Test 12
27	13: *In-class Essay (263-64)*	13: *In-class Essay (263-64)*	13: Using Troublesome Words (246-49)	13: Using Troublesome Words (250-52)	13: Using Troublesome Words (265)
28	13: Using Troublesome Words (253-56)	13: Using Troublesome Words (257-61)	13: Using Troublesome Words (262)	Review	Test 13
29	14: *Biographical Sketch (283-85)*	14: Capitalization† (266-70)	14: Capitalization (270-75)	14: Capitalization (275-77)	14: Capitalization (277-79)
30	14: *Biographical Sketch (283-85)*	14: Capitalization (279-81)	14: Capitalization (281-82)	Review	Test 14
31	15: Punctuation† (286-89)	15: Punctuation (289-91)	15: Punctuation (291-93)	15: Punctuation (294-95)	15: Punctuation (295-97)
32	15: Punctuation (298-304)	15: Punctuation (305-9)	15: Punctuation (310-14)	Review	Test 15
33	15: *Letter to the Editor (315-17)*	16: *Report Evaluation (329-31)*	16: Spelling (318-22)	16: Spelling (322-24)	16: Spelling (325-27)
34	15: *Letter to the Editor (315-17)*	16: *Report Evaluation (329-31)*	16: Spelling (327-28)	Review	Test 16
35	FINAL REVIEW AND FINAL EXAMINATION				
36					

Chapters 17-20 are reference chapters. Teach material from these chapters throughout the semester whenever it is appropriate for your students.

* The topics in italics refer to writing lessons and assignments within the chapter.

† If necessary, adjust the schedule to teach Chapter 14 (Capitalization) and Chapter 15 (Punctuation) before your students take any standardized achievement test.

‡ These page numbers refer to enrichment sections of the student text including critical thinking, writing across the curriculum, and English language history. Assign these pages if time allows.

Suggested Teaching Schedule: One Semester

Week	Day One	Day Two	Day Three	Day Four	Day Five
1	1: Sentences (xii-7)	1: Sentences (7-12)	1: Sentences (13-21) 1: *Book Jacket (22-23)*	Test 1‡ (23)	2: Nouns (24-32) 2: *Observation Journal (44-47)*
2	2: Nouns (33-37)	2: Nouns (37-42)	Test 2 (47)	3: *Ads and Announcements (77-81)*	3: Verbs (48-55)
3	3: Verbs (55-62)	3: *Ads and Announcements (77-81)*	3: Verbs (62-68)	3: Verbs (68-72)	3: Verbs (72-77) 2: *Observation Journal (44-47)*
4	Test 3 (80-81)	4: *Letter to a Pen Pal (98-99)*	4: Pronouns (82-88)	4: Pronouns (88-98)	Test 4
5	5: *Found Poems (121-23)*	5: Adjectives (100-107)	5: Adjectives (108-16)	5: Adjectives (116-20)	Test 5 (124-25)
6	5: *Found Poems (121-23)*	6: Adverbs (126-33)	6: Adverbs (134-40)	6: *Family Tradition Report (140-41)*	Test 6 (141)
7	6: *Family Tradition Report (140-41)*	7: Prepositions, Conjunctions, Interjections (142-51)	7: Prepositions, Conjunctions, Interjections (151-60)	7: *Process Writing (161)*	Test 7
8	7: *Process Writing (161)*	8: Phrases and Clauses (169-74)	8: Phrases and Clauses (169-74)	8: *Dramatizing a Scene (175-80)*	Test 8 (181)
9	MIDTERM REVIEW AND MIDTERM EXAMINATION				
10	9: Subject-Verb Agreement (182-86)	9: Subject-Verb Agreement (186-91)	9: Subject-Verb Agreement (191-94) 9: *Taking Notes (194-95)*	8: *Dramatizing a Scene (175-80)*	Test 9
11	9: *Taking Notes (194-95)*	10: Pronoun-Antecedent Agreement (196-99) 10: *Defining Terms (186-91)*	10: Pronoun-Antecedent Agreement (200-203) 10: *Defining Terms (186-91)*	10: Pronoun-Antecedent Agreement (204-5, Review)	Test 10 (207)
12	11: Using Pronouns (208-14)	11: Using Pronouns (214-19)	11: Using Pronouns (219-26)	11: *Giving Directions (227-28)*	Test 11 (229-31)
13	12: Using Adjectives and Adverbs Correctly (232-34) 11: *Giving Directions (227-28)*	12: Using Adjectives and Adverbs Correctly (234-39)	12: Using Adjectives and Adverbs Correctly (239-41, Review)	12: *Explaining the Rules (242-44)*	Test 12 (245)
14	13: Using Troublesome Words (246-53)	13: Using Troublesome Words (254-62)	Test 13 (265)	13: *In-class Essay (263-64)*	14: Capitalization†
15	14: Capitalization (275-82)	Test 14	14: *Biographical Sketch (283-85)*	15: *Letter to the Editor (315-17)*	15: Punctuation† (286-91)
16	15: Punctuation (291-300)	15: Punctuation (301-7)	15: Punctuation (307-14)	Test 15	16: Spelling (318-24)
17	16: Spelling (325-28)	16: *Report Evaluation (329-31)*	Test 16	14: *Biographical Sketch (283-85)*	15: *Letter to the Editor (315-17)*
18	FINAL REVIEW AND FINAL EXAMINATION				

Chapters 17-20 are reference chapters. Teach material from these chapters throughout the semester whenever it is appropriate for your students.

* The topics in italics refer to writing lessons and assignments within the chapter.

† If necessary, adjust the schedule to teach Chapter 14 (Capitalization) and Chapter 15 (Punctuation) before your students take any standardized achievement test.

‡ These page numbers refer to enrichment sections of the student text including critical thinking, writing across the curriculum, and English language history. Assign these pages if time allows.

Chapter 3

3-3

1.

banker | called | police

2.

policemen | arrived

3.

captain | showed | plans

men

4.

He | unfolded | map

5.

He | told | orders

policemen

6.

men | ran

7.

They | surprised | thieves

8.

thieves | gave | funds

police

9.

police | arrested | thieves

10.

police | handed | money

banker

3-5

1.

James Naismith | was \ teacher

2.

he | was \ responsible

3.

He
and boss | were \ eager

4.

legacy | is \ basketball

5.

baskets | were \ hoops

6.

ball | was \ soccer ball

7.

players | were \ members

8.

sport | was \ popular

9.

popularity | is \ greater

10.

kids
and athletes | are \ enthusiastic

3-7

1.

Andre | goes

2.

He | is \ freshman

3.

He | appears \ tall

4.

Andre | gives | effort

team

5.

| squad | remains \ undefeated |

6.

| sister | participated |

7.

| LaTasha | played | flute |

8.

| she | is \ cheerleader |

9.

| parents | come |

10.

| They | support | Calvary High |

3-8

1.

| work | is \ *Beowulf* |

2.

| author | remains \ unknown |

3.

| language | is \ Old English |

4.

| Beowulf | seems \ strong *and* courageous |

5.

| opponent | was \ Grendel |

6.

| roar | sounded \ ferocious |

7.

| He | looked \ fierce |

8.

| He | appeared \ stronger |

9.

| Beowulf | became \ hero |

10.

| people | were \ thankful |

Chapter 4
4-9

1.

| Brenda | has invited | everyone |

2.

| we | May bring | anything |

3.

| Somebody | will want | salad |

4.

| No one | offered | cake \ us |

5.

| anyone | Is bringing | anything |

6.

| everybody | Is coming |

7.

| Some | will be \ late |

8.

| everything | Is \ ready |

9.

| Someone | dropped | hamburgers |

10.

| work | will be \ nothing |

Chapter 5
5-8

1.

Christians | should develop | life
a / strong / daily / prayer

2.

God | desires | prayers
The / daily

3.

prayer | is \ resort
a / last

4.

prayer | benefits | welfare
Intercessory / the

5.

Jesus | is \ intercessor
the / heavenly

6.

God | hears | request
a / sincere

7.

answer | does come
An / immediate

8.

plans | outweigh | ones
The / infinite / finite / human

9.

We | must offer | request
an / earnest / heartfelt

10.

prayers | produce | result
Godly / fervent / the

Chapter 6
6-3

1.

Duane | reads | Bible
Daily / his

2.

Duane | finishes | devotions
always / nearly / his

3.

Proverbs | is \ choice
usually / Duane's

4.

Duane | likes | language
the / beautiful / exceptionally

5.

He | studies | verses
carefully / the

6.

Duane | memorizes | passages
also / many / Proverbs

7.

8.

9.

10.

Chapter 7

7-3

1.

2.

3.

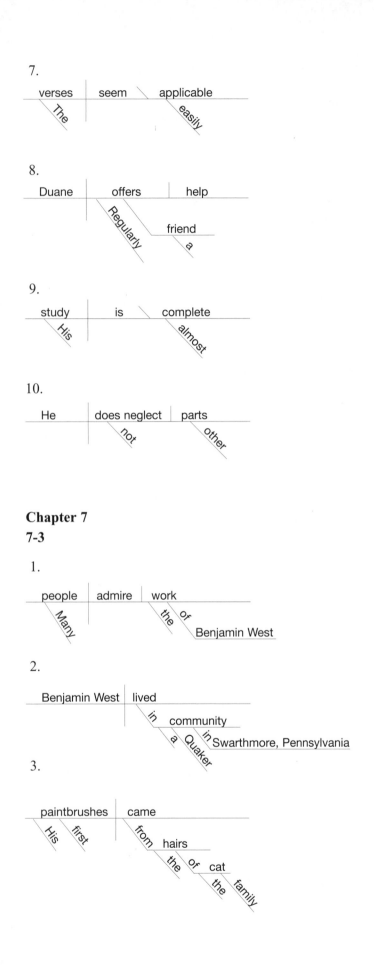

4.

5.

6.

7.

8.

9.

10.

7-11

1.

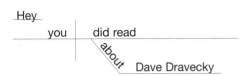

Hey | you | did read
about Dave Dravecky

2.

Dave | played
for San Diego Padres (the) and San Francisco Giants (the)

3.

Wow

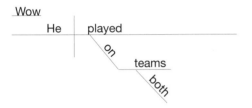

He | played
on teams both

4.

please

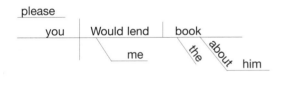

you | Would lend | book
me the about him

5.

story | is — realistic / yet amazing
His

6.

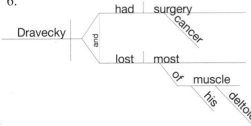

Dravecky | had | surgery (cancer) and lost | most of muscle his deltoid

7.

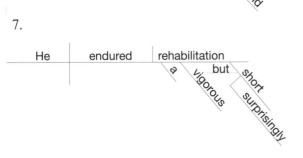

He | endured | rehabilitation
a vigorous but short surprisingly

8.

Yes

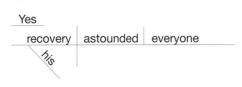

recovery | astounded | everyone
his

9.

comeback | surprised — doctors his and teammates his
His quick to baseball

10.

Good

you | Did enjoy | story
his

Chapter 8
8-3

1.

foods | stay \ fresh
Frozen for periods of time long

2.

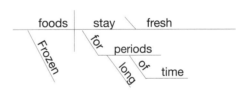

cooks | buy | food in bulk and freeze | part for later of it
Many or
they | make and freeze | meals whole

Diagram Answers **449**

3.

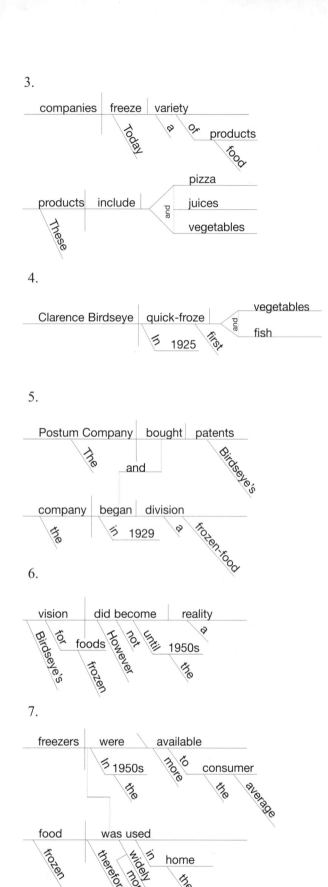

4.

5.

6.

7.

8.

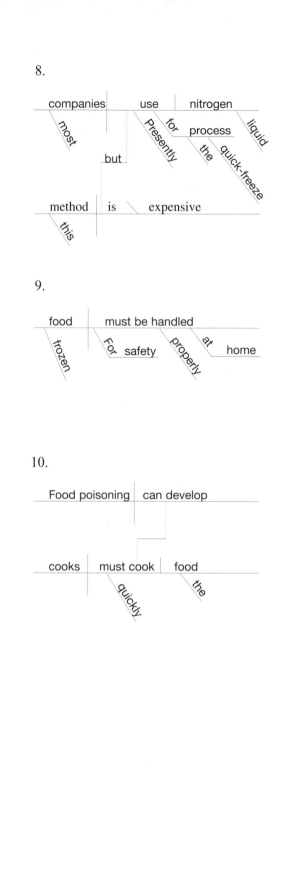

9.

10.

Scope and Sequence

Writing & Grammar 7 for Christian Schools, Third Edition

Parts of Speech (and Verbals)	Noun; pronoun; verb—simple tense and perfect tenses; adjective; adverb; preposition; conjunction; interjection
Sentence Structure	Sentence patterns—S-InV, S-TrV-DO, S-TrV-IO-DO, S-LV-PN, S-LV-PA; introduction to dependent clauses; sentence types—declarative, interrogative, imperative, exclamatory; clause structure—simple, compound, complex; sentence errors—fragments, comma splices, fused sentences
Mechanics	Capitalization; punctuation; spelling
Usage	Subject-verb agreement; pronoun-antecedent agreement; pronoun reference; troublesome words (homophones, homonyms, etc.)
Writing Skills	Writing process—planning, drafting, revising and proofreading, publishing; paragraph development—fact, example, statistic, incident/anecdote, sensory detail, reason; paragraph organization—chronological, spatial, order of importance; style—precise words, showing not telling
Examples of Writing Projects	**description:** biographical sketch **exposition:** in-class essay, science report evaluation **narration:** family tradition report, drama scene **persuasion:** letter to editor **poetry:** found poem
Study & Reference Skills	dictionary—guide words, entry word, syllabification, pronunciation, definition, function label, etymology; library—types of materials, call number, alphabetizing, Dewey Decimal system, Library of Congress system, card catalog, computer catalog; reference tools—dictionary, thesaurus, biographical dictionary, gazetteer, encyclopedia, almanac, atlas, book of quotations, Bible concordance, *Readers' Guide to Periodical Literature;* parts of a book—title page, copyright page, table of contents, list of illustrations, acknowledgements, introduction/preface, text, bibliography, appendix, glossary, index; scheduling study time; memory techniques; reading comprehension—definitions, restatements, examples, word parts; test-taking strategies—classroom tests, standardized tests

Correlation with National Standards

WRITING & GRAMMAR 7 for Christian Schools, Third Edition

Standards for the English Language Arts, by the International Reading Association and the National Council of Teachers of English, Copyright 1996 by the International Reading Association and the National Council of Teachers of English. Reprinted with permission.

Standards for the English Language Arts	WRITING & GRAMMAR 7 for Christian Schools	Other BJU Press series and products
1. Students read a wide range of print and non-print texts to build an understanding of texts, of themselves, and of the cultures of the United States and the world; to acquire new information; to respond to the needs and demands of society and the workplace; and for personal fulfillment. Among these texts are fiction and nonfiction, classic and contemporary works.	ST*: 4, 6-7, 13-14, 17, 18-20, 26, 33-34, 38-39, 41, 51-52, 56-57, 59, 68, 70, 72, 78, 83-85, 90, 92-93, 96-97, 103, 106-7, 109, 112, 115-18, 131, 136, 145-46, 148, 153-54, 158-59, 165-66, 170, 172-73, 189, 199, 202-04, 212, 218-19, 225-26, 235, 239-41, 253, 262, 274-75, 280-82, 288-89, 290-96, 302-3, 309, 311-14, 321, 329-35	*Literature* series
2. Students read a wide range of literature from many periods in many genres to build an understanding of the many dimensions (e.g., philosophical, ethical, aesthetic) of human experience.	ST: 1, 22-23, 25, 49, 101, 127, 143, 163	*Literature* series
3. Students apply a wide range of strategies to comprehend, interpret, evaluate, and appreciate texts. They draw on their prior experience, their interactions with other readers and writers, their knowledge of word meaning and of other texts, their word identification strategies, and their understanding of textual features (e.g., sound-letter correspondence, sentence structure, context, graphics).	ST: 22-23, 80-81, 124-25, 140, 160, 174, 229-30, 329-35, 359, 362-63, 365	*Literature* series *Vocabulary* series
4. Students adjust their use of spoken, written, and visual language (e.g., conventions, style, vocabulary) to communicate effectively with a variety of audiences and for different purposes.	ST: 21, 43, 77-79, 98-99, 120, 161, 175-80, 206-7, 227-28, 242-44, 245, 283-85, 315-17, 357, 378, 386 TE*: 157, 201, 276	*Vocabulary* series *Sound Speech* *Performing Literature*
5. Students employ a wide range of strategies as they write and use different writing process elements appropriately to communicate with different audiences for a variety of purposes.	ST: 22-23, 44-46, 77-79, 98-99, 121-23, 140-41, 161, 175-80, 194-95, 204-6, 227-28, 242-44, 263-64, 265, 315-17, 375-89	*The Writer's Toolbox*

6.	Students apply knowledge of language structure, language conventions (e.g., spelling and punctuation), media techniques, figurative language, and genre to create, critique, and discuss print and non-print texts.	ST: 3-20, 21, 23, 26-42, 47, 51-76, 84-97, 102-18, 128-39, 141, 144-59, 164-74, 183-94, 197-204, 209-26, 233-41, 247-62, 267-82, 287-314, 319-28, 366-67 TE: 201, 276	*Literature* series
7.	Students conduct research on issues and interests by generating ideas and questions, and by posing problems. They gather, evaluate, and synthesize data from a variety of sources (e.g., print and non-print texts, artifacts, people) to communicate their discoveries in ways that suit their purpose and audience.	ST: 44-46, 140-41, 161, 205-6, 283-85, 377 TE: 192	*Literature* series *The Writer's Toolbox* *Writing from Research*
8.	Students use a variety of technological and information resources (e.g., libraries, databases, computer networks, video) to gather and synthesize information and to create and communicate knowledge.	ST: 337-43, 349-56	*Literature* series *The Writer's Toolbox* *Writing from Research*
9.	Students develop an understanding of and respect for diversity in language use, patterns, and dialects across cultures, ethnic groups, geographic regions, and social roles.	ST: 4, 8-9, 15, 30, 35, 36, 40, 61, 62, 66-67, 71, 83, 92-93, 95, 118, 137-38, 171-72, 181, 193	*Literature* series *Vocabulary* series
10.	Students whose first language is not English make use of their first language to develop competency in the English language arts and to develop understanding of content across the curriculum.	ST: (ESL Notes): 4, 6, 28, 37, 39, 99, 111, 116, 180, 237 TE: 3, 4, 13, 22, 30, 35, 37, 39, 52, 54, 62-63, 72, 86, 89, 102, 115, 121, 128, 141, 144, 164, 183, 195, 197, 205, 237, 267, 271, 287, 305, 312, 337, 353, 355, 359	
11.	Students participate as knowledgeable, reflective, creative, and critical members of a variety of literacy communities.	ST: 99, 180, 242-44 TE: 21, 22-23, 77-79, 103, 111-12, 123-124, 127, 148, 157, 160-61, 170-71, 173, 179, 194-95, 201, 205-8, 227-29, 234, 238, 254, 312, 314-17	*Literature* series *Sound Speech* *Performing Literature*
12.	Students use spoken, written, and visual language to accomplish their own purposes (e.g., for learning, enjoyment, persuasion, and the exchange of information).	[NCTE and IRA explain that this standard describes students' using classroom skills outside of the classroom (i.e., lifelong learning). Students have met this goal when they freely choose to discuss, to write, and to read outside of the classroom.]	

*ST refers to pages in the Student Text; TE refers to pages in the Teacher's Edition.

WRITING & GRAMMAR 7
Support Materials CD Information

Getting Started

Viewing the *Support Materials CD* for WRITING & GRAMMAR 7, Third Edition, requires Adobe Acrobat Reader compatible with version 5.0 or higher. Various versions of Acrobat Reader for Windows are provided on the CD. Acrobat Reader for Macintosh operating systems, Acrobat Reader in languages other than English, and the most recent version of Acrobat Reader for Windows are available for free download at www.adobe.com. Internet access is required.

Installing Adobe Acrobat Reader for Windows

1. Insert the CD. If the CD does not start automatically, use Windows Explorer to open the CD's file listing.

2. Double-click on Startup.exe and follow the installation instructions on the screen.

Installing Adobe Acrobat Reader for Macintosh (requires Internet access)

1. Insert the CD. Open the "Reader" folder and then the "Mac" folder.

2. Double-click on the appropriate installation file for your operating system version.

3. Double-click on the file that is copied to your computer and follow the installation instructions on the screen.

Note: We recommend that you first view the To the Teacher file to become familiar with this product. Start Acrobat Reader and then open the file "TeacherInformation.pdf" from the CD.

System Requirements

Windows

Intel Pentium processor

Microsoft Windows 95 OSR 2.0, Windows 98 SE, Windows Millennium Edition, Windows NT 4.0 with Service Pack 5, Windows 2000, or Windows XP

64MB of RAM

24MB of available hard-disk space

Additional 70MB of hard-disk space for Asian fonts (optional)

Macintosh

PowerPC processor

Mac OS 8.6, 9.0.4, 9.1, or Mac OS X

64MB of RAM

24MB of available hard-disk space

Additional 70MB of hard-disk space for Asian fonts (optional)